D0843542

Ethics Training in Action

An Examination of Issues, Techniques, and Development

A volume in
Ethics in Practice
Robert A. Giacalone, *Series Editor*

Ethics Training in Action

An Examination of Issues, Techniques, and Development

edited by

Leslie E. Sekerka

Menlo College

INFORMATION AGE PUBLISHING, INC.

Charlotte, NC • www.infoagepub.com

Library of Congress Cataloging-in-Publication Data

A CIP record for this book is available from the Library of Congress
http://www.loc.gov

ISBN: 978-1-62396-463-4 (Paperback)
      978-1-62396-464-1 (Hardcover)
      978-1-62396-465-8 (ebook)

CONTENTS

SECTION I

OVERVIEW

SECTION II

CURRENT ISSUES

SECTION III

TECHNIQUES AND ASSESSMENT

SECTION IV

FIELD APPLICATIONS

SECTION V

LEADERSHIP AND DEVELOPMENT

PREFACE

Leslie E. Sekerka

Ensuring that ethics is a part of performance in business enterprise is no small task. Being less unethical is not enough—we need to work at being more ethical. Management needs to create systems and processes that support ethical achievement. To design a workplace where responsibility, accountability, and doing the right thing are genuinely valued and practiced, educational training programs are needed to cultivate ethical awareness and personal development. Underscoring the importance of regulations, while also moving to ensure that employees understand what's right and wrong in their job and can apply this knowledge to their daily operations, is just a beginning.

Recognizing a need to go beyond compliance, today's managers have expanded their efforts to frame training as a forum for values-based education and individual moral competency development. With the infusion of mandatory requirements for ethics training programs in some firms and self-imposed initiatives in others, we see a range of educational deliverables and varied commitment ethical performance expectations. To advance ethics in practice, a closer look at ethics training in the workplace is warranted.

The book is laid out in five sections, starting with an overview of the science of training and empirically identified best practices. We then take a look at the current issues managers face in the workplace, specifically targeting challenges in global ethics and workplace bullying. Techniques and assessment are examined, presenting several tools for building ethical

Ethics Training in Action, pages ix–x
Copyright © 2014 by Information Age Publishing
All rights of reproduction in any form reserved.

strength and helping to support their marked success through planned and measured engagement. A look at several field applications provides empirical study of two unique organizational contexts, small firms and public administration. The book concludes with a focus on ideas to help promote ongoing leadership and development.

Given that most firms only emphasize a compliance-based approach toward ethics training, there is vast room for additional development, improvement, and growth in this domain. Training people to be less bad is not good enough. As a volume within IAP's Ethics in Practice series, the authors attempt to better understand ethics training in organizational settings by taking a focused look at the nature of training itself and what tools are currently being used, and to promote management interest in the topic. If we expect to see ethical performance, the prevention of unethical behavior is simply not enough. Managers need to create an environment where employees have a desire to be ethical in the workplace. Toward this end, ethics training is a unique venue where ethical performance goals can be communicated and encouraged, and the skills to support such achievement can be further developed.

Managers and practitioners reading this book will garner specific trends and techniques, which can inform, guide, and improve their efforts to develop ethical decision making and ethical action within their organizations. Academic scholars will find this book useful, providing insight as to where additional research is needed.

ACKNOWLEDGEMENTS

Special thanks to the *James Hervey Johnson Charitable Educational Trust* for their unwavering commitment to advance ethics education. Thanks also go to Kirk Hanson and Jim Balassone, whose work at Santa Clara University's Markkula Center for Applied Ethics has provided ongoing insight and support. The reviewers and editorial team were exceptionally helpful, with special acknowledgements to Robert Giacalone, George Johnson, Lucy Sekerka and Dana Tomasino who shared their talent and dedication. Finally, to our contributors as well as other scholars and practitioners, we appreciate your steadfast pursuit of knowledge that moves to advance adult moral development in organizational settings.

SECTION I

OVERVIEW

CHAPTER 1

ENHANCING BUSINESS ETHICS

Prescriptions for Building Better Ethics Training

Lauren E. Benishek and Eduardo Salas

The twenty-first century has borne witness to a growing list of business scandals, which have collectively harmed millions of employees. These scandals weaken public confidence in capital markets, damage trust in professional institutions, undermine the rectitude of corporate America (Adler, 2002), and inspire concern that there is an ethics crisis in the West (Sims, 1992). Widespread media coverage and publication of numerous high-profile scandals have business managers, academicians, and the public at large wondering at the cause of corporate wrongdoing and how future transgressions can be avoided (Treviño & Brown, 2004). Global awareness of these scandals has the public demanding that private and public organizational entities and the members who represent them act in accordance with high ethical and moral standards (Sims, 1992). According to the 2011 Edelman Trust Barometer, only 46% of United States consumers trust businesses to

Ethics Training in Action, pages 3–29
Copyright © 2014 by Information Age Publishing
All rights of reproduction in any form reserved.

do what is right (Edelman, 2011). In response, organizations have renewed efforts to improve their ethical image (Weber, 2007). The prevalence of unscrupulous behavior in the workplace suggests that many rather than few would benefit from interventions aimed at promoting ethical behavior and limiting unethical behavior. To this end, organizations have implemented formal codes of conduct articulating their expectations of ethical behavior among employees, created mandatory ethics training programs to promote employee awareness of and commitment to ethical behavior, and appointed integrity officers tasked with the responsibility of policing and promoting ethical behavior (Weber, 2007).

WHAT ARE ETHICS AND WHY DO THEY MATTER?

The word *ethics* is derived from the Greek word *ethos*, meaning character or custom. It is hard to define *business ethics*, as the term itself has many nuances (Ferrell & Fraedrich, 1991), and several definitions of business ethics have been set forth in the literature (see Table 1.1). However, what these definitions each indicate is that, when applied to corporations, ethics signifies a code describing moral integrity (Sims, 1992).

Business ethics may be approached at two levels. The first level encompasses ethical norms that are commonly accepted within and across organizations and seeks to understand why they work. The second level involves assessment of beliefs regarding what is right and wrong, good and bad, and held to be morally true. The distinction between these two levels is that of observation and philosophy. Applied ethics deal with how ethical codes are manifested in behavior, whereas the domain of theoretical ethics is in understanding how value systems are perceived (Arthur, 1986). Theoretical ethics are outside the purview of this chapter, which is focused on improving business conduct through the application of business ethics.

Business is reliant on applied ethical practices—ethics facilitate order in the often chaotic conditions under which organizations must operate

TABLE 1.1 Definitions of Business Ethics

Definition	Source
"Patterns of business conduct that are accepted as good within the particular environment where they are applied."	Arthur (1986, p. 322)
"Moral principles and standards that guide behavior in the world of business."	Ferrell & Fraedrich (1991, p. 5)
"Inquiry into the nature and grounds of morality where the term morality is taken to mean moral judgments, standards and rules of conduct."	Taylor (1975, p. 1)

(Arthur, 1986). Yet ethical behavior is a constant challenge that has profound impact on organizational dynamics and performance (Sims, 1992). The ethical challenges organizations face fall into two broad categories (Stark, 1993). The first challenge involves navigating situations in which the right course is evident, but where real-world pressures lead employees to behave unethically. As unethical behavior becomes illegal, it is easier to identify it as "wrong" and worthy of some corrective and/or punitive action. Unfortunately, many ethics concerns fall in a moral grey area in which appropriate behavior is ambiguous. Confusion regarding what does or does not constitute ethical behavior represents the second challenge in business ethics. It is not always clear what is "right" or "wrong" under some circumstances, and failure to choose the "correct" path may seriously compromise an organization's position. Badaracco (1992) described this area as not involving "issues of right versus wrong" but "conflicts of right versus right" (p. 65). Regardless of whether ethical behavior is clear or ambiguous, failing to adhere to ethical standards may place a company at risk for criticism or punishment, which is why ethics remains an important topic within businesses around the globe.

WHY ETHICS TRAINING IS NECESSARY

Over three quarters of the United States' major corporations are actively trying to build ethics into their organizations (Stark, 1993). Past research suggests that organizations must rely on their cultural environment to promote employee ethicality (e.g., Brass, Butterfield, & Skaggs, 1998; Sims, 1991; Treviño & Nelson, 1999; Treviño, Butterfield, & McCabe, 1998). Formalized corporate policies and programs convey organizational values (Grossman & Salas, 2011) and provide normative guidance to employees for demonstrating acceptable behaviors and attitudes (Valentine & Fleischman, 2004). Together, ethics policies (e.g., codes of ethics) and programs (e.g., ethics training) establish, represent, and sustain organizational culture. Many companies use an institutionalized code of ethics to signal their ethical position (Schwartz, 2001; Valentine & Barnett, 2002; Valentine & Fleischman, 2004). However, as Palmer and Zakhem (2001) have stated, "Merely having standards is not enough, a company must make the standards understood, and ensure their proper dissemination within the organizational structure" (p. 83). Ethics training may be an integral complement to institutionalized ethics codes as it creates awareness of these codes (Izzo, 2000; LeClair & Ferrell, 2000; Loe & Weeks, 2000; Minkes, Small, & Chatterjee, 1999; Palmer & Zakhem, 2001; Valentine & Fleischman, 2004), facilitates development of an ethical climate within organizations (Bohren, 1992; Hyman, Skipper, & Tansey, 1990), and positively influences ethical decision processes (Jones & Hiltebeitel, 1995). Supporting this notion, Valentine and Fleischman (2004) found that organizations whose employees are aware of corporate ethical values tend to have formalized ethics training programs in place.

In addition to promoting awareness of formalized codes of ethical conduct, ethics training is often intended to improve employees' ethical knowledge and decision-making ability (LeClair & Ferrell, 2000). Despite its purported importance, the utility of ethics courses and training has been the topic of some debate (Thompson, 1990). Discussion in the literature has addressed the value of ethics training in business education and organizations (Delaney & Sockell, 1992). Some observers proposed that ethics courses make mangers more ethically sensitive (Laczniak, 1983), while others insisted on the uselessness of ethics training (Levin, 1989). Putting a seeming end to the speculative debate, extant empirical evidence indicates that ethics training in organizations does indeed have a positive effect on ethical behavior (e.g., Delaney & Sockell, 1992; Ferrell, Fraedrich, & Ferrell, 2002). Some authors have suggested that training interventions advance individuals' moral reasoning patterns, allowing them to better integrate the interests of others in their final decisions (Baxter & Rarick, 1987). Evidence tends to support this argument, showing that ethics training affects the usage of ethical principles in decision making (Hiltebeitel & Jones, 1992), improving moral reasoning in students (Loe & Weeks, 2000) and cognitive moral development in business professionals (Penn & Collier, 1985). This encouraging evidence helps explain why ethics training is increasingly common in corporations internationally (Weber, 2007) and underscores the importance of developing ethics training programs that are instructionally sound.

Because ethics training is a common tool in organizations, creating effective ethics training programs should be of concern to organizational stakeholders. Decisions regarding the design and implementation of ethics training should be made based on the best evidence available to instructional designers. Fortunately, there is a well-established science that prescribes exactly how training should be designed and implemented in order to achieve optimal results, and which can be applied to the development of ethics training programs. The focus of this chapter is to provide an overview of the science of training and forward practical, evidence-based guidelines for designing and delivering successful organizational ethics training.

DEFINITIONS OF TRAINING AND LEARNING

Before describing the science of training, a few definitions are necessary. Simply stated, training refers to "the planned and systematic activities designed to promote the acquisition of knowledge (i.e., need to know), skills (i.e., need to do), and attitudes (i.e., need to feel)" (Salas, Tannenbaum, Kraiger, & Smith-Jentsch, 2012, p. 77). Although a desired outcome of training, learning is not synonymous with training. Instead, learning is the "process of acquiring new knowledge and behaviors as the result of practice, study, or experience" (Salas et al., 2012, p. 77). Training will not always affect learning, and much learning takes place outside of formal training environments. In order to promote learning, training must be effective. Effective training creates relatively permanent changes in cognition, behavior, and affect (Kraiger, Ford, & Salas, 1993) through the provision of information, demonstration, practice opportunities, and timely feedback. On the other hand, trainees may come away from ineffective training having failed to learn. Fortunately, as we discuss next, carefully and systematically planning training increases the likelihood that training participants will learn from the experience and apply what they have learned to their jobs.

OVERVIEW OF THE SCIENCE OF TRAINING

The training evidence base suggests standard principles for designing, implementing, and evaluating training programs that may be applied to the development of ethics training. Creating successful ethics training initiatives requires an understanding of the science-based principles behind effective training practices. First, we provide a brief overview of the state of the science of training.

In the first review chapter of the training literature, Campbell (1971) characterizes the field as "voluminous, nonempirical, non-theoretical, poorly written, and dull" (p. 565). Since then, there has been much advancement in the science of training. We now know from over 40 years of pointed investigation that, regardless of the content, well-designed training works (Arthur, Bennett, Edens, & Bell, 2003; Salas & Cannon-Bowers, 2001; Salas et al., 2012) and that the way training is designed, developed, and implemented influences its ultimate effectiveness (Salas & Cannon-Bowers, 2001; Salas et al., 2012).

Theoretical Drivers

Since Campbell's (1971) assessment of the state of training science, researchers have articulated theoretical models that provide a richer picture and description of training (Kozlowski & Salas, 1997; Tannenbaum & Yukl, 1992) and that have expanded our view of training to include both micro (e.g., individual-level) and macro (e.g., organizational-level) perspectives (Salas et al., 2012). It is now understood that training effectiveness is influenced by a range of factors spanning multiple organizational levels (e.g., individual, team/entity, and organizational).

One notable theoretical development is the concept of training transfer (Salas et al., 2012). *Transfer* has a range of meanings across a number of disciplines. For example, in the cognitive science domain, transfer is used to refer to how well learning on one task facilitates learning on another (e.g., Gick & Holyoak, 1983). However, this chapter employs the definition of transfer as it is used in the training domain, which describes the application of trained skills in the job performance environment. In other words, transfer refers to how well training participants use knowledge, skills, and attitudes (KSAs) learned during training in their regular work environment to perform their job responsibilities. This is, in fact, the ultimate goal of training: to generalize new KSAs to a typical performance context. In ethics training, this is analogous to behaving more ethically in the workplace as a result of learning what is expected of employees and how to consistently engage ethical thinking, behavior, and attitudes.

In their model of training transfer, Baldwin and Ford (1988) articulate how various organizational, individual, and design factors influence learning and subsequent transfer of learned KSAs to the work environment. Organizational (e.g., transfer climate, support, opportunity to perform, follow-up) and individual (e.g., cognitive ability, self-efficacy, motivation, perceived utility of training) characteristics in addition to training design features (e.g., behavioral modeling, error management, realistic training environments) directly and indirectly affect how much is learned during training and how well learned KSAs ultimately transfer to the work environment (Grossman & Salas, 2011). It is therefore wise to pay attention to these factors when designing and delivering training.

Older research outlining the training process (e.g., Goldstein, 1991) ignored the multilevel factors that affect training effectiveness. More recent work includes the advancement of training effectiveness models that considers these issues and contributes to an understanding of how to best train learners under a variety of conditions (e.g., Colquitt, LePine, & Noe, 2000; Ford, Smith, Weissbein, Gully, & Salas, 1998; Noe, 1986). Such theoretical advances have changed our view of training to that of a system (Salas et al., 2012). Training is not just a one-time event; science suggests that the best training programs are the result of a systematic process. Employing a programmatic instructional design approach increases the odds of observing desirable training outcomes (Goldstein, 1991, 1993; Salas, Wilson, Priest, & Guthrie, 2006); otherwise it is shooting in the dark and hoping the final training program is successful. Training may be conceptualized as a system consisting of three general stages: (1) before, (2) during, and (3) after (e.g., Gregory, Feitosa, Driskell, Salas, & Vessey, 2013). Table 1.2 provides an overview of what happens during each stage.

TABLE 1.2   Elements of the Before, During, and After Stages of Training

Before	During	After

• Needs Analysis
  – Task Analysis
  – Person Analysis
  – Organizational Analysis
• Planning & Design
• Development of Materials
• Preparation of learning
  environment
	• Information
	• Demonstration
	• Practice
	• Feedback
		• Training Evaluation
		• Transfer

Pre-training refers to the planning stage that occurs before training is administered to participants and is the most important phase for ensuring the success of ethical training courses. Prior to training, instructional designers must plan and create the training program. This includes conducting a training needs analysis to specify who and what will be trained as well as what individual and situational characteristics may impede training effectiveness and transfer, designing the course content and evaluation plan, developing the training materials, and preparing the training climate for learning. In pre-training, the scope of the ethical training program is defined and the instructional objectives of the program are articulated. Some questions that may be answered during pre-training include: Is the organization ready for ethics training? What topics need to be covered in training? Will the training teach employees the corporate code of ethics and how to report unethical behavior safely? Will it go beyond this to attempt to enhance employees' ethical decision-making capability? When and where will training be conducted? Who will attend training? How will it be determined that the training worked? The answers to these and related questions are critical to designing appropriate and effective ethics training courses.

The second stage, which takes place during training, entails actual implementation of the instructional course. At this time, trainees participate in the training that was designed and developed during the pre-training stage. Instructional principles and strategies should be built into the training course materials prior to implementation, but during training the ethics instructor must ensure that the training experience includes information, demonstration, practice, and feedback.

Targeted KSAs should be demonstrated during training to provide training participants with an understanding of how KSAs are executed in practice. Demonstrating both positive and negative KSA examples will promote greater learning in training participants and provide them with concrete examples to guide them when transferring learning to the work context (Taylor, Russ-Eft, & Chan, 2005). Similarly, multiple demonstrations of trained KSAs representing a variety of ability levels will improve training effectiveness. Following demonstration, training participants should be allowed to practice the behaviors they observed (Taylor et al., 2005). Practice opportunities should require that trainees engage in the same cognitive processes they would use on-the-job, as this will encourage training transfer after training (Taylor et al., 2005). Committing errors during practice should be encouraged to improve experience with error management and promote greater learning (Keith & Frese, 2008). Feedback in response to practice performance should be constructive, timely, and focused on behavior, not on personal traits (Smith-Jentsch, Zeisig, Acton, & McPherson, 1998).

After training, evaluation of learning and training effectiveness is conducted and training participants are expected to transfer what they learned into practice. Training evaluation should follow the evaluation plan formulated in pre-training. Transfer may be facilitated through organizational support of employees to use what they have learned. Over time, learners will likely experience skill decay, possibly as much as 92% in a year (Arthur, Bennett, Stanush, & McNelly, 1998). Skill decay may be reduced by providing employees with reminders of the value of ethics to the organization and periodic refresher training as needed.

SCIENCE-BASED PRINCIPLES FOR SUCCESSFUL ETHICS TRAINING

We now offer a set of seven science-based principles for ensuring successful ethics training (see Table 1.3). Discussion of these principles is organized in accordance with the before-during-after framework discussed above.

Before Training

Training Needs Analysis

The first step in any training development effort should be a training needs analysis (TNA). A TNA is a diagnosis of what needs to be trained, who needs to be trained, and within what organizational system the training will take place. Outcomes of a proper TNA include (1) projected learning objectives, (2) guidance for training design and delivery, (3) plans for training evaluation, and (4) information about the organizational factors that may influence learning and transfer.

It is important to note that training is not a panacea for organizational troubles. A well-conducted TNA will provide evidence of whether training is

TABLE 1.3   Evidence-based Principles for Successful Ethical Training Interventions

Before Training

Principle 1	Conduct a systematic training needs analysis, including task, person, and organizational analyses, prior to the design and delivery of ethics training.
Principle 2	Ensure ethics training content and strategy is appropriately matched to training needs.
Principle 3	Create an ethics training program evaluation plan.
Principle 4	Prepare the environment for learning.

During Training

Principle 5	Employ pedagogically sound instructional strategies, including information presentation, demonstration, practice, and feedback, during ethics training.

After Training

Principle 6	Foster an environment that facilitates transfer and sustainment of ethical behavior on the job.
Principle 7	Evaluate ethics training.

an appropriate solution for current organizational needs. Some problems may be better solved using other organizational strategies and methods, such as selection practices. For example, perhaps an organization's ethics problem stems from a knowingly corrupt upper management who persists in unethical activities anyway. In this scenario, it may be better to hire new corporate leadership instead of spending resources on rehabilitation of individuals who are unlikely to reform and who are an organizational liability. On the other hand, a TNA may reveal that unethical behaviors are due to employees being unaware of a formal ethics code and the policies in place for reporting unethical behavior. In this scenario, a training initiative to inform employees about the corporate code of ethics and available channels for anonymously reporting unethical behavior is an appropriate strategy.

The training literature articulates three components of a proper TNA: task analysis, person analysis, and organizational analysis. We describe each of these below.

Task analysis. A task analysis answers the question: What needs to be trained? Task analysis specifies the elements of a job, determines the task requirements, and identifies the particular knowledge, skills, and attitudes (KSAs) required to successfully complete a job or task. It is beyond the scope of the current chapter to provide a description of how a task analysis may be conducted, but there are a variety of procedures suggested in the literature. For further information on how to conduct a task analysis see Brannick, Levine, and Morgeson (2007).

Person analysis. Person analysis answers the questions: Who needs to be trained? What are the individual characteristics of those who need to be trained? Specifically, a person analysis identifies who has (and who lacks) the requisite skills to perform the task as identified during the task analysis. This step allows instructional designers to tailor training experiences for employees in need of training. It is especially useful when resources are scarce and training attendance must be necessarily limited as it identifies employees for whom training is critical.

A person analysis may also be used to elucidate characteristics of trainees (e.g., morality, personality) that may influence training effectiveness. Person characteristics such as motivation to learn (Baldwin, Magjuka, & Loher, 1991; Tannenbaum, Mathieu, Salas, & Cannon-Bowers, 1991), self-efficacy (Chen, Gully, Whiteman, & Kilcullen, 2000; Colquitt et al., 2000; Ford, Kozlowski, Kraiger, Salas, & Teachout, 1997; Mathieu, Tannenbaum, & Salas, 1992; Quiñones, 1995), and goal orientation (Ford et al., 1997; Phillips & Gully, 1997) are known to affect learning outcomes resulting from training. Information collected during a person analysis may be used to determine who would be most likely to benefit from training and what training strategies may be most useful given the profile of trainee's characteristics.

Organizational analysis. This final step in TNA answers the questions: What are the organization's training priorities? Is the organization ready for training? Is training the most appropriate solution to organizational problems? What are the possible organizational barriers to effective training? This element of TNA investigates the organization's strategy, culture, norms, limitations, resources, and stakeholder (e.g., leadership and stockholders) support of training initiatives.

Organizational analysis includes two components: strategic alignment and environmental readiness. Strategic alignment involves examining corporate objectives and priorities, critical competencies in which the organization must excel in order to compete in its market; identifying the positions and functions instrumental to corporate success; and establishing a corporate learning strategy (Tannenbaum, 2002). Studying organizational goals and culture will help instructional designers determine whether ethics training is an appropriate solution for the current organizational climate. For example, an organizational analysis should consider the utility of alternative methods for promoting ethics in the workplace. If awareness of the corporate code of ethics is an issue, it may be possible to use organization-wide correspondence to promote awareness regarding the corporate stance on business ethics. However, if the objective is to teach employees how to make ethical decisions, training may be a necessary strategy.

The second component of organizational analysis, environmental readiness, assesses the work environment for barriers to training effectiveness. For example, the literature is clear that organizational support improves learning and application of trained KSAs on the job (Grossman & Salas, 2011; Rouiller & Goldstein, 1993; Tracey, Tannenbaum, & Kavanagh, 1995) and that support varies widely among organizations (Flynn, Eddy, & Tannenbaum, 2005; Holton, Chen, & Naquin, 2003; Tannenbaum, 1997). Awareness of the organizational characteristics that may hinder training effectiveness prior to the design and delivery of training allows instructional designers to develop training programs that are resilient to certain barriers and/or create contingency plans for avoiding these barriers.

Unfortunately, despite its usefulness for informing training design and delivery, TNA is frequently skipped because it can be expensive and time consuming. This is a grievous omission, likely to result in less effective training and a waste of resources. Ethics training programs that are planned in response to a TNA will be more effective. Therefore,

> **Principle 1:** *Conduct a systematic training needs analysis, including task, person, and organizational analyses, prior to the design and delivery of ethics training.*

Training Design

Training design should be guided by the results of a TNA (Salas & Stagl, 2009). After conducting a thorough TNA, instructional designers will be able to determine whether business ethics training is a viable solution for addressing organizational needs. If so, the next step in the training system will be to design the training program. Training design involves planning the instructional program itself and addresses concerns such as what content the training will cover, how this content will be delivered to learners, and what instructional strategies will be used to facilitate maximal learning. Results from a TNA are helpful in this step as they can be used to establish a set of instructional learning objectives for the training program. Learning objectives outline what the training will address and impose boundaries on the training content. Identifying learning objectives based on TNA results ensures that the final training program will be an appropriate fit with the organization and its needs (Goldstein & Ford, 2002). Establishing this connection between the training program content and organizational needs provides a strong foundation for an effective training program.

When specifying learning objectives, it must be remembered that training content should fully encompass all information that employees must know in order to behave ethically on the job, as identified in the TNA. In other words, training content should not be deficient of essential information related to the training purpose. When training fails to address critical information, employees do not learn as much as they should and training effectiveness suffers. Alternatively, instructional designers should be cautioned against including unnecessary information in the training program.

Including such information contaminates the training program and may detract from critical information. For instance, if a TNA indicated that employees are generally aware of the corporate code of ethics and its content but they are not acting ethically because they lack the necessary decision-making skills, then addressing the corporate code of ethics in detail unnecessarily contaminates the training program. In this case, it would be unwise to focus training resources on training corporate policy; instead, training should be limited to improving participants' ethical decision-making ability.

In addition to ensuring that training content is poignant and complete, instructional designers should be aware of what information is *need-to-know* versus *need-to-access* (Salas et al., 2012). Need-to-know information refers to information that employees must know without reference aids in order to be able to perform their jobs at an acceptable level. For example, corporate ethics standards are need-to-know information because employees must know them in order to perform their job at some minimally accepted ethical standard. Need-to-access information, on the other hand, is information that employees do not need to know off the cuff. Procedures for reporting ethical misconduct exemplifies information that is need-to-access. In general, employees do not need to know the details of the formal process to report instances of misconduct in order to perform their duties effectively; however, when it becomes necessary to file a formal report regarding a co-worker's misconduct, employees need to know where they can access instructions for submitting a formal report. It should be a goal of training to disseminate information that is need-to-know. This includes training where need-to-access information can be obtained when it is needed but excludes training of specific details of information that is need-to-access.

Incorporating characteristics of effective training into instructional strategy will help business ethics training programs to have lasting results. Fortunately, Noe and Colquitt (2002) offered a useful list of design characteristics that can be incorporated into effective training strategies: (1) training participants understand the objectives, purpose, and intended outcomes of training; (2) training content (e.g., examples, exercises) is meaningful and relevant to work experiences; (3) participants are provided instructional aids to help them learn, organize, and recall training content; (4) practice opportunities are provided in a safe environment; (5) feedback is provided by multiple sources, including trainers, observers, peers, and/or the task itself; (6) participants have the opportunity to observe and interact with other training participants; and (7) the training program is efficiently coordinated. It is recommended that instructional designers purposefully design business ethics training strategies to incorporate these advantageous elements.

Principle 2: *Ensure ethics training content and strategy is appropriately matched to training needs.*

Evaluation Plan

It is often simply assumed that a given training program works. The possibility that participants fail to learn from training or, worse, that training actually damages employee behavior is rarely evaluated in practice. However, ineffective or harmful training causes organizations to misuse valuable resources (e.g., money, employee time) on a program that does not provide lasting desired performance changes. Because no organization wants to needlessly throw away resources, it is important to conduct training evaluation, which is the systematic collection of data to support training effectiveness (Kraiger et al., 1993). Training evaluation provides empirical evidence for a training program's strengths and weaknesses and allows inferences to be made regarding the utility of the program for meeting organizational objectives and needs (Alvarez, Salas, & Garofano, 2004). Although results of program evaluation will not be apparent until after training takes place, it is important to establish an evaluation strategy prior to conducting training to ensure that the necessary data needed to complete a comprehensive evaluation is collected at appropriate time points. In other words, planning evaluation in advance of training allows instructional designers to create a rigorous evaluation strategy that fits the purpose, within the boundaries of the situation (Aguinis & Kraiger, 2009; Sackett & Mullen, 1993).

An evaluation plan describes what will be measured, how it will be measured, and when it will be measured. Evaluation frameworks are invaluable tools for evaluation planning, and it is recommended to adopt one in order to facilitate the planning process. A number of evaluation frameworks have been forwarded throughout the years, but Kirkpatrick's (1976, 1994) is the most common framework used for evaluating organizational training. Kirkpatrick's (1976) framework consists of four levels of evaluation: (1) reactions, (2) learning, (3) behavior, and (4) results. Collectively, these levels represent different areas for evaluating training effectiveness.

In the Kirkpatrick (1976, 1994) framework, reactions refer to learners' attitudes towards the training program. Learner attitudes toward training may include assessment of whether learners enjoyed training (i.e., training satisfaction) as well as whether learners believe they learned from training. It is often easiest to evaluate training through learner reactions as reaction data can be collected with simple self-report surveys. Reactions data also can render important insights regarding training effectiveness, as learner satisfaction with training does lead to greater knowledge gains (Sitzmann, Brown, Casper, Ely, & Zimmerman, 2008). In other words, learners actually learn more from training that is enjoyable. Learner dissatisfaction with training may indicate that training needs to be redesigned to improve learner motivation and engagement as a mechanism for subsequent learning.

Kirkpatrick (1976, 1994) refers to learning as changes in KSAs resulting from participation in training. After reactions, learning is the second most common level at which training is evaluated. There are a number of ways in which learning may be assessed, but arguably the most common method is through declarative knowledge tests. The popularity of declarative knowledge measures is likely due to the relative ease and objectivity with which such tests can be developed and administered. Behavioral observation is another method for assessing learning. However, observations are subjective in nature. Ratings can be influenced by idiosyncratic rater biases, which can make observations an unreliable source for individual performance (Landy & Farr, 1980). The already somewhat subjective nature of ethics may make the use of observational ratings especially difficult when measuring learning from ethics training. Should observations be used for the purpose of measuring ethics raters should be trained to avoid committing common rating errors? The use of behaviorally anchored rating scales (BARS) is also recommended to help reduce idiosyncratic rating errors by explicitly associating different rating levels to behavioral anchors (Smith & Kendall, 1963). Whatever method employed, measuring learning is critical in determining whether ethics training has met the predetermined learning objectives and aligns with organizational needs.

Level 3 of Kirkpatrick's framework, labeled *behaviors*, entails assessment of learners' ability to apply their knowledge gains. As discussed above, transfer of learned KSAs to the organizational environment is the crux of training. Savvy instructional designers understand that effective training programs must not only affect learning but must also facilitate transfer of learned KSAs. Unfortunately, while intrinsically tied to employees' ability to demonstrate desired behaviors at work, learning does not automatically translate to improved employee ethical behavior. Therefore, it is of paramount importance that on-the-job use of trained KSAs is measured. Behaviors should be measured during training as well as in the work context. Measuring behaviors during or immediately following the conclusion of training when participants are still in the training environment will provide insight into whether training is able to affect participant behavior in general. Should participants be unable to perform during training it is unlikely they will be able to do so on-the-job. Such findings would require training designers to make improvements to the ethics program perhaps by including more varied practice and feedback opportunities to participants. However, if participants demonstrate ethical behaviors while in the training environment but not in the work context, organizations may need to consider additional explanations for employees' failure to transfer. While training may still need to be redesigned to better elicit transfer-appropriate processing from participants during training, other explanations may include a perceived lack of supervisor support or an unethical organizational climate. Measuring behaviors both during and after training will enable training designers to make well-informed decisions regarding ethics training.

Lastly, in Kirkpatrick's (1976, 1994) evaluation framework, results refer to the impact training has on the organization. In other words, results are the organizational benefits incurred by training employees. For example, in the ethical training context organizations may expect a reduction in lawsuits or an improvement in public image as a result of a more ethical workforce. Unfortunately, organizational benefits may be subjective and are notoriously difficult to measure. Measuring results usually requires some creativity and planning. Often it may only be possible to measure anticipated organizational impact indirectly with proxy measures.

Ideally, evaluation plans will include measurement of all four levels of Kirkpatrick's (1976, 1994) framework. Instructional designers must determine what is feasible to measure in their organizations and should plan to evaluate the outcomes of greatest importance to organizational stakeholders (e.g., upper level management, business owners, shareholders, etc.). Each of these levels should then be measured via multiple measurement methods (e.g., self-report, objective measures). Multi-method measurement generates a more accurate understanding of training and promotes confidence in conclusions regarding its effectiveness.

Principle 3: *Create an ethics training program evaluation plan.*

Learning Climate

Before training is conducted, efforts must be made to generate a climate that is conducive to learning. There are a number of ways a learning climate can be created. Organizations must communicate early and often about the purpose of training, establish an appropriate attendance policy, explain why certain employees are expected to attend, and promote organization-wide support of training (Salas et al., 2012).

Learners develop expectations before training, and learners with unmet expectations demonstrate lower self-efficacy, motivation, and commitment to use of training on the job (Sitzmann, Bell, Kraiger, & Kanar, 2009; Tannenbaum et al., 1991). When promoting training, caution should be taken to avoid overselling training. Communications regarding training prior to its implementation should focus on its benefits as opposed to (alleged) deficits in employees (Salas et al., 2012). Framing training as an opportunity rather than a test or punishment reduces learner anxiety (Martocchio, 1992) and promotes mastery orientation, which improves learning (Ford et al., 1998). Pre-training communications should, therefore, be honest yet positive.

A training attendance policy should be established prior to training. Setting an attendance policy, however, can be tricky. Employees often take attendance policies as signals of the organization's opinion about training. This may sometimes have unintended implications, so how the attendance policy is framed matters. For example, employees may view mandatory training more positively if organizational attitudes towards training are generally positive, as this may signal that the training is important (Tannenbaum & Yukl, 1992). We caution instructional designers against selective mandatory ethical training attendance. Such policies may inadvertently suggest that some employees are more unethical than others, and this may cause employees required to attend to become stigmatized, embarrassed, and resentful. Instead, we recommend that, when conducting ethics training, attendance is either mandated or voluntary for all organizational employees. We shall leave this decision up to top organizational management, but should training be made mandatory, the attendance policy should not only identify who is required to attend training but should also specify why.

As noted above, organizational support of training influences training effectiveness. In fact, one study found that as little as one misdirected comment by a team leader regarding the usefulness of training is enough to prevent learning and transfer (Smith-Jentsch, Salas, & Brannick, 2001). Instead, organizations should prepare and encourage supervisors and mentors to discuss organizational ethics and the benefit of ethics training for employees (Salas et al., 2012).

Principle 4: *Prepare the environment for learning.*

During Training

Ethical training programs should include four instructional elements to promote the greatest amount of learning within training participants (Salas & Cannon-Bowers, 2001). These elements are: information, demonstration, practice, and feedback (Kraiger, 2003). Information involves presentation of what learners need to know and be able to do at the end of training. In ethics training, information includes an explanation of what ethics are and why they are important. Information may also involve a description of what ethical behavior is. Demonstration, on the other hand, shows learners the informational concepts being addressed during instruction. It allows learners to absorb the content in another way and makes it salient to them. For optimal learning and transfer, demonstration should include both positive and negative exemplars (Taylor et al., 2005). In business ethics training, this involves examples demonstrating both ethical and unethical behaviors. Providing learners with demonstrations of both ideal and undesirable behavior allows them to understand the difference and recognize both. For topics like ethics, which are inherently ambiguous and confusing, demonstration of good and bad behavior is particularly important.

Effective training programs also include a practice element. Well-designed training builds in opportunities for learners to practice what they have learned during the training event to allow enhanced development of the knowledge, skills, and attitudes being trained. To further improve the utility of the practice exercises, instructors should provide both negative and positive feedback to learners. Ellis and Davidi (2005) found that when post-event discussion includes discussion of both successful and unsuccessful performance during practice events, learners develop a better understanding of the environment and what constitutes effective performance than when post-event discussions focus solely on unsuccessful performance. Including information, demonstration, practice, and feedback strategies during ethics training will facilitate learning and post-training transfer to the job context. It is therefore important to include these elements in all training programs.

Principle 5: *Employ pedagogically sound instructional strategies, including information presentation, demonstration, practice, and feedback, during ethics training.*

After Training

Transfer

Positive transfer is the supreme purpose of training (Baldwin & Ford, 1988; Goldstein & Ford, 2002). Instructional designers create training programs to teach learners specific KSAs that are intended to improve relevant work behaviors (i.e., transfer). Although employees may gain new KSAs through training, this learning alone does not guarantee transfer. In fact, many organizations report a failure to effectively improve KSAs and anticipate future training needs (IBM, 2008). When learning occurs but fails to transfer, training loses its organizational value, becoming a waste of organizational resources and employee time. This phenomenon has been called the "transfer problem" (Grossman & Salas, 2011; Michalak, 1981). Estimates indicate that as little as 10% of training costs transfer to the job (Georgenson, 1982). To avoid this waste and reduce the gap between training efforts and organizational outcomes, organizational leadership should make efforts to create a work environment that is supportive of training transfer. Such an environment would provide a positive transfer climate, support training participants' use of ethics upon return to work, offer opportunities to perform, and follow up with additional opportunities to learn (Grossman & Salas, 2011).

Transfer Climate

Transfer climate is the observable or perceived organizational atmosphere that inhibits or facilitates the use of learned KSAs (Rouiller &

Goldstein, 1993). A positive transfer climate is one that facilitates the use of learned KSAs at work, whereas a negative transfer climate inhibits the use of learned KSAs. Perceptions of a positive transfer climate encourage training participants to more readily apply their learned competencies on the job (Salas et al., 2006). Further evidence is found in a qualitative exploratory study in which training participants indicated that an unsupportive transfer climate is the largest inhibitor to transfer (Gilpin-Jackson & Bushe, 2007). Participants were tentative to use learned KSAs at work when they dreaded violating organizational norms. It is therefore desirable to create the experience of a positive transfer climate. Characteristics of such an environment can be classified into two categories: situational cues and consequences (Rouiller & Goldstein, 1993). Broadly, situational cues prompt training participants to use new KSAs and include things such as clearly established goals, peer and supervisor support, equipment availability, and job aids (i.e., tools that assist job performance; Salas et al., 2006). Consequences consist of positive and negative feedback as well as punishment. Consequences include rewards for the use of correct KSAs and remediation for incorrect use.

Support

Just as it is important for organizations to encourage management and leadership to promote the value of training prior to training implementation, management and leadership should continue to support the use of learned KSAs on the job after training has concluded and employees return to work. Leadership, supervisor, and peer support are critical to training transfer as they significantly influence the likelihood of training participants to adopt learned competencies on the job (Grossman & Salas, 2011). Training participants who receive high levels of supervisor support transfer more KSAs one year following training than those who reported lower levels of support (Cromwell & Kolb, 2004). There are a number of different ways in which trained employees can be supported, such as by facilitating goal setting (Burke & Hutchins, 2007; Taylor et al., 2005); offering recognition, encouragement, and rewards for utilizing trained skills (Kontoghiorghes, 2001; Salas & Stagl, 2009; Salas et al., 2006); delivering feedback (Lim & Johnson, 2002); and having supervisors participate in training (Gilpin-Jackson & Bushe, 2007; Lim & Johnson, 2002; Saks & Belcourt, 2006). Peer support has also been shown to facilitate transfer (e.g., Blume, Ford, Baldwin, & Huang, 2010; Chiaburu & Marinova, 2005; Cromwell & Kolb, 2004). For instance, Hawley and Barnard (2005) showed that transfer improves when training participants network with peers and discuss course content. Interestingly, there is little evidence to suggest that one type of support is superior to another. One recent study found no difference between the provision of feedback by peers versus supervisors (Van den Bossche, Segers, & Jansen,

2010). We therefore recommend that organizations utilize as many avenues of support as they are capable of providing to recently trained employees.

Opportunity to Perform

In order for transfer to occur, trained employees need opportunities to practice and apply learned KSAs to the job context (Burke & Hutchins, 2007). A lack of performance opportunities has been shown to reduce employees' use of learned KSAs on the job (e.g., Clarke, 2002). The sooner after training employees are able to practice learned KSAs in the workplace the more likely these competencies will transfer (Salas et al., 2006). Supervisors should minimize the delay between training and opportunities to perform by modifying training participants' workloads and allowing them to practice their learned KSAs during their normal schedules (Clarke, 2002).

Follow-up

Learning does not end with the conclusion of formal training (Grossman & Salas, 2011). As trained employees return to work and are provided opportunities to perform on the job, post-training feedback can help these individuals sustain and improve upon their learned competencies (Baldwin, Ford, & Blume, 2009). Trained employees should reflect on their learning experience (Grossman & Salas, 2011) and can enlist involvement of their peer support network to facilitate discussion and goal setting for using and sustaining their learned skills.

Given the importance of training transfer to training effectiveness, organizations should be committed to improving the probability that trained employees will be able to appropriately use learned KSAs in the workplace. We therefore recommend that organizations use the strategies discuss above to foster a positive transfer environment.

> **Principle 6:** *Foster an environment that facilitates transfer and sustainment of ethical behavior on the job.*

Evaluation

After training is conducted, instructional designers should execute the evaluation plan developed during pre-training and collect the data needed to assess training effectiveness. As discussed above, evaluation has a very important role in the training system (Kraiger et al., 1993). Evaluation identifies "a training program's successes and failures with regard to content and design, changes and learners, and organizational payoffs" (Alvarez et al., 2004, p. 388). In other words, it specifies what is working in a training program and what can be improved in future iterations of the program for either new organizational members or as refresher training for employees experiencing skill decay. Conducting a thorough evaluation of a business ethics training program allows instructional designers and organizational stakeholders to make decisions regarding its current utility and continued use. Findings from training evaluation should be communicated to management, including results regarding participant reactions to training, learning, subsequent transfer of learned KSAs, and relevant organizational results.

When planned in advance, evaluation should be a smooth process. However, should instructional designers fail to articulate an evaluation plan during pre-training, meaningful evaluation can still be conducted (Kraiger, 2002; Kraiger, McLinden, & Casper, 2004; Sackett & Mullen, 1993; Tannenbaum & Woods, 1992). Sackett and Mullen (1993) suggest there are two classes of training evaluation. The first class is aimed at understanding how much change has occurred in training participants from pre-training to post-training. Change-oriented evaluations require a comparison between pre-training and post-training scores in order to ascertain whether participants experienced a change in reactions, learning, and/or behaviors from pre-training to post-training. The second class of training evaluation seeks to determine whether a specific level of performance has been reached through participation in training. Participants' post-training ability is compared to benchmark scores, which represent a desired performance standard. The focus of these performance-oriented evaluations is not on whether participants' scores changed from pre-training to post-training, but whether training helps participants perform at an expected level of competency. The answer to this query may be of particular value in the case of business ethics as it may not matter whether employees become slightly more ethical after participating in training if they still do not adhere to an organization's ethical standard.

Both classes of training evaluation answer important questions regarding training effectiveness. The key distinction, according to Sackett and Mullen (1993), is that change-oriented evaluations are designed to assess training utility; that is, whether the training is capable at all of improving business ethics. Performance-oriented evaluations, on the other hand, may be used to assess both the effectiveness of the ethics training program as well as the individual participants. Ideally, instructional designers will determine in advance of training whether the requirements of their situation call for the measurement of change, achievement, or both. However, both classes of evaluation may be planned post-hoc, if necessary.

Performance-oriented evaluations lend themselves more easily to post-hoc planning than change-oriented evaluations. Performance-oriented evaluations can be conducted solely with post-training data, making it relatively simple for instructional designers to plan a robust evaluation after training implementation. For change-oriented evaluations, determining an evaluation plan prior to conducting training is the easiest way to obtain the data needed to calculate change scores. However, it may still be possible to measure change if there are archival data available from which comparable pre-training scores can be acquired. Instructional designers should be cautious when planning a change-oriented evaluation post-hoc, however. There is no guarantee that complete and relevant archival data exist or that access to this data will be granted (Shultz, Hoffman, & Reiter-Palmon, 2005). Using archival data may also be risky when less valid proxy measures must be used. The use of such data could lead instructional designers and organizational leadership to make incorrect inferences about training effectiveness by concluding that the training program is more or less effective than it is in reality (Shultz et al., 2005; Shadish, Cook, & Campbell, 2002). Instructional designers can avoid these pitfalls by planning training evaluation prior to training implementation, but training evaluation should always be conducted.

Principle 7: *Evaluate ethics training.*

CONCLUSION

Business ethics training is a useful tool in promoting ethical behavior in organizations (e.g., Delaney & Sockell, 1992; Ferrell, Fraedrich, & Ferrell, 2002) during a time when some are concerned we may be amidst an ethics crisis in the West (Sims, 1992). Ethics training may not only increase employees' ability to make ethical decisions and act ethically, but it may also demonstrate an organizational commitment to ethical business practices (Weber, 2007). Given these corporate trends, we have discussed the science of training and forwarded seven scientifically based principles for conducting business ethics training programs in an effort to guide development of effective ethics training.

REFERENCES

Adler, P. S. (2002). Corporate scandals: It's time for reflection in business schools. *Academy of Management Executive, 16*(3), 148–149.

Aguinis, H., & Kraiger, K. (2009). Benefits of training and development for individuals and teams, organizations, and society. *Annual Review of Psychology, 60*, 451–474.

Alvarez, K., Salas, E., & Garofano, C. M. (2004). An integrated model of training evaluation and effectiveness. *Human Resource Development Review, 3*, 385–416.

Arthur, H. B. (1986). Making business ethics useful. *Strategic Management Journal, 5*, 319–333.

Arthur, W., Jr., Bennett, W., Jr., Edens, P. S., & Bell, S. T. (2003). Effectiveness of training in organizations: A meta-analysis of design and evaluation features. *Journal of Applied Psychology, 88,* 234–245.

Arthur, W., Jr., Bennett, W., Jr., Stanush, P. L., & McNelly, T. L. (1998). Factors that influence skill decay and retention: A quantitative review and analysis. *Human Performance, 11*(1), 57–101.

Baldwin, T. T., & Ford, J. K. (1988). Transfer of training: A review and directions for future research. *Personnel Psychology, 41,* 63–105.

Baldwin, T. T., Ford, J. K., & Blume, B. D. (2009). Transfer of training 1988–2008: An updated review and agenda for future research. *International Review of Industrial and Organizational Psychology, 24,* 41–70.

Baldwin, T. T., Magjuka, R. J., & Loher, B. T. (1991). The perils of participation: Effects of choice of training on trainee motivation and learning. *Personnel Psychology, 44,* 260–267.

Badaracco, J. L., Jr. (1992). Business ethics: Four spheres of executive responsibility. *California Management Review, 34*(3), 64–79.

Baxter, G. D., & Rarick, C. A. (1987). Education for the moral development of managers: Kohlberg's stages of moral development and integrative education. *Journal of Business Ethics, 6*(3), 243–248.

Blume, B. D., Ford, J. K., Baldwin, T. T., & Huang, J. L. (2010). Transfer of training: A meta-analytic review. *Journal of Management, 39,* 1065–1105.

Bohren, J. (1992). Reinforcing ethics at work. *The Human Resource Professional, 4,* 55–58.

Brannick, M. T., Levine, E. L., & Morgeson, F. P. (2007). *Job and work analysis: Methods, research and applications for human resource management* (2nd ed.). Thousand Oaks, CA: Sage Publications.

Brass, D. J., Butterfield, K. D., & Skaggs, B. C. (1998). Relationship and unethical behavior: A social network perspective. *Academy of Management Review, 23,* 14–31.

Burke, L., & Hutchins, H. M. (2007). Training transfer: An integrative literature review. *Human Resource Development Review, 6,* 263–296.

Campbell, J. P. (1971). Personnel training and development. *Annual Reviews of Psychology, 22,* 565–602.

Chen, G., Gully, S. M., Whiteman, J. A., & Kilcullen, B. N. (2000). Examination of relationships among trait-like individual differences, state-like individual differences, and learning performance. *Journal of Applied Psychology, 85,* 835–847.

Chiaburu, D. S., & Marinova, S. V. (2005). What predicts skill transfer? An exploratory study of goal orientation, training self-efficacy and organizational supports. *International Journal of Training and Development, 9,* 110–123.

Clarke, N. (2002). Job/work environment factors influencing training effectiveness within a human service agency: Some indicative support for Baldwin and Ford's transfer climate construct. *International Journal of Training and Development, 6,* 146–162.

Colquitt, J. A., LePine, J. A., & Noe, R. A. (2000). Toward an integrative theory of training motivation: A meta-analytic path analysis of 20 years of research. *Journal of Applied Psychology, 85,* 678–707.

Cromwell, S. E., & Kolb, J. A. (2004). An examination of work-environment support factors affecting transfer of supervisory skills training to the workplace. *Human Resource Development Quarterly, 15,* 449–471.

Delaney, J. T., & Sockell, D. (1992). Do company ethics training programs make a difference? An empirical analysis. *Journal of Business Ethics, 11*(9), 719–727.

Edelman. (2011). *2011 Edelman trust barometer.* Retrieved from http://www.sustainablebrands.com/digital_learning/research/2011-edelman-trust-barometer-findings

Ellis, S., & Davidi, I. (2005). After-event reviews: Drawing lessons from successful and failed experience. *Journal of Applied Psychology, 90,* 857–871.

Ferrell, O. C., & Fraedrich, J. (1991). *Business ethics: Ethical decision making and cases.* Boston, MA: Houghton Mifflin Company.

Ferrell, O. C., Fraedrich, J., & Ferrell L. (2002). *Business ethics: Ethical decision-making and cases.* Boston, MA: Houghton Mifflin Company.

Flynn, D., Eddy, E. R., & Tannenbaum, S. I. (2005). The impact of national culture on the continuous learning environment: Exploratory findings from multiple countries. *Journal of East–West Business, 12,* 85–107.

Ford, J. K., Kozlowski, S. W. J., Kraiger, K., Salas, E., & Teachout, M. (Eds.). (1997). *Improving training effectiveness in work organizations.* Mahwah, NJ: Erlbaum.

Ford, J. K., Smith, E. M., Weissbein, D. A., Gully, S. M., & Salas, E. (1998). Relationships of goal-orientation, meta-cognitive activity, and practice strategies with learning outcomes and transfer. *Journal of Applied Psychology, 83,* 218–233.

Georgenson, D. L. (1982). The problem of transfer calls for partnership. *Training and Development Journal, 36,* 75–78.

Gick, M. L., & Holyoak, K. J. (1983). Schema induction and analogical transfer. *Cognitive Psychology, 15,* 1–38.

Gilpin-Jackson, Y., & Bushe, G. R. (2007). Leadership development training transfer: A case study of post-training determinants. *Journal of Management Development, 26,* 980–1004.

Goldstein, I. L. (1991). Training in work organizations. In M. D. Dunnette & L. M. Hough (Eds.), *Handbook of industrial and organizational psychology* (Vol. 2, pp. 507–619). Palo Alto, CA: Consulting Psychologists Press.

Goldstein, I. L. (1993). *Training in organizations: Needs assessment, development and evaluation* (3rd ed.). Belmont, CA: Brooks/Cole.

Goldstein, I. L., & Ford, J. K. (2002). *Training in organizations* (4th ed.). Belmont, CA: Wadsworth Thompson Learning.

Gregory, M. E., Feitosa, J., Driskell, T., Salas, E., & Vassey, W. B. (2013). Designing, delivering, and evaluating team training in organizations: Principles that work. In E. Salas, S. I. Tannenbaum, D. Cohen, G. Latham (Eds), *Developing and enhancing teamwork in organizations: Evidence-based best practices and guidelines* (pp. 441–487). San Francisco, CA: Jossey-Bass.

Grossman, R., & Salas, E. (2011). The transfer of training: What really matters. *International Journal of Training and Development, 15*(2), 103–120.

Hawley, J. D., & Barnard, J. K. (2005). Work environment characteristics and implications for training transfer: A case study of the nuclear power industry. *Human Resource Development International, 8,* 65–80.

Hiltebeitel, K. M., & Jones, S. K. (1992). An assessment of ethics instruction in accounting education. *Journal of Business Ethics, 11*(1), 37–46.

Holton, E. F., III, Chen, H.-C., & Naquin, S. S. (2003). An examination of learning transfer system characteristics across organizational settings. *Human Resource Development Quarterly, 14,* 459–482.

Hyman, H. R., Skipper, R., & Tansey, R. (1990). Ethical codes are not enough. *Business Horizons, 33,* 15–22.

IBM. (2008). *Unlocking the DNA of the adaptable workforce: The IBM Global Human Capital Study.* Milwaukee, WI: IBM.

Izzo, G. (2000). Compulsory ethics education and the cognitive moral development of salespeople: A quasi-experimental assessment. *Journal of Business Ethics, 28*(3), 223–241.

Jones, S. K., & Hiltebeitel, K. M. (1995). Organizational influence in a model of the moral decision process of accountants. *Journal of Business Ethics, 14*(6), 417–431.

Keith, N., & Frese, M. (2008). Effectiveness of error management training: A meta-analysis. *Journal of Applied Psychology, 93,* 59–69.

Kirkpatrick, D. L. (1976). Evaluation. In R. L. Craig (Ed.), *Training and development handbook,* (2nd ed., pp. 294–312). New York, NY: McGraw-Hill.

Kirkpatrick, D. L. (1994). *Evaluating training programs: The four levels.* San Francisco, CA: Berrett-Koehler. (Original work published 1959)

Kontoghiorghes, C. (2001). Factors affecting training effectiveness in the context of the introduction of a new technology: A U.S. case study. *International Journal of Training and Development, 5,* 248–260.

Kozlowski, S. W. J., & Salas, E. (1997). A multilevel organizational systems approach for the implementation and transfer of training. In J. K. Ford, S. W. J. Kozlowski, K. Kraiger, E. Salas, & M. S. Teachout (Eds.), *Improving training effectiveness in work organizations* (pp. 157–210). Mahwah, NJ: Erlbaum.

Kraiger, K. (2002). Decision-based evaluation. In K. Kraiger (Ed.), *Creating, implementing, and maintaining effective training and development: State-of-the-art lessons for practice* (pp. 331–375). San Francisco, CA: Jossey-Bass.

Kraiger, K. (2003). Perspectives on training and development. In W.C. Borman, D. R. Ilgen, & R. J. Klimoski (Eds.), *Handbook of psychology: Volume 12, Industrial and organizational psychology* (pp. 171–192). Hoboken, NJ: Wiley.

Kraiger, K., Ford, J. K., & Salas, E. (1993). Application of cognitive, skill-based, and affective theories of learning outcomes to new methods of training evaluation. *Journal of Applied Psychology, 78,* 311–328.

Kraiger, K., McLinden, D., & Casper W. J. (2004). Collaborative planning for training impact. *Human Resource Management Review, 43,* 337–351.

Laczniak, G. (1983). Business ethics: A manager's primer. *Business, 33*(1), 23–29.

Landy, F. J., & Farr, J. L. (1980). Performance rating. *Psychological Bulletin, 87*(1), 72–107.

LeClair, D. T., & Ferrell, L. (2000). Innovation in experiential business ethics training. *Journal of Business Ethics, 23*(3), 313–322.

Levin, M. (1989, November 25). Ethics courses: Useless. *The New York Times,* pp. 23.

Lim, D. H., & Johnson, S. D. (2002). Trainee perceptions of factors that influence learning transfer. *International Journal of Training and Development, 6,* 26–48.

Loe, T. W., & Weeks, W. A. (2000). An experimental investigation of efforts to improve sales students' moral reasoning. *The Journal of Personal Selling and Sales Management, 20*(4), 243–251.

Martocchio, J. J. (1992). Microcomputer usage as an opportunity: The influence of context in employee training. *Personnel Psychology, 45,* 529–551.

Mathieu, J. E., Tannenbaum, S. I., & Salas, E. (1992). Influences of individual and situational characteristics on measures of training effectiveness. *Academy of Management Journal, 35,* 828–847.

Michalak, D. F. (1981). The neglected half of training. *Training and Development Journal, 35,* 22–28.

Minkes, A. L., Small, M. W., & Chatterjee, S. R. (1999). Leadership and business ethics: Does it matter? Implications for management. *Journal of Business Ethics, 20*(4), 327–335.

Noe, R. A. (1986). Trainees' attributes and attitudes: Neglected influences on training effectiveness. *Academy of Management Review, 11,* 736–749.

Noe, R. A., & Colquitt, J. A. (2002). Planning for training impact: Principles of training effectiveness. In K. Kraiger (Ed.), *Creating, implementing, and maintaining effective training and development: State-of-the-art lessons for practice* (pp. 53–79). San Francisco, CA: Jossey-Bass.

Palmer, D. E., & Zakhem, A. (2001). Bridging the gap between theory and practice: Using the 1991 federal sentencing guidelines as a paradigm for ethics training. *Journal of Business Ethics, 29,* 77–84.

Penn, W. Y., Jr., & Collier, B. D. (1985). Current research in moral development as a decision support system. *Journal of Business Ethics, 4*(2), 131–136.

Phillips, J. M., & Gully, S. M. (1997). Role of goal orientation, ability, need for achievement, and locus of control in the self-efficacy and goal setting process. *Journal of Applied Psychology, 82,* 792–802.

Quiñones, M. A. (1995). Pre-training context effects: Training assignment as feedback. *Journal of Applied Psychology, 80,* 226–238.

Rouiller, J. Z., & Goldstein, I. L. (1993). The relationship between organizational transfer climate and positive transfer of training. *Human Resource Management, 45,* 229–247.

Sackett, P. R., & Mullen, E. J. (1993). Beyond formal experimental design: Towards and expanded view of the training evaluation process. *Personnel Psychology, 46,* 613–627.

Saks, A. M., & Belcourt, M. (2006). An investigation of training activities and transfer of training in organizations. *Human Resource Management, 45,* 629–648.

Salas, E., & Cannon-Bowers, J. A. (2001). The science of training: A decade of progress. *Annual Review of Psychology, 52,* 471–499.

Salas, E., & Stagl, K. C. (2009). Design training systematically and follow the science of training. In E. Locke (Ed.), *Handbook of principles of organizational behavior: Indispensible knowledge for evidence-based management* (2nd ed., pp. 59–84). Chichester, UK: Wiley.

Salas, E., Tannenbaum, S. I., Kraiger, J. K., & Smith-Jentsch, K. A. (2012). The science of training and development in organizations: What matters in practice. *Psychological Science in the Public Interest, 13*(2), 74–101.

Salas, E., Wilson, J. R., Priest, H. A., & Guthrie, J. (2006). Training in organizations: The design, delivery and evaluation of training systems. In G. Salvendy (Ed.), *Handbook of human factors and ergonomics* (pp. 472–512). Hoboken, NJ: John Wiley & Sons.

Schwartz, M. (2001). The nature of the relationship between corporate codes of ethics and behavior. *Journal of Business Ethics, 32,* 247–262.

Shadish, W. R., Cook, T. D., & Campbell, D. T. (2002). *Experimental and quasi-experimental designs for generalized causal inference.* Boston, MA: Houghton Mifflin.

Shultz, K. S., Hoffman, C. C., & Reiter-Palmon, R. (2005). Using archival data for I-O research: Advantages, pitfalls, sources, and examples. *The Industrial-Organizational Psychologist, 42*(3), 31–37.

Sims, R. R. (1991). The institutionalization of organizational ethics. *Journal of Business Ethics, 10,* 493–506.

Sims, R. R. (1992). The challenge of ethical behavior in organizations. *Journal of Business Ethics, 11*(7), 505–513.

Sitzmann, T., Bell, B. S., Kraiger, K., & Kanar, A. M. (2009). A multilevel analysis of the effect of prompting self-regulation in technology-delivered instruction. *Personnel Psychology, 62,* 697–734.

Sitzmann, T., Brown, K. G., Casper, W. J., Ely, K., & Zimmerman, R. D. (2008). A review and meta-analysis of the nomological network of trainee reactions. *Journal of Applied Psychology, 93*(2), 280–295.

Smith, P. C., & Kendall, L. M. (1963). Retranslation of expectations: An approach to the construction of unambiguous anchors for rating scales. *Journal of Applied Psychology, 47*(2), 149–155.

Smith-Jentsch, K. A., Salas, E., & Brannick, M. T. (2001). To transfer or not to transfer? Investigating the combined effect of trainee characteristics, team leader support, and team climate. *Journal of Applied Psychology, 86,* 279–292.

Smith-Jentsch, K. A., Zeisig, R. L., Acton, B., & McPherson, J. A. (1998). Team dimensional training: A strategy for guided team self-correction. In J. A. Cannon-Bowers & E. Salas (Eds.), *Making decisions under stress: Implications for individual and team training* (pp. 271–297). Washington, DC: American Psychological Association.

Stark, A. (1993). What's the matter with business ethics? *Harvard Business Review, 7*(3), 38–48.

Tannenbaum, S. I. (1997). Enhancing continuous learning: Diagnosing findings from multiple companies. *Human Resource Management, 36,* 437–452.

Tannenbaum, S. I. (2002). A strategic view of organizational training and learning. In K. Kraiger (Ed.), *Creating, implementing, and maintaining effective training and development: State-of-the-art lessons for practice* (pp. 10–52). San Francisco, CA: Jossey-Bass.

Tannenbaum, S. I., Mathieu, J. E., Salas, E., & Cannon-Bowers, J. A. (1991). Meeting trainees' expectations: The influence of training fulfillment on the development of commitment, self-efficacy, and motivation. *Journal of Applied Psychology, 76,* 759–769.

Tannenbaum, S. I., & Woods, S. B. (1992). Determining a strategy for evaluating training: Operating within organizational constraints. *Human Resource Planning, 15*(2), 63–81.

Tannenbaum, S. I., & Yukl, G. (1992). Training and development in work organizations. *Annual Review of Psychology, 43,* 474–483.

Taylor, P. W. (1975). *Principles of ethics: An introduction to ethics* (2nd ed.). Encino, CA: Dickenson.

Taylor, R. J., Russ-Eft, D. F., & Chan, D. W. L. (2005). A meta-analytic review of behavior modeling training. *Journal of Applied Psychology, 90,* 692–709.

Thompson, B. L. (1990). Ethics training enters the real world. *Training, 27*(10), 82–94.

Tracey, J. B., Tannenbaum, S. I., & Kavanagh, M. J. (1995). Applying trained skills on the job: The importance of work environment. *Journal of Applied Psychology, 80,* 239–252.

Treviño, L. K., & Brown, M. E. (2004). Managing to be ethical: Debunking five business ethics myths. *Academy of Management Executive, 18*(2), 69–81.

Treviño, L. K., & Nelson, K. A. (1999). *Managing Business Ethics.* New York, NY: Wiley.

Treviño, L. K., Butterfield, K., & McCabe, D. (1998). The ethical context in organizations: Influences on employee attitudes and behaviors. *Business Ethics Quarterly, 8,* 447–476.

Valentine, S., & Barnett, T. (2002). Ethics codes and sales professionals' perceptions of their organizations' ethical values. *Journal of Business Ethics, 40,* 191–200.

Valentine, S., & Fleischman, G. (2004). Ethics training and businesspersons' perceptions of organizational ethics. *Journal of Business Ethics, 52,* 381–390.

Van den Bossche, P., Segers, M., & Jansen, N. (2010). Transfer of training: The role of feedback in supportive social networks. *International Journal of Training and Development, 14,* 81–94.

Weber, J. A. (2007). Business Ethics Training: Insights from Learning Theory. *Journal of Business Ethics, 70*(1), 61–85.

CHAPTER 2

BEST PRACTICES
IN ETHICS TRAINING

A Focus on Content and Context[1]

Leslie E. Sekerka

With ever-increasing global competition and the economic demands of our time, there is added pressure for employees to achieve ambitious performance goals while also addressing more complex ethical issues. As corporations in the United States try to face these concerns, leaders must understand and follow existing, new, and revised regulations. This means that those responsible for organizational ethics education and training must ensure that employees understand the rules and apply ethical practices in their everyday workplace routines.

It is important not only that organizations develop and communicate their ethical standards, but that they also disseminate this information throughout the organizational structure and be certain that it is fully understood by employees at every level (Palmer & Zakhem, 2001).

We know that awareness of proper conduct can be achieved via ethics training (Chen, Sawyers, & Williams, 1997; Izzo, 2000; Loe & Weeks, 2000). Moreover, ethics programs in organizations must go beyond the teaching

Ethics Training in Action, pages 31–56

of requirements and standards: They must also help employees learn how to effectively recognize and respond to common ethical problems experienced in the workplace. Training can actually shape company culture (LeClair & Ferrell, 2000), which can help employees have more positive perceptions of organizational ethics than do those working for firms without such training (Valentine & Fleischman, 2004).

To develop their efforts, organizations can base their programs on a variety of philosophical frameworks. As described by Bowan (2004), if an organization desires ethical behavior, its management will likely develop a program grounded in the moral philosophy of consequentialist or nonconsequentialist ethics (cf. Christians, Fackler, Rotzoll, & McKee, 2001; DeGeorge, 1986; Donaldson & Werhane, 1999). The former, often referred to as utilitarianism, guides people to determine the appropriate course of ethical action based on the perceived consequences. The latter, known as a deontological approach, determines the ethics of a situation by the principles or duties involved, rather than examining potential outcomes. These foundational perspectives can range widely, producing different program purposes and objectives, leading to multifaceted pedagogical approaches (LaFollette, 2007). For example, a focus on teaching compliance and a duty to perform one's job with ethical standards is likely to be grounded in a *deontological* approach. Here, the ethics program would help employees understand the rules, regulations, policies, and procedures deemed central to effective task accomplishment. Some describe how this may be the dominant and potentially exemplary approach for general ethics training (cf. Bowan, 2004); however, other programs may be grounded in *consequentialism.* In such cases the concern would be to have employees think about the long-term implications, outcomes, and ultimate consequences of workplace decisions and actions. Another approach might be to encourage people to think about how their actions can impact others and helping them consider how to achieve outcomes that exceed personal and organizational goals to benefit the "greater good." This idea, and the notion that moral judgment and action require practice to become habituated into daily routines, would represent a virtue ethics approach. Clearly, ethics programs may draw upon multiple frameworks to achieve their training goals and objectives, but are likely to be grounded in a central core philosophy.

Given that an ethics program has a specific purpose derived from a moral foundation, what makes it successful? More than a decade ago, Knouse and Giacalone (1997) outlined what was needed. To achieve ethics training success, they suggested that the program must:

- Help people understand ethical judgment philosophies and decision-making heuristics
- Address areas of ethical concern within their industry/profession

- Teach the organization's ethical expectations and rules
- Help people to understand their own ethical tendencies
- Take a realistic view, while also elaborating on difficulties in ethical decision making
- Have people use the material in the workplace, then return to training for additional work to analyze their application

Are these components featured in today's ethics training? How might these guidelines be manifest in organizations today? To ascertain current perceptions of what are considered effective practices for in-house ethics training, a study was undertaken to answer these questions:

1. What are the commonly reported best practices in organizational ethics education and training today?
2. Are these practices being utilized by organizations in the Silicon Valley region of the Western United States?
3. When comparing best practices with current efforts, what trends emerge that can inform and guide program improvements?

Before continuing with a description of the study, a word about best practices: What are they? A best practice is a technique, process, or methodology that, based on research and experience, reliably leads to a desired outcome. The reason for identifying best practices and applying them is to reduce error and dysfunction and to provide an effective means toward improvement. A criticism is that they are inherently historical; they have effectively contributed to the achievement of some *past* objective. Therefore, current conditions do not ensure repeated success, which is especially relevant in today's rapidly changing workplace environments. But it can also be argued that because a best practice has stood the test of time, it is steadfast and durable. While the adoption rate is not as high as might be expected (Ungan, 2004), an examination of best practices can add value by instilling awareness and promoting idea generation that may contribute to organizational learning.

The intention of this work was not to determine program effectiveness, nor to validate the usefulness of any particular practice. Rather, the goal was to identify practice trends in ethics education and training today. From there, the intention was to help those responsible for training to garner insight for potential program improvement. As an action research investigation, the inquiry was designed to be a catalyst for dialogue—to serve as a platform for ethics program networking to influence collective organizational development among the participants.

The first phase identified 65 best practices in organizational ethics education and training as reported in academic and practitioner journals.

The second phase was an inquiry conducted with ten companies in the western United States, in the Silicon Valley region of California. Leaders within these companies expressed an interest in ethics program improvement. Interviews were conducted with an ethics official representing each organization with a goal to: (1) understand the nature of their in-house program; (2) determine which best practices are currently being used, assess their value and, given the findings; and (3) consider the adoption of practices to improve their program. A review of each phase of the study is presented, beginning with the methods, followed by analyses, findings, and a discussion with suggestions for future directions.

METHODS AND ANALYSES

Phase one of the study examined the literature using ProQuest, ABI/Inform, ERIC, and the Business and Company Resource Center databases. Academic, educational, and practitioner journals were included, but the inquiry was restricted to articles published within the last five years. A variety of search strings and their derivations were used to identify the practices (e.g., "ethics training and organizations," "organizational ethics," "business ethics and training," "management education," and "ethics education best practices"). The author and five research assistants worked independently to procure articles and cull best practices in organizational ethics education and training, focusing on key areas including business management, education, human resources, organizational behavior, psychology, and training and development. A technique, process, or method was considered a potential "best practice" if it was referenced in an academic, practitioner, or training journal as an effective ethics training practice or a useful process to support ethics training in an organizational setting.

Once the preliminary list of practices was identified (over 400 items), the author (lead researcher) used qualitative analysis techniques to combine similar items. The best practices were distilled and then clustered by themes (cf. thematic analysis; Boyatzis, 1998). Ultimately, groupings were formed around related practices and were then named as the final main themes (e.g., *core issues, delivery form,* and *ongoing communications*). The final thirteen themes were then sorted by central concept, which formed two main categories (labeled Content and Context). Content describes the type of material and delivery form utilized, and context describes the application of content and to communicate, assess, and measure ethics in the organization. For example, under content is the theme of *Situations and Scenarios,* which consisted of several best practice items such as: (1) "Uses ethical challenges or cases actually faced in the organization as the focus of training" and (2) "Solicits employees to submit areas of concern, key issues, stories, or ideas to use in training." Under context is the theme of *ethical risk assessment*, which consisted of several best practice items such as (1) "Conducts formal risk assessments to identify areas of ethical risk" and (2) "Line managers have specific responsibility for managing areas of ethical risk."

Phase two began with the preparation of an interview script with open-ended questions to learn more about the participating organizations (e.g., type, structure, size) and their current ethics education and training programs. As an action research project, where participants take an active role in the development of the inquiry and its findings, the preliminary script and best practice list were examined by several participants, along with two ethics scholars and an organizational development practitioner. The script and best practice list were pretested with two members of the sample population and three students. This effort simplified the script and added clarity to the questions and items, resulting in a final list containing 40 content and 25 context best practice items. The thematic grouping of *actions of the board* was not a best practice culled from the literature, but it was deemed worthwhile based upon participant request (i.e., to include various items related to this topic). Therefore, in the spirit of action research, these items were included in the general inquiry.

Ten corporations were invited to participate in the study based on their membership in a regional ethics organization in the Western United States. Referred to as the "partnership," the alliance brings together executives and scholars in a forum designed to increase participants' knowledge about how to effectively manage ethics in their organizations. Breaking issues in business and organizational ethics are discussed, and members benefit from sharing experiences with leading companies and hearing from scholars who share the latest research. Members sustain involvement because they find that their engagement has helped them implement innovative ideas and to expand their social networks, which enables them to better address complex ethical issues that emerge within their global business operations. The group is based in the Silicon Valley area of California, a region known for its innovative products and services in the field of technology. Partnership members are responsible for the ethics education and training within their organizations and expressed an interest in learning more about current best practices in ethics programming.

Eight of the ten organizations currently enrolled in the partnership were engaged (one was not available for an interview and one was dropped because it was a different industry type from all the others). Participant roles varied, including VP of Human Resources, CEO, Director of Ethics, General Counsel, and other ethics officials. The companies ranged in size from 900 to 150,000 employees, all engaged in international markets that focus on service and manufacturing in technology.

The author (also lead researcher) conducted all of the interviews. The participants were guided through the script and then discussed the 69 specific practices identified in Phase 1 and 2 of the study (65 best practices and 4 requested items). Participants were asked to indicate the presence of each item (yes, no, or limited, coded as 1, 0, and .25, respectively) and, if the practice was employed, its degree of value or perceived importance to the organization (using a 1–7 Likert scale, 1 = not at all to 7 = extremely). If the practice was not used, participants indicated if they would like to adopt it (1 = yes, 0 = no). The tape-recorded interviews lasted 60–90 minutes and were transcribed verbatim.

Quantitative analysis was used to prepare descriptive statistics, and qualitative methods were used to analyze the transcripts to construct interview summaries. The first step was to identify the best practices utilized within each organization, providing a kind of ethical "check-up" for each of the participating organizations. The second step was to identify patterns in the overall dataset. Because no values were assigned to the best practice items by the researcher, no judgments were made as to the effectiveness of any program. Rather, the list served as an inventory to facilitate a comparison between recognized best practices and the various programs under study. This helped highlight areas of strength and challenges for potential future program development. The transcripts were summarized independently by two research assistants (blind to any identifiers) using open coding from ground theory technique (Strauss & Corbin, 1990). This information provided explanatory details about the nature of each organization and its training program.

Findings

Framework

The interview summaries provided an overview of each organization's program, including its intent and purpose. In describing the core message of their program, participants revealed that communicating specifics related to rules, policies, standards of conduct, and government regulations shape the central purpose of the ethics training. Consistent throughout the organizations studied was a primary motive to prevent unethical action by elevating awareness of what principled action is expected for employees. This deontological approach was underscored by a general belief that formal rules and principles are aligned with a personal and organizational duty to "do the right thing" in the workplace. A shared concern for establishing awareness of the organization's values could be viewed as a representation of virtue ethics within the programs, but only one organization actually articulated the importance of using training (and other means) to help employees develop and exercise their ethical strength. The potential benefits of utilitarianism, considering multiple long-term consequences for effective decision making, were rarely mentioned. When this philosophy emerged, it was only in the context of specialized training sessions or retreats for senior level managers or executives.

The interview summaries also provided general information about the structure, culture, and ethical climate of each organization. For example, three organizations position their ethics group within their legal department. Here we see that a focus on regulation and compliance are especially pronounced, affirming a deontological approach. The other organizations positioned their programs either as an independent functional unit (three) or located it within their human resource department (two). In the latter five organizations, participants not only described the importance of training for cultivating awareness of rules and attending to compliance-based requirements, but they were also interested in the educational aspects of training. For example, in these organizations there was a more explicit concern for helping employees learn the rules and values as well as how to apply them. In these cases, the organization seemed to adopt a broader-based ethical philosophy, one that attempts to address several frameworks.

Use of Best Practices

The mean scores for presence (actual use) and value (level of importance) were calculated for each best practice item, providing insights by category, theme, and item across the sample. Tables 2.1 and 2.2 describe this information in detail. As might be expected, the strength of presence is often associated with higher values. But this is not always the case. In describing the findings, the highs and lows (in terms of presence and value) will be highlighted, along with several examples where inconsistencies emerge. This includes times when a practice is low in presence but highly valued. Such an examination will provide areas for additional exploration, which will be addressed in the discussion section.

If an item was not present in the organization, the participant did not place a value on its use, but rather stated whether or not they desired the adoption of the particular best practice. The final column reflects the number of companies that indicated a desire to adopt some or all of the best practices if they were not currently in use.

Content Category

Of the seven themes in the content category, *Core Issues* is clearly dominant, with five of the six best practice items very high in presence. Mean scores for presence are ≤ .91 (out of 1) and mean scores for value are ≤ 6.25 (out of 7). Within this theme the item "*Explains that whistleblowers are protected from retaliation*" is the strongest, present in all eight organizations (1.0)

TABLE 2.1   Best Practices by Content and their Application (N = 8)[a]

Best Practices by Content: Themes and Items (40)	Best Practice Presence Mean (0–1)	Best Practice Value Mean (1–7)	Companies that Desire Adoption (0–8)
1. Core Issues (6)			
Explains that whistleblowers are protected from retaliation.	1.00	6.75	0
Addresses values and ethics topics that go beyond compliance.	0.91	6.88	0
Covers confidential reporting channels (e.g., anonymous telephone line).	0.91	6.63	0
Addresses compliance issues such as rules, regulations, and laws that apply to employees and their jobs.	0.91	6.50	0
Covers key areas, selected because ethical problems often occur in these areas.	0.91	6.25	0
Addresses how to achieve performance goals ethically.	0.19	5.33	5
2. Specific and Explicit Behaviors (5)			
Designed to promote values and positive ethical behavior.	1.00	6.63	0
Designed to prevent unethical and illegal behavior.	0.88	6.57	0
Defines what it means to be ethical and how to apply ethics into everyday activities.	0.88	6.00	1
Describes exact level of accountability ascribed to each employee, explicitly identifying expected behaviors.	0.47	5.50	2
Employees learn how to openly discuss the implications of their actions, practicing transparency and openness as part of workplace routines.	0.28	6.00	4
3. Target Audience (11)			
All employees receive core E&T program that explains the company's ethics philosophy and underscores how rules are consistent and equal among all levels.	0.91	6.88	0
Provides ethics training during the first week of new employee orientation.	0.91	6.25	0
Varies by level, function and role: Special focus for new employees.	0.88	6.43	1
Certain employees, in areas of ethical risk, receive more frequent ethics E&T.	0.75	6.50	0
Every employee participates in ethics E&T annually.	0.50	6.50	2

(continued)

TABLE 2.1 Best Practices by Content and their Application (cont.)

Best Practices by Content: Themes and Items (40)	Best Practice Presence Mean (0–1)	Best Practice Value Mean (1–7)	Companies that Desire Adoption (0–8)
Mixes hourly and management personnel in sessions.	0.47	5.17	2
Varies by level, function and role: Special focus for first level supervisors.	0.31	6.00	1
Varies by level, function and role: Special focus for midlevel managers.	0.19	5.67	3
Has an ethics E&T for vendors, suppliers, and business partners.	0.19	5.33	2
Varies by level, function and role: Special focus for senior executives.	0.16	6.50	6
Varies by level, function and role: Special focus for BoDs.	0.00	NA	4
4. Focus on Learning Styles (4)			
Demonstrates how to use the resources (helpline, websites, etc.) to report allegations.	0.88	6.00	1
Uses a variety of tools to address various learning styles.	0.53	5.80	2
Uses games or other techniques designed to encourage employees to have fun.	0.38	5.67	4
Makes use of videos or acted out situations which demonstrate appropriate ethical behavior.	0.31	6.25	0
5. Situations and Scenarios (3)			
Uses ethical challenges or cases actually faced in the organization as the focus of the training.	0.88	6.14	1
Solicit employees to submit areas of concern, key issues, stories, or ideas to use in training.	0.38	5.00	2
Company solicits employees before or during the training to offer personal cases.	0.28	5.00	2
6. Ongoing Reflection, Practice, and Dialogue (5)			
Helps employees to use critical thinking or an ethical decision-making process to determine the moral action.	0.78	5.43	1
Has employees practice ethical situations that involve choosing between two right paths.	0.41	5.00	4
Includes periods of reflection and sharing ideas during session.	0.31	5.20	3
Has employees practice ethical decision-making, posing questions to help them resolve their ethical challenges.	0.25	4.75	4

(continued)

TABLE 2.1   Best Practices by Content and their Application (cont.)

Best Practices by Content: Themes and Items (40)	Best Practice Presence Mean (0–1)	Best Practice Value Mean (1–7)	Companies that Desire Adoption (0–8)
Uses role playing or other techniques to encourage emotional awareness.	0.03	3.00	5
7. Delivery Form (6)			
Uses online training for values and ethics topics beyond compliance.	0.75	7.00	0
Uses online training for compliance topics.	0.75	6.83	1
Uses face to face training for values and ethics topics beyond compliance.	0.38	5.83	1
Uses face to face training for compliance topics.	0.38	5.67	1
Conducted by the supervisor of each work group for his or her employees.	0.16	6.50	3
Conducted in-house by line management.	0.16	6.00	3

[a] Presence is based upon 0 = no, 1 = yes, or .25 = limited; Value (importance) is based upon a 1–7 Likert scale (1 = not at all to 7 = extremely); Desired Adoption represents the number of companies who do not have one or more of the best practice items within a given theme, but would like to adopt one or more of them.

Note: A "0" value indicates that this best practice is not being used.

TABLE 2.2   Best Practices for Context and their Application (N = 8)[a]

Best Practices by Context: Themes and Items (25)	Best Practice Presence Mean (0–1)	Best Practice Value Mean (1–7)	Companies that Desire Adoption (0–8)
1. Raising Questions and Promoting Awareness (9)			
Ethics information is available in multiple languages.	0.88	6.29	1
Tracks information provided by reporting mechanisms.	0.88	5.86	0
Maintains online website with frequently asked ethics Q&A.	0.88	5.71	1
Ethics information, including the code of conduct, is provided in written form to all employees.	0.78	6.57	0
Provides an anonymous telephone hotline where employees can ask questions, get advice, and report concerns.	0.75	6.67	0

(continued)

TABLE 2.2   Best Practices for Context and their Application (cont.)

Best Practices by Context: Themes and Items (25)	Best Practice Presence Mean (0–1)	Best Practice Value Mean (1–7)	Companies that Desire Adoption (0–8)
Provides an ethics email service where employees can ask questions, get advice, and report concerns.	0.75	6.67	1
Appoints ethics officers within business units or in each location.	0.34	6.00	0
Employees are solicited for suggested changes in the organization's code of ethics and other ethics information.	0.25	6.00	2
Ethics information is posted where employees will encounter it daily.	0.13	6.00	3
2. Commitment to the Code (3)			
Code is signed by all employees.	0.78	6.00	0
Distributes ethics codes to vendors, suppliers, and business partners.	0.34	5.80	1
Employees are asked to resign the code each year.	0.31	5.50	0
3. Program Effectiveness (4)			
Conducts an annual employee survey to measure ethical attitudes and culture.	0.50	6.25	3
Requires all E&T participants to complete program evaluations.	0.28	5.33	4
Poses questions before and after an E&T session to measure impact on ethical thinking.	0.28	4.00	4
Conducts exit interviews include questions about ethical behavior observed.	0.13	7.00	6
4. Ethical Risk Assessment (2)			
Conducts formal risk assessment to identify areas of ethical risk.	0.38	6.00	3
Line managers have specific responsibility for managing areas of ethical risk.	0.06	6.00	5
5. Link Ethics with Performance (3)			
Managers develop skill sets and competencies to attain successful ethical performance.	0.31	5.80	4
Ethical actions are explicitly included in employees' performance evaluations.	0.31	5.25	3
Recruiting practices evaluate the ethical character of candidates.	0.25	6.50	4
6. Ongoing Communications (4)			
Includes ethics content in internal publications to all employees at least once a month.	0.13	6.00	5

(continued)

TABLE 2.2 Best Practices for Context and their Application (cont.)

Best Practices by Context: Themes and Items (25)	Best Practice Presence Mean (0–1)	Best Practice Value Mean (1–7)	Companies that Desire Adoption (0–8)
Requires line managers to include ethical topics in staff meetings at least once quarterly.	0.06	6.50	4
Requires event planners to include ethics content in companywide conferences and other events.	0.03	7.00	3
Sends special ethics communications to all employees at least once a month.	0.03	6.00	5
Actions of the Board (4)[b]			
BoDs explicitly focus on issues of compliance.	1.00	6.25	0
BoDs explicitly focus on issues beyond compliance.	0.56	5.83	1
BoDs encourage transparency.	0.38	7.00	0
BoDs align senior leader performance with ethics.	0.03	7.00	3

[a] Presence is based upon 0 = no, 1 = yes, or .25 = limited; Value (importance) is based upon a 1–7 Likert scale (1 = not at all to 7 = extremely); Desired Adoption represents the number of companies who do not have one or more of the best practice items within a given theme, but would like to adopt one or more of them.
[b] The theme of *Actions of the Board* (4) was not a best practice identified in Phase One, but was added to the Context category by participant request.
Note: A "0" value indicates that this best practice is not being used.

with very high value (6.75). The other items that comprise this theme have to do with specific areas covered in the training, such as compliance, rules, regulations, values, confidential reporting channels, and other salient ethics issues. The only item not present in most organizations within this theme was "*Addresses how to achieve performance goals ethically*" (.19), yet it too is somewhat valued (5.33).

Moving in order of greatest strength of overall presence in the content category, we next see that the theme of *Specific and Explicit Behaviors* follows. Here, three of the five best practice items have mean scores for presence ≤ .88 with relatively high values (≤ 6.00). While the best practice "*Designed to promote values and positive ethical behavior*" is present in all eight organizations (1.00) and highly valued (6.63), several other items such as "*Describes exact level of accountability ascribed to each employee, explicitly identifying expected behaviors*" and "*Employees learn how to openly discuss the implications of their actions, practicing transparency and openness as part of workplace routines*" lack consistent inclusion in the organizations' ethics programs (.47

and .28 respectively), yet their value remains fairly high (at 5.50 and 6.00 respectively).

Target Audience, Focus on Learning Styles, and *Situations and Scenarios* are themes that tend to have several best practice items with strong presence, but show much less inclusion overall. For example, *Target Audience* has four items that are fairly strong at ≤ .75. It is clear that new employees are a primary focus (presence .91 and value 6.25), and that describing the ethical philosophy and how the rules apply to all employees is present in most of the organizations (.91) and very highly valued (6.88). Yet seven additional items within this theme vary from .50 to 0 in presence. For example, only half of the organizations apply the item "*Every employee participates in ethics E&T annually*" (.50), valuing it highly (6.50), but with adoption only desired by two of four organizations. As a theme, targeting the audience is a best practice that describes how training must be directed to specific roles, shaping the content based upon level (e.g., new employees, supervisors, managers, executives). We see that this does not typically occur, except for in the training directed towards new employees. But this is not because it is not valued; in fact, "*Varies by level, function, and role: Special focus for Board of Directors*" is not performed in any of the organizations and is desired for adoption by half (four companies). Why this discrepancy may have occurred is addressed in the discussion section.

For the *Focus on Learning Styles* theme, the item "*Demonstrates how to use the resources (helpline, websites, etc.) to report allegations*" has the highest mean presence (.88) and value (6.00). But again, we see in this theme that there are more items that are valued but not included as much as the organizations would like. An example is the item "*Uses a variety of tools to address various learning styles*" (presence .53 and value 5.80), with two organizations desiring its adoption. Another item, "*Makes use of videos or acted out situations which demonstrate appropriate ethical behavior,*" has a presence of .31 with a strong value (6.25). Interestingly, the presence for "*Uses games or other techniques designed to encourage employees to have fun*" did not have a robust presence (.38), yet it was highly valued (5.67), and four organizations wanted to see this adopted.

For the theme of *Situations and Scenarios,* only one of the three items had both a strong presence and value (.88 and 6.14 respectively), that being "*Uses ethical challenges or cases actually faced in the organization as the focus of the training.*" The other two items focus on having employees become actively engaged in the process, soliciting them for their personal cases (ethical challenges) or areas of concern. The inclusion of these two best practice items was limited (.38 and .28), and they are only somewhat valued (each at 5.00). Only two organizations wanted this type of employee participation included.

For the sixth theme in the content category, *Ongoing Reflection, Practice, and Dialogue*, only one of the five items showed a strong presence, while others dip to as low as .03 usage. The item "*Helps employees to use critical thinking or an ethical decision-making process to determine the moral action*" has the greatest inclusion (.78) and is deemed as being somewhat valued (5.43). The item with the next highest strength of presence (.41), "*Has employees practice ethical situations that involve choosing between two right paths,*" reflects a lower value, as compared to the first item (5.0). The best practice "*Has employees practice ethical decision-making, posing questions to help them resolve their ethical challenges*" is not regularly present (.25) nor highly valued (4.75), but those who do not have this practice desire its adoption (four organizations). While only one firm had the theme "*Uses role playing or other techniques to encourage emotional awareness*" (.03) and its value was quite low (3.00), five organizations desired its adoption. This reflects that most training asks employees to engage in bounded ethical decision making effort, deciding what action(s) to take between several choices. For the most part, the training is not a generative process where employees help to co-create the learning effort, can ask questions, and have the opportunity to engage in the practice of ethical decision-making through interaction. These observations are affirmed by the additional findings associated with the final theme, described next.

In the final content theme of *Delivery Form*, we see that the organizations typically use online training to provide compliance, values, and ethics content (.75 presence), which is deemed high in value (6.83–7.00). Also valued highly (5.67–5.83), yet used substantially less (.38), is the face-to-face delivery form. In addition, having the training conducted by in-house line management or by the supervisor of each work group was a valued best practice (6.00–6.50), but rarely present (.16). Taken together, the best practice items for this theme were valued highly (5.67–7.00).

Overall, the findings for the content category suggest that organizations are doing a good job at including content to address rules, regulations, and compliance requirements, while simultaneously bringing forward a focus on values. Targeting specialized audiences within the organization is under-addressed, except when it comes to new employee training, which appears to be a consistent practice. Techniques proffered as effective that require a face-to-face interactive environment (e.g., role playing, posing questions, sharing ideas during a session) present mixed values by the few organizations that currently include them, but are typically desired for adoption if not currently in use. Opportunities for improvement appear to reside most abundantly within the themes that *Target Audience*, provide *Ongoing Reflection, Practice and Dialogue*, and extend the *Delivery Form*.

Context Category

Looking now to the context category, these themes represent the framework and setting for the ethics training program within the organization. The first theme, *Raising Questions and Promoting Awareness*, shows a strong presence. Three of the nine items reflect a mean presence of .88 with values ≤ 5.71. These best practices include sharing information in multiple languages, tracking ethics concerns reported, and maintaining an online employee website with ethics information. Three additional items included in this theme, "*Ethics information, including the code of conduct, provided in written form to all employees*," "*Provides an anonymous telephone hotline where employees can ask questions, get advice, and report concerns*," and "*Provides an ethics email service where employees can ask questions, get advice, and report concerns*," are also present (.75–.78) with very high values (6.57–6.67). Not typically present (.34–.13) but valued (6.00) were three additional items: "*Appoints ethics officers within business units or in each location*," "*Employees are solicited for suggested changes in the organization's code of ethics and other ethics information*," and "*Ethics information is posted where employees will encounter it daily*." This last item was considered by most of the participants as being "old-fashioned," given the dissemination of ethics information via the company website (as per above).

Most of the organizations studied have some level of a *Commitment to the Code*, referring to their in-house document that describes the company standards of conduct and general ethical guidelines for employees. While the first item in this theme, "*Code is signed by all employees*" has a high presence (.78) and value (6.00), the other two best practices have a rather low presence (.31–.34) and are only somewhat valued (5.50–5.80). This reflects a limitation in organizational efforts to share ethics information to vendors, suppliers, and business partners. In addition, employers infrequently ask employees to recommit to the company code after their initial signing (when first employed).

The remaining themes in the context category show substantially less presence, as compared to those in content, yet their value scores remain comparable. These themes, *Program Effectiveness, Ethical Risk Assessment, Link Ethics with Performance*, and *Ongoing Communications*, have no representation in three of the organizations studied (no presence of any of the best practice items). But despite their limited presence, there is a strong desire for their adoption. For example, in the theme of *Program Effectiveness*, only half (.50) of the organizations "*Conduct an annual employee survey to measure ethical attitudes and culture*," yet this best practice is a valued item (6.25), and three organizations desire its adoption. Perhaps the most striking observation is that the presence score for "*Conducts exit interviews that include questions about ethical behavior observed*" is .13, yet its value is 7.00 and six of the eight organizations desired its adoption. Missing from most organizations are the best practice items for the theme of *Ethical Risk Assessment,* especially *"Line managers have specific responsibility for managing areas of ethical risk,"* which has a very low mean presence (.06). Again, it is valued (6.00) despite limited use, with six organizations desiring its adoption. For the theme of *Link Ethics with Performance* we see a similar pattern: low presence for the three items (.25–.31), with a reasonably high value (5.25–6.50), and desired adoption by those who do not currently use the practices (three or more organizations). The last theme of *Ongoing Communications* follows suit. All four best practice items show little presence (.03–.13), possess very high value (6.00–7.00), and adoption is generally desired by those who do not currently employ them. An example is *"Requires line managers to include ethical topics in staff meetings at least once quarterly,"* which has a very low presence (.06), high value (6.50), and is desired by four organizations.

Actions of the Board was not a best practice theme based upon those identified in Phase 1 of the study. It was added based upon participant request and provides additional insight. Only one of the four items in this theme is typically present, yet the items appear to merit inclusion, when comparing their values to other context-related themes. Consistent with other findings related to performance, the item that explicitly links ethics and performance for the board of directors lacks presence (.03) but was highly valued (7.00). Conversely, the best practice item *"Board of Directors explicitly focus on issues of compliance"* was present in all of the organizations (1.00) with a value of (6.25).

Overall, the thirteen themes that address the content and context of ethics training reflect areas where improvements are needed. To understand where opportunities reside, we can look at when best practices are not being used and their adoption is desired. Moreover, the inconsistencies and patterns that emerged among several themes point to the need for closer examination. Reviewing the overall findings in concert with the qualitative interview data will provide greater insight toward the development of recommendations.

DISCUSSION

Findings suggest that specific strengths as well as challenges exist in both content and context areas for ethics education and training. Overall, the eight organizations studied show more representation of the best practices for the Content category, as compared to the Context category. Figures 2.1 and 2.2 display percentages of best practices present in each organization by category. In Figure 2.1 we see that two of the organizations studied use more than 65% of the best practice items for content, with another five organizations using nearly 50%, and one using 46%. The representation of best practices is not as favorable for the context category, where only one

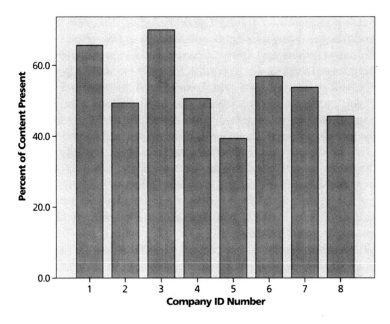

Figure 2.1 Percent of best practices by content. *Note:* $n = 8$; Based upon best practice themes listed under Content (40).

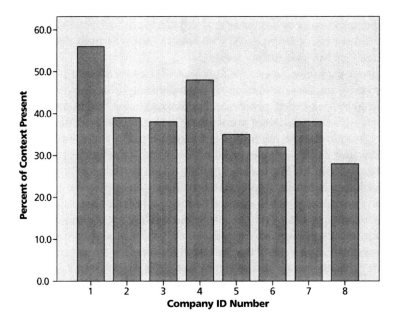

Figure 2.2 Percent of best practices by context. *Note:* $n = 8$; Based upon best practice themes listed under Context (25), not including Actions of the Board.

organization uses 56% of the best practice items, followed by another at 48%, and the remaining six organizations range in utilization between 28 to 39%. To better understand these outcomes, the findings are examined, noting where improvements are needed. This will help build a general picture of the overall program efforts, which contributes to informed next steps.

Looking to the content category, the organizations included material that covers both compliance and values-based topics. The general focus is to make people aware of the organization's rules and its code of conduct, and to make it clear that each employee is held responsible for applying these regulations and standards in the workplace. There is not much effort to try and develop or educate most employees—that is, helping people learn and explore ethical frameworks, understand their use and application, and expand their ethical competencies as they relate to more effective decision making and behavior.

While new employees receive formal indoctrination that includes a focus on ethics, unless you are a senior executive, in direct sales, or have been targeted for special attention (based upon areas of vulnerability or in cases where unethical activities have occurred), it is unlikely that you will be engaged in face-to-face training where reflection, practice, and ongoing dialogue are cultivated. In addition, organizations are not as inclusive as they could be, limiting employee involvement in the ethics program's development, content, and form. For example, employees are rarely solicited for their personal cases or concerns and will likely not be in an interactive dialogue during the training itself. This relates to the form of delivery, which is typically one-way via online method.

A closer examination reveals that four of the seven content themes currently being implemented in most organizations bring forward key issues related to salient ethical problems. Furthermore, we find that scenarios associated with the workplace are used to help employees understand these concerns and relate to them during the training. For example, participants describe how their online tutorial sessions link specific desired behaviors to ethical action. Employees are typically asked to navigate through a series of questions where they are directed to choose an appropriate response by applying corporate rules to correctly address a series of issues. But knowing the rules and applying them in an online session is not the same as learning how to recognize, work through, openly discuss, and resolve an ethical dilemma (where there may not be one right solution to an issue).

This underscores an inconsistency in the findings around delivery form and the desire to educate and develop employees for ethical decision making and moral action. We know that face-to-face delivery is considered a critical element in training because it promotes interaction, shared reflection, and dialogue, which are needed for the practice of moral agency (cf. Piper, Gentile, & Parks, 1993; Sekerka, 2008). While organizations expect this capability for all employees and affirm that the rules and standards apply equally to all levels, they are not investing in ethical development at all levels. While participants value face-to-face training, it is limited and not always desired by those who do not have it. And yet, by the same token, the findings show that those responsible for training want employees to be able to practice, reflect, and share ideas during the process. To unpack this incongruence, the interview summaries reflect how participants describe face-to-face delivery as prohibitive, based upon multiple costs (both in time and money from multiple venues). Several participants were quite frank, suggesting they agreed that this would be particularly effective, but is beyond their capacity, given the resources that they have been provided. The data show that half of the sample (four companies) would like to adopt best practices to cultivate *Ongoing Reflection, Practice, and Dialogue.* However, the participants were very clear that face-to-face sessions are typically reserved for special groups because of the expense, and they consider this form beyond their means in terms of resources. They also added that it would take employees away from their regular duties, adding even more cost to such an initiative.

To address this challenge, perhaps merging best practices can be considered, combining several so that they can be attended to in part (if not in totality). For example, face-to-face delivery could be used to teach first-level supervisors how to create face-to-face discussions about ethics in their workgroups. This could potentially weave several under-addressed and highly valued best practice items together (e.g., having in-house line management conduct face-to-face training with their staff, where employees practice ethical decision-making and exercise dialogue and inquiry to help resolve ethical challenges). Unfortunately, there is a tendency to wait to employ these methods until problems have occurred. Participants candidly described how their organizations tend to promote more personalized ethics training when they are in a reactionary mode, working to rectify unethical behaviors. Only then does it become unilaterally employed throughout the employee base. Some organizations employ many of these best practices and strengthen them, going beyond legal compliance requirements such as those set forth by the Sarbanes-Oxley Act of 2002 (e.g., Section 806, whistleblower protection). Leaders may wish to get more aggressive about ethical development in their organizations, acting in a proactive manner to prevent unethical action through more educational and developmentally focused initiatives.

In seeking an explanation for the disparity between the presence of content and context themes, participants described the difficulties companies face in linking ethics with performance—specifically with tracking, measurement, and assessment. While special awards are given ubiquitously for exemplary ethical behaviors, employers seem to be at a standstill when it comes to connecting performance objectives with identifying ethical risk, transparent practices, and overall ethical achievement. More than half of the companies want to adopt best practices that link ethics with performance, but they expressed concern about how they could actually implement these items. Because most companies do not have ethical components associated with task accomplishment (e.g., risk assessment), it makes tracking ethical actions highly subjective. For example, one participant described how when "ethics" has been included in the performance review processes, it was a general question about the person's character. Typically, everyone was given high marks unless they were blatantly unethical. Obviously this did not distinguish ethical performance.

It appears that the lack of focus on the development of ethical competencies makes linking ethics to performance difficult. Therefore, to improve this area, a fruitful approach might be to address several best practices simultaneously. For example, by implementing metrics for items under *Specific and Explicit Behaviors* and *Ethical Risk Assessment* (e.g., "*Conducts risk assessment to identify areas of ethical risk*"), employees' ethical competencies could be assessed, and personal accountability could become part of their performance objectives.

As with other best practices implemented, communication tends to be one-way. While employees can report ethical issues through formal reporting mechanisms, participants revealed that these are not necessarily the key sources for garnering important ethics information. Firms are required to have reporting processes, mandated via compliance regulations in the U.S. But truly cultivating an open and trusting ethical culture is how information becomes shared on a regular basis. This is when transparency, reflection, and dialogue can become normal features of everyday task operations. Participants shared how training must be complemented with a workplace environment that is guided by its organizational leaders. They described different circumstances reflecting how people watch and emulate the behavior and attitudes set by the "tone at the top."

On this point, a number of participants expressed frustration about how to sustain ongoing ethics communications within their organizations. They seemed troubled by how to keep ethics on the agenda, making it fresh and interesting, and ensuring that leadership continually incorporates ethics into their regular communiqués. Again, participants mentioned that until there is a specific problem, those responsible for training find it difficult to make a case for bolstering ethics programming—beyond existing compliance requirements. The finding that ethics education and training at the board of director level is focused solely on compliance suggests that this is an area for improvement. One participant described how they tried to implement training at this level but it was considered problematic, so they did not wish to adopt the practice. Two of the participants affirmed that it would be a good idea to link ethics to performance at the highest levels, and three wanted to see performance aligned with ethics at every level. But by the same token, they were reserved about who would be responsible for implementing this responsibility (which prohibited desired adoption).

Those responsible for ethics training believe that the organizational context must support the program content, but there is much room for development. Here, another trend was that several of the context themes reflected low means for presence and high means for value. If employees are expected to comply with regulations and exercise corporate values in their daily task actions, then processes that promote dialogue, identify ethical risks, and link ethics with performance are needed. In short, the best practices linked with these themes cannot be woven into the culture and climate of the organization without focused leadership support.

Looking at the themes in aggregate, we can see how strengths and challenges are observable in both the content and context categories (see Table 2.3). Given the 2008 market collapse, global competition, and added pressure to focus on sustainability, organizations will likely be required to attend to more regulatory requirements in the years to come. This reality, combined with potentially less funding for ethics education and training, may constrict rather than expand the use of these best practices. Those responsible for training will have to become efficient with their resources and work to develop creative solutions. For example, those responsible for training can help to ensure that line managers know how to foster ethical awareness and behavior in the daily actions of those they supervise. Perhaps a viable strategy might be to invest in face-to-face training for those who assume these roles, with a specific focus on emphasizing ethical reflection and dialogue as a part of routine interactions. When discussing a project at a group or quarterly meeting, supervisors can then demonstrate transparency, bringing forward and addressing the ethical risks, outlining the implications of pending decisions, and encouraging open conversation and debate. A "train the trainer" process that is filtered throughout the organization from top-down and bottom-up can help integrate and infuse ethics as a practice and foster shared ownership of the initiative.

While participants were adamant about the inclusion of core values in their programs, some participants looked to the ethical history of their organization to influence its current identity and employee behaviors. This is a potentially dangerous assumption, believing that employees can transfer values as content knowledge without the development of workplace routines and social norms that cultivate an active identity through their own daily actions. Again, this points to the importance of establishing an ongoing dialogue, one that instills individual and collective attention to achieve ethical performance in daily task actions. The overarching picture of ethics education and training in this study suggests that a shift in how we view

TABLE 2.3   Strengths and Challenges in Organizational Ethics Content and Context

Content	Context
Strengths	
• Address key compliance requirements, such as reporting channels and whistleblower protection. • Focus on prevention of unethical behavior and promotion of values. • Describe and define ethics as applicable to daily tasks. • Use relevant issues that target problem areas. • Use of online delivery reaches all employees, typically upon hire and then biannually.	• Reporting mechanisms are in place. • Code of Conduct ethics policy is easily accessible, typically through a website that also provides supplemental question/answer section. • Code of Conduct is available in multiple languages and typically signed by all employees.
Challenges	
• Online delivery promotes awareness but does not encourage reflection, practice, and dialogue. While outcomes associated with face-to-face delivery are desired, time, interest, and resources restrict applications to special groups or when problems arise. • Training efforts can become siloed (e.g., in legal departments), detracting from ethics integration and a competency development approach. • Organizations assume employees will exercise values in resolving ethical challenges: "We only hire ethical people." • No ethics training for vendors, suppliers, and partners. • Employees are not petitioned for their personal stories or for insights on cases or issues to be used in training.	• Lack a sustained ethics message in corporate communications (e.g., publications, events, announcements, and leadership messages). • Employees are not included in the process of ethics program efforts, training, and Code of Conduct development. • Ethical risk assessment tools are rarely applied. • Managers do not explicitly assume responsibility for handling areas of ethical risk (a reaction orientation dominates: focused attention on problems after they emerge). • Ethical issues are not regularly addressed at staff meetings. • The link between ethics and performance goals is vague—if present. • Focus is on training rather than education; the goal is to disseminate information rather than to foster personal and organizational development.

ethical awareness and development in the workplace may be warranted. Rather than being contained as a one-way activity, perhaps ethics officials can foster a more open and interactive process. The idea is to have employees participate in discussing their ethical issues with others, helping to create a context where values can be applied to ethical decision making and where ethical competencies can be practiced and honed.

LIMITATIONS AND CONCLUSION

The intent of this research was not to validate best practices but to generate a better understanding of how ethics education and training is being conducted in several organizations. Readers should be reminded that presence and value were not precise measurements, but based upon input from in-house ethics program experts. Thus, if a participant said that a particular best practice was in use, or present in a limited way, the numerical scoring provides insight rather than measurement precision. A complete review and analyses of the organizations' processes, practices, and procedures was beyond the scope of this study. But important understandings can be gleaned from such processes, which should be undertaken in future research.

A limitation was a small sample of self-selected companies, drawn from one particular region of the U.S. Moreover, these firms are involved in the technology industry and have similar interests to actively pursue the cultivation of an ethical workplace as members of an ethics partnership group. This puts some constraints on the generalizability of the findings. Additional empirical work is needed to test the validity of the best practices in different types of organizations with a consideration of demographics, size, industry type, and culture. Despite the shortcomings, the findings show how the programs studied compared to reported best practices. Results were shared with the participants, which contributed to collective dialogue regarding further development of their efforts and planned initiatives.

The implications suggest that a focus on ethical content is essential. But the treatment of content alone is an incomplete approach. The assumption that providing information ensures ethical behavior is risky—at best. This presumes that describing what people should do enables them to proceed accordingly. While a deontological approach helps to ensure that rules are known and that it is the employee's duty to adhere to them, how to recognize and attend to ethical challenges presumes a great deal of personal awareness and the development of competencies that support effective ethical decision making. Therefore, people need environments that also support and encourage the practice of ethical reflection, dialogue, and moral agency.

Practitioners and researchers need to work together to create additional activities that cultivate process norms that help develop ethical thinking in support of personal accountability and moral development in the workplace. A greater focus on context implies that supervisors and managers need to bring forward ethical issues in staff meetings, become aware of and responsible for areas of ethical risk, and link ethical practice to organizational goals and personal performance. In particular, heightened emphasis on ethical or moral competency development will help employees exercise ethics as an active "practice" rather than seeing ethics as a form of forced compliance.

Some of the participants, those managing ethics programs and the accompanying training efforts, expressed that employees "should already know how to be ethical." And, that "if people do not know how to be ethical it is not the company's responsibility to teach them how to behave appropriately." Some expanded upon this matter, explaining their belief that "you cannot teach ethics or morals to adults; people either learn ethical thinking as children—or they do not." These same participants were quite emphatic that their company "only hires ethical people." Given these beliefs and attitudes, it seems all the more important to be reminded that organizational contexts can inadvertently create and support social norms that unwittingly encourage unethical decision making and wrongdoing.

Given the right context, we know that ordinary people can participate in uncharacteristic amoral behavioral shifts, transformations that enable them to engage in unethical decisions and acts (Zimbardo, 2007). We are all vulnerable to the conscious or unconscious demands of our social milieu. Zimbardo's work, coupled with the latest evidence in the media reported on the nightly news, elevates the urgency for people to learn how to pay attention to the ethical considerations of their daily decisions. This includes the ability to conceptualize the potential consequences of their decisions and actions. In addition, learned habits of self-regulation can impact the long-term success—or failure—of people and their organizations. Given that personal awareness is key, perhaps leaders, managers, and trainers can begin to think about using the best practices outlined in this article as ways to help employees continue to integrate ethics into their workplace routines by encouraging the practice of reflection and dialogue in their everyday activities. The best practice themes and the associated items that have been outlined in this work provide ideas for how to commence.

Ethics as a habit of choice, a capability that needs to be exercised to be sustained, must be affirmed as a continual activity and message. Communication from leadership and evaluation mechanisms must reinforce the critical nature of ethical performance. With a focus on both content and context, organizational ethics programming can help employees at every level experience ethics as a core element of personal and organizational success. Ethics education and training will truly own its name when the goal is not only to disseminate information, but also to foster development at the individual and organizational levels.

ACKNOWLEDGMENTS

Special thanks go to Rick Bagozzi and Kirk Hanson, who were instrumental in the development of this research. Editorial assistance was kindly provided by Lucy Sekerka. Gratitude is also extended to the participants, giving time and support which made this inquiry possible.

NOTE

1. Permission has been granted by John Wiley & Sons Ltd. to use elements of this chapter that appeared in the original work by Sekerka (2009).

REFERENCES

Bowan, S. A. (2004). Organizational factors encouraging ethical decision making: An exploration into the case of an exemplar. *Journal of Business Ethics, 52,* 311–324.

Boyatzis, R. E. (1998). *Transforming qualitative information.* Thousand Oaks, CA: Sage.

Chen, A. Y. S., Sawyers, R. B., & Williams, P. F. (1997). Reinforcing ethical decision making through corporate culture. *Journal of Business Ethics, 16,* 855–865.

Christians, C. G., Fackler, M., Rotzoll, K. B., & McKee, K. B. (2001). *Media ethics: Cases and moral reasoning* (6th ed.). New York, NY: Longman.

DeGeorge, R. T. (1999). *Business ethics* (5th ed.). New York, NY: Macmillan.

Donaldson, T., & Werhane, P. H. (1999). *Ethical issues in business: A philosophical approach* (6th ed.). Upper Saddle River, NJ: Prentice Hall.

Izzo, G. (2000). Compulsory ethics education and the cognitive moral development of salespeople: A quasi-experimental assessment, *Journal of Business Ethics, 28,* 223–241.

Knouse, S. B., & Giacalone, R. A. (1997). The six components of successful ethics training. *Business and Society Review, 98,* 10–13.

LaFollette, H. (2007). *The practice of ethics.* Oxford, UK: Blackwell Publishing.

LeClair, D. T., & Ferrell, L. (2000). Innovation in experiential business ethics training. *Journal of Business Ethics, 23,* 313–322.

Loe, T. W., & Weeks, W. A. (2000). An experimental investigation of efforts to improve sales students' moral reasoning. *Journal of Personal Selling and Sales Management, 20,* 243–251.

Palmer, D. E., & Zakhem, A. (2001). Bridging the gap between theory and practice: Using the 1991 federal sentencing guidelines as a paradigm for ethics training. *Journal of Business Ethics, 29,* 77–84.

Piper, T. R., Gentile, M. C., & Parks, S. D. (1993). *Can ethics be taught?* Cambridge, MA: Harvard University Press.

Sekerka, L. E. (2008, March). *Are managers curious about ethics? A process to prepare managers for moral agency.* Paper presented at the Western Academy of Management Annual Meeting, Oakland, CA.

Sekerka, L. E. (2009). Organizational ethics education and training: A review of best practices and their application. *International Journal of Training and Development, 13*(2), 77–95.

Strauss, A., & Corbin, J. (1990). *Basics of qualitative research: Grounded theory procedures and techniques.* Thousand Oaks, CA: Sage.

Ungan, M. (2004). Factors affecting the adoption of manufacturing best practices. *Benchmarking: An International Journal, 11*(5), 504–520.

Valentine, S., & Fleischman, G. (2004). Ethics training and businesspersons' perceptions of organizational ethics. *Journal of Business Ethics, 52,* 381–390.

Zimbardo, P. (2007). *The Lucifer effect: Understanding how good people turn evil.* New York, NY: Random House.

SECTION II

CURRENT ISSUES

CHAPTER 3

THE TALL ORDER
OF TACKLING RELATIVISM
IN ETHICS TRAINING
FOR INTERNATIONAL FIRMS

Marianne M. Jennings

Yes, but bribery is accepted in most cultures. So goes the response when an ethics officer undertakes the tall order of training employees in companies with international operations on the nuances of the Foreign Corrupt Practices Act (FCPA). A devotion to the "when in Rome" analogy of moral relativism is not limited to bribery issues. Companies with international operations are filled with the comfort "everybody does it" gives to employees, something that leaves ethics officers nervous as they face the daunting task of countermanding the heavy hand of cultural norms. If ethics officers are relying upon compliance training alone to handle complex international ethical issues, they will find that they are grappling with employees working in countries outside the United States and the issues they raise (and in some cases, prefer not to raise) by following this mantra: They are like toddlers by a swimming pool; they must not be left unattended. The over-

Ethics Training in Action, pages 59–81
Copyright © 2014 by Information Age Publishing
All rights of reproduction in any form reserved.

whelming responsibility of one-on-one supervision is not much better than challenging the "when in Rome" ethical theorists.

A compliance training program on international issues simply will not get employees where they need to be, which is somewhere above that lowest common denominator of "go with the flow, at least until you get caught." The mantra of "reliance on compliance" does not serve companies well. Over the past few years, Avon, Siemens, Ikea, KBR, IBM, Morgan Stanley, Tyson Foods, HP, and BAE have all grappled with FCPA charges and/or settlements. At these companies, the employees fully understood their legal and ethical obligations. For example, at Siemens, the employees who were responsible for the cash disbursements used in the company's multination, multiyear bribery strategy were so familiar with the prohibitions against bribery that they joked about their conduct, with former Siemens employee, Reinhard Siekaczek, explaining, "I would have never thought I'd go to jail for my company. Sure, we joked about it, but we thought if our actions ever came to light, we'd get together and there would be enough people to play a game of cards" (Schubert, 2008, p. SB1).

They also realized that they were engaged in bribery. To eliminate the nagging feeling of noncompliance, the group of five men handling the cash payments just referred to their company's bribes as "useful expenditures" (Schubert, 2008). At Avon, the dribs and drabs of continuing FCPA investigations that uncovered more and more violations led to the company's continuing performance decline, and, ultimately, a change in the top leadership. When Avon's FCPA investigation was broadened, the company's stock dropped 5% (Byron, 2011).

Yes, bribery is everywhere, and yes, the employees had been trained. Suppliers for Apple were aware of the company's labor standards (Graham, 2012). Mattel's production factories in China understood that lead-based paint could not be used for children's toys (Zamiska, 2007). Still, these international operations ignored contract terms and did business, well, as they all were doing business in their self-created Rome.

How does a company with international operations get the message of ethics beyond "when in Rome" across to employees? Reliance on compliance, a focus on the rules, will not get them where they need to be. A company that covers the nuts and bolts of FCPA compliance with regularity and vigor is a company at risk for an FCPA violation. Technical compliance does not rein in Roman expatriates. There are four key knowledge components in effective training for companies with international operations. The first component is an overarching theme of "No matter where we are in the world, we do business the same way." This theme cuts off the debate of cultural relativism and sets the tone for the remainder of the components. The second component is instruction in the *why* behind the nitty-gritty rules of compliance, or why employees should worry about something more than compliance; that is, ethics as *everybody does it* is a classic form of rationalization that gives employees ethical comfort about their conduct. However, training that goes beyond relativism teaches employees to develop an ethical mind, one that is capable of analyzing and understanding that we do not worry about ethical issues for the sake of feeling good about ourselves. This component of training focuses on the consequences of violations of those rules and seeks to hold employees accountable for those consequences. The third component of training focuses on the economic cycle, a cycle that trains employees in understanding the full-cycle costs of relativistic approaches to international business. The fourth and final component takes the training into strategic directions, teaching employees the futility of relativistic conduct for growth and long-term survival. Following what everyone else does is antithetical to strategy, which should be unique and not easily duplicated. Following the Roman herd in international operations is not a strategy of distinction.

NO MATTER WHERE WE ARE, BUSINESS IS BUSINESS

The list of scholars and practitioners who have attempted to develop an international code of ethics is long and distinguished. The shortcomings in these attempts have come because of the inevitable bow to the "when in Rome" theory. Donaldson labored mightily in his much-cited work to develop a simple, uniform standard, but ended up stuck in the mud with his allowance for "wiggle room" (Donaldson, 1996). Training employees with the notion that you have "wiggle room" on your business decisions in other countries is akin to placing a target on the offices and plants in which they work. Trouble is coming; the only variable is time—that is, how much wiggling they do and how far beyond just a simple wiggle they go. The attempt was a good one, but Donaldson ultimately ended up at an "it depends" conclusion on what was right and what was wrong and even that point was determined on a country-by-country basis.

The first task in any training is to develop the topics that should be covered. For international training in this area of one ethical standard worldwide, the topics most companies must cover are:

- Bribery
- Money laundering
- Factory/operations conditions and worker rights
- Safety standards

Bribery

The Myth of Cultural Norms and the Reality of Laws

Employees do take comfort in the international urban legend, "Everybody pays bribes." However, reliance on this glib assertion is misplaced. This much-repeated and relied-upon norm can actually be disputed factually. There is not a country in the world that does not make bribery a crime. In other words, *accepted in culture* is not the same as *accepted by law*. What may be interpreted as cultural acceptance of bribery may actually be a perception created by a lack of resources for prosecution of bribery cases. The resulting spotty approach to enforcement is often mistaken for tolerance and acceptance of bribery. Training should include a reminder that individual data sets on cultural acceptance are often flawed. The perception of cultural acceptance is often based on a lack of information about actual enforcement activities. In other words, perception of cultural acceptance of bribery is mistaken. What people may be perceiving is an inability to adequately enforce a higher norm. Table 3.1 (Transparency International, 2012) presents a list of the countries that criminalize bribery of foreign officials, with their criminal statutes largely modeled after the United States' FCPA. Not only is bribery within these countries a crime, but bribery by their citizens of officials of other countries is also prohibited.

In some of the countries on this list, the legislation goes beyond the FCPA. For example, Mexico prohibits solicitation payments. In addition to this list,

TABLE 3.1 Countries with Criminal Statutes Prohibiting Bribery

Argentina	France	Panama
Australia	Germany	Peru
Austria	Greece	Poland
Belgium	Guatemala	Portugal
Brazil	Hungary	Romania
Bulgaria	Iceland	Russia
Canada	Ireland	Slovak Republic
Chile	Israel	Slovenia
China	Italy	South Africa
Colombia	Jamaica	South Korea
Costa Rica	Japan	Spain
Czech Republic	Luxembourg	Sweden
Denmark	Mexico	Switzerland
Dominican Republic	Netherlands	Turkey
El Salvador	New Zealand	United Kingdom
Estonia	Nicaragua	United States
Finland	Norway	Uruguay

there are conventions that will result in more countries making bribery a criminal offense. The African Union has its African Convention on Preventing and Combating Corruption, which requires criminalization and which has been signed by 45 member countries (List of Countries, 2010; see Table 3.1). Beyond the issues of misperceptions of acceptance and realities of prosecution is an issue of norms. Bribery violates what has been called a hypernorm, or a social standard that is necessary for social efficiency (Dunfee & Donaldson, 2002).With acceptance of a hypernorm against bribery comes a shift in thinking. From this point, bribery can become a salient ethical issue and people begin to grasp the economic consequences of such actions and the fact that corruption is economically devastating (see Part III for specifics related to the economic consequences of bribery) (Salbu, 1999).

There is also a difference between cultural practices and legalities. For example, in the United States, we all speed when driving, but that cultural practice does not mean that we are not held accountable for compliance when there is an accident. In the case of an accident, our conduct is not evaluated on the basis the norm. Rather, we are held to the simple standard of the rule, the law on speeding. Our liability and responsibility is based on compliance, not on accepted cultural norms.

So it is with bribery. That bribery goes on each day in countries around the world does not mean that its practitioners are free from consequences. Relativism gives comfort, but it does not give its practitioners a free pass when the legal standard is breached and discovered. Consider China, where execution is the punishment when government officials take bribes. China takes a backseat to no one in terms of its punishments for bribery. Swift action in all countries when a scandal unfolds is actually the norm because of the need to keep and attract business. Recently, when a pattern of alleged bribery by Walmart was uncovered in Mexico, the retailer's proposed stores were not only halted in Mexico but also in the United States until the issues related to its activities in Mexico could be further investigated (Banjo, 2012).The United States has been a leader in joining with other countries to fight bribery. As stated by Gold, "U.S. companies that are paying bribes to foreign officials are undermining government institutions around the world. It is a hugely destabilizing force" (Gold & Crawford, 2008, B1).

If a company is doing business with this simple standard, "We comply with the laws of each country where we do business," then bribery has already been addressed. No matter where the company does business, bribery is prohibited. If we are to adhere to our credo of doing business in the same fashion in all countries, we are bound to the simple principle of obeying the law.

Everyone Does It
Some pushback in training and practice comes as employees, immersed in the culture, see bribery in a culture, despite legalities. Bribery is practiced,

accepted, and fairly successful in getting people what they want. For example, in Russia, a country that is deep into the fourth quartile in terms of corruption in Transparency International's index, bribery has even made it down to the retail level.[1] Russians pay doctors money to get in for treatment. Company divisions that operate in such a culture are bound to push back when bribery is so pervasive.

The means used to address bribery as a way of life need to go beyond training. Enforcement of company rules on bribery is a key component. For example, Alcoa overcame the cultural norms with its Russian operations by terminating the Russian leaders who engaged in bribery on behalf of the company. Once the employees realized that there would be no winking tolerance of bribery, they found other ways to do business.

Dealing with the Nuances

As clear as "no bribes" seems to be, training still needs to focus on bribery nuances, or the types of behaviors that employees feel comfortable with because they have not actually engaged in hand-to-hand cash payments. There is evolving creativity in terms of companies avoiding the cash-to-hand situation, such as payments to consultants, payments to shell corporations (with payments from the corporation then made to government officials), payments to custom officials in order to have them undervalue goods, and making government officials silent partners in companies and organizations run by the company trying to win a government contract (Crawford, 2010). The following list provides examples of bribery nuances that have landed FCPA violations and provide training discussion fodder:

- UTStarcom, Inc., a U.S. telecommunications company, agreed to pay a $3 million fine for violations of the FCPA. The Justice Department complaint alleged that from 2002–2007 the company paid about $7 million for Chinese government officials (those who work for the biggest government-owned telecoms in China: China Netcom, China Telecom, and China Mobile) to visit the United States. The visits were called "training sessions," but were held in Hawaii and Las Vegas. The Justice Department complaint also alleges that no training ever took place. One U.S. Securities and Exchange Commission (SEC) official referred to the use of "training sessions" as a standard industry practice (SEC, 2009).
- In addition to the trips, UTStarcom also provided the following to officials or their family members: tuition for universities, assistance in obtaining travel visas, and payments to consultants who were able to then win business for the company (SEC, 2009).
- Lucent Technologies, another U.S. telecommunications company, also paid a fine for FCPA violations based on Justice Department

allegations that the company had arranged, from 2000–2003, for 1,000 Chinese government employees to inspect Lucent plants and attend "training sessions." Instead, however, the government employees traveled to Las Vegas, Disneyland, and the Grand Canyon (SEC, 2010).

- The United Kingdom subsidiary of Aon, Aon, Ltd., was spending money to train officials at a state-owned insurance company in Costa Rica. However, the SEC's complaint alleged that a "significant portion" of the funds were used for travel for the officials and their spouses to Paris, Monte Carlo, and Cologne, and that the activities at these locations involved neither training nor education (SEC, 2011b).
- Paid board positions for government employees who are responsible for making decisions about using a firm's products and/or services
- Challenges with the cultural relativism of gift-giving

Dealing with pressures to incorporate gift-giving also stems from executive and sales employees who insist that they cannot do business without offering and receiving gifts. Accepting the premise that *it's a gift culture* means the unleashing of creativity linked to this thought, "It depends on the meaning of the word 'gift.'" For example, Orthofix International settled FCPA charges in 2012. The complaint in the case alleged that the company's Mexican subsidiary, Promeca, funneled $317,000 to Mexican officials in exchange for obtaining and retaining sales contracts for health care and social services. The most interesting part of the case is that Promeca employees explained that they referred to the payments as "chocolates." The employees obtained the funds for the "chocolates" through cash advances that were issued for "chocolates." The use of this term allowed the employees to continue the payments comfortably because they were simply giving "gifts." The SEC's position was that Promeca's training and promotional budgets were so high that an investigation was warranted, particularly into the cash advances and the references to "chocolates." Chocolates graduated to televisions, laptops, appliances, and one lease of a Volkswagen Jetta (SEC, 2012).There is a difference between a box of chocolates and a Volkswagen Jetta, but a culture of gifts knows few bounds, and the definition of a gift tends to grow with each transaction.

Training for employees in countries where there is a gift culture begins with an international standard for the company. The type of gifts appropriate for giving and the disposition of gifts received are the first two critical components of such an international standard. Many companies do not permit employees to retain gifts received; those gifts are returned to the corporation and, in some cases, are sold, with proceeds donated to charity. On the giving side, company policies vary. On the strict control end of the scale, after the "no gifts" standard, some companies have a uniform gift (which changes from year to year), with the distribution of and access to the chosen gift being controlled by the company.

At the other end of the scale are the companies that permit gift-giving to be handled on an individual office basis. However, "each office decides" turns into Rome and introduces what Orthofix experienced: a wide range of gifts that seem to grow in cost as well as a lack of internal controls designed to identify and limit funds for gifts. The SEC's harshest penalties are imposed on those companies that are not properly recording transactions, a void that allows gifts to turn into bribes.

Money Laundering

Since the 1980s, countries that desire trade relations, economic development that comes with new market participants, or even the support of the World Bank have all had to develop the types of banking systems, regulations, and regulatory enforcement that allow for the monitoring of funds and funds transfers. Even in the most primitive of cultures, the desire for World Bank funding has resulted in controls, supervision, and prosecution, as international banks have insisted upon the same standards in banking operations with partner banks. If a company is doing business the same way around the world, these types of controls and supervision would be a prerequisite to operations in any country. If companies are doing business in the same manner around the world in terms of cash flow and management, they would require employees to perform the same types of "know thy customer" standards that are required for operations in the United States. Large cash transfers may be culturally common in other countries, but those countries are not operating without regulatory supervision and controls. Inasmuch as these funds can be the lifeline for bribery, monitoring is often the key to loosening corruption's grip on businesses and economies in those countries (Alsever, 2006).

Money laundering does not carry the ethical complexity of bribes and gifts. The secret transfer of money to rogue nations enables their activities. Ethics training in money laundering involves the easier task of providing employees with the background on red flags. For example, large transactions that occur in certain countries (e.g., Mexico, Iran, and Cuba) are the types of transfers that require employee reporting. In addition, continuing transfers to a certain entity or entities can be a red flag. For example, in the HSBC case, the transfers were all made to *casas de cambio* (Barrett, 2012). Large cash purchases, as well as bulk-cash transactions, are also red flags that employees should be trained to question.

Training should emphasize the role of employees in giving voice to ethical malfeasance—that is, raising the red flag. Employees offer the front-line defense through their willingness to refuse those transactions when clients and sources cannot be verified, to report transfers made surreptitiously (in a concealed manner), and to raise questions when unusual transactions arise. The 2012 example of Standard Chartered, the fifth largest bank in the United Kingdom, is instructive. New York's banking regulator reviewed 30,000 internal memos, emails, and other documents at Standard Chartered and has alleged that the bank handled $250 billion in illegal transactions with Iran. Although the bank has vigorously disputed the charges, emails reveal that bank officials asked certain references to be deleted from external audit reports so that regulators' interest would not be piqued regarding the transactions. The inaction of employees and internal and external auditors resulted in the continued practice and now the regulatory action (Rappaport, 2012).

Factory Operations and Worker Rights

One of the flaws in reasoning related to factory conditions and worker rights, relativistic though the thought may be, is the thinking that "when in Rome, we operate our factories using Roman standards." If a company has pledged to operate with a universal standard, those Roman standards will not only undermine a universal approach but will likely find the company the target of media reports and worker rights activists (Ballinger & Olsson, 1997).For example, the *New York Times* published a front-page story on Apple's low pay in the United States. The classic international sales versus wages comparison appeared graphically: Apple's sales per square foot are $5,647, and the average pay of a sales employee in the United States is $11.91 per hour (Segal, 2012). That story followed months of stories about the suicides among workers in the Foxconn (an Apple supplier) plants in China, which resulted in student protests, an audit of the factories, and changes in supplier agreements and operations (Porter, 2012).

Clearly, factory conditions will not be identical around the world, but it is still possible to have a universal code that the company can honor if the basic tenets of that code include the following:

- Factory and supplier plant and operations conditions do not impair the health of workers
- Factory and supplier work hours and schedules do not result in health problems in workers
- Factory and supplier supervisory standards create an atmosphere of dignity for workers

- Factory and supplier wages are at a living wage
- Factory and supplier conditions are consistent, as determined on the basis of unannounced inspections
- Factories, operations, and suppliers offer workers opportunities for training, education, and advancement

Within this list there is no straitjacket of an absolute wage figure or the simplistic adherence to local laws, something that would permit the relativistic standard that contributes to factory conditions that do indeed harm workers. Rather, this list of universal values is the company's credo that operations do not harm workers: We respect those who work for us or for our suppliers, and we use our presence there as a means for their economic and educational advancement. The credo leaves no "wiggle room" for simply meeting local standards. Rather, the standards are clear before any operations begin in the country, whether by the company itself or its suppliers.

Training should focus on supplier contract terms that include the company's values as well as on inspection methods, including coverage of regularity and the element of surprise, with both the FCPA/bribery training and the training on money laundering, the recordkeeping function remains critical. Notification of violations, worker complaints, and even local press coverage constitute the database each office should be maintaining, with systems for reporting information to the corporate office and processes for institutionalization of reforms prompted by the data. For example, the suicides at the Foxconn factories were an initially slow but steady beat in terms of media coverage. Coverage began in business publications and then crossed over into the social media, a step that resulted in the protests and reforms. The first stories appeared in February 2011, but the audits did not begin until February 2012 (Barboza, 2011; Martin, 2012). The company weathered a year of negative reports before it took action. A company policy on collection of news stories is part of the institutionalization of the credo. Company training on steps to be taken advances the credo, results in swift corrective action, and avoids the boycotts that come from the sweatshop issues.

Safety Standards

There are three words that underscore the importance of universal safety standards: Union Carbide and Bhopal. What is often lost in the folklore about the Bhopal accident is that one of the workers at the plant simply made a mistake in responding to a problem that arose in part of the plant's equipment (Union Carbide Corp. Gas Plant Disaster, 1987). The plant met the safety standards of the Indian government. However, those standards were well below safety standards that Union Carbide followed for plants in the United States, such as allowing residences to spring up too close to the plant. In addition, safety was compromised by the lack of training for those who were operating the plant. The mistaken response to an equipment issue was perhaps an inevitable result of the lack of experience and absence of ongoing training among the workers and supervisory staff at the plant.

Before constructing plants in other countries, whether utility, chemical, or manufacturing, companies should develop a universal credo related to safety. Such a credo covers the requirements for staffing, training, compliance with code and construction standards that minimize risk for workers and residents, and the right of ongoing monitoring of operations.

An interesting example is BP's construction of the Deepwater Horizon oil rig, located off the coast of Louisiana. At hearings on the explosion and spill of Deepwater, held by the U.S. House of Representatives, other oil company CEOs testified that BP did not follow appropriate design standards in drilling the well (Schmitt, 2010). A *Wall Street Journal* study (Chaza, Faucon, & Casselman, 2010) found that BP used a risky design that was cheaper for Deepwater Horizon and also for one out of three of its deepwater wells. The so-called long-string design is one that is cheaper and faster to construct because this design uses a single pipe for bringing the oil to the surface. Experts testified that the result of using one long pipe is that natural gas accumulates around the pipe and can rise unchecked. Most experts recommend the long-string design for low-pressure wells only, not wells such as Deepwater Horizon. The experts also noted that long-string drilling is particularly risky as a design when a company is drilling in areas with which it has no familiarity. BP drilled Deepwater Horizon in the Gulf of Mexico, an area about which it had little experience or knowledge.

This type of safety issue, one that results from unfamiliarity with the topography or geography of an area, is one that affects all types of production and construction issues. Training related to safety standards requires more than "meet local laws." The four principles outlined here are designed to help companies avoid being a Union Carbide or a BP, with the resulting impact on the companies' share price, its capitalization and, most importantly, the often permanent damage to its reputation. The loss of that reputational capital impairs the company's ability to continue to do business in the country where the accident occurs as well as expansion into other countries because of the loss of trust these major accidents produce.

Once universal standards have been established in the company and used as the basis for international ethical standards, training is not such a tall order. In addition, training will be explicitly peppered with the "Yes, but what about..." questions that take employees back to cultural differences. The goal in training is to establish the company's position that there are no "in Rome" standards. The standards of training are standards that provide employees with clear lines for all international operations.

BEHIND THE SCENES

Perhaps one of the most surprising revelations for employees in training is that, more than occasionally, ethics and business success *do* walk on the same side of the street. This segment of training is designed to provide motivation for compliance with higher and uniform international ethical standards from a very basic premise: There are compelling economic and social reasons that demand ethical conduct in international operations. The economic and social problems that spring from ethical lapses should give us all pause and should be covered in training. Consequences of unethical conduct are used to make the case for ethical choices.

Surrendering Power

When a company engages in bribery, it surrenders power to the government official and/or a bureaucracy. The government official or bureaucracy now has control over the company in that it is able to demand increasing amounts of corrupt payments without the normal economic constraints of competitive pricing and transparency (Abaroa, 1999). The company enters into a deal with someone whose self-interest carries no checks and balances. The company also has no protection or assurance that the government official will not create new obstacles to the company's progress within that country (Reinikka & Svensson, 2002). For training purposes, the message is simple: Once you pay there is no way out and there are no price ceilings. Bribery, therefore, increases costs.

In addition, a rather perverse result of bribery is that companies that do bribe actually end up expending more time and money in handling regulators and regulatory issues than do firms that do not pay bribes (Choi & Thum, 2003). Some studies suggest that even grease payments increase the amount of time and money companies that make such payments spend in terms of regulatory compliance. These results appear to spring from the same theme, referred to as the *ratchet effect*: once government officials know that a company is willing to pay, they use their regulatory power to extract more from that firm (Svensson, 2001).

Lower Growth Rates

Nothing hits home in training more than the simple admonition that if employees do not comply with the company's standards against bribery, then the company will make less money. Companies that engage in bribery do experience lower growth rates. The direct ratio is that for every one percent increase in bribery there is a three percent reduction in firm growth rate (Fisman & Svensson, 2007). The studies in this area all conclude that there is no evidence that bribery results in some form of competitive advantage. Interestingly, the conclusions of the studies appear to be that bribery leads to reduced sales. The reasons for the impact on sales are not yet clearly established but could be related to the diverted time spent dealing with government officials and their demands, as noted in the discussion about the impact of paying bribes on regulatory relationships.

Bribery's Impact on Company Culture

Employees who witness the payment of bribes will engage in the same type of rule-breaking behavior that follows all rule-breaking by managers. When managers engage in bribery, they signal that self-serving behaviors are acceptable in the company culture. That signal then results in employees engaging in self-serving behaviors, which could be anything from embezzlement to abuse of travel expenses to the use of firm resources for personal benefit (Vitell, Dickerson, & Festervand, 2000). Bribery benefits the few at the expense of many—employees see that the company loses discounts and other pricing benefits because individual managers have engaged in bribery (Ostas, 2007).

The Impact of Bribery on External Relationships

As noted earlier, bribery remains a concern even in those countries where companies perceive that bribery is acceptable. The issue in these countries is: How long will it be before the corrupt government is removed and change can result? The movement toward elimination of bribery appears to be vibrant in all cultures. Once the elimination movement succeeds, the new government is less likely to do business with companies that have engaged with previous corrupt officials. For example, when the corrupt Suharto regime was removed in Indonesia, the companies that had worked with the Suharto regime were met with great resistance. Those companies were unable to market successfully in Indonesia once the corruption had been removed (Kantor, 2001). This phenomenon, known as social rebuke, indicates that bribery brings results only in the short term and that there are long-term consequences that must be paid when the corruption is removed from a country that a company has perceived as one in which bribery was accepted and necessary for business advancement.

Apart from the inability to do business with new governments when there is political change in countries, companies also find that they may be shunned by other transnationals that do not want to be tainted by dealings with a company known for its relationships with a corrupt, and now defunct, regime (Meyer & Sinani, 2009). In addition, the reach of the bribery laws is such that those who are in joint ventures may find themselves criminally responsible for the actions of their partner associations, even though none of their own employees or agents has engaged in bribery. Constructive knowledge can bring criminal and/or civil liability to joint venture alliances, so companies choose carefully when it comes to transnational relationships (Marceau, 2007).

Economic Development Consequences

Beyond the harm that comes to companies in earnings, costs, and reputation is the more significant harm bribery imposes on the countries where businesses engage in bribery. Table 3.2 presents a list of countries that have

TABLE 3.2 Countries Ranked with the Least Amount of Bribery

1. New Zealand
2. Denmark
3. Finland
4. Sweden
5. Singapore
6. Norway
7. Netherlands
8. Australia
9. Switzerland
10. Canada
11. Luxembourg
12. Hong Kong
13. Iceland
14. Germany
15. Japan
16. Austria
17. Barbados
18. United Kingdom
19. Belgium
20. Ireland
21. Bahamas
22. Chile
23. Qatar
24. United States
25. France
26. Santa Lucia

the least amount of bribery present in their economies, as determined by Transparency International (2011). Now compare this list of low-bribery nations with a list of the countries ranked as having the most bribery (Table 3.3).

Even the most cursory glance illustrates a profound distinction between the economic development of the countries in the first list versus the economic development of the countries in the second list. Somalia is wrestling with pirates. The other nations in the top five of the most-corrupt list face challenging human rights issues. Permanent economic stability eludes all of the countries in the most corrupt list. Former Treasury Secretary Robert Rubin, who worked to have the World Bank establish the types of controls that make bribery difficult said, "Corruption and bribery benefit a few at the expense of many" (Johnson, 2005, p. 1). Within these countries there is concentration of wealth and a system of corruption that precludes advancement through merit. Lori Weinstein, the lawyer from the U.S. Department of Justice who handled the Siemens bribery case, explained, "Crimes of official

TABLE 3.3   Countries Ranked with the Greatest Amount of Bribery

1. Somalia
2. Korea (North)
3. Myanmar
4. Afghanistan
5. Uzbekistan
6. Turkmenistan
7. Sudan
8. Iraq
9. Haiti
10. Venezuela
11. Equatorial Guinea
12. Burundi
13. Libya
14. Democratic Republic of Congo
15. Chad
16. Yemen
17. Kyrgyzstan
18. Guinea
19. Cambodia
20. Zimbabwe
21. Paraguay
22. Papua New Guinea
23. Nepal
24. Laos
25. Kenya

corruption threaten the integrity of the global marketplace and undermine the rule of law in host countries" (see Department of Justice, 2010).

Training of employees requires an understanding of how corruption undermines economic systems. Figure 3.1 illustrates the delicate balance the four-legged stool of an economic system must have in order to keep investment, production, and purchasing going (Jennings, 2011).

Everyone in the system (the groups represented by the four legs of the stool) must be ethical. If corruption seeps into one leg, the economic system becomes unbalanced. For example, if customers become corrupt, as when customers submit fraudulent insurance claims, the economic system is affected as rates go up, insurance becomes less available, and some insurers are forced out of the marketplace. In the United States, the current wave of reforms at the federal level (post-2008 market collapse) is the result of perceived corruption by business in their operations in the economic system. The reforms were needed in order to rebuild investor trust in markets and draw their funds back to investments, investments that provide capital for businesses to start and grow.

Government corruption also interferes with market forces in the determination of types of products and goods sold. Jennings and Smeltzer (1998) explain the resulting problem as follows: Suppose, for example, that the sale of a firm's product is determined not by perceived consumer value but rather by access to consumers, which is controlled by government officials. That is, your company's product cannot be sold to consumers in a particular country unless and until you are licensed within that country. Suppose

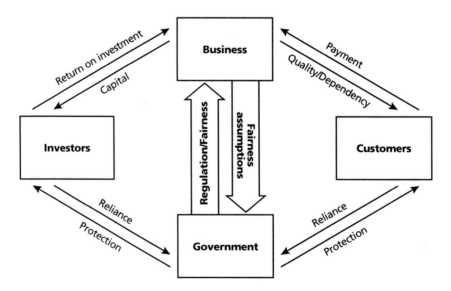

Figure 3.1 The components of economics systems.

further that the licensing procedures are controlled by government officials and that those officials demand personal payment in exchange for your company's right to even apply for a business license. Payment size may be arbitrarily determined by officials who withhold portions for themselves. The basic values of the system have been changed. Consumers no longer directly determine the demand (Jennings & Smeltzer, 1998).

Both those who take risks and those who work within the system as employees must have a certain level of trust in their fates. If their effort and investment can be taken away through government power, their willingness to participate in the system declines. Investors withdraw their funds and employees lose the stability of ongoing and vibrant places of employment. In developing countries where there are "speed" or grease payments and resulting corruption by government officials, the actual money involved may not be significant in terms of the nation's culture. However, such activities and payments introduce an element of demoralization and cynicism that thwart entrepreneurial activity when these nations most need risk-takers to step forward. As Brazil struggled during the mid-1990s to stabilize its economy, a businessman from Sao Paulo observed, in response to the corruption that had consumed the country, "The fundamental reason we can't get our act together is we're an amoral society" (Kamm, 1994, p. A1).

Apart from the training in the impact of corruption on the economic development of other countries is a necessary grounding in the social impact of corruption. Table 3.4 presents a comparison of the devastation of the earthquakes in Haiti and Chile, earthquakes that were just months apart.

The photographs of the devastation in the two countries following the earthquakes show a remarkable distinction in terms of the damage. The full collapse of the buildings and homes in Haiti stands in stark contrast to the damaged buildings in Chile that were still standing. The initial observation most make in trying to determine root cause is that there are building code differences that would explain the significantly greater loss of human life and structural damage in Haiti. The reality is that the building codes in the two countries are not all that different. What was different was

TABLE 3.4   Hurricane Damage by Comparison of Countries

Haiti	Concepcion, Chile
7.0 RS	8.8 RS
52 aftershocks	130 aftershocks
230,000 deaths	521 deaths
300,000 injured	Limited injuries
1,000,000 homeless	300,000 homeless
250,000 residences destroyed	370,000 homes damaged

the enforcement of those codes and the elimination in Chile of the direct contact between inspectors and builders that results in waived inspections, standards, and enforcement. By taking away the contacts and opportunities that result in kickbacks and waived standards, Chile was able to enforce its building codes. Training that includes these types of dramatic illustrations prick the conscience and help employees to understand that relativism provides a false sense of comfort. These simple examples spell out the implications of corruption, and one such implication that human life can be at risk through these "in Rome" standards. Employees are forced to think about "everybody does it" risks in ways they had not imagined because of their facile dismissal through their norms approach to doing business.

A Justice Department official made a poignant observation about companies and their decisions to do business "as they do in Rome": "If the only way that a company can conduct business in a particular location is to do so illegally, then the company shouldn't be doing business there" (Lewis, 2007, p. A18).

Ethics and Costs in the Economic Cycle

Whether used in supply chain or in economics (and the labels used in these disciplines may vary), there is a real cost in the production cycle for goods and services. An example that Donaldson uses in his attempt to develop an international code of ethics involves the cost of removal of asbestos from a ship and helps to illustrate the economic or product cycle. A company that needs to have one of its ships cleaned of all asbestos can have the removal work undertaken in the United States or Europe, but removal done in Western countries involves significant costs because of the mandated safety precautions that keep the asbestos from harming the workers, becoming embedded in clothing, and, thereby, being transferred to other areas. However, the company could sail the ship to the west coast of Africa and have the removal done by workers in a country that does not yet have the regulations for asbestos removal. The cost would be about one-tenth of what the removal would cost in the United States. Employees looking at the immediate cost savings conclude that sailing the ship to Africa is the best way to have the asbestos removal done.

In this situation, there are significant cost savings that can come from "doing as the Romans do." However, such an analysis overlooks an important piece of cost information. Focusing only on the immediacy of the 90% cost increase, employees will, for their budgets' sake and the possible commendations that follow for such savings, go with removal on the west coast of Africa. However, product or economic cycle costs take into account the costs of developing goods and/or services from cradle to grave, or until disposal of the goods. One of the costs within every cycle focuses on the nature of the product itself and the risk it presents to others. Under both the economic and supply chain theory of the cycle, there is a true cost of business use or development of a good. The true economic cost includes the danger the product presents to workers, customers, and society. Markets require accountability for that cost. The use of the substantially discounted African removal crew does not avoid that high cost. Rather, the decision to go with the African removal merely postpones the true cost of this part of the cycle. Under the cycle theory, the true cost eventually emerges. Further, the longer the length of time spent taking advantage of the mispriced discount operations, the greater the increase in the true cost.

Drawing on the asbestos removal example to illustrate the possible outcomes, the true cost includes whatever health damage is done to the workers who undertake the risky task without knowledge of the need for precautions and, as a result, experience health problems. There would also be the costs of removal of asbestos from any physical areas in which the asbestos fibers landed due to the lack of precautions taken by the discount removal operations. The longer companies take advantage of the discount removal, the greater the number of workers affected. The greater the number of workers affected, the higher the true cost climbs. The true cost of the cycle is thus a simple notion of pay now or pay later, but in either case the market demands reimbursement for the societal costs that result from business activities. If this story sounds familiar, the true cost of asbestos was not factored in for 30 years of low-cost Johns-Manville operations. The end result is that Manville (the company's name now) has had to assign 25% of its profits in perpetuity in order to pay for the health and removal costs of 40 years of postponing the costs of worker and on-site precautions in the production, use, and installation of asbestos (Devlin v. Johns-Manville Corp., 1985). The true cost factors in the societal costs of the economic shortcuts that "when in Rome" decisions often allow, albeit temporarily.

Interestingly, these cycle costs usually emerge in the context of social activism. Social activism carries the additional challenge for companies of managing the public relations and regulatory aspects of the newspaper headline revelations of the company's discounted approach to minimizing costs in an unregulated area or country, despite compelling safety issues.

Ethics and Strategic International Advantage

By definition, an effective strategy is one that is unique and not easily duplicated. There is nothing unique about "everyone does it," and the fact that everyone is already doing it is an indication that the strategy is easily duplicated. Bribery is an example of conduct that is antithetical to effective strategy. A competitor can simply up the ante and win the contract or obtain access to services or officials in a particular country. However, there is another impact when companies rely on the facile strategy of bribery, an impact that was clear to Siemens executives once its years-long run of bribery was ended through multinational prosecutions for its activities. Because those within the company had relied on bribery for so long in winning contracts, they lost the skill sets necessary for winning contracts and customers through effective deal packaging, negotiations, and customer service. Imagine a sales force without marketing and customer relations skills. Siemens was faced with the task of trying to win customers and contracts without even an understanding of what had evolved in international sales transactions over the five years of its bribery practices when it was absent from the competitive field, a field that requires skill sets lost in the too-easy "when in Rome" strategy. Peter Löscher, the CEO tapped to take over the leadership role following the settlement of the FCPA charges, summed up the company's precarious position: "We are great innovators but not the best marketers," and "There is a lot of work to be done" (Raghavan, 2009, p. 122).

There are additional examples of the catch-up required once the "when in Rome" conduct is ended by government intervention. For example, Tyson Foods settled its FCPA charges related to its payment to veterinarians in Mexico in order to obtain their certification of Tyson's chickens for production. Following the settlement, Tyson could no longer rely on the rubber stamp of the paid vets and had to focus on production standards. Following years of reliance on government complacency, the catch-up on production quality necessarily impacts earnings (Securities Exchange Commission, 2011a).

FINAL THOUGHTS

If there were one simple phrase to summarize this approach to training employees who work in international operations, that phrase would be, "Teach them the why behind the rules." This approach to training focuses on why employees should step beyond cultural norms and rationalization to doing business with the backdrop of economic and strategic implications of their conduct. With training that demands analyses of consequences, employees are more likely to develop a commitment to ethical and compliance standards because they understand the implications of the blissful ignorance that surrounds moral relativism. There are consequences for the facile choices that follow the "when in Rome" notion. Those consequences affect the company's long-term ability to succeed, the economic development of the countries in which they do business, and, in too many cases, can result in health and social issues for the citizens of those Roman nations. One final result of "why"-based training is that employees begin to understand that we are not asking them to worry about ethics for compliance purposes. We are asking them to worry about ethics because the long-term success of the company and their jobs are dependent upon ethical choices in all aspects of international operations.

NOTE

1. Russia is 154 in the ranking of 178 countries.

REFERENCES

Abaroa, R. M. (1999). Towards 2005: Profits, people, and the future of the regulatory state in the free market. *Journal of Law and Policy in International Business, 30*, 131–136.

Alsever, J. (2006, November 27). Chiquita cleans up its act. *Fortune*, 73–74.

Ballinger, J., & Olsson, C. (Eds.). (1997). *Beyond the swoosh: The struggle of Indonesians making Nike shoes*. Uppsala, Sweden: ICDA/Global Publications Foundations.

Banjo, S. (2012, June 13). Walmart review includes India, South Africa. *Wall Street Journal*, p. B3.

Barboza, D. (2011, February 23). Workers poisoned at Chinese factory wait for Apple to fulfill a pledge. *New York Times*, pp. B1, B7.

Barrett, E. P. (2012, July 17). Senate probe faults HSBC. *Wall Street Journal*, pp. B1, B2.

Byron, E. (2011, May 4). Avon's stock is hit by new worries. *Wall Street Journal*, p. B4.

Chazan, G., Faucon, B., & Casselman, B. (2010, June 30). Saftey and cost drives clashed as CEO Hayward remade BP. *Wall Street Journal*, p. A1.

Choi, J. P., & Thum, M. (2003). The dynamics of corruption with the ratchet effect. *Journal of Public Economics 87*, 427–439.

Crawford, D. (2010, April 15). H-P executives face bribery probes. *Wall Street Journal*, p. B1.

Department of Justice. (2010, May 19). Retreived from www.sec.gov/litigation

Devlin v. Johns-Manville Corp., 495 A.2d 495 (N.J. Super. 1985).

Donaldson, T. (1996, September). Values in tension: Ethics away from home. *Harvard Business Review*, 48–62.

Dunfee, T. W., & Donaldson, T. J. (2002). Untangling the corruption knot: Global bribery viewed through the lens of integrative social contract theory. In N. E. Bowie (Ed.), *The Blackwell guide to business ethics* (pp. 61–76). Oxford, UK: Blackwell.

Fisman, R., & Svensson, J. (2007). Are corruption and taxation really harmful to growth? Firm level evidence. *Journal of Development & Economics 83*, 63–75.

Gold, R., & Crawford, D. (2008, September 12). U.S., other nations step up bribery battle. *Wall Street Journal*, pp. B1, B6.

Graham, J. (2012, March 30). Report slams Apple supplier. *USA Today*, p. 1B.

Jennings, M. M., & Smeltzer, L. M. (1998). Why an international code of business ethics would be good for business. *Journal of Business Ethics, 16*, 57–66.

Jennings, M. M. (2011). *Business ethics: Case studies and selected readings.* Cincinnati, OH: Cengage.

Johnson, M. (2005). *Syndromes of corruption: Wealth, Power, and Democracy.* Cambridge, UK:

Cambridge University Press.

Kamm, T. (1994, February 4). Why does Brazil face such woes? Some see a basic ethical lapse. *Wall Street Journal,* p. A1.

Kantor, M. (2001). International project finance and arbitration with public sector entities: When is arbitrability a fiction? *Fordham International Law Journal, 24,* 1126–1146.

Lewis, N. A. (2007, August 16). Inquiry threatens ex-leader of security agency. *New York Times,* p. A18.

List of Countries Which Have Signed, Ratified/Accepted to the African Convention on Preventing and Combating Corruption. (2010, June 8). Retrieved from http://www.africa-union.org/root/au/documents/treaties/List/African%20on%20Combating%20Corruption.pdf

Marceau, J. F. (2007). A little less conversation, a little more action: Evaluating and forecasting the trend of more frequent and severe prosecutions under the Foreign Corrupt Practices Act. *Fordham Journal of Corporate & Financial Law, 12,* 285–310.

Martin, S. (2012, February 14). Inspections begin at Apple factory. *USA Today,* p. 2B.

Meyer, K. E., & Sinani, E. (2009). When and where does foreign direct investment generate positive spillovers? A meta-analysis. *Journal of International Business Studies, 40,* 1075–1094.

Ostas, D. T. (2007). When fraud pays: Executive self-dealing and the future of self-restrain. *American Business Law Journal, 44,* 571–601.

Porter, E. (2012, March 7). Dividends in pressing Apple over labor. *New York Times,* pp. B1, B5.

Raghavan, A. (2009, April 27). No more excuses. *Forbes.* pp. 121–122.

Rappaport, L. (2012, August 7). Big bank examined over Iran dealings. *Wall Street Journal,* pp. A1, A8.

Reinikka, R., & Svensson, J. (2002). Measuring and understanding corruption at the micro level. In D. Della Porta & S. Rose-Ackerman (Eds.), *Corrupt exchanges: Empirical themes in the politics and political economy of corruption* (pp. 134–146). Baden-Baden, Germany: Nomos Verlagsgesellschaft.

Salbu, S. R. (1999). The Foreign Corrupt Practices Act as a threat to global harmony. *Michigan Journal of International Law, 20,* 419–450.

Schmitt, J. (2010, June 16). Oil execs: BP didn't meet standards. *USA Today,* p. 1B.

Schubert, S. (2008, December 28). Where bribery was just a line item. *New York Times,* p. SB1.

Securities Exchange Commission. (2009, December 31). *Litigation Release No. 21357.* Retrieved from www.sec.gov: http://www.sec.gov/litigation/litreleases/2009/lr21357.htm

Securities Exchange Commission. (2010, December 27). *Litigation Release 21795.* Retrieved from http://www.sec.gov/litigation/litreleases/2010/lr21795.htm

Securities Exchange Commission. (2011a, February 10). Retrieved from www.sec.gov/litigation

Securities Exchange Commission. (2011b, December 20). *Litigation Release 22203.* Retrieved from http://www.sec.gov/litigation/litreleases/2011/lr22203.htm

Securities Exchange Commission. (2012, July 10). *www.sec.gov.* Retrieved from http://www.sec.gov/litigation/complaints/2012/comp-pr2012-133.pdf

Segal, D. (2012, June 24). Apple's retail army, long on loyalty but short on pay. *New York Times,* pp. A1, A18.

Svensson, J. (2001). The cost of doing business: Firms' experiences with corruption. In R. Reinikka and P. Collier (Eds.), *Uganda's recovery: The role of farms, firms, and government* (pp. 319–341). Washington, DC: World Bank.

Transparency International. (2011). *2011 Corruption Perception Index.* Berlin: Transparency International.

Transparency International. (2012). *Trends in anti-bribery laws.* Transparency International. Retrieved from *www.sec.gov/litigation.*http://www.transparency.org/whatwedo/answer/trends_in_anti_bribery laws

Union Carbide Corp. Gas Plant Disaster, 809 F.2d 195 (2nd Cir. 1987); cert. denied, 484 U.S. 871 (1987) (Federal Appellate Court and U.S. Supreme Court 1987).

Vitell, S. J., Dickerson, E. B., & Festervand, T. A. (2000). Ethical problems: Conflicts and beliefs of small business professionals. *Journal of Business Ethics, 28,* 15–27.

Zamiska, N. (2007, August 14). Owner of Chinese toy factory kills himself. *Wall Street Journal,* p. A2.

CHAPTER 4

CROSS-CULTURAL CHALLENGES WITH ETHICS TRAINING IN CHINA

Stephan Rothlin and Dennis McCann

INTRODUCTION

For over a decade, educators at the Center for International Business Ethics (CIBE: www.cibe.org.cn) have been conducting ethics training for Chinese and non-Chinese managers in the Peoples Republic of China. In addition to forming a core group of workshop facilitators, we produced a standard package of course modules designed to address the needs of managers working in firms that operate in China. The seminars provide guidance for Chinese and foreign businesses, including state-owned enterprises (SOEs) and privately owned companies. They are meant to help our clients and their managers achieve various goals—among them, creating an organizational code of ethics, developing personal growth strategies in order to strengthen the corporate culture, designing anti-corruption campaigns, and deepening their understanding of what it means to be a moral leader (Hanson & Rothlin, 2010). The challenges we have faced in conducting these classes are formidable and have required workshop facilitators to

Ethics Training in Action, pages 83–101
Copyright © 2014 by Information Age Publishing
All rights of reproduction in any form reserved.

adopt methods of presentation specially adapted to fit learning styles commonly found among the Chinese managers whom we seek to serve.

In offering our reflections on the CIBE's ethics training initiative, we have four goals in mind:

1. understand and respond constructively to the pervasive cynicism in China that dismisses ethics training as useless
2. integrate the cultivation of virtue into ethics training as a complement to policies and programs focused on compliance with the law
3. encourage further exploration into strategies designed to make ethics training more effective pedagogically
4. establish ethics training as a key channel for change, especially in stimulating value system awareness and fostering creative insight toward organizational ethics

We believe that these goals can be achieved, and with positive outcomes for our partners and participants. Our suggestions for achieving them involve orienting ethics training seminars to ancient Chinese wisdom, as reflected in the insights of Confucian virtue ethics. We find that invoking the wisdom of Confucian tradition activates the participants' own sense of moral integrity, honesty, compassion, empathy, and sincerity (Tiwald, 2010; Yu, Tao, & Ivanhoe, 2010). By crossing the bridge connecting business ethics to the core tenets of Chinese culture, we can enhance the participants' capacity for absorbing the specific lessons that the training sessions are designed to offer.

One example of the practical significance of appealing to Confucian tradition is to challenge common misperceptions among Chinese about the rule of law. Confucianism historically contrasts with what is known in China as "legalism"—understood as the attempt to achieve organizational compliance with policies through the use of exemplary punishments. Legalism is the opposite of what international businesses regard as the rule of law, since legalism seeks to achieve compliance through arbitrary and excessive measures designed to provoke fear of reprisals against nonconformity. Confucianism rejects legalism precisely because it recognizes how counterproductive such reprisals are likely to be. The rule of law, in Confucian teaching, achieves compliance by internalizing legal norms and administrative policies through the practice of social virtues, which we will explore further on in this presentation. Overcoming legalism through the cultivation of Confucian virtue, therefore, is a primary objective in ethics training seminars sponsored by the CIBE.

That China is fast becoming a major player in a globalizing economy where the rule of law is increasingly respected thus confirms the relevance of virtue ethics. Since Chinese people are now doing business all over the world, it is important not only for them, but for all their business partners, to appreciate the persistence of Chinese moral wisdom and to learn how to live by it in today's world (Enderle, 2001). Many scholars have recognized that virtue ethics is one key element in developing appropriately Chinese models of business ethics (Romar, 2002; Touval, 2007). Understanding the ancient Way (*Dao*) of China and its enduring power (*De*) is a major philosophical achievement. But the challenge remains how to use this power to come to grips with China's amazingly complex recent history, as routinely encountered by anyone trying to do business there.

Conducting the ethics training seminars has given the CIBE a unique vantage point on the difficulties of relating theory to practice. The frank interaction between instructors and participants, as well as among the participants themselves, has given us a privileged opportunity to rediscover just how deeply China's history influences the attitudes and responses of everyone involved. In what follows, the quotations from workshop organizers and participants are taken from our unpublished notes from interviews held before and after the workshops. We find in their responses opportunities for appreciating both the persistence of traditional Chinese morality and the emergence of major obstacles against taking it seriously. As much as possible we will strive to present an objective description of our participants' responses within the training seminars, while refraining as much as possible from finger pointing. We hope to be direct in our descriptions of the challenges involved in developing and conducting such seminars, but also diligent in exploring ways to address them constructively.

AT A CIBE ETHICS TRAINING WORKSHOP

One of the CIBE's first clients is a major multinational corporation (MNC) in the food industry, with both production and distribution facilities in China. Over the past thirty years, this firm has established itself in 19 countries, with more than two-thirds of its plants now operating beyond the borders of its original home. Most of this dramatic growth has come through mergers and acquisitions, which have compounded the problem of maintaining a corporate culture based on common values. Our client entered the China market only six years ago, with one such acquisition of another MNC's operations. Among the challenges faced in China was learning to understand and respect Chinese cultural values, including popular food tastes, in order to provide products that would truly meet the expectations of Chinese consumers. Meeting this challenge prompted our client to seek more effective integration of Chinese cultural values into the firm's overall corporate culture, so that management in China could be both flexible in response to local customs and tastes, and yet consistent with the core values that had guided its success in other areas.

One of the firm's executives noted how "entering China was undoubtedly a huge challenge for our company," because the firm hoped to remain "faithful to our values and philosophy while being flexible in adapting to a new culture that we are constantly learning." In order to meet this challenge, the firm relied upon local leadership and talent in order to create a "mixing of, and interaction between, the two cultures." The hope was to stimulate a mutual learning process that enables us to understand the market and facilitate problem solving. The firm engaged the CIBE to conduct a training workshop for a select group of its managers, in order to facilitate this "mutual learning process."

We found that the firm's strong corporate culture already provided significant resources for developing virtue ethics among their employees. The core value animating its operations was respect for persons, a commitment not only observed in its routine management practices but also in its approach to corporate social responsibility (CSR). The company envisions becoming an "inclusive enterprise," one pledged, for example, "to eliminate social, cultural and physical barriers that limit the development of persons with disabilities." Such employment policies are meant to reflect the firm's understanding of CSR, which it defines as "a social vision based on policies and programs to perform beyond their legal obligations, always taking into consideration the expectations of the community." There are four basic elements to their CSR vision: commitments to the health of its customers, to the environment, to its associates or employees, and to society. The company's website features reports on specific initiatives taken to fulfill these commitments: among them, participation in various reforestation programs and the development of innovative factories fueled by ecologically sustainable sources of renewable energy—for example, wind and solar power.

These are clear and credible expressions of the values that our client also wants to promote in its China operations. The task assigned to the CIBE training seminars was to orient the client's Chinese staff to its core values. We meant to help the firm's employees integrate these values into their own emerging sense of personal integrity and professional identity, consistent with the development of Chinese culture. When the first of these seminars was held in a two-day event in Beijing in 2008, approximately twenty managers participated. The seminar opened with an address from the general director outlining the key values animating the firm's corporate culture. This was followed by small group discussions focused on the questions, "What are the key values in my life? What happens after death? What are the five things in my life I cherish most?" The point of this initial discussion was to help participants take ownership of the seminar, by inviting them to reflect on their own values as responses to everyone's concern about the meaning of life and death. Following the first group discussion, a representative from the firm's human resources department made a general presentation relating these values to each participant's commitment to the firm, after which there was a second round of small group discussions. True to the firm's core values, the first day concluded with a discussion on taking good care of one's health.

While this first day's schedule may seem routine for anyone familiar with ethics training seminars internationally, the second day's clearly reflected the fact that this was a seminar tailored to the needs and expectations of Chinese managers. It opened with a presentation, given by a CIBE advisory board member then teaching at Renmin University, on "The Person: The Social and Spiritual Value of Each Person in Chinese Tradition." This talk made the case for a close alignment between the client's core value of "Personalism" and the tradition of Confucian humanism. A follow-up presentation by the same speaker on "Discovering the Meaning of Life: What are the Key Chinese and Western Values?" was followed by small group discussion on "Which Are My Chinese Values? What Can I Learn from Other Values?" On the second day, then, Chinese tradition was closely linked with the participants' personal values and professional sense of identity, as these had emerged in the discussions of the first day. The program concluded with a session focused on best practices in cross-cultural management. A colleague from the Communication University in Beijing led these discussions, designed to secure practical outcomes from the training exercise. What could be taken away from the seminar to assist each manager's pursuit of a "successful and meaningful life" thus became the topic of the final small group discussions.

Though the training seminar was well thought out, a product of close collaboration between the CIBE and its client, the results were less than perfect. While the CIBE seminar continued the client's longstanding practice of offering a "Personal Development Training" exercise for all its employees, at the time such were unheard of in China. Perhaps their novelty helps account for the fact that, even now, it is hard to get a sense of what participants really think about them. While the client's executive leadership in China is still committed to expanding the workshops, there also seems to be a consensus that organizing a training seminar in venues lacking opportunities for recreational activities, such as casino gambling, is not likely to be welcomed by local staff. The effort to design and conduct effective personal development seminars has also been retarded by recent turnovers among staff working for the client's human resources department, who normally collaborate closely with CIBE in producing the seminars. The bottom line is that despite the great expectations that accompanied the first CIBE seminar, it has had no measurable impact on the firm's efforts to resist the rising tide of corruption in China, or the pervasive cultural attitudes that have contributed to it. The client's hope of strengthening its corporate culture by foregrounding the integration of Chinese cultural values within it is still a dream waiting to be fulfilled (Weaver, 2001).

ACKNOWLEDGING THE LESSONS OF EXPERIENCE

Despite the modest results that the CIBE can report at this time, there are certain basic lessons that ought to be noted by colleagues planning similar training sessions in and for China. The first of these is learning to remove any barriers to effective communication that may have inadvertently been built into the way in which the program is structured.

The language barrier is the most obvious one, and overcoming it involves much more than recruiting trainers who are competent in Putonghua (Selmer, 2006). While Chinese people usually are quite moved by sincere efforts to understand their culture and learn their language, even a foreigner who has mastered these is not likely to present the best face for a training seminar in China. The foreigner making his or her presentation in Putonghua may elicit a rebuttal, typically starting with the phrase "In China..." followed by the listing of a number of points that the presenter stands accused of missing. Such reactions have the effect, if not the intent, of giving fellow attendees sufficient reason to dismiss the foreigner's presentation. The point is to prove that the foreigner—especially one who would like to display some special expertise—has no clue about the situation in China. On the other hand, questions such as "How can he/she really know anything about our situation?" combined with increasing self-assertiveness may also indicate that the participants are trying to find secure footing in a conversation in English (at best their second language). Having been forced out of their comfort zone, they hope to execute a dignified retreat back into it, by expressing their criticisms in Putonghua.

Faced with such challenges, the most prudent approach to overcoming the language barrier is to work closely with local professionals. We learned this lesson when one of us was asked by a Chinese colleague to give a joint lecture with him before both Chinese and Swiss students. Whenever I made a statement about China I asked my colleague to confirm his agreement with my argument. After the lecture ended, I realized that some of the Chinese students had been greatly irritated by what I had said concerning subtle differences between the Swiss and themselves. With the nodding approval of my Chinese colleague I pointed out that Europeans generally feel much more at ease in expressing their opinions directly. What irritated the students was their sense that they were now being challenged to step out of their cultural comfort zone in order to be as blunt and direct in their interactions as their Western counterparts allegedly were. Thanks to the support of my Chinese colleague, the challenge, though initially unwelcome, now elicited a constructive response. One would not be wrong to conclude that the success of a training exercise—as well as other ventures in China—depends on working with trusted Chinese colleagues whose participation not only makes for a more balanced presentation but also confers legitimacy on the foreign expert.

That Chinese resentments must be taken seriously is clear from the numerous occasions when poorly designed training seminars suggest insensitivity to local needs. One of us recalled an incident from his early experiences in China: "I remember the discomfort I felt when I was dragged into a seminar where a CEO on a visit in China insisted that the Chinese participants would have to listen to a video of the firm's President and founder. Since most of the participants were not really fluent in English, almost no one could actually figure out what the person flickering on the screen was actually trying to say." Such a performance may indeed justify the impression that training exercises are a waste of time. But even if serious attempts are made to anticipate the needs of Chinese participants, the difficulties of effective communication are generally underestimated.

The language barrier, however, is closely related to the difficulties involved in getting participants to take ownership of the training seminar. The first seminar conducted for our MNC client in the food industry attempted to address this challenge by designing the sessions with sufficient time for small-group discussion. But we discovered still more barriers to taking ownership, such as the passive-aggressive behavior involved in cell phone use. It is not unusual for participants to play with their cell phones throughout the training exercise, with the result that cell phones are constantly ringing, and people are constantly leaving the room in order to return phone calls perceived as really relevant for business. Just as it is now common, even in Chinese cinemas, for the audience to be urged to turn off their cell phones for the duration of the movie, so the effective trainer will insist, when the ground rules are being discussed, that cell phones be silenced until either the seminar is finished or the group has begun a scheduled break. Of course, if participants are urged to refrain from using cell phones during the sessions, the training instructors must also discipline themselves to respect the coffee and tea breaks that provide the needed opportunities for participants to respond to urgent business calls. If the participants are allowed sufficient time and space for business calls, cell phone use during the seminar sessions can be minimized.

Success in assisting participants to take ownership of the training seminar depends not simply on establishing appropriate ground rules for all concerned, but also on the degree of coordination between the seminar's producers and the client's executive leadership. While this clearly is true for all training seminars, there are distinctive challenges to be addressed in understanding and working with the leadership, particularly in Chinese firms. It helps to know something of China's social history, particularly the unmistakably hierarchical worldview and social structures that survive and even flourish in contemporary China. Given the hierarchical character of Chinese corporate culture and organizational behavior, typically evident in both private and public enterprises, a successful training exercise must enjoy strong backing from the top leadership.

To be sure, support from the top is also necessary in the West. However, there are subtle differences in the ways such support is established that need to be respected. For example, social rituals have great significance in Chinese culture, as in observing proper table manners, or maintaining an appropriate seating order, and so on—matters that Western "common sense" about how to get things done in business often tends to ignore. Such rituals persisted well beyond the Imperial phase of China's history, survived the Cultural Revolution, and even today in an era of economic and social reform they are regarded as neither frivolous nor superfluous (Yang, 1994). Moreover, since in China the eyes of subordinates seem to be even more fixed on the leader than in the West, the corporate leader who has ultimate authority over the training seminar is expected not only to preside over the opening ceremonies, but also, and more importantly, to acknowledge visibly its success in the closing ceremonies.

Once the firm's CEO demonstrates his or her support for the training seminars, successful implementation depends on working with a trusted intermediary or facilitator. The ideal facilitator must be capable not only of assessing the leadership's specific objectives in sponsoring the training but also of communicating clearly these goals and how they will bring added value to those invited to participate. Crucial to the success of a training program is adequate preparation, in which the specific needs of the target group are identified and thoroughly understood, with particular attention given to any recent conflicts that may have prompted the call for training. It is also important to win over the support and confidence of the person— usually from the human resources department—who will work with the facilitator to secure logistical support for the seminar. Once a good working relationship is established, it is much easier to adjust to the specific needs of the invited participants as they emerge. Attention to details is much appreciated, particularly in Chinese contexts. Once participants are confident that the trainers are sensitive to their needs, the way is opened for addressing the challenges that occasioned the seminar itself.

Some training firms operating in China have attempted to adapt their training seminars to the Chinese situation, but with very mixed results. They may have assumed that Chinese whose families have emigrated or who have worked overseas will automatically have adapted to internationally recognized practices—for example, honoring a corporate code of ethics (Snell, Chak, & Chu, 1999). While overseas Chinese may be more familiar with international best practices, local participants may still dismiss them as foreigners. Their presumed usefulness in facilitating interactions with local staff may turn out to be limited. For similar reasons, one cannot assume that facilitators coming from Hong Kong or Taiwan will be any more successful in developing smooth working relationships with mainland Chinese.

Motivating employees and cadres to actively participate requires a level of personal credibility that can respond persuasively to hard-nosed skepticism, reflecting local conditions. Whoever is conducting the training seminars—whether they are Chinese based locally or overseas or foreign experts—must persuade participants that the information given about CSR or business ethics, for example, will have a positive impact on the firm's "bottom line." The persuasion must come early and effectively to capture the participants' attention. The instructor needs to spell out very clearly which tangible benefits for the long-term profitability of a firm will be enhanced, and how they will be enhanced, through such a training exercise. It is also important to appeal to personal incentives, for example, the fact that participants generally are eager to obtain the certificates they will earn upon successful completion of the exercise. The effective training instructor therefore will underscore the fact that full participation is required in order to obtain this certificate and that a strict attendance policy will be enforced throughout the seminar.

In the end, the success of an ethics training seminar depends on creating an atmosphere in which people from different cultural backgrounds feel at ease, one in which arrogant and disrespectful behavior towards those coming from another culture becomes unthinkable (Li, 2011). This requires a substantial effort from everyone involved. Success in such efforts results from establishing a genuine dialogue where everyone is willing to learn from one another, an attitude that, once established, is likely to be maintained throughout the seminar and may even carry over into workplace routines. The high degree of availability for genuine listening to each other obviously requires not only flexibility and mutual respect, but also self-discipline among both presenters and participants.

ACHIEVING CONSISTENCY
WITHIN THE CORPORATE CULTURE

Given the persistence of hierarchical social practices in China, it is not surprising that corporate cultures—regardless of how successful elsewhere—may have to adapt to challenges specific to doing business in China. Recall the case involving our client in the Chinese food industry. When this client invited us to provide training seminars, their hopes were shaped by the corporate culture by which they had flourished prior to coming to China. Consistent with that culture, they assumed that all employees should be on an equal footing in the seminar sessions. But this aspect of the client's corporate culture could not be owned in China, since Chinese managers are generally convinced that they lose face if and when they are reduced to the same level as their subordinates. When we tried to conduct a seminar conforming to the client's egalitarian assumptions, we learned just how counterproductive this idea could be. In reviewing the first seminar, we recommended a more modest approach adapted to local cultural norms, one that respected the principle of hierarchy by offering a workshop exclusively for the firm's local leadership teams.

When adapting the corporate culture to social expectations in China, it is important to understand the widespread drive for short-term profit (which by no means is limited to China) that is likely to animate the participants' routine attitudes and behavior at work. For a long time, especially during the so-called Cultural Revolution between 1966 and 1976, China was cut off from the rest of the world and ideologically dominated by a version of Marxism "with Chinese characteristics." With the shift toward economic reform under Deng Xiaoping, the repressed desire for material wealth became a dominant feature of Chinese society. The shift in cultural values, however, was not simply about wealth and its acquisition. It carried with it an extremely pragmatic "bottom-line" attitude toward all other human values and relationships. Whatever may have the smell of being too idealistic, or too Western, will almost certainly be rejected.

The overall climate seems reminiscent of a "gold rush," now focused on grabbing as much money, power, and prestige as possible, as well as the status symbols indicating their acquisition, namely, the cars, condominiums, recent telecommunication gadgets, and whatnot. This gold rush mentality, of course, exists in some tension with another very powerful cultural factor that training instructors must bear in mind. That is, they should expect to hear criticism of various aspects of Chinese culture, including the discrepancy between the "gold rush" attitude and traditional Confucian values. While such criticism may be resented when it comes from foreigners, this does not imply that all critical remarks are out of bounds in a training seminar. On the contrary, facilitators should try to cultivate a healthy climate of confidence, which would allow all participants to air their own mixed feelings about the "gold rush" and its distorting effects on doing business in China. The point of such frank and open discussion should be made crystal clear. As the firm adapts to local conditions in China, it must face the question of how its own best interests may be aligned with the gold rush mentality.

The challenge, of course, is to find the right balance between the firm's corporate culture and the expectations of its local employees, including their personal stake in China's gold rush. What we have learned in conducting ethical training seminars is as much about what doesn't work as what does. Responding critically but constructively to the gold rush mentality, however, is but one small part of the process of rethinking the firm's corporate culture. Whatever may be perceived as evidence of a "colonial hangover"—for example, a lack of appreciation of Chinese culture and customs and the arrogance of Westerners assuming that their role consists in telling others what to do—should be avoided. Cross-cultural ventures—such as conducting the training seminars—often get trapped in a form of historical amnesia that simply masks how much resentment is still harbored in typical Chinese attitudes based on the threat of foreign aggression, real or imagined. As a Polish friend remarked about his own country, we may find ourselves working with colleagues caught up in a pervasive mood swing between an inferiority complex and aggressive new claims of superiority. In China, the old fear of foreigners and foreign domination is giving way to a widespread feeling that now is the time for China to take the leading role on the world stage once more. Whatever the sources of this resurgence of nationalistic pride, it is important for the success of the training seminars to send as many signals as possible that everyone involved respects and welcomes China's reemergence in the world.

REDISCOVERING CONFUCIAN VIRTUE ETHICS

One very promising way to demonstrate such an appropriate respect for Chinese cultural values is to follow the central government's lead in restoring the role of Confucian tradition in moral education. At first this effort seemed intended to extend China's "soft" power internationally, by establishing Confucian Institutes all over the world as well as creating Confucian Academies within China. But recently various leaders in the CCCP have called for developing a form of "cultural therapy" based on Confucian values in order to resist corruption and sustain the process of economic and social reform (Cheng & Liu, 2011). This represents an important turning point away from the Cultural Revolution, which reviled Confucius as a bourgeois philosopher whose values were judged incompatible with revolutionary ideology. Though criticism of the Cultural Revolution often remains a taboo subject (HRIC, 2005; Li, 2001; Pye, 1986), the quiet rehabilitation of Confucius and his teachings now underway in China provides a unique opportunity for developing an approach to training seminars that recognizes the perennial importance—especially in China—of cultivating the social virtues.

Confucian moral teaching begins with a realistic assessment of human nature, in its propensity for both good and evil. Though the tradition offers various explanations of the deeper relationship between the two, it clearly affirms the basic goodness of human nature and relies upon the more or less spontaneous emotional responses of people to prompt us toward doing good things. Mencius, inspired by the teachings of Confucius, points out the universality of compassion: "All men have a mind which cannot bear to see the sufferings of others" (Mencius, 2A6:1). In order to demonstrate the reality of the compassion naturally occurring in human beings, Mengzi tells a story about what happens when "men suddenly see a child about to fall into a well." They "without exception experience a feeling of alarm and distress." Without calculating any reward they might obtain for doing so, they rush to save the child (Mencius, 2A6:3). From this observation, Mengzi infers that normal people contain within themselves the "sprouts" from which the basic virtues grow. Like sprouts the virtues must be cultivated in order to flourish. Natural dispositions become virtues through processes of self-cultivation, identified by Confucian tradition as the Way (Yu, 1998).

In Confucian teaching, for example, each human being (*ren*) has the opportunity to become genuinely humane (*ren*). Considered as a virtue, *ren* is usually translated as "benevolence," or more concretely as knowing and loving people. Goodness or happiness—the goal of humane living—cannot be achieved without taking responsibility for one's relationships with other people, which are governed by the five basic virtues: in addition to benevolence (*ren*), Confucius spoke of righteousness (*yi*), ritual propriety or proper conduct (*li*), wisdom (*zhi*), and sincerity (*xin*). While there are differences—some subtle and some profound—between the understanding of these five in Chinese tradition and their meanings in Western philosophy, they converge in a Golden Rule shared by both Chinese and Western morality, namely: "Do unto others as you would have them do unto you" (Matthew 7:12 and Confucius: The Analects 15:24). Although there is much philosophical controversy over the differences between positive and negative formulations of the Golden Rule, and whether Confucian tradition contains both formulations, or even should contain them, the point remains that the *Dao* leading to all moral virtues consists in the practice of reciprocity (*xu*) (Nivison, 1996).

One important feature in Chinese virtue ethics is that reciprocity is perceived and practiced within social relationships, each of which has indispensable moral significance. Thus Confucian tradition sees self-cultivation occurring within a process described as the "rectification of names" (*zhengming*). The names refer to the five basic relationships in which each of us finds himself or herself in life: parent and child, elder sibling and younger sibling, husband and wife, elder friend and younger friend, and ruler and subject. Rectification in any of these relationships entails that a person should live up to the responsibilities inherent in the name. Notice that there is also a hierarchical progression in the sequence of relationships. A person becomes fully human, starting from his or her relationships with parents, proceeding through the family, and then exercised in friendships, and ultimately in the embrace of one's duties to the Emperor, considered as the Son of Heaven and the embodiment of the people as a whole. Guided by a general sense of benevolence, each person makes progress toward greater humanity by observing the rules of propriety (*li*) objectively determined for each relationship. Successful rectification, thus, is the result of a process of self-cultivation that is meant to allow a person's inherently moral nature to become increasingly clear and effective. The cultivation of virtue becomes possible because humanity is inherently good (Mengzi); it is necessary because uncultivated goodness is so easily corrupted (Xunzi).

Teaching and learning the Way of the virtues must begin by identifying the "sprouts" within oneself and others, and then nurturing these to full maturity. How might that be done? If a sprout or a seedling is to grow, it must be weeded, watered, and exposed to sunlight—and all of these in just the right amount. Weeding suggests the exercise of self-control, what Mengzi describes as lessening one's desires (Mencius, 7B:35). Unruly desires, that is, seemingly uncontrollable impulses that threaten to upset the heart-mind's (*xin*) natural serenity, must not be allowed to dominate the self. Some form of yoga or meditation practice is usually recommended at this point. Watering suggests the need for nourishment, in this case, perhaps, establishing a regular program of reading Confucian texts designed to strengthen the heart-mind's natural propensity for goodness. Exposure to sunlight suggests public accountability, even in one's process of self-cultivation. Thus it is always wise to have a mentor or, if you will, a guru, spiritual director, or teacher (*shifu*). This also suggests, in China's current situation, that ethics training seminars can and ought to be regarded as an extension of the ancient *Dao* of Confucian virtue ethics.

Though the chief sprout to be cultivated in each person's life may be identified as filial piety (*xiao*), or the respect properly shown toward parents and teachers, Confucian virtue ethics extends by analogy through all the social relationships in which a mature person is likely to find himself or herself. However obsolete we may consider the *Zhengming*'s ruler/subject relationship as a guide to social practices in a modern society, its relevance consists in the fact, as previously noted, that Chinese organizations remain strongly hierarchical. Sincerity or personal loyalty (*xin*) represents the maturation of the sprout of filial piety (*xiao*), now practiced in the context of organizational behavior. Such sincerity must flow from inner dispositions, and simply cannot be reduced to external compliance. This is why Confucianism's ideal of moral leadership depends upon self-cultivation rather than exclusive reliance on compliance with the law.

BEYOND MERE COMPLIANCE: CULTIVATING CONFUCIAN SOCIAL VIRTUES

In light of this brief sketch of Confucian virtue ethics, workshop instructors can design exercises that relate Confucian teaching to the participants' own experiences. As is evident in the outline of the program we organized for our client in the food industry, the seminars should seek to create "teachable moments" in which participants can take a critical look at the enduring significance of Confucian virtues in their own lives. A useful contrast may be developed by urging participants, for example, to reflect on how "modern" Chinese respond to the need to care for their parents. In extreme cases, some Chinese who moved to the cities may not remember where their parents live and may be most reluctant to pay them regular visits. Integrating aged parents into their own homes may appear to them as a totally outdated, crazy idea. If participants can be encouraged to have frank discussions among themselves about what filial piety (*xiao*) may and may not entail for them in a modernizing China, they may be open to giving the cultivation of Chinese virtues a serious hearing. Once their own residual sincerity (*xin*) has been engaged, they may be better disposed to think more broadly about their responsibilities—personal, corporate, and social.

The need to overcome outmoded "colonial" approaches to ethics training may also be found in addressing problems of compliance. A number of firms, which are more and more threatened by the U.S. Foreign Corrupt Practices Act and other anti-corruption legislation internationally, try to fix their problems by simply instructing their employees in the requirements of the law. The main concern seems to be to convey a message that illegal and corrupt behavior will be severely punished, and that an increasing number of firms are indeed meting out punishments before they themselves are punished. In a culture—such as China's—where exemplary punishment is still regarded as an effective deterrent, it is certainly crucial to try to instill a sense of respect for the rule of law. Nevertheless, as China's history also suggests, an exclusive reliance on "legalism" in order to obtain compliance is inevitably counterproductive for various reasons, among them the tendency of exemplary punishment to perpetuate confusion between the rule of law and rule by law. Confucian virtue ethics, on the other hand, commends itself precisely for being the only method of minimizing corruption that has proven effective in the long run. One need only recall the social conditions in which Confucius began his teaching, and the reasons it was institutionalized as an alternative to "legalism" during the Imperial period.

When addressing the problem of corruption, usually China's gift-giving culture emerges as a key bone of contention. In the different "anti-corruption summits" that are routinely organized in major cities such as Hong Kong, Beijing, and Shanghai, a concern about appropriate gifts and entertainments usually emerges as one of the biggest challenges (St. Clair & Norris, 2012). While it is certainly important for multinational corporations to be as precise as possible in spelling out their policies on gifts, a host of other issues need to be addressed, beyond indicating what is an appropriate price level for gifts. To be sure, China is not the only culture in which traditional gift-giving practices are often used as a cover for bribery. As some studies confirm, bribers know how to mimic the traditional etiquette of gift-giving rituals (Yang, 1994). Nevertheless, for reasons already given here, preventing or minimizing corruption should not require a wholesale repudiation of traditional gift-giving practices.

All concerned should recognize first of all the positive side of gift-giving in Asian cultures. As a social practice, gift-giving is the ritually appropriate way to acknowledge hierarchical relationships and their ethical burden. Accepting a gift can create the kind of loyalty that is taken for granted in family life, but now extended through relationship building (*guanxixue*) to important contacts outside the family circle. For two business organizations to ritually exchange gifts on appropriate occasions, such as Chinese New Year celebrations, is to pledge mutual support by demonstrating it ritually, as if they were brothers. The role of gift-giving in traditional Chinese culture cannot be regulated by imposing a limit on the amount spent for the gift. The touchstone is sincerity (*xin*) as signified in the thoughtfulness of the gift as well as its ritual appropriateness. Confucian tradition well equips Chinese people to recognize the difference between gifts that are sincerely offered and other bids that are gifts in name only. The difference between gifts and bribes is specifically recognized in the Book of Mencius (Book 2B, Chapter 3). Here the priority of virtue ethics is clear, though admittedly there will be major difficulties translating the ethics of Chinese gift-giving practices into legalistic guidelines that take little or no account of the sincerity of the parties involved.

Another example in which the relevance of Confucian virtue ethics may be seen concerns the role of alcohol consumption in closing business deals. "Zero-tolerance" policies are usually ineffective because they may be misunderstood as a rude refusal to interact socially. It is standard custom in China, especially in rural areas, for banquets to include a lot of ritual drinking, particularly between courses. Some of the toasts involve all the participants at once, but others may invite specific individuals to participate in "bottoms-up" rituals. It is in the vital interest of firms doing business in China to communicate appropriate policies in this area. There is nothing in Confucian teaching that would make a virtue of excessive drinking or pressuring certain individuals to participate in practices masquerading as traditional rituals. While the cultivation of good social relationships (*guanxixue*) certainly is valued in Confucian tradition, the abuse of *guanxi*—that is, cultivating relationships only for strategic purposes—is an abuse, particularly regarding the generous Chinese impulse toward hospitality that flows directly from the cultivation of benevolence (*ren*). A shrewd follower of Confucius will remain alert to the different games that others are playing during such meals, as when one party may be observed deliberately targeting members of the other negotiating party, to secure strategic advantages—personal as well as corporate—rather than develop genuine friendship.

Another example indicating the need to draw a distinction between the use and abuse of Chinese cultural values is the problem of "nepotism," arising from a misunderstanding of the Confucian virtue of sincerity or personal loyalty (*xin*). As a famous Chinese saying puts it: "When somebody is elevated to heaven, even his dog will follow." That means when someone gets promoted to high office, it is perceived as normal that family and clan members will get privileged treatment. Everyone has heard of the dominant roles that sons, daughters, nieces, nephews, and so on of top leaders may play in the government. Qualified or not, they will be hired for whatever positions become available, and they may not be expected to perform at the same level as other employees not so well connected. Though numerous conflicts of interest may emerge from this practice, rarely is it even recognized as a problem. It is therefore useful to take a close look into an amazingly complex social reality where the boundaries between private and public spheres seem to be more blurred than in the West.

While even acknowledging nepotism as a problem may be a considerable achievement, once participants look more deeply into it, they may also be persuaded to recognize an inevitable downside to Confucian moral teaching, which stresses the importance of respect for parents and close family members. Indeed, in our ethics training seminars we have witnessed constructive dialogues in which Chinese participants have pointed out some positive features of nepotism. For example, if an accountant comes from the same village as her boss it becomes very difficult for her to embezzle the firm's funds without completely ruining her reputation. Even so, for the dialogue to reflect genuine reciprocity (*xu*), participants should be led to explore reasonable limits to the practice of nepotism, and the ethical questions it raises about the sincerity of a firm's commitment to any of the basic Confucian virtues. Recognizing it as a problem and developing strategies for minimizing it should become one of the goals for a successful training session (Lovett, Simmons, & Kali, 1999; Verhezen, 2008).

Genuine dialogue may result in achieving another crucial learning outcome: that each participant becomes aware of his or her own potential for changing a given business culture and for overcoming preconceived ideas about how reality should work. It is often said—contrary to all the historical evidence—that there is no way to change Chinese culture. If training seminars are to become part of the change that people hope for, we must aim higher than merely absorbing some lessons about business etiquette in China and realize that the simple step of becoming friends can be transformative, in both corporate as well as personal relationships. The key factor in becoming friends is to establish an appropriate level of trust. It is crucial for a Chinese to feel personal loyalty, to be sure that a friend is on his or her side. The Confucian way of cultivating the virtues, acknowledging the role of relationships in becoming a fully realized human person, while honoring the rituals by which such relationships are maintained and enhanced, is well suited to creating the kind of personal loyalty that expands the comfort zone in which a corporate culture can achieve its full potential. Those who would conduct ethics training seminars in and for China should recognize the contribution that Confucian virtue ethics can make toward achieving their goals.

CONCLUSION: RESPONDING TO A THIRST FOR TRUTH

Recently we conducted a training seminar for a state-owned company in Chengdu, Sichuan Province. What makes it memorable is the fact that the participants, mostly middle managers in their 30s and 40s, came from different cities, among them Guangzhou, Shanghai, Beijing, and Taipei. There was an amazing mix of different Chinese cultures and a rare atmosphere of frank sharing. This in itself was surprising in an environment where people are not used to sharing their own feelings and emotions, knowing that someone may have been assigned the task of reporting each detail to higher authorities. It came to us as a surprise that the participants ranked *truth* as the most desirable value in their final evaluation. This unusual outcome may indicate a genuine desire to find a safe space in which something may be learned that is worth taking home. In stark contrast to the idea that a training seminar just teaches a few pointers about management and compliance, we found that people are genuinely interested in going beyond propaganda, slogans, and the sometimes sophisticated web of lies that surrounds us, in order to get some concrete and relevant answers to questions which are vital to their work lives. The surprisingly open way in which managers coming from different cultural backgrounds in China shared their insights and hopes seems to reflect a deeper thirst for truth—one that an organization's leadership team must learn to respect instead of fear, and take appropriate steps to sustain, for the sake of the firm's own development.

These few comments about specific challenges involved in conducting training seminars in China are intended to highlight the potential for genuine change within firms and institutions. The discussion here is obviously preliminary, and meant to stimulate further attempts to understand, without prejudice, China's complex social reality and reach a genuinely positive appreciation of its local cultures and values. It is intended to counter cynical views of China's business environment that depict it as a brutal, cutthroat affair devoid of any sense of law and basic decency. A contrasting perspective on doing business in China—one that is alert to the persistence of traditional Confucian values such as benevolence, righteousness, appropriate behavior, wisdom, and personal sincerity, and seeks to support new ways of honoring these in a common pursuit of truth—should enable all concerned to take a more realistic approach to the challenges and possible pitfalls enterprises face when doing business in a cultural environment undergoing rapid transformation.

REFERENCES

Cheng, Y., & Liu, B (2011, October 25). China explores cultural therapy to cure social ills. Retrieved from http://news.xinhuanet.com/english2010/china/2011-10/25/c_131212258.htm

Confucius: The Analects. (1979). Translated with an Introduction by D. C. Lau. London: Penguin Books.

Enderle, G. (2001). Is it time for business ethics in China? *International Business Ethics Review, 4*(1), 3–5. Retrieved from http://business-ethics.org/articles/Global%20Business%20Ethics%20Programs.pdf

Hanson, K. O., & Rothlin, S. (2010). Taking your code to China. *Journal of International Business Ethics, 3*(1), 69–80. Retrieved from http://www.scu.edu/ethics/publications/ethicalperspectives/Code-to-China.pdf

HRIC. (2005). The cultural revolution as legacy and precedent. *China Rights Forum, 4*, 37–40. Retrieved from http://hrichina.org/sites/default/files/oldsite/PDFs/CRF.4.2005/CRF-2005-4_Revolution.pdf

Li, X. (2001). The Chinese cultural revolution revisited. *The China Review, 1*(1), 137–165. Retrieved from http://www.chineseupress.com/chinesepress/promotion/China%20Review/5-Li.pdf

Li, Y. (2011). Cross-cultural communication within American and Chinese colleagues in multinational organizations. *Proceedings of the New York State Communication Association, 2010*, Art.7. Retrieved from http://docs.rwu.edu/nycsaproceedings/vol2010/iss1/7

Lovett, S., Simmons, L. C., & Kali, R. (1999). Guanxi versus the market: Ethics and efficiency. *Journal of International Business Studies, 30*, 231–247.

Mencius. (1970). Translated with an Introduction by D. C. Lau. London: Penguin Books, 1970

Nivison, D. (1996). Golden rule arguments in Chinese moral philosophy. In D. Nivison & B. W. Van Norden (Eds.), *The ways of Confucianism: Investigations in Chinese philosophy* (pp. 59–76). Chicago, IL: Open Court Publishing Company.

Pye, L. W. (1986). Reassessing the cultural revolution. *The China Quarterly, 108*, 597–612. Retrieved from http://www.jstor.org/stable/653530

Romar, E. J. (2002). Virtue is good business: Confucianism as a practical business ethics. *Journal of Business Ethics, 38*, 119–131.

Selmer, J. (2006). Language ability and adjustment: Western expatriates in China. *Thunderbird International Business Review, 48*, 347–368. doi:10.1002/tie.20099

Snell, R. S., Chak, A. M.-K., & Chu J. W.-H. (1999). Codes of ethics in Hong Kong: Their adoption and impact in the run up to the 1997 transition of sovereignty to China. *Journal of Business Ethics, 22*, 281–309.

St. Clair, N. S., & Norris, J. T. (2012). Business ethics and social responsibility in contemporary China. *Journal of Academic and Business Ethics, 5.* Retrieved from http://www.aabri.com/manuscripts/111005.pdf

Tiwald, J. (2010). Confucianism and virtue ethics: Still a fledging in Chinese and comparative philosophy. *Comparative Philosophy, 1*(2), 55–63. Retrieved from http://www.comparativephilosophy.org/index.php/ComparativePhilosophy/article/view/52/79

Touval, A. (2007, July). Instilling business ethics in China. *Shanghai Business Review,* 66. Retrieved from http://www.itapintl.com/pdf/InstillingBusinessEthicsIn-China.pdf

Verhezen, P. (2008). *Guanxi*: Networks or nepotism? The dark side of business networks. Retrieved from http://www.verhezen.net/thoughts_publications/Guanxi%20Networks.pdf

Weaver, G. R. (2001). Ethics programs in global business: Culture's role in managing ethics. *Journal of Business Ethics, 30,* 3–15.

Yang, M. M. (1994). *Gifts, favors, and banquets: The art of social relationships in China.* Ithaca, NY: Cornell University Press.

Yu, J. (1998). Virtue: Confucius and Aristotle. *Philosophy East and West, 48,* 323–347. Retrieved from http://www.jstor.org/stable/1399830

Yu, K., Tao, J., & Ivanhoe, P. J. (Eds.). (2010). *Taking Confucian ethics seriously: Contemporary theories and applications.* Albany, NY: State University of New York Press.

CHAPTER 5

ETHICS TRAINING AND THE PREVENTION OF WORKPLACE BULLYING

Creating a Healthy Work Environment

Denise Salin

Workplace bullying is a form of unethical behavior that violates generally accepted norms of behavior. It has been defined as "harassing, offending, or socially excluding someone or negatively affecting someone's work" (Einarsen, Hoel, Zapf, & Cooper, 2011, p. 22). Typically, for something to be defined as bullying, researchers also require that the negative acts occur repeatedly and regularly over a period of time and that the person(s) at the receiving end do not feel able to defend themselves successfully. Bullying can take many different forms and may include work-related negative acts, personal harassment, and social exclusion (Notelaers, 2010). Work-related bullying includes, but is not limited to, unjustified criticism, the sabotaging of a colleague's work, or withholding of relevant information. Personal harassment includes gossip and rumors. Offensive and insulting comments about one's person, attitudes, or political or religious convictions are other examples.

Ethics Training in Action, pages 103–119
Copyright © 2014 by Information Age Publishing
All rights of reproduction in any form reserved.

Bullying is characterized by repeated and prolonged exposure to predominantly psychological mistreatment (Einarsen et al., 2011). While the individual acts may seem trivial on their own, the accumulated effect of repeated negative acts may still be considerable. Bullying is typically an escalating process, where the number and severity of negative acts increase over time. Many employees will occasionally experience some negative behavior in the workplace, such as having their opinion ignored in a meeting, being unjustly criticized, or experiencing that somebody has attempted to take credit for their work. This does not mean we should call all of them victims of bullying. Using advanced statistical methods, Notelaers, Einarsen, De Witte, and Vermunt (2006) have shown that while some employees can be grouped into clear victim or no-bullying clusters, the majority of employees fall in between. This means that they experience some degree of negative acts in their workplace, but are not systematically mistreated to the extent required by most definitions of bullying.

National culture may also impinge upon the forms that bullying takes. In Anglo-Saxon countries, bullying is often associated with a tyrannical style of management, and the vast majority of targets report being bullied by managers (e.g., Hoel & Cooper, 2000; Namie, 2007). This chapter will focus predominantly on bullying by managers.

The aim of this chapter is to present workplace bullying as a form of unethical behavior that can be reduced with ethics training. I discuss how ethics training can help managers to avoid such behavior themselves, how it can help third parties to develop the moral courage to intervene, and how it can help managers to prevent bullying behavior in their units by creating a healthy work environment. The work begins with a short review of why bullying is an important ethical issue and why it is important that managers take action. As a subsequent step, the causes of workplace bullying are discussed. That section shows that not all bullying is carried out by evil perpetrators desiring to harm their colleagues and subordinates. Based on both the serious consequences of bullying and the need to understand factors that may contribute to it, a case is then made for seeing bullying as a serious ethical problem that can be reduced through proper ethics training. Having reviewed the literature, I then turn to what trainers need to consider and factors that may affect the successfulness of training programs. Key takeaways are presented to advance future research and further this concern.

WHY SHOULD WE CARE ABOUT BULLYING?

Drawing a line between what does and does not constitute bullying is a complex issue. Whether something is bullying or not is determined not only by the acts included, but also by how frequently and systematically they occur. Different researchers have put forward different criteria and cut-off points, leaving many practitioners with a sense of confusion. However, what researchers seem to be very much in agreement on is that acts of bullying have severe detrimental effects on those concerned (Nielsen & Einarsen, 2012; Salin, 2013). This seems to be the case also for rather "mild" forms of repeated negative acts in the workplace. Workplace bullying can have serious consequences for both victims and observers and can affect their lives very negatively. In the long run, these effects may also impact on the bottom line of individual companies and can result in societal costs.

The health consequences of bullying have been demonstrated in many studies and there is ample evidence for negative effects on both mental and physical health. Typical symptoms associated with bullying are anxiety, depressive symptoms, as well as various psychosomatic ailments (Hansen & the Nordic Bullying Network Group, 2011; Hauge, Skogstad, & Einarsen, 2010). For instance, studies demonstrate that targets of bullying are more likely to have sleep difficulties and impaired sleep quality (Hansen et al., 2011; Notelaers et al., 2006) and to use more sleep-inducing drugs and sedatives (Vartia, 2001). Interview studies also indicate that symptoms of chronic diseases, such as diabetes, asthma, and hypertension, may get worse as a result of bullying (Hallberg & Strandmark, 2006). Bystanders also report effects on their health, although these are not as strong as for the victims (Hoel & Cooper, 2000; Lutgen-Sandvik, Tracy, & Alberts, 2007). Symptoms include general stress and mental stress reactions (Vartia, 2001). Given that for each victim of bullying there are multiple third parties who either witness the bullying themselves or hear about it, a high number of employees are indirectly affected.

In addition to health effects, bullying may jeopardize the quality of life for those concerned in many other ways. Bullying has been shown to have detrimental effects on general self-esteem and social life. Many victims of bullying experience shame, guilt, and decreased self-confidence as a result of the process (Hallberg & Strandmark, 2006; Lewis, 2004; Vartia, 2001). This may in turn affect the victims' social lives, causing them to withdraw from social contacts and resulting in even stronger feelings of isolation (Hallberg & Strandmark, 2006).

Bullying may further interfere with the victims' ability to do their work well and, in the worst cases, may even lead to expulsion from work life (Leymann, 1996). Victims may report problems with memory and concentration, which typically affect work performance. Bullying may also affect the way that victims work and the meaning that work and career has for them (MacIntosh, Wuest, Gray, & Cronkhite, 2010). Bullying may typically include taking away interesting work tasks, giving impossible deadlines, not giving credit for work done, and withholding information needed to perform well. When combined with sleep problems, health effects, and depletion of energy, it is hardly surprising that the quality of work suffers. Such impacts are often accompanied by a lack of perceived self-efficacy, lower self-confidence, and reduced job satisfaction.

Different withdrawal behaviors at work can then be expected. Given the nature of bullying, it is understandable that many victims consider leaving their jobs. Many studies have established a link between bullying and intention to leave (e.g., Djurkovic, McCormack, & Casimir, 2004; Hauge et al., 2010; Hoel & Cooper, 2000). When victims become depleted of energy and when possible rumors and gossip have been spread about them, it may become increasingly difficult for them to find a new job. This may make the victims feel even further trapped. The possibility of expulsion from work life—through early retirement, unemployment, permanent work-disability, and disability pension—thus becomes a real risk (Leymann, 1996; Salin, 2013).

Effects on employee well-being, job satisfaction, and work ability also have financial implications for organizations. Bullying can lead to costs in many different ways. Two obvious costs are sickness leave and replacement costs due to increased turnover of personnel. In a report commissioned by the International Labour Organization (ILO) Hoel, Sparks, and Cooper (2001, p. 49) attempted to calculate the costs of bullying, using Great Britain as an example. Based on statistics available, they calculated that the costs for increased absenteeism alone amounted to £1.5 billion annually and replacement costs because of bullying to £380 million annually. It is worth noting that these estimates for Great Britain are already more than ten years old. Also, it is a very conservative estimate, as bullying may indirectly lead to many other costs for employers. For example, bullying may lead to decreases in employee productivity, motivation, and creativity. Bad publicity and lengthy internal investigations or even litigation are other possible costs. This demonstrates why taking this unethical behavior seriously and providing training to combat it also may have a positive effect on the bottom line.

THE CAUSES OF BULLYING

Victims of bullying often portray bullies as psychopaths driven by a desire to harm others. This is also visible in the titles of many popular books on workplace bullying: for example, *The Bully-Free Workplace: Stop Jerks, Weasels, and Snakes From Killing Your Organization* (Namie & Namie, 2011); *Surviving Bullies, Queen Bees & Psychopaths in the Workplace* (Barnes, 2012); or *The No Asshole Rule: Building a Civilized Workplace and Surviving One That Isn't* (Sutton, 2010). However, when trying to look at alleged bullies more systematically, we can conclude that there is little academic research about perpetrators. Rayner and Cooper (2003) even called this aspect a "black hole," and little research has been conducted since. Obviously, few perpetrators self-report as bullies and volunteer to take part in studies.

Narcissism and lack of social competencies have both been reported to increase the risk of engaging in bullying behavior (see, for example, Zapf & Einarsen, 2011). Narcissistic leaders are those with a high but unstable self-esteem, whereas leaders with low social competences often have difficulties controlling their emotions and seeing things from other individuals' perspective. Men engage in more bullying than women (Hauge, Skogstad, & Einarsen, 2009). Studies also show that being the recipient of bullying oneself is associated with an increased risk of engaging in bullying behavior (Hauge et al., 2009). This shows that bullying often has a trickle-down effect—that is, those who are bullied are more likely to use an abusive management style themselves.

While victims may see perpetrators as evil persons out to get them, interviews with alleged perpetrators reveal that being labeled a bully can be extremely stressful and surprising for many informants. Crawshaw (2012), who has interviewed and coached what she labels as abrasive managers, claims that a majority of the alleged bullies "are blinder than bats" (p. 85) and often lack the empathy and social skills needed to realize how their acts may harm others. In an Australian study, Jenkins, Winefield, and Sarris (2011) interviewed managers and supervisors accused of bullying and similarly found that most of them were shocked by the allegations. Instead, they themselves saw their behavior as a reasonable reaction to difficult and tense situations. In fact, the allegations had a major effect on their lives, including loss of confidence and trust and difficulties in returning to managerial work.

As argued above, it is important to remember that not all bullying occurs because of malevolent, psychopathic perpetrators who desire to harm others. In fact, a major issue in social psychology has been to try to explain why good people may turn "evil" (e.g., Zimbardo, 2007). Certain social situations—for example, ones involving extreme power, powerful pressure, or expectations of obedience (cf., Giacalone & Promislo, 2010; Milgram, 1975; Zimbardo, 2007)—have been shown to influence individuals to commit immoral acts. Also in bullying research, Heinz Leymann (1996), a Swedish pioneer of bullying research, has strongly argued that more or less anybody can become a bully or a victim and that organizational factors and leadership are the main causes of bullying. This has spurred a great interest in the "work environment hypothesis," and empirical studies support the role of work environmental characteristics as risk factors of bullying (see Salin, 2003; Salin & Hoel, 2011 for summaries).

In terms of work environment factors, studies highlight the significance of role ambiguity, role conflict, and unclear goals (Baillien, Neyens, & De Witte, 2008; Hauge, Skogstad, & Einarsen, 2007; Notelaers, De Witte, & Einarsen, 2010; Salin & Hoel, 2011). Bullying seems to thrive where expectations are unclear or unpredictable and where employees perceive contradictory demands and expectations. High demands, coupled with low control (cf., Karasek's [1979] job demand-control model) seem to increase the risk (Baillien, Rodriguez-Munoz, De Witte, Notelaers, & Moreno-Jimenez, 2011; Notelaers et al., 2013). Stress and high time pressures lower the threshold for aggression and allow less time for constructive problem solving (Baillien et al., 2008; Hauge et al., 2007). Not only victims report an association between being bullied and a stressful work environment; self-reported bullies also work in environments characterized by more role conflict and interpersonal conflicts (Hauge et al., 2009).

Research on workplace bullying further highlights the role of leadership and reward systems (Hoel, Glasø, Hetland, Cooper, & Einarsen, 2010; Salin & Hoel, 2011). Whereas a laissez-faire style of leadership—that is, a very passive leadership style—may provide fertile soil for bullying among colleagues, a very autocratic leadership style may itself be perceived as bullying. Noncontingent leadership—where punishment is used arbitrarily—is also associated with an elevated risk of bullying. In competitive environments, an undesired effect of some reward systems may be an incentive to try to get rid of colleagues and subordinates perceived as threats or liabilities. Ethical leadership, on the other hand, has been shown to decrease the risk of bullying (Stouten, Baillien, Van den Broeck, Camps, DeWitte, & Euwema, 2010). Ethical leaders are leaders who demonstrate integrity and high ethical standards and considerate and fair treatment of employees (Brown, Treviño, & Harrison, 2005). Further, they hold employees accountable for ethical conduct. Ethical leaders are also described as leaders who are honest, trustworthy, fair, principled in decision making, and ethical in their personal life (Treviño, Brown, & Hartman, 2003).

Organizational culture may further help us explain why some organizations are more prone to bullying than others. While few organizations explicitly condone or encourage bullying, in some organizations there might be an indirect acceptance of bullying as a way of achieving results, ensuring compliance, or socializing and testing new employees (Salin & Hoel, 2011).

Finally, some researchers have tried to identify a typical victim profile, assuming that victim characteristics may increase the risk of bullying. However, the results are mixed. While some studies find that certain personality traits, such as introversion and neuroticism, are associated with a higher risk (e.g., Coyne, Seigne, & Randall, 2000), a review of the literature shows that there is no general victim profile (Zapf & Einarsen, 2011). In contrast, there are different subgroups of victims, the majority of which do not differ from the general population in terms of personality (Glasø, Matthiesen, Nielsen, & Einarsen, 2007).

Corporate scandals, such as ENRON, have increased the general public's awareness of ethical dilemmas, but also highlighted the role of whistleblowers. Whistleblowers are employees who witness wrongdoing and report it to someone who can effect action (Matthiesen, Bjørkelo, & Burke, 2011). While some high-profile whistleblowers may be seen by the general public as "heroes" demonstrating civil courage, they also risk retaliation from organizational members. Such retaliatory acts may involve ostracism, ridicule, or job content deterioration and may over time develop into full-scale bullying (Matthiesen et al., 2011). Being a whistleblower and reporting illegal, immoral, or illegitimate practices may thus be a risk factor for being subject to bullying. A Norwegian study comparing whistleblowers and non-whistleblowers did in fact report that the probability of being exposed to bullying was nearly three times higher for whistleblowers, 9.4% vs. 3.2%, respectively (Matthiesen, Bjørkelo, & Nielsen, 2008).

ETHICS TRAINING AS A MEANS OF REDUCING THE RISK OF BULLYING

Many different factors—both individual and contextual—contribute to bullying. Managers can play a key role in reducing the risk of bullying (1) by being aware of their own behavior and how it is interpreted by their subordinates, (2) by taking swift action when seeing bullying occurring in the organization, and (3) by creating a healthy work environment that reduces the risk of bullying among colleagues. Training can be helpful in giving managers tools to address all three aspects.

Avoiding Bullying Behavior: Developing an Ethical Leadership Style

As discussed previously, many bullies see themselves as tough-minded executives determined to push their employees to ultimate performance, rather than as persons seeking to inflict harm (cf., Crawshaw, 2007, 2012; Jenkins et al., 2011). Increasing awareness of what kind of behavior can be seen as bullying and clearly signaling that this is unacceptable are therefore important first steps.

Codes of conduct are typically used as a way of clarifying desirable and ethical behavior in the workplace. These highlight what kind of behavior is considered appropriate and inappropriate in the work context. Antibullying training typically includes presentations of what bullying is and listing what kind of behavior is considered undesirable and unacceptable. This is in line with the finding by Sekerka (2009) that many organizations emphasize a compliance-based approach when it comes to ethics training. This kind of deontological approach highlights principles and duties involved.

To increase the chances of the training being successful, it is important that trainees understand how training is relevant to successful job performance (Salas, Tannenbaum, Kraiger, & Smith-Jentsch, 2012). When it comes to bullying, this implies that it is important that instructors can clearly convince participants of the negative consequences of workplace bullying. On a general level, this means making participants aware of how bullying may affect employee well-being, employee attitudes, and employee behavior (including willingness to stay and productivity). On a more personal level, it means making participants aware that bullying behavior may reduce their effectiveness as managers and may result in lower performance appraisals, thereby representing a potential obstacle to career ambitions. Instead, improving one's social skills should be presented as something that may further the participants' career interests.

As many managers may resort to bullying because they believe it is the best way to get employees to give their utmost, it is important that managers also receive general leadership training on alternative and more effective ways of boosting employee motivation and performance (cf., Crawshaw, 2012). This may include sessions on giving constructive and actionable feedback (Cannon & Witherspoon, 2005), effective goal-setting (Locke & Latham, 2002), and promoting justice to reduce stress (Greenberg, 2004). As with training in general, for leadership training to be effective it is important that participants are not only provided information about appropriate leadership behaviors, but also given demonstrations and the chance to practice themselves. Also, feedback about their own performance will increase the effectiveness of the training (cf., Salas et al., 2012).

Intervening in Bullying: Building Moral Courage to Take Action

We see that a key feature of antibullying training is to increase managers' and employees' awareness of their own behavior. Bystanders and third parties play an important role in the process and may through their action or inaction have a role in the escalation or de-escalation of the problem. Third parties can be, for example, colleagues, managers, or human resources (HR) professionals. Depending on their position, their possibilities to enact efficient responses may vary. Ethics training may be instrumental for all of them in terms of increasing their willingness and perceived responsibility to take action.

Third parties can choose from a range of different actions, from siding with the perpetrator or privately advising or supporting the target to openly confronting the perpetrator or alerting (top) management to the issue (cf., Bowes-Sperry & O'Leary-Kelly, 2005). Third-party reactions in cases of harassment and bullying are influenced by many different aspects

(Bowes-Sperry & O'Leary-Kelly, 2005; O'Reilly & Aquino, 2011; Skarlicki & Kulik, 2005). These include the perceived severity and impact of the behavior and attributes of the target and third party. Third-party reactions are also influenced by the how third parties attribute responsibility and to what extent they feel they have a personal responsibility to act.

Ethics training can—and should—address many of these factors, thereby increasing the chance that third parties will intervene. First of all, this highlights the need to make third parties clearly aware of the severity of workplace bullying and its likely consequences. This will affect third parties' chances of correctly identifying bullying and will affect their perceptions of moral intensity. Moral intensity describes the degree to which the third party perceives a moral imperative in the event (cf., Bowes-Sperry & O'Leary-Kelly, 2005), and the higher the moral intensity, the higher the likelihood will be that third parties take action.

A second step for the third party is typically to try to determine who is to blame. In cases of both harassment and bullying, there is oftentimes a tendency to blame the victim and assume that the target has provoked the behavior through his or her own behavior. This may partly be explained by our "belief in a just world" (cf., Lerner, 1980): Most people need to believe in a world where people get what they deserve, or, in other words, deserve what they get. Admitting that an innocent employee gets mistreated or bullied shatters this view. To challenge the tendency to blame the victim and thereby one's own justification for not taking action, ethics training needs to make participants aware of the real causes of bullying and to help third parties see beyond target characteristics or target behaviors.

As a third step, ethics training needs to address third parties' perceptions of responsibility and their moral courage to intervene. O'Reilly and Aquino (2011) argue that those who see being a moral person as central to their self-concept will feel more obliged to show concern for distant others. They will also react with more moral anger when seeing violations. It is important to note that situational cues can also affect judgments and behavior (Aquino, Freeman, Reed, Lim, & Felps, 2009). This seems to indicate that regularly reminding employees of codes of conduct and desirable behavior may make employees likely to behave more ethically and react more forcefully when seeing others do the opposite.

Sekerka and Godwin (2010) define professional moral courage as fortitude to pursue a moral path when faced with a dilemma, even when choosing that route may be risky or costly to that employee. They argue that this moral courage is the critical link between knowing what is right and actually doing it. However, they further argue that moral courage is not a trait that you either have or do not have, but rather a muscle that can be trained. When giving ethics training to third parties it is therefore important that participants are provided with tools that will help them dare to take action.

Sekerka and Godwin (2010) present advice on how to exercise one's moral muscle and how this can be used in ethics training. These points are relevant also for antibullying training. This may include helping third parties use reflective pause to avoid instinctive responses to witnessing bullying behavior, such as trivializing it or blaming the victim for what has happened. Further, it may involve training third parties to honestly examine their own motives for intervening or not intervening. Finally, it may involve third parties beforehand going over different scenarios, thinking through alternatives, and reaffirming their desire to do the right thing—that is, a form of "moral preparation."

Using case descriptions of bullying situations as a basis for discussion may be one way of preparing third parties. However, asking participants to identify and share actual cases they have witnessed and reflect upon what they could have done is likely to be even more effective (cf., Sekerka & Godwin, 2010, on a balanced experiential inquiry method). This kind of preparation will also increase participants' self-efficacy—in other words, their confidence that they can successfully perform a specific behavior in a specific situation. Self-efficacy has been argued to increase the desire to act with moral courage (cf., Sekerka & Bagozzi, 2007).

It is important to develop coworkers', supervisors', and HR professionals' understanding of bullying and their moral courage to intervene. However, for these efforts to be successful, the attitudes held by managers and top management are crucial. Salas et al. (2012) showed that one of the predictors of whether training in general results in behavioral changes and improved performance is whether supervisors support the training and give the participants the chance to truly apply the new skills. Organizational attitudes towards bullying therefore need to be addressed in addition to training individual employees. When deciding whether or not to take action, third parties will also consider the possible costs for them. D'Cruz and Noronho (2011), who studied bullying in Indian call centers, found that many bystanders at first tried to protect targets from bullying. However, after facing retaliation, many of them turned silent. For third-party training to be successful, it is important that participants feel that they truly have managerial support to implement their training. When training third parties to take action, measures to counter possible retaliation should also be taken to protect third parties desiring to act.

Preventing Bullying: Building a Healthy Work Environment

In addition to helping managers avoid bullying behavior themselves and encouraging third parties to speak up, ethics training can help managers create work conditions that reduce the risk of bullying. As discussed in a previous section, the quality of the work environment is a major predictor of the risk of bullying.

Stouten and colleagues (2010) showed that ethical leadership was negatively associated with bullying partly because ethical leadership addresses the design of the work environment. In companies with ethical leaders employees reported more manageable workloads and a better work environment. Training that seeks to help leaders develop ethical leadership and improved work conditions is more likely to contribute to less bullying in those departments. Based on our knowledge of risk factors (e.g., Hauge et al., 2007; Notelaers et al., 2010; Salin & Hoel, 2011), leaders can reduce the risk of bullying by improving role and goal clarity, setting attainable work targets and reasonable workloads, increasing perceptions of job security, and improving work-related feedback.

A healthy work environment not only reduces the risk of bullying, but may further shield victims of bullying from some of the negative consequences. For instance, it has been hypothesized that perceived organizational support and procedural justice may moderate the association between bullying and negative impacts on well-being and employee attitudes (cf., Parzefall & Salin, 2010). When employees genuinely feel that the organization supports them and takes measures to correct unfair treatment, employees may be better equipped to cope with inappropriate treatment by a deviant bully.

Ethics training can also help managers build organizational climates and cultures that do not even indirectly encourage bullying. Making sure that reward systems do not even indirectly encourage bullying is one important aspect of this (Salin & Hoel, 2011). Also, the significance of role models is crucial. Employees learn certain behavioral patterns by observing others in the organizations, and by observing how others are rewarded. Employees who see superiors engage in mistreatment are more likely to enact similar behavioral patterns themselves (cf., Robinson & O'Leary-Kelly, 1998). Coaching abrasive managers to learn more constructive forms of leadership is therefore likely also to influence other (future) managers in the organization.

Building a culture that does not accept bullying involves a clear code of conduct and antibullying policies (cf., Rayner & Lewis, 2011). A number of points should be included (Richards & Daley, 2003; Salin, 2008). These include:

1. An explicit commitment to a bullying-free environment and zero tolerance for bullying
2. A definition of the kinds of behavior that are regarded as bullying and those that are not
3. A statement of the consequences of breaching the organizational codes of conduct

4. A clarification of responsibility borne by the various actors involved
5. An explanation of the procedure for making and investigating infor-mal and formal complaints

In a study of Finnish municipalities, Salin (2008) found that antibully-ing documents quite often turned out to contain not only identical advice, but even identical sentences. This indicates that organizations often rely on a copy-paste strategy. However, for an antibullying policy to be effective, relevant to a particular organizational context, and seen as legitimate, it is important to incorporate top managers and staff from all levels in the process of developing and implementing it (cf., Richards & Daley, 2003). Communicating, monitoring, and regularly reviewing the policy are cru-cial steps, as well (Rayner & Lewis, 2011). What is important to remember is that antibullying policies can be helpful tools also for third parties—in-creasing both their willingness and perceived competence to take action.

CONCLUSIONS AND KEY TAKEAWAYS

This work has explained why bullying is an important ethics challenge for or-ganizations, and why management needs to address this issue. The discussion offers different ways in which ethics training can reduce the risk and negative impact of bullying. This review has highlighted five important points:

1. Ethics training must clearly define what kind of behavior is accept-able and unacceptable within the organization. Participants need to understand what the organizations' code of conduct means in prac-tice. A rule-based, compliance-based approach is not sufficient. Man-agers need to understand the detrimental effects that bullying can have not only on employee well-being and productivity, but in the long run also for organizational success and for their own careers. During ethics training, improved social skills should therefore be presented as a way of enhancing the participants' career prospects.
2. Training should not only seek to end undesirable behavior, but, above all, help managers (and co-workers) develop alternative behav-ioral strategies to reach their targets. This includes training on giving actionable feedback, making decisions in a fair and transparent manner, and handling conflicts constructively and without delay. Dur-ing the training it is important that managers have a chance to truly practice new skills and get feedback on their progress. They also need to receive support in applying the skills in their day-to-day tasks.
3. By helping third parties increase their confidence and willingness to intervene, bullying may be halted and stopped at an early stage.

This involves increasing awareness of the moral intensity and severe negative impact of bullying behavior. Third parties also need to learn about the factors contributing to bullying. Finally, it is crucial to strengthen third parties' moral courage to take action when faced with moral dilemmas. Helping third parties prepare by discussing possible responses based on either fictive cases or real cases that the participants themselves have encountered may increase third parties' moral preparedness.

4. The risk of bullying can be reduced by investments in a healthy work environment. Training that helps managers to reduce role ambiguity and role conflict, clarify goals, and set reasonable workloads will also reduce the risk of bullying. Clear codes of conduct, antibullying policies, and ethical role models also help to create a healthy workplace culture.

5. To make antibullying training effective, there has to be clear top management support for it. It is crucial that reward systems do not even indirectly encourage bullying. Similarly, for antibullying training to result in behavioral changes, there must be mechanisms to ensure that those who speak up about bullying are not punished for doing so.

This chapter has presented workplace bullying as a form of unethical behavior and has discussed how ethics training can reduce its risk. A healthy work environment will not only result in increased job satisfaction and improved employee well-being, but also lower turnover, lower absenteeism, and better employee performance. In the long run, efforts to curb bullying are therefore also likely to have a positive effect on the bottom line.

REFERENCES

Aquino, K., Freeman, D., Reed, A., Lim, V., & Felps, W. (2009). Testing a social-cognitive model of moral behavior: The interactive influence of situations and moral identity centrality. *Journal of Personality and Social Psychology, 97,* 123–141.

Baillien, E., Neyens, I., & De Witte, H. (2008). Organizational, team related and job related risk factors for workplace bullying, violence and sexual harassment in the workplace: A qualitative study. *International Journal of Organisational Behaviour, 13,* 122–146.

Baillien, E., Rodriguez-Munoz, A., De Witte, H., Notelaers, G., & Moreno-Jimenez, B. (2011). The demand–control model and target's reports of bullying at work: A test within Spanish and Belgian blue-collar workers. *European Journal of Work and Organizational Psychology, 20,* 157–177.

Barnes, P. (2012). *Surviving bullies, queen bees & psychopaths in the workplace.* Seattle, WA: Amazon Digital.

Bowes-Sperry, L., & O'Leary-Kelly, A. M. (2005). To act or not to act: The dilemma faced by sexual harassment observers. *Academy of Management Review, 30,* 288–306.

Brown, M. E., Treviño, L. K., & Harrison, D. A. (2005). Ethical leadership: A social learning perspective for construct development and testing. *Organizational Behavior and Human Decision Processes, 97,* 117–134.

Cannon, M., & Witherspoon, R. (2005) Actionable feedback: Unlocking the power of learning and performance improvement. *Academy of Management Executive, 19,* 120–134.

Coyne, I., Seigne, E., & Randall, P. (2000). Predicting workplace victim status from personality. *European Journal of Work and Organizational Psychology, 9,* 335–350.

Crawshaw, L. (2007). *Taming the abrasive manager: How to end unnecessary roughness in the workplace.* San Francisco, CA: Jossey-Bass.

Crawshaw, L. (2012). Coaching abrasive leaders: Contradictory tales of the Big Bad Wolf. In N. Tehrani (Ed.), *Workplace bullying: Symptoms and solutions* (pp. 132–148). New York, NY: Routledge.

D'Cruz, P., & Noronha, E. (2011). The limits to workplace friendship: Managerialist HRM and bystander behaviour in the context of workplace bullying. *Employee Relations, 33,* 269–288.

Djurkovic, N., McCormack, D., & Casimir, G. (2004). The physical and psychological effects of workplace bullying and their relationship to intention to leave: A test of the psychosomatic and disability hypotheses. *International Journal of Organization Theory and Behavior, 7,* 469–497.

Einarsen, S., Hoel, H., Zapf, D., & Cooper. C. L. (2011). The concept of bullying and harassment at work: The European tradition. In S. Einarsen, H. Hoel, D. Zapf, & C. L. Cooper (Eds.), *Bullying and harassment in the workplace: Developments in theory, research, and practice* (2nd ed., pp. 3–39). Boca Raton, FL: CRC Press.

Giacalone, R., & Promislo, M. (2010). Unethical and unwell: Decrements in well-being and unethical activity at work. *Journal of Business Ethics, 91,* 275–297.

Glasø, L., Matthiesen, S. B., Nielsen, M., & Einarsen, S. (2007). Do targets of workplace bullying portray a general victim personality profile? *Scandinavian Journal of Psychology, 48,* 313–319.

Greenberg, J. (2004). Stress fairness to fare no stress: Managing workplace stress by promoting organizational justice. *Organizational Dynamics, 33,* 352–365.

Hallberg, L., & Strandmark, M. (2006). Health consequences of workplace bullying: Experiences from the perspective of employees in the public service sector. *International Journal of Qualitative Studies on Health and Wellbeing, 1,* 109–119.

Hansen, Å. M., & the Nordic Bullying Network Group. (2011). *State of the art report on bullying at the workplace in the Nordic countries.* TemaNord 2011:515. Copenhagen, Denmark: Nordic Council of Ministers.

Hauge, L. J, Skogstad, A., & Einarsen, S. (2007). Relationships between stressful work environments and workplace bullying: Results of a large representative study. *Work & Stress, 21,* 220–242.

Hauge, L. J, Skogstad, A., & Einarsen, S. (2009). Individual and situational predictors of workplace bullying: Why do perpetrators engage in the bullying of others? *Work & Stress, 23*, 349–358.

Hauge, L. J., Skogstad, A., & Einarsen, S. (2010). The relative impact of workplace bullying as a social stressor at work. *Scandinavian Journal of Psychology, 51*, 426–433.

Hoel, H., & Cooper, C. (2000). *Destructive conflict and bullying at work.* Report produced by the Manchester School of Management. Manchester, UK: University of Manchester, Institute of Science and Technology.

Hoel, H., Sparks, K., & Cooper, C. L. (2001). *The cost of violence/stress at work and the benefits of a violence/stress-free working environment.* Geneva, Switzerland: International Labour Organisation.

Hoel, H., Glasø, L., Hetland, J., Cooper, C., & Einarsen, S. (2010). Leadership styles as predictors of self-reported and observed workplace bullying. *British Journal of Management, 21*, 453–468.

Jenkins, M., Winefield, H., & Sarris, A. (2011). Consequences of being accused of workplace bullying. An exploratory study. *International Journal of Workplace Health Management, 4*, 33–47.

Karasek, R. A. (1979). Job demands, job decision latitude, and mental strain: Implications for job redesign. *Administrative Science Quarterly, 24*, 285–308.

Lerner, M. J. (1980). *The belief in a just world: A fundamental delusion.* New York, NY: Plenum Press.

Lewis, D. (2004). Bullying at work: The impact of shame among university and college lecturers. *British Journal of Guidance & Counselling, 32*, 281–299.

Leymann, H. (1996). The content and development of mobbing at work. *European Journal of Work and Organizational Psychology, 5*, 164–185.

Locke, E. A., & Latham, G. P. (2002). Building a practically useful theory of goal setting and task motivation. *American Psychologist, 57*, 705–717.

Lutgen-Sandvik, P., Tracy, S. J., & Alberts, J. K. (2007). Burned by bullying in the American workplace: Prevalence, perception, degree and impact. *Journal of Management Studies, 44*, 837–862.

MacIntosh, J., Wuest, J., Gray, M. M., & Cronkhite, M. (2010). Workplace bullying in health care affects the meaning of work. *Qualitative Health Research, 20*, 1128–1141.

Matthiesen, S. B., Bjørkelo, B., & Burke, R. (2011). Workplace bullying as the dark side of whistleblowing. In S. Einarsen, H. Hoel, D. Zapf, & C. L. Cooper (Eds.), *Bullying and harassment in the workplace: Developments in theory, research, and practice* (2nd ed., pp. 301–324). Boca Raton, FL: CRC Press.

Matthiesen, S. B., Bjørkelo, B., & Nielsen, M. B. (2008). *Klanderverdig atferd og varsling i norsk arbeidsliv* [Wrongdoing and whistleblowing in Norwegian work life]. Bergen, Norway: University of Bergen.

Milgram, S. (1975). *Obedience to authority: An experimental view.* New York, NY: Harper & Row.

Namie, G. (2007, September). *US workplace bullying survey.* Bellingham, WA: Workplace Bullying Institute and Zogby International.

Namie, G., & Namie, R. F. (2011). *The bully-free workplace: Stop jerks, weasels, and snakes from killing your organization.* Hoboken, NJ: Wiley.

Nielsen, M. B., & Einarsen, S. (2012). Outcomes of exposure to workplace bullying: A meta-analytic review. *Work & Stress, 26,* 309–332.

Notelaers, G. (2010). *Workplace bullying: A risk control perspective.* Unpublished doctoral dissertation, University of Bergen, Bergen, Norway.

Notelaers, G., De Witte, H., & Einarsen, S. (2010). A job characteristics approach to explain workplace bullying. *European Journal of Work and Organizational Psychology, 19,* 487–504.

Notelaers, G., Einarsen, S., De Witte, H., & Vermunt, J. (2006). Measuring exposure to bullying at work: The validity and advantages of the latent class cluster approach. *Work & Stress, 20,* 288–301.

Notelaers, G., Baillien, E., De Witte, H., Einarsen, S., & Vermunt, J. K. (2013). Testing the strain hypothesis of the demand control model to explain severe bullying at work. *Economic and Industrial Democracy, 34,* 69–87.

O'Reilly, J., & Aquino, K. (2011). A model of third parties' morally motivated responses to mistreatment in organizations. *Academy of Management Review, 36,* 526–543.

Parzefall, M., & Salin, D. (2010). Perceptions of and reactions to workplace bullying: A social exchange perspective. *Human Relations, 63,* 761–780.

Rayner, C., & Cooper, C. (2003). The black hole in bullying at work research. *International Journal of Management and Decision Making, 4,* 47–64.

Rayner, C., & Lewis, D. (2011). Managing workplace bullying: The role of policies. In S. Einarsen, H. Hoel, D. Zapf, & C. L. Cooper (Eds.), *Bullying and harassment in the workplace: Developments in theory, research, and practice* (2nd ed., pp. 327–340). Boca Raton, FL: CRC Press.

Richards, J., & Daley, H. (2003). Bullying policy: Development, implementation and monitoring. In S. Einarsen, H. Hoel, D. Zapf, & C. Cooper (Eds.), *Bullying and emotional abuse in the workplace: International perspectives in research and practice* (pp. 247–258). London, UK: Taylor & Francis.

Robinson, S. L., & O'Leary-Kelly, A. (1998). Monkey see, monkey do: The influence of work groups on the antisocial behavior of employees. *Academy of Management Journal 41,* 658–672.

Salas, E., Tannenbaum, S. I., Kraiger, K., & Smith-Jentsch, K. A. (2012). The science of training and development in organizations: What matters in practice. *Psychological Science in the Public Interest, 13*(2), 74–101.

Salin, D. (2003). Ways of explaining workplace bullying: A review of enabling, motivating and precipitating structures and processes in the work environment. *Human Relations, 56,* 1213–1232.

Salin, D. (2008). The prevention of workplace bullying as a question of human resource management: Measures adopted and underlying organizational factors. *Scandinavian Journal of Management, 24,* 221–231.

Salin, D. (2013). Bullying and well-being. In R. Giacalone & M. Promislo (Eds.), *Handbook of unethical work behavior: Implications for individual well-being* (pp. 73–88). Armonk, NY: M.E. Sharpe.

Salin, D., & Hoel, H. (2011). Organizational causes of bullying. In S. Einarsen, H. Hoel, D. Zapf, & C. L. Cooper (Eds.), *Bullying and harassment in the workplace: Developments in theory, research, and practice* (2nd ed., pp. 227–243). Boca Raton, FL: CRC Press.

Sekerka, L. E. (2009). Organizational ethics education and training: A review of best practices and their application. *International Journal of Training and Development, 13*, 77–95.

Sekerka, L. E., & Bagozzi, R. (2007). Moral courage in the workplace: Moving to and from the desire and decision to act. *Business Ethics: A European Review, 16*, 132–149.

Sekerka, L. E., & Godwin, L. (2010). Strengthening professional moral courage: A balanced approach to ethics training. *Training & Management Development Methods, 24*, 563–574.

Skarlicki, D. J., & Kulik, C. T. (2005). Third party reactions to employee (mis)treatment: A justice perspective. *Research in Organizational Behavior: An Annual Series of Analytical Essays and Critical Reviews, 26*, 183–229.

Stouten, J., Baillien, E., Van den Broeck, A., Camps, J., DeWitte, H., & Euwema, M. (2010). Discouraging bullying: The role of ethical leadership and its effects on the work environment. *Journal of Business Ethics, 95*(S1), 17–27.

Sutton, R. I. (2010). *The no asshole rule: Building a civilized workplace and surviving one that isn't.* New York, NY: Business Plus.

Treviño, L. K., Brown, M., & Hartman, L. P. (2003). A qualitative investigation of perceived executive ethical leadership: Perspectives from inside and outside the executive suite. *Human Relations, 56*, 5–37.

Vartia, M. (2001). Consequences of workplace bullying with respect to the wellbeing of its targets and the observers of bullying. *Scandinavian Journal of Work and Environmental Health, 27*, 63–69.

Zapf, D., & Einarsen, S. (2011). Individual antecedents of bullying: Victims and perpetrators. In S. Einarsen, H. Hoel, D. Zapf, & C. Cooper (Eds.), *Bullying and harassment in the workplace: Developments in theory, research, and practice* (2nd ed., pp. 177–200). Boca Raton, FL: CRC Press.

Zimbardo, P. G. (2007). *The Lucifer effect: Understanding how good people turn evil.* New York, NY: Random House.

CHAPTER 6

EMBEDDED SUSTAINABILITY

Creating Ethical Habits
through Personal Engagement

Lindsey N. Godwin and Nicole S. Morris

You can never have an impact on society if you have not changed yourself.
—Nelson Mandela (Francis, 2012, p. 33)

Employees in today's organizations face a wide array of ethical challenges on a daily basis. From complying with ever-changing rules and regulations to navigating continually shifting social relationships with both internal and external organizational stakeholders, the ethical obstacles and opportunities are vast. Compounding these challenges is the fact that in order to be considered an ethical business, corporations are now also being called upon to contribute to society as a whole by defining their stakeholders in a much more holistic sense than in the past (Bolton, Kim, & O'Gorman, 2011). The stakeholder groups to which businesses are now ethically accountable extend beyond just a myriad of people (stockholders, customers, suppliers, etc.) to also include the natural environment (Driscoll & Starik, 2004; Rushton, 2002). Indeed, it is not only new regulations, but also customers who are now actively holding businesses accountable for their sustainability efforts all the way through their supply chain (Ernst &

Ethics Training in Action, pages 121–138
Copyright © 2014 by Information Age Publishing
121

Young, 2008). People are beginning to realize that protecting the natural environment is not simply a nice thing to do; it has become a moral imperative, because "how we use natural resources and the levels of our consumption will affect our future security as a local and global community" (Reid, 2009, p. 70). Some have even argued that sustainability could become an overarching global ethic against which all businesses are measured as being ethical or not (Rushton, 2002). Given that organizational ethics are "a company's adoption of desired ethical standards and business practices" (Valentine & Fleischman, 2008, p. 160), then it is perhaps no wonder that sustainability[1] issues are increasingly becoming an important element of the standards and practices organizations are seeking to integrate into their culture (Thomas & Lamm, 2012).

Sustainability has perhaps become a significant emphasis in the business ethical environment not only because of external pressures, but because it has been shown to drive organizational innovation (Nidumolu, Prahalad, & Rangaswami, 2009) and contribute to an organization's overall financial performance (Orlitzky, Schmidt, & Rynes, 2003). A company's commitment to sustainable actions has been shown to attract new employees (Albinger & Freeman, 2000; Montgomery & Ramus, 2007; Turban & Greening, 1997), strengthen employee commitment (Bolton et al., 2011; Peterson, 2004), and lead to increased job satisfaction (Peloza, 2009). Furthermore, employees are more engaged, creatively involved, and have higher quality relationships with their coworkers when they work for organizations that are considered good corporate citizens (Glavas & Piderit, 2009). Given the mounting evidence that suggests that sustainability leads to a number of desired organizational outcomes, it is no wonder that 93% of CEOs see sustainability as important to their company's future success (Accenture & UN Global Compact, 2010). Thus, the pressing question for businesses today is no longer, *Should we embed sustainability into our company?*, but rather, *How can we embed sustainability across the organization?* (Bertels, Papania, & Papania, 2010; Laszlo & Zhexembayeva, 2011).

Building on the argument that "sustainability requires responsible, ethical choices everywhere in daily life" (Ehrenfeld, 2005, p. 25), our chapter aims to guide organizations as they explore how to incorporate sustainability as a theme into organizational ethical training programs in order to foster sustainability-related actions among employees. Valentine and Fleischman (2008) posit that ethics programs "establish attitudes about the acceptability of a company's broader ethical obligations to society" (p. 161), and as such, they are the critical mechanism through which organizations can help cultivate the specific ethical behaviors aimed at positively impacting the natural environment. While organizations "can help 'steer' ethical behavior through the design of their products and services" (e.g., by installing water-conserving toilets in office buildings), employees "must make a conscious and obvious choice every time" they are faced with an opportunity to act sustainably or not (Ehrenfeld, 2005, p. 25), just as they must decide to act ethically or not every time they are confronted with any ethical dilemma. Thus, we contend that sustainability-related behaviors (e.g., recycling materials, reducing consumption, being a conscientious steward of natural resources at an individual and organizational level, etc.) are merely an important practical demonstration of ethics in action. When individual employees choose to act in a sustainable manner, they are illustrating how an organization's espoused ethical values (e.g., "we say we do good things for others") can actually become the company's enacted ethical values (e.g., "we are having a measurable impact on improving the environment for others"). Training is critical and necessary to help cultivate these specific ethical behaviors on a consistent basis.

Organizations are increasingly experimenting with a variety of approaches to answer this call to action and build a culture of sustainability, where "organizational members hold shared assumptions and beliefs about the importance of balancing economic efficiency, social equity, and environmental accountability" (Bertels et al., 2010, p. 10). Benson and Ross (1998) found that embedding a culture of ethical conduct requires leveraging a variety of practices within the organization. Likewise, in their analysis of nearly 200 sources, Bertels et al. (2010) identified a myriad of ways that organizations are currently attempting to embed sustainability into their organizational culture—from creating new policies, to identifying sustainability champions within the organization, to benchmarking and piloting new products, to providing corporate-wide training. It is this latter approach that our chapter focuses upon—sustainability training.

While sustainability training has been identified as an important approach organizations can undertake (Buysse & Verbeke, 2003; Haugh & Talwar, 2010), its form varies widely—much like all ethics training programs—from intense immersion programs for new hires to individual courses that cover topics from sustainability policies, program goals, and operational procedures (Maon, Lindgreen, & Swaen, 2009). While some companies are beginning to move beyond a myopic focus on technical knowledge and are beginning to leverage trainings that aim at changing employees' behaviors (Holton, Glass, & Price, 2010), many companies—particularly multinationals—continue to frame sustainability (and ethics training in general) in a compliance-oriented manner (Kolk, 2008). Unfortunately, when organizations focus their sustainability training on the acquisition of technical knowledge or policy compliance, they are less likely to create an embedded culture of sustainability in their organization or to create lasting change (Dunphy, Griffiths, & Benn, 2003), similar to how traditional ethics training that focuses only on rules and compliance does little to actually cultivate moral decision making and action (Sekerka, 2009). Furthermore,

Nord and Fuller (2009) argue that what is lacking in both our research and practice alike is an employee-centered view of organizational change related to sustainability and corporate social responsibility. They argue that companies focus on overarching organizational strategies, which are typically delivered as a top-down approach. An employee-centered approach, on the other hand, is one that can be initiated at all levels of the organization and one that can be accomplished through "small steps" as opposed to a grand organizational strategy (Nord & Fuller, 2009, p. 281). Hence, a culture of sustainability remains an unrealized goal for many companies because they do not know how best to motivate employees to engage in sustainability initiatives at a personal level (Laughland & Bansal, 2011).

To truly foster sustainability in any organization, individuals within must be committed to embedding sustainability not just as a broad, external corporate strategy, but also as personal daily practices (Laszlo & Zhexembayeva, 2011). In many respects, implementing eco-efficient operations in a manufacturing plant—where behaviors are monitored and standardized— may be easier than trying to get a single employee to recycle the soda can she drank at lunch. Even when motivation may exist, we know from theory and practice that changing employee behavior is challenging. Yet, if sustainability is truly to become embedded at every level of an organization, old, ineffective routines of individual employees must shift into new, effective, sustainable habits. To accomplish this feat, we argue that organizations need to frame sustainability education as opportunities to actually change behavior and incorporate sustainability habits into daily actions. Fostering sustainability-related behaviors needs to become the end goal of employee-driven intentional change efforts.

After an overview of intentional change theory, we discuss how this theory offers an effective framework for creating sustainability trainings that result in real, enduring behavioral changes among employees. We then describe a specific training approach referred to as personal sustainability projects (PSPs), which applies intentional change theory to assist organizations in fostering a culture of sustainability. More specifically, PSPs are designed to cultivate employees' commitment to engaging in sustainability "nano-practices," which consist of the many small things that one can do each day that ultimately contribute to a lifestyle that embraces a commitment to sustainability (Werbach, 2009). Modeled on work done by Saatchi & Saatchi with companies including Wal-Mart, Duke Energy, and McDonald's, we explore how PSPs can be used as an important aspect of ethics training to make sustainability issues tangible for employees by building not only commitment, but actionable habits toward sustainable behaviors in the workplace. The chapter concludes with a discussion on implications for organizations as they seek to foster cultures of sustainability.

FOSTERING INTENTIONAL CHANGE IN EMPLOYEES

Understanding and encouraging behavioral change among employees is a task as old as organizations themselves. While providing a full literature review on theories of change is beyond the scope of this chapter, it is important to note that since the early work by Lewin (1947), various scholars have suggested that change happens over time, and that lasting change is developed through a series of stages (e.g., Boyatzis, 1999; Norcross, Krebs, Prochaska, 2011; Prochaska & DiClemente, 1983). For example, Prochaska and DiClemente (1983) introduced an early model of intentional change called the transtheoretical model of change (TTM), which has since been used to develop interventions to promote health behavior change (Prochaska, DiClemente, & Norcross, 1992). Their model focuses on the decision making of the individual and describes how people modify a problem behavior or acquire a positive behavior. While TTM and other change models have provided an array of descriptions for the "how" of the personal change process, they have not fully expounded on the "why"; as such, "the actual change process remains in a black box" (Boyatzis, 2008, p. 300). One theory that does begin to dive into both the "how" and "why" of intentional change is Boyatzis' intentional change theory (ICT), which we offer here as a framework for cultivating the adoption of sustainability-related behaviors in employees.

Originally called self-directed learning (Boyatzis, 1999; Boyatzis & Kolb, 1969; Goleman, Boyatzis, & McKee, 2002), ICT posits that adults learn what they want to learn, and thus only change behaviors they really *want* to change; the behavior change must be internalized individually. Thus, no amount of managerial nagging or external incentives will produce enduring behavioral change if employees do not really want to make the change. McKee, Johnston, and Rotondo (2008, p. 2) succinctly summarize the five major elements of ICT as:

1. Creating a personal vision
2. Assessing where you are today (your "real" self)
3. Analyzing the gaps between your vision and where you are today
4. Experimenting and practicing new behaviors
5. Asking for support from trusted others

As Boyatzis (2002) explains, the ICT process involves a sequence of discoveries that correspond to each of these steps. First, to create a personal vision, an individual must discover who they want to become, their "ideal self." There is mounting evidence to suggest that having a clearly articulated aspiration helps motivate personal change (Boyatzis & Akrivou, 2006). Goal-setting literature (Locke & Latham, 1990) has added evidence to our understanding of the importance of personal goals in the individual change process. Our personal visions for what we want to achieve or become are very powerful motivators; as Aristotle once wrote, "A vivid imagination compels the whole body to obey it" (cited in Cooperrider & Whitney, 1999, p. 258). Medical research lends support to the power of positive imagery, where placebo effect studies reinforce the "important therapeutic use of imagery, namely, the use of positive future images to activate positive physical changes" (Jaffe & Bresler, 1980, p. 47). Similarly, other studies have shown improvements in performance for athletes who engage in positive imagery exercises (Woolfolk, Parrish, & Murphy, 1985). At all levels of organizational systems, positive imagery is arguably an important prerequisite for positive action (Cooperrider, 2003).

The second discovery in ICT involves becoming aware of one's "real self" and comparing it to the ideal self. Before you can achieve your goals and ideal vision for the future, it is critical to have an accurate understanding of where you are today (Ashford, Blatt, & VandeWalle, 2003). According to Taylor (2006), the real self consists of two main elements: (1) accurate self-knowledge of one's own competencies and (2) accurate assessments of one's competencies as reported by others (p. 644). Thus, the real self is comprised of both self-reflections as well as external data points from others. The real self not only serves as a "check-point" against which an individual can measure progress toward his or her goals; it also helps provide motivation to change (Taylor, 2006, p. 646). Rooted in early work on cognitive dissonance (Festinger, 1957), Higgins' self-discrepancy theory (1987) suggests that when individuals experience a gap between their real self and their ideal self, they experience emotional discomfort and are thus internally motivated to reduce the discrepancy. In other words, comparing where you are currently with where you want to be in the future helps motivate you to make changes in the pursuit of the ideal self.

The third discovery entails the creation of a change agenda—or a plan that details how the individual will move from their current real self toward their ideal self. Research has demonstrated that individuals who set behavioral change goals are more likely to make progress toward their desired behaviors compared to individuals who do not (Leonard, 1996). In a summary of over 35 years of goal-setting research, Locke and Latham (2002) explain how goals impact behaviors in four distinct ways: (1) by directing our attention toward the goal, (2) by energizing us to put forth effort, (3) by encouraging persistence, and indirectly (4) by encouraging the use of strategic methods to accomplish the goal. According to Boyatzis, this creation of a change agenda using a goal-oriented approach helps move individuals into a "learning orientation (that) arouses a positive belief in one's capability and the hope of improvement" (2002, p. 25).

Next comes putting one's change agenda into action by experimenting and practicing new behaviors. Actively trying out new ways of acting is the cornerstone to truly learning something (or in this case changing one's behavior), as "knowledge is created through the transformation of experience" (Kolb, 1984, p. 41). Experiential activities have been shown to be especially important in the context of ethics training, as such approaches help individuals actively practice new, desired behaviors (Laditka & Houck, 2006; Sanyal, 2000; Sekerka, Godwin, & Charnigo, 2012). Research has also shown that experiential activities are effective in helping to cultivate not only positive intentions to engage in sustainable behaviors, but also follow-through on those intentions (Mittelstaedt, Sanker, & VanderVeer, 1999).

The final discovery in ICT suggests that the cultivation and leveraging of supportive relationships will enhance every other step in the change process. Our relationships "give us a sense of identity, guide us as to what is appropriate and 'good' behavior, and provide feedback on our behavior" (Boyatzis, 2002, p. 27). Professionals who leverage multiple relationships to help them achieve their goals are more likely to make progress on those goals compared to individuals who rely on only one relationship (Wheeler, 1999). Career development literature further supports the importance of building and using a "constellation" of multiple developmental relationships (Higgins & Thomas, 2001) to create mentoring networks (versus depending on a single mentor) from which one can garner support for personal development (Higgins & Kram, 2001). Figure 6.1 illustrates ICT, showing how these discoveries can be conceptualized as an ongoing cyclical process (Boyatzis,

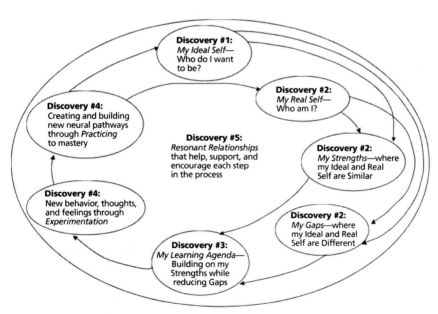

Figure 6.1 Boyatzis' Theory of Intentional Change (From Boyatzis, 2006).

1999). According to Goleman et al. (2002), "The steps [of ICT] do not un-fold in a smooth, orderly way, but rather follow a sequence, with each step demanding different amounts of time and effort" (p. 109).

Insights from ICT suggest that ethical trainings aimed at encouraging enduring behavior changes among employees be designed in such a way as to incorporate these five elements. One such approach involves having employees create personal sustainability projects—a method to which we now turn our attention.

PERSONAL SUSTAINABILITY PROJECTS

While structured in a variety of ways, the concept of personal sustainabil-ity projects (PSPs) has been gaining momentum in various companies under different naming conventions. These initiatives can range from for-malizing a commitment to recycling, use of alternative transportation, or healthy lifestyle changes. For example, one of the largest PSP programs was launched in one of the biggest companies in the country: Wal-Mart. In collaboration with the sustainability consulting agency, Saatchi & Saat-chi S (http://www.saatchis.com), Wal-Mart launched a massive, voluntary PSP program. Adam Werbach, leader of the personal sustainability projects for Wal-Mart, explains that these involve getting employees to commit to "something that's a repeated action that's good for you, your community, and the planet" (Grist, 2008, n.p.). According to Barbaro (2007), this work has already involved more than 50% of their employees, representing a $30 million commitment where:

> The company is training—and paying—hundreds of employees to recruit their colleagues, holding off-site retreats for participants (a rarity for hourly workers) and tracking workers' progress in written reports that measure par-ticipation rates. During a workshop...managers and hourly workers spent five hours at the zoo learning about environmental sustainability, a lesson that included tips on reducing carbon emissions and consuming healthier, more environmentally friendly food. By the end of the day, each employee had written down a pledge—or, in the program's parlance, a personal sustain-ability practice.

Saatchi & Saatchi S is also working with other companies, launching a variety of PSP-type projects, many less complex than those at Wal-Mart. One of the simplest forms of PSPs is their "DOT" or "Do One Thing" initia-tive. Just as the name implies, "Each person is encouraged to choose one thing to pursue regularly. It can be anything from cycling to work or doing laundry with cold water. We call this DOT—Do One Thing. One person's DOT may stand alone, but connect a billion DOTs together and you'll see a movement of change happening." (http://www.saatchis.com/ideas). One does not need to be a part of an organization to create a DOT pledge, but can do so on their own via their website, which showcases the various promises made to date and aims to inspire one billion people to make a pledge.

The work being done at Wal-Mart with PSPs, as well as the general DOT calls-to-action, is inspirational. Yet, there are many companies that want to encourage sustainable behaviors among their employees but do not have the resources of Wal-Mart, while others perhaps want to do something a little more structured than the DOT, everyone-on-their-own approach. The good news is that there are many ways in which an organization can use the concept of PSPs to encourage employees to engage in the creation of sustainable behaviors. Regardless of how vast a scope the organization wants to take, however, we suggest that using the five major elements of ICT outlined above as a guiding framework will help ensure that the PSPs actually result in enduring behavioral change. Thus, we posit that the five steps for creating an impactful PSP include:

1. Articulating a personal sustainability vision
2. Assessing one's current environmental impacts
3. Creating SMART sustainability change commitments
4. Experimenting with new sustainable behaviors
5. Sharing stories and celebrating successes with others

First, employees need to create a personal sustainability vision for themselves—a vision that helps them imagine what a more sustainable lifestyle in the "ideal" would look like. As discussed above, a clear vision of their desired, more sustainable future becomes the driving force to help move them toward that desired future image. Their visions could be focused on images of their work habits, or more broadly to include sustainable habits in their daily personal life as well. To help facilitate the creation of this vision, employees can be asked to reflect on questions such as:

- Imagine it is 2015 and your workplace has become a completely sustainable office. It is a model for all other organizations in their pursuit of sustainability. You and your coworkers are engaged in daily practices—both big and small—that when considered cumulatively create the ideal sustainable workplace. Imagine yourself coming into the office on a Monday morning: What do you see? What does the office look like? What are you seeing that is new, different, changed, or better? What specifically are you doing differently?
- Now, with this future in mind, what is one step, the smallest step you could take today, to move your organization forward in its sustainability goals?

• What is one bigger and bolder step you might consider, something you may not have ever yet considered?

The method of having employees engage in such a visioning process can be done in a variety of ways. Depending on the time and resources an organization has, employee retreats may be dedicated solely to facilitating the articulation of personal sustainability visions. On the other end of the spectrum, employees can engage in this process on their own with the aid of some reflective prompts such as the ones mentioned above.

Once their personal sustainability vision is crafted (or even in parallel with the visioning process), employees need to also get a sense of where they are in comparison to their ideal vision for the future. As ICT suggests, this involves establishing the baseline of the "real self," or a starting point from which the employee can measure movement toward their vision of the future. Employees can easily take inventory of the sustainability behaviors they are already engaged in (e.g., "I have a water bottle at my desk that I will often refill instead of buying a new plastic bottle") and begin to see what actions they are—or are not—taking in relationship to their ideal vision of a more sustainable future. As noted above, however, self-assessment is only one part of establishing the real self (Taylor, 2006). Employees need to consider objective assessments from others regarding their behaviors as well. This can be done by asking coworkers (or even friends and family if individuals are focused on improving sustainable behaviors in their personal life) to give them feedback on behaviors they notice them doing—or not doing (e.g., "You fill up your water bottle every day, but I notice that you always leave your light on when you leave your office for a meeting"). Incorporating feedback from others is helpful in creating a realistic assessment of current behaviors that the employee may want to change.

There are also a variety of tools readily available to help employees quantitatively measure their current status in relation to a variety of sustainable behaviors. Online questionnaires called "ecological footprint calculators" are one such resource that employees can use to establish a numeric baseline with respect to their sustainability behaviors. These tools can be used to help employees "estimate the impact of an individual's lifestyle on the planet by converting levels of consumption into the amount of land needed to sustain production levels and lifestyle choices" (Franz & Papyrakis, 2010, p. 391). These calculators are typically free (see examples at: http://www.earthday.org/footprint-calculator or http://myfootprint.org) and easy to use. Although the majority of them focus on helping an individual assess the carbon footprint of their overall lifestyle, there are also those geared specifically to examine organizational behaviors as well, such as the Environmental Protection Agency's "office carbon footprint tool" (http://www.epa.gov/osw/partnerships/wastewise/carboncalc.htm), or those created

by consulting firms like The Green Office (http://www.thegreenoffice
.com/carboncalculator/calculator). While there are ongoing debates
about the effectiveness of these tools (Franz & Papyrakis, 2010), as well as
the need to standardize the equations used by these calculators (Padgett,
Steinemann, Clarke, & Vandenbergh, 2008), they do present another form
of personal feedback that an individual can use to get a sense of where they
are at the present with regard to sustainability behaviors.

As suggested by ICT, the next step in creating a PSP is to compare one's
ideal vision of the future with their assessment of their real self in the present
and to create a personal change agenda. During this process, the employee
actually sets a number of personal sustainability change commitments that
they will commit to over a given period of time. There is a wide array of
resources available to help employees get ideas for commitments they can
make, from websites with tips for how to "go green at work" (e.g., http://
www.treehugger.com/htgg/how-to-go-green-at-work.html) to books such as
Carlson's (2009) *Green Your Work*, and Clift and Cuthbert's (2008) *Greening
Your Office: From Cupboard to Corporation*. Such resources can be made available to employees to give them ideas to foster personal commitment to
goals they may want to consider.

While there are a plethora of approaches for writing effective goals, we
suggest that these change commitments be framed using the SMART goal
model. "SMART" is an acronym commonly used to denote goals that are
specific, measurable, attainable, realistic, and time-bound (Gudger, 2011).
Crafting goals in such a way has been shown to help increase goal attainment in a variety of contexts (Bovend'Eerdt, Botell, & Wade, 2009; Conzemius & O'Neill, 2005). Table 6.1 provides some example goals that have
been evolved into SMART sustainability commitments.

As with the visioning process, the method of crafting SMART sustainability commitments can be done in a variety of ways, either collectively or

**TABLE 6.1   Evolving Generic Sustainability Goals into SMART
Sustainability Commitments**

Original Sustainability Commitment	SMART Sustainability Commitment
I will use less energy when I am in my office	I will turn the thermostat in my office down to 68 degrees when I am working during the week, and down to 65 degrees when I leave for the weekends.
I will commute with colleagues more often.	I will carpool with at least two other coworkers at least three times a week.
I will throw less stuff away during the day.	I will put all my scrap paper into the recycling receptacle at the end of each day before I go home.

individually. What is important, however, is that employees are made aware of the SMART goal framework and given examples of how to create goals using this approach.

After an employee's sustainability commitments are in place, employees start putting their SMART plans into action. This step in the process can go on indefinitely (which is actually a mark of success in creating a culture of sustainability), as each employee may have different timelines for their various goals. During this time, employees can be encouraged to both implement their existing commitments, as well as perhaps adding new ones—especially once specific goals are met. Thus, they are always referring to, updating, and expanding their sustainability commitments as they work to move from the present into their desired future. Organizations can help support employees as they experiment with new sustainable behaviors by helping them track the impact of their behaviors. Again, depending on resources available in the organization, they can invest in various eco-feedback technologies to assist employees in monitoring the consequences of their new, sustainable behaviors. There are a variety of such technologies that are designed to "provide feedback on individual or group behaviors with a goal of reducing environmental impact" (Froehlich, Findlater, & Landay, 2010, p. 10). Some companies are investing in workplace footprint trackers that display real-time, visual energy monitoring via online dashboards so that employees can see, minute by minute, how actions like turning off the lights are actually impacting overall energy consumption. Software companies like AngelPoints (who are partners with the sustainability firm that has been working with Wal-Mart on their PSP program) have created new web-based platforms for employees to easily track their progress on actions that are having a positive impact on the environment, allowing them to chart both individual as well as team progress across various categories (Fleischer, 2009). Most recently, during the Clinton Global Initiative Annual Meeting in September 2010, Wal-Mart has pledged to license, for free distribution, a "My Sustainability Plan" toolkit to organizations across the globe to foster the engagement of employees in the commitment to sustainability (Wal-Mart, 2011). Such tools help employees appreciate the tangible impact that their actions are having, which in turn helps motivate them to continue their actions.

Finally, as ICT suggests, the most effective way for each of these various stages to occur is in the context of trusting and supportive relationships (Boyatzis, 2002). Thus, we suggest it is important that employees share stories and celebrate their successes with other colleagues in the organization. As discussed earlier, having a personal support system helps to enhance success on goals. The collective sharing of successes among colleague networks helps foster positive emotions such as pride, hope, and optimism, which have been shown to initiate upward spirals toward increasing emotional well-being in organizations (Fredrickson, 2003). Organizations can help facilitate this important step in a number of ways. Using a formalized approach, employees can be assigned to each other as eco-coaches, for example, to help support and be accountable to each other. Taking a less formal, more social approach, organizations can simply create opportunities for employees to connect and share their progress with each other. From online forums to report-outs at meetings, there are numerous ways that employees can help support each other to reach their sustainability goals.

IMPLICATIONS AND TAKEAWAYS

As organizations today strive to create ethical cultures that include a focus on sustainability issues, there are a variety of approaches they can take. A "portfolio" approach that offers a "combination of different practices, including formal and informal, strategic and tactical, top-down and bottom-up" is most likely to truly embed sustainability across an organization (Bertels et al., 2010, n.p.). One key component to such an approach is involving employees in sustainability trainings (Buysse & Verbeke, 2003; Haugh & Talwar, 2010). We have suggested in this chapter that in order for these trainings to lead to enduring behavioral changes, however, they should incorporate the insights of intentional change theory. For those responsible for creating ethics trainings in organizations, PSPs offer organizations one such approach that they can customize to meet the needs of their particular employees. There are many benefits to implementing PSPs: namely, they are customizable, cost-effective, and commitment and collaboration building.

- *Customizable.* As discussed above, while we propose that ICT be used as a framework for designing PSPs, each "step" in the process can be conducted in a manner that makes the most sense for a specific organization. From having large group retreats to individualized reflective activities for employees to complete on their own, the stages outlined here can be delivered in a variety of ways.
- *Cost-effective:* Although a company can invest significant resources in promoting organization-wide PSPs, as has Wal-Mart, there need not be a large monetary investment to launch such trainings. External consultants can be hired to help guide the process, or internal trainers (or even inspired employees) can be empowered to introduce "home-grown" trainings. Several free resources have already been highlighted in the context of this chapter. Tracking tools can be purchased to help employees monitor their progress, or low-tech spreadsheets can be used. Given that PSPs can be launched with very little financial investment and can result in actual cost savings

for a company (e.g., through reduced waste, decreased electricity usage, etc.), they can prove to be very cost-effective.

- *Commitment and Collaboration Building:* Because PSPs allow employees to focus on things they are passionate about by setting personalized sustainability goals for themselves, they cultivate intrinsic motivation for sustainable behaviors at work. They also help increase employee buy-in to overarching organizational sustainability commitments by providing a venue for employees to see that even small personal changes can have significant outcomes. Given the relational emphasis of the PSPs, they also help build collaborative relationships, which in turn can have a positive impact on teamwork within the organization. As employees track and celebrate their successes collectively, they are reinforcing a culture of shared accomplishments.

As discussed above, sustainability behaviors are a demonstration of ethics in action, illustrating how espoused ethical values become enacted ethical values within an organization. Such behaviors are not only being demanded from consumers, but are also yielding positive impacts within organizations. Yet, if organizations want to foster these kinds of specific ethical behaviors, they need to provide employees with the opportunity to cultivate sustainable habits in the workplace. Using ICT as a framework, personal sustainability projects can be used as a form of ethics training in organizations to help make sustainability issues tangible for individuals, and to build not only commitment for, but also follow-through on sustainable behaviors in the workplace and beyond.

NOTE

1. For purposes of this chapter, we are using Bertels, Papania, and Papania's definition of business sustainability to refer to "managing the 'triple bottom line.' This includes decision-making that takes into consideration financial, social, and environmental risks, obligations and opportunities" (2010, p. 9).

REFERENCES

Accenture & UN Global Compact. (2010). A new era of sustainability: UN Global Compact-Accenture CEO study. Retrieved from http://www.unglobalcompact.org/docs/news_events/8.1/UNGC_Accenture_CEO_Study_2010.pdf

Albinger, H., & Freeman, S. J. (2000). Corporate social performance and attractiveness as an employer to different job seeking populations. *Journal of Business Ethics, 28*, 243–253.

Ashford, S. J., Blatt, R., & VandeWalle, D. (2003). Reflections on the looking glass: A review on research on feedback-seeking behavior in organizations. *Journal of Management, 29,* 773–799.

Barbaro, M. (2007). At Wal-Mart, lessons in self-help. *The New York Times.* Retrieved from http://www.nytimes.com/2007/04/05/business/05improve. html?pagewanted=all&_r=0

Benson, J. A., & Ross, D. L. (1998). Sundstrand: A case study in transformation of cultural ethics. *Journal of Business Ethics, 17,* 1517–1527.

Bertels, S., Papania, L., & Papania, D. (2010). Embedding sustainability in organizational culture: A systematic review of the body of knowledge. *Network for Business Sustainability.* Retrieved from http://www.nbs.net/wp-content/uploads/ dec6_embedding_sustainability.pdf

Bolton, S., Kim, R., & O'Gorman, K. (2011). Corporate social responsibility as a dynamic internal organizational process: A case study. *Journal of Business Ethics, 101,* 61–74.

Bovend'Eert, T. J., Botell, R. E., & Wade, D. T. (2009). Writing SMART rehabilitation goals and achieving goal attainment scaling: A practical guide. *Clinical Rehabilitation, 23,* 352–361.

Boyatzis, R. E. (1999). Self-directed change and learning as a necessary meta-competency for success and effectiveness in the 21st century. In R. Sims & J. Veres (Eds.), *Keys to employee success in the coming decades* (pp. 15–32). Westport, CT: Greenwood Publishing.

Boyatzis, R. E. (2002). Unleashing the power of self-directed learning. In R. R. Sims (Ed.), *Changing the way we manage change: The consultants speak* (pp. 13–32). Westport, CT: Quorum Books.

Boyatzis, R. E. (2008). Leadership development from a competency perspective. *Consulting Psychology Journal, 60,* 298–313.

Boyatzis, R., & Akrivou, K. (2006). The ideal self as the driver of intentional change. *Journal of Management Development, 25,* 624–642.

Boyatzis, R. E., & Kolb, D. A. (1969). *Feedback and self-directed behavior change.* Unpublished Working Paper #394-69. Sloan School of Management, MIT.

Buysse, K., & Verbeke, A. (2003). Proactive environmental strategies: A stakeholder management perspective. *Strategic Management Journal, 24,* 453–470.

Carlson, K. (2009). *Green your work.* Avon, MA: Adams Media.

Clift, J., & Cuthbert, A. (2008). *Greening your office: From cupboard to corporation.* White River Junction, VT: Green Publishing.

Conzemius, A., & O'Neill, J. (2005). *The power of SMART goals: Using goals to improve student learning.* Bloomington, IN: Solution Tree Press.

Cooperrider, D. L. (2003). Positive image, positive action: The affirmative basis of organizing. In D. L. Cooperrider, P. F. Sorenson, Jr., T. F. Yaeger, & D. Whitney (Eds.), *Appreciative inquiry: An emerging direction for organization development* (pp. 31–55). Champaign, IL: Stipes Publishing.

Cooperrider, D. L., & Whitney, D. (1999). *Appreciative inquiry: Collaborating for change.* San Francisco, CA: Barrett-Koehler.

Driscoll, C., & Starik, M. (2004). The primordial stakeholder: Advancing the conceptual consideration of stakeholder status for the natural environment. *Journal of Business Ethics, 49,* 55–73.

Dunphy, D., Griffiths, A., & Benn, S. (2003). *Organizational change for corporate sustainability.* London, UK: Routledge.

Ehrenfeld, J. (2005). The roots of sustainability. *MIT Sloan Management Review, 46*(2), 23–25.

Ernst & Young. (2008, September). Ready or not, here comes sustainability. *Top of Mind: Issues Facing Technology Companies* (Issue 1). Retrieved from http://www.ey.com/Publication/vwLUAssets/Industry_Technology_Ready_or_not_here_comes_sustainability/$FILE/Technology_Ready_or_not_here_comes_sustainability.pdf

Festinger, L. (1957). *A theory of cognitive dissonance.* Stanford, CA: Stanford University Press.

Fleischer, D. (2009, October 30). Employee engagement: AngelPoints launches new personal sustainability practice (PSP) tool. *Green Impact.* Retrieved from http://greenimpact.wordpress.com/2009/10/30/employee-engagement-angelpoints-launches-new-personal-sustainability-practice-psp-tool/

Francis, L. (2012). Obama, Mandela & Doctor King, Jr.: Inspirational quotes to inspire the world today. Charleston, SC: CreateSpace.

Franz, J., & Papyakis, E. (2010). Online calculators of ecological footprint: Do they promote or dissuade sustainable behaviour? *Sustainable Development, 19,* 391–401.

Fredrickson, B. L. (2003). The value of positive emotions. *American Scientist, 91,* 330–335.

Froehlich, J., Findlater, L., & Landay, J. (2010, April 10–15). *The design of eco-feedback technology.* Paper presented at Computer–Human Interaction conference, Atlanta, GA. Retrieved from http://dub.washington.edu/djangosite/media/papers/tmpssyQcm.pdf

Glavas, A., & Piderit, S. K. (2009). How does doing good matter? Effects of corporate citizenship on employees. *Journal of Corporate Citizenship, 36,* 51–70.

Goleman, D., Boyatzis, R. E., & McKee, A. (2002). *Primal leadership: Realizing the power of emotional intelligence.* Boston, MA: Harvard Business School Press.

Grist. (2008). Adam Werbach calls for a new movement of a billion consumers. Retrieved from www.grist.org/article/the-birth-of-blue

Gudger, J. (2011). *SMART Goals: The ultimate goal setting guide.* Seattle, WA: Amazon Digital Services.

Haugh, H., & Talwar, A. (2010). How do corporations embed sustainability across the organization? *Academy of Management Learning and Education, 9,* 384–396.

Higgins, E. T. (1987). Self-discrepancy: A theory relating self and affect. *Psychological Review, 94,* 319–340.

Higgins, M. C., & Kram, K. E. (2001). Reconceptualizing mentoring at work: A developmental network perspective. *Academy of Management Review, 26,* 264–288.

Higgins, M., & Thomas, D. (2001). Constellations and careers: Toward understanding the effects of multiple developmental relationships. *Journal of Organizational Behavior, 22,* 223–247.

Holton, I., Glass, J., & Price, A. (2010). Managing for sustainability: Findings from four company case studies in the UK precast concrete industry. *Journal of Cleaner Production, 18,* 152–160.

Jaffe, D. T., & Bresler, D. E. (1980). The use of guided imagery as an adjunct to medical diagnosis and treatment. *Journal of Humanistic Psychology, 20*(4), 45–59.

Kolb, D. A. (1984). *Experiential learning: Experience as the source of learning and development.* Englewood Cliffs, NJ: Prentice-Hall.

Kolk, A. (2008). Sustainability, accountability and corporate governance: Exploring multinationals' reporting practices. *Business Strategy and the Environment, 17,* 1–15.

Laditka, S. B., & Houck, M. M. (2006). Student-developed case studies: An experiential approach for teaching ethics in management. *Journal of Business Ethics, 64,* 157–167.

Laszlo, C., & Zhexembayeva, N. (2001). *Embedded sustainability: The next big competitive advantage.* Stanford, CA: Stanford University Press.

Laughland, P., & Bansal, T. (2011). The top ten reasons why businesses aren't more sustainable. *Ivey Business Journal,* January/February. Retrieved from http://www.iveybusinessjournal.com/topics/social-responsibility/the-top-ten-reasons-why-businesses-aren't-more-sustainable#.USKFRI55iy4

Leonard, D. (1996). *The impact of learning goals on self-directed change in management development and education.* Unpublished doctoral dissertation, Case Western Reserve University, Cleveland, OH.

Lewin, K. (1947). Frontiers in group dynamics. *Human Relations, 1,* 5–41.

Locke, E. A., & Latham, G. P. (1990). *A theory of goal setting and task performance.* Englewood Cliffs, NJ: Prentice Hall.

Locke, E., & Latham, G. (2002). Building a practically useful theory of goal setting and task motivation: A 35-year odyssey. *American Psychologist, 57,* 705–717.

Maon, F., Lindgreen, A., & Swaen, V. (2009). Designing and implementing corporate social responsibility: An integrative framework grounded in theory and practice. *Journal of Business Ethics, 87,* 71–89.

McKee, A., Johnston, F., & Rotondo, S. (2008). Intentional change: The power of emotion. *Executive Matters.* Retrieved from http://membersonly.amamember.org/newsletters_archive/2008/exec-matters-june08.pdf

Mittelstaedt, R., Sanker, L., & VanderVeer, B. (1999). Impact of a week-long experiential education program on environmental attitude and awareness. *Journal of Experiential Education, 22,* 138–148.

Montgomery, D. B., & Ramus, C. A. (2007). *Including corporate social responsibility, environmental sustainability, and ethics in calibrating MBA job preferences.* Stanford Graduate School of Business, Research Paper No. 1981.

Nidumolu, R., Prahalad, C. K., & Rangaswami, M. R. (2009). Why sustainability is now the key driver of innovation. *Harvard Business Review, 87*(9), 57–64.

Norcross, J. C., Krebs, P. M., & Prochaska, J. O. (2011). Stages of change. *Journal of Clinical Psychology: In Session, 67,* 143–154.

Nord, W., & Fuller, S. (2009). Increasing corporate social responsibility through an employee centered approach. *Employee Responsibilities and Rights Journal, 21,* 279–290.

Orlitzky, M., Schmidt, F., & Rynes, S. L. (2003). Corporate social and financial performance: A meta-analysis. *Organizational Studies, 24,* 403–441.

Padgett, J. P, Steinemann, A. C., Clarke, J. H., & Vandenbergh, M. P. (2008). A comparison of carbon calculators. *Environmental Impact Assessment Review, 28,* 106–115.

Peloza, J. (2009). The challenge of measuring financial impacts from investments in corporate social performance. *Journal of Management, 35,* 1518–1541.

Peterson, D. K. (2004). The relationship between perceptions of CSR and organizational commitment. *Business & Society, 43,* 296–319.

Prochaska, J. O., & DiClemente, C. C. (1983). Stages and processes of self-change of smoking: Toward an integrative model of change. *Journal of Consulting and Clinical Psychology, 51,* 390–395.

Prochaska, J. O., DiClemente, C. C., & Norcross, J. C. (1992). In search of how people change: Applications to addictive behaviors. *American Psychologist, 47,* 1102–1114.

Reid, R. (2009). The moral imperative for sustainable communities. *Public Management, 91*(4), 68–72.

Rushton, K. (2002). Business ethics: A sustainable approach. *Business Ethics: A European Review, 11,* 137–139.

Sanyal, R. N. (2000). An experiential approach to teaching ethics in international business. *Teaching Business Ethics, 4,* 137–149.

Sekerka, L. E. (2009). Organizational ethics education and training: A review of best practices and their application. *International Journal of Training and Development, 13,* 77–95.

Sekerka, L. E., Godwin, L. N., & Charnigo, R. (2012). Use of Balanced Experiential Inquiry to build ethical strength in the workplace. *Journal of Management Development, 31,* 275–286.

Taylor, S. (2006). Why the real self is fundamental to intentional change. *Journal of Management Development, 25,* 643–656.

Thomas, T. E., & Lamm, E. (2012). Legitimacy and organizational sustainability. *Journal of Business Ethics, 110,* 191–203.

Turban, D. B., & Greening, D. W. (1997). Corporate social performance and organizational attractiveness to prospective employees. *Academy of Management Journal, 40,* 658–672.

Valentine, S., & Fleischman, G. (2008). Ethics programs, perceived corporate social responsibility and job satisfaction. *Journal of Business Ethics, 77,* 159–172.

Wal-Mart. (2011). Global Responsibility Report. Retrieved from http://www.walmart stores.com/sites/responsibilityreport/2011/goal3_sell_products.aspx

Werbach, A. (2009). *Strategy for sustainability: A business manifesto.* Boston, MA: Harvard Business Press.

Wheeler, J. V. (1999). *The impact of social environments on self-directed change and learning.* Unpublished doctoral dissertation, Case Western Reserve University, Cleveland, OH.

Woolfolk, R. L., Parrish, M., & Murphy, S. (1985). The effects of positive and negative imagery on motor skill performance. *Cognitive Therapy and Research, 9,* 335–341.

SECTION III

TECHNIQUES AND ASSESSMENT

CHAPTER 7

ORGANIZATIONAL ETHICS PROCESS AND ASSESSMENT

Intervening to Improve Interventions

Richard Charnigo and Leslie E. Sekerka

You are what you measure.
—Dan Ariely, b. 1968

Business ethics commands a sustained interest among practitioners and academic researchers. Even so, ethics training remains largely understudied. Moreover, the actual benefits of training are rarely fully realized due to the lack of carefully designed program assessment. Although there is some scholarly work to describe the evaluation of ethics interventions (e.g., Ajuwon & Kass, 2008), the literature in this area is surprisingly limited. More focus is directed to content, which is often commercially driven (e.g., online programs), legally mandated (e.g., external governmental regulations), or imposed through policy (e.g., internal rules for a corporation). Notably absent from the discourse is the empirical assessment of ethics interventions. Focused study to understand ethics training effectiveness, examining learning outcomes and behavioral change, calls for attention among academics and practitioners alike.

Ethics Training in Action, pages 141–165
Copyright © 2014 by Information Age Publishing
All rights of reproduction in any form reserved.

While the Ethics Resource Center (ERC; see http://www.ethics.org) tracks information related to organizational ethics (e.g., whistleblowing activity), the influence of ethics training programs in organizations is rarely considered. Training evaluations typically ask participants about their perceptions, posing questions about the facilitator, accommodations, and how much participants valued the session. According to the *State of Compliance: 2012 Study*, a study by PricewaterhouseCoopers (PwC) and Compliance Week, measuring ethics training effectiveness is a key problem for management (Kelly, Bernstein, & Kipp, 2012). Acknowledging challenges in confirming that ethics programs are effective, a partner with PwC stated, "Compliance officers today know that just tracking calls to the hotline isn't enough. Compliance officers really need overall assurance that their program is effective. Getting that assurance requires a combination of multiple metrics and insights" (Kelly et al., 2012, p. 12). An overarching concern with ethics training is that surprisingly little is done to build employee competency for effective decision making or to encourage employees' desire to engage in ethical action (cf., Sekerka, 2009). To address this concern, managers need to consider both the process tools utilized in their ethics programming and the assessment of training deliverables.

In this chapter we advocate a more thoughtful focus on ethics training delivery and assessment. This focus entails formulating an assessment plan and determining what outcomes need to be measured (as well as how to measure them) *before* the training is provided. Our primary rationale in this chapter is to help managers and organizational members discover whether and how an ethics program is effective. To begin, proposing a binary answer to the question of effectiveness (yes or no) would be a vast oversimplification. For example, an ethics program may succeed in familiarizing participants with regulatory content but fail to encourage employees' desire to engage in ethical action. An ethics program may build ethical awareness among mid-level employees but may not do so for lower-level staff. The program may alter behaviors in the short-term, but not cultivate learning, growth, and development, reflecting changes over time. When managers and organizations seek a nuanced answer to the question of training effectiveness, the need for a more deliberate approach to training assessment becomes quite clear. With a more granular and carefully designed assessment effort, managers can acquire insight toward greater efficacy or, if the program is deficient, they can justify expenses to improve it (monetary and otherwise).

Assessment serves at least two secondary purposes. One, as Salas, Tannenbaum, Kraiger, and Smith-Jentsch (2012) contend, the evaluation debriefing can be of benefit to trainees. When feedback is presented as a vehicle for personal development, fostering awareness and encouraging improvement, this can help strengthen the ethical health of the organization. Two, whatever is learned from the assessment, if widely disseminated (e.g., via best practices), will work to benefit other organizations (e.g., drawing upon established methods with quantified success) as well as academic researchers (e.g., providing empirical insight to foster theoretical development and spur additional inquiry).

A major issue is that ethics training is rarely designed to address the needs of adult learners (e.g., Delaney & Sockell, 1992), thus unlikely to be evaluated for its effectiveness in meeting such needs. For instance, employees presumably experience greater benefit from ethics training if they comprehend how the training applies to specific issues that they actually encounter. Yet management is often more concerned about whether an ethics program mitigates legal risk (e.g., LeClair & Ferrell, 2000) than about employee comprehension per se. While the mitigation of legal risk is a legitimate goal, building an organizational culture of ethical strength does not emerge from rule-based initiatives alone (cf., Sekerka, 2012). In addition, the expected outcomes of a training program may not align with its actual impacts on an organization and its employees (Sekerka & Zolin, 2007). Managers cannot assume that exposure to content results in the material being fully understood, learned, and applied. Of course, these considerations underscore the need for assessment.

The purpose of this chapter, then, is to highlight and discuss important issues related to process assessment of ethics interventions. (We use the term *intervention* throughout this chapter to reference any ethics training initiative conducted in an organizational setting, as this may be considered a form of organizational development.) To support this undertaking, we often use for illustration a particular mode of organizational ethics training called *balanced experiential inquiry* (BEI). The BEI process has been employed to instigate ethical reflection and dialogue in a variety of organizations, including business, academic, and government settings (Sekerka & Godwin, 2010).

Given our dual focus on process and assessment, the chapter is presented in two parts. Part I provides an overview of BEI, explicating an example of ethics training process that is based upon adult learning and experiential learning theories. This technique underscores how management learning can be particularly effective when both positive and negative workplace experiences are tapped, generating learning from both strength- and deficit-based inquiry. Part II describes prerequisites for and logistics of empirically assessing intervention effectiveness. First, assessors need to develop a theory regarding how the intervention may affect target outcomes. By implication, this suggests that managers need to consider the use of valid and reliable measurement tools that capture the social or behavioral constructs that support their target outcome goals. The logistics of empirical assessment include careful protocol design, working to limit unintended biases, and applying appropriate statistical modeling techniques to analyze the resulting data. We conclude by identifying implications for organizational ethics assessment and proposing questions for future research.

CONTENT AND PROCESS

Adult Learning

A focus on ethics has become a mainstay of employee training over the past two decades, mainly because of regulatory demands, but also due to technological advances (e.g., LeClair & Ferrell, 2000; Mayrath, Clarke-Midura, Robinson, & Schraw, 2012). Paradoxically, this evolution in training may have reduced its effectiveness. The predominant form, online delivery, is convenient and economical but generally patterned after traditional coursework models (cf., Sekerka & Godwin, 2010; Sekerka, Godwin, & Charnigo, 2012). Employees are prompted by software to digest content, with mastery defined in accordance with an external motivation (e.g., a passing grade to certify unit completion). Despite its ease, low cost, and directness, this approach has severe limitations in both process and content.

A typical ethics coursework model is derived from primary, secondary, and undergraduate higher education. Therefore, this model rarely addresses the needs of adult learners. Indeed, Knowles (1968) highlights an important distinction for adult education by juxtaposing the words *andragogy* and *pedagogy*. The former pertains to helping adults learn, whereas the latter—which contains the Greek root word for child—underlies the coursework model. As per Knowles (1980), Merriam (2001) articulates the key principles for andragogy, describing how adult learners can:

1. direct their own learning
2. draw upon personal life experiences as resources
3. address dynamic needs related to social roles
4. problem-solve and troubleshoot
5. draw upon their own internal motivations.

The coursework model does not adhere to these principles and so does not meet the needs of adult learners. For example, consider the first principle. Students in primary, secondary, and undergraduate higher education usually follow a specified curriculum into which they have no input and are often expected to assimilate material delivered in a lecture format. These students, and adult learners engaged in similarly patterned coursework, therefore do not direct their own learning.

The relevance of life experiences to adult learning has been emphasized by several management and executive education scholars (Brookfield,

1986; Laditka & Houck, 2006; Sanyal, 2000; Weick, 1995). Perhaps most notably, Kolb (1984) defines adult learning as a four-step process that begins with a concrete experience (first step) and, following reflection (second) and abstract conceptualization (third), culminates in active experimentation with new actualized behavior (fourth). To the extent that ethics training follows a coursework model, the suggested experiential learning process is largely omitted.

Following a template derived from primary, secondary, and undergraduate higher education entails the selection of course material by either the instructor or the organization, usually without substantive participant involvement. Moreover, the chosen content may impose barriers to adult learning in general and to ethical action in particular. As Sekerka (2009) observes, content in ethics training is frequently oriented toward compliance with and information about policies related to regulatory adherence. While scholars (e.g., LeClair & Ferrell, 2000) note that minimizing legal risk (associated with regulatory adherence) can be beneficial, an excessively legalistic orientation is problematic. A tight focus on rules-based ethics may reduce the sort of overt malfeasance that is explicitly proscribed by regulations. However, this result falls short of instilling a desire to determine and pursue what is right, let alone developing the moral competencies necessary to achieve ethical action.

For example, the competency of *professional moral courage* (PMC) is characterized not by an employee's or a manager's rigid devotion to regulations but rather by his or her resolution to engage in ethical action, despite the potential for adverse personal consequences (Sekerka, Bagozzi, & Charnigo, 2009). Moreover, PMC is acquired not (merely) by avoiding malfeasance in the workplace. Instead, PMC involves learning how to recognize and use emotions as signals, to understand oneself and others, to practice the suspension of initial reactions in favor of reflective pauses for insight and deliberation, to evaluate motives and manage desires, and to rehearse ethical decision making in anticipation of future ethical challenges (Sekerka, McCarthy, & Bagozzi, 2011).

Perhaps most worrisome is that reliance upon legal compliance to shape an organization's ethical culture may actually discourage ethical behavior. Researchers have found that, in organizational settings where formal structures rely solely on rules to support moral action, employees may learn to justify deviations from policies to accomplish performance targets. In turn, an orientation towards rule-bending can become normalized and part of an organization's accepted culture (Sekerka & Zolin, 2007). Several authors contend that ethical performance is highly dependent on employees having some degree of personal control or autonomy (Ashkanasy, Windsor, & Trevino, 2006; Granitz, 2003; Ryan, 1982; Sekerka & Bagozzi, 2007). This is in juxtaposition to employees who are rigidly constrained by policies and correspondingly motivated by rewards and punishments to achieve what the organization defines as ethical action (cf., Kashdan & Fincham, 2004; Tenbrunsel, 1998).

A final point regarding process, especially salient to this chapter, is that ethics training is not always accompanied by explicit identification of target outcomes, much less assessment of intervention effectiveness. One commendable example, involving an ethics workshop for human subjects researchers, is provided by Ajuwon and Kass (2008). This workshop was preceded and followed, both immediately and one month later, by assessments measuring knowledge of research ethics, applications of ethical principles, institutional review board operations, and ethical reasoning. The acquisition of such knowledge may not necessarily transfer into superior moral reasoning on the job. However, managers cannot hope to maximize ethical strength without assessing the effectiveness of ethics training, despite the difficulties and expenses of so doing. Toward this end, we provide guidance concerning the measurement and methodological challenges of assessment in Part II of this chapter.

A Balanced Experiential Approach

Balanced experiential inquiry (BEI) is an alternative approach to ethics training that overcomes the aforementioned limitations regarding process and content (Sekerka & Godwin, 2010; Sekerka, Godwin, & Charnigo, 2012). The word *balance* refers to participants' acknowledgment of both strengths and weaknesses in addressing ethical challenges, at both the individual and organizational levels. Importantly, BEI welcomes the "good" and the "bad" (and even the "ugly," referring to particularly difficult ethical challenges). In short, BEI draws upon participants' personal experiences, favorable and unfavorable, to promote ethical awareness and personal moral development.

As described by Sekerka, Brumbaugh, Rosa, and Cooperrider (2006), organizational development is typically pursued using either a diagnostic or an appreciative inquiry framework. The former is geared toward questions that work to problem-solve, whereas the latter emphasizes organizational and member strengths that support growth and development. These authors' empirical investigation revealed that both frameworks have desirable, complementary effects on target outcomes. A study by Sekerka, Zolin, and Goosby-Smith (2009) revealed that favorable developmental themes emerge from both positive and negative entry points, provided that inquiry does not force participants to focus solely on their own negative aspects as the source for change. Intervention processes that focus only on the negative (where problems have occurred), or solely on the positive (where excellence has been achieved) may be too narrow for adult moral development. Efforts to assess such intervention processes may be similarly insufficient. For instance, if an ethics training process emphasizes only the negative (what not to do), then the selection of target outcomes may be skewed toward the avoidance of overt malfeasance rather than fully encompassing the various facets of character strength in ethical decision making. Similarly, a focus solely on the positive may inadvertently shroud problem areas that need to be addressed.

Participants in BEI engage in a workshop process aligned with Kolb's (1984) paradigm for adult learning. The coursework model is not adopted, there is no instructor per se, and employees use their own experiences (good and bad) as the platform for learning and discovery. A skilled, well-prepared facilitator helps participants to direct their own learning, based upon their personal repertoire of ethical challenges (i.e., workplace ethics issues they have actually experienced). Rather than the instructor providing specific content, adult learners create and shape the context for much of the learning material.

In the first step of BEI, each participant privately identifies a personal ethical challenge that he or she faced—a concrete experience (Kolb, 1984). Employees then reflect on what they did as well as on what they were thinking and feeling during the challenge. Participants are also asked to describe what happened and what the final outcome was. Regardless of whether an employee responded to the challenge with an ethical action, the examination of his or her own personal case depicts the moral competencies that were used, avoided, or unrecognized as he or she navigated an ethical decision-making trajectory.

After this internal reflection period, participants form pairs and share their ethical challenge scenarios and personal reflections with their partners. The facilitator meets with each pair to support their dialogue and gain insight into key issues within their organization. While still in pairs, participants consider what factors blocked or supported their ability to respond with ethical action, with attention given to both internal (e.g., their own emotions and convictions) and external factors (e.g., management and other aspects of the organization). During this shared reflection period and subsequent abstract conceptualization (Kolb, 1984), participants exercise the competencies shown to be associated with moral action (Sekerka & Godwin, 2010). More specifically, they practice reflective pauses, emotional signaling, and openly (and hopefully honestly) evaluating their personal motives.

Participants then engage in a group discussion. Depending upon the time allocated for BEI (typically two to three hours), the facilitator solicits a number of volunteers to share their ethical challenges and reflections with the entire group. Some barriers to ethical action are explicitly identified by the presenters themselves, while others emerge via group questions and comments. Using a whiteboard or flipchart, the facilitator diagrams the ethical challenges, how they were approached, what thoughts and feelings were experienced, where moral competencies for ethical decision making were exercised, and where competencies might have been exercised—but were not. This group discussion exercises and hones the competencies needed for ethical action (Sekerka, McCarthy, & Bagozzi, 2010). Participants then consider how they will overcome the factors that have been identified as impeding ethical action in their organization and how they plan to develop and sustain ethical strength, which may entail creating new processes. This completes the Kolb (1984) experiential learning cycle, moving adult learners on to the experimentation stage, helping them to consider and demonstrate support mechanisms and new behaviors.

Besides participants' consideration of both the favorable and unfavorable aspects of how people address their ethical challenges, BEI seeks balance in several other respects. Participants ponder factors that promote and elements that curtail ethical action at both the individual and organizational levels. The process reveals both internal and external circumstances driving participants toward or away from "doing the right thing." Finally, participants weigh their individual perceptions against those that emerge during the group discussion.

Field Study

A field study was conducted to empirically assess the effects of BEI in a military management setting (Sekerka, McCarthy, & Bagozzi, 2011; Sekerka, Godwin, & Charnigo, 2012). The participants, 169 officers in the United States Navy Supply Corps, completed a variety of measures before and after BEI. The officers participated in small groups (12 to 15 people) with similar distributions of military rank. Measures included: (1) a curiosity scale (Kashdan, Rose, & Fincham, 2004), (2) a desired moral approbation scale (Ryan & Riordan, 2000), and, for some participants, (3) positive and negative affect scales (a brief version of the PANAS-X, Watson & Clark, 1999).

Participants expressed significantly greater curiosity after BEI. This change was driven by increases in exploration and, to a lesser degree, flow. Participants also perceived significantly less need for moral approbation (i.e., approval for moral action) after BEI. This decrease was driven by reduced need for praise from others; the changes in the needs for self-approval and for avoiding blame from others were comparatively modest. Participants felt significantly less sluggish after the activity, and there was a decrease of lesser magnitude in fear (e.g., toward reporting an ethical concern). In contrast, participants felt significantly greater excitement after the session. Although changes on other emotions were not significant, they were in all but one case consistent with BEI diminishing negative emotions and augmenting positive ones.

If emotions (e.g., excitement), desired moral approbation, and curiosity lie on a causal pathway to ethical decision making, then this empirical study provides some support for the idea that BEI may enhance ethical development in organizational settings. However, further investigations are required to obtain more definitive support for this idea. Implementing these investigations necessitates confronting measurement and methodology issues. For example, ethical decision making must be quantified, and there must be some basis for asserting that improved ethical decision making is attributable to BEI and not just the attention received by participants. Importantly, these measurement and methodology issues are not only germane to quantifying the impact of BEI on ethical behavior but also relevant to assessing the effects of other ethics interventions on a variety of target outcomes.

ISSUES IN ASSESSMENT

Articulating Constructs

A prerequisite for conducting an empirical investigation on the effects of ethics training is to identify target outcomes on a theorized causal pathway. Figure 7.1 depicts this idea, reflecting anticipated cause-and-effect patterns from ethics training. The formality of theoretical explication may vary, depending on whether a practitioner or academic researcher is conducting the study.

Among practitioners, theory is often based on what is desired from trainees and how the intervention accomplishes this goal. For instance, participants may be expected to become curious about ethics in the workplace. The intervention may fulfill this expectation by enhancing participants' interest in ethical issues. Explicitly identifying learning objectives is essential, along with determining what constructs are to be measured for assessment purposes. Here, the word construct refers to an intangible quality that may be inferred using, for example, a scale in which respondents indicate their agreement/disagreement with various items. Such a scale is often referred to as an instrument and serves as a tangible proxy for the underlying construct. For brevity, people often say that the scale measures the construct. For instance, curiosity is a construct that can be measured using the scale of Kashdan et al. (2004).

The social or behavioral science literature can provide helpful guidance regarding theory related to the intervention and the identification of relevant constructs. Indeed, Salas and colleagues (2012) stress that training theories provide practitioners with a "wealth of knowledge on the components

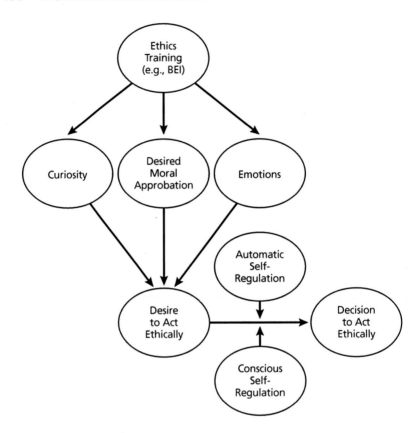

Figure 7.1 A theoretical causal pathway from ethics training to ethical action. We assume that, like BEI, most ethics training processes prompt some level of ethical awareness. Hence, ethics training is anticipated to initiate a causal pathway culminating in the decision to act ethically and involving multiple mediators and moderators along the way.

critical to [a] training system" (p. 78). For example, consider the hypothesis that BEI fosters ethical decision making. While there is already some empirical evidence that BEI favorably impacts curiosity, reduces the need for external praise for ethical action, and favorably influences emotional feeling, a variety of suppositions may be proposed that complete the link from intervention to ethical action. Moreover, these suppositions may vary across organizational contexts and populations. For instance, applying Rest's (1986) decision-making paradigm in a management setting, Sekerka and Bagozzi (2007) propose that a desire to act ethically may translate into a decision to engage in ethical action, subject to the influence of self-regulation (see Figure 7.1). Curiosity, desired moral approbation, and emotions precede the desire to act ethically, which in turn precedes ethical decision making. Additionally, two forms of self-regulation favorably influence the link from the desire to the decision to act ethically.

While the pathway in Figure 7.1 is plausible, our objective here is not to assert its correctness. Rather, we wish to exemplify the articulation of target outcomes and a theorized causal pathway as important preliminary steps for conducting and assessing ethics training. Once this foundational work is complete, the process of finding or constructing valid and reliable measurement instruments can begin.

Valid and Reliable Measures

Many texts (e.g., DeVellis, 2012; Nunnally & Bernstein, 1994; Rust & Golombok, 2008) and research papers (e.g., Singhapakdi, Vitell, Rallapalli, & Kraft, 1996; Turker, 2009) describe construct measurement in social and behavioral science. While their collective wisdom cannot be distilled into a few pages, we highlight some key ideas vital to measuring constructs in a theorized causal pathway. We also draw upon our own efforts in scale development as we discuss the selection and use of measurement tools. One construct that we have previously studied and also consider below is professional moral courage (PMC), which entails a virtuous ethical response action when facing an ethical challenge in the workplace. In addition, while proposing new scales to measure ethical decision-making (and other target outcomes for an ethics intervention) is an ambitious task that lies beyond the scope of this chapter, we do mention that other researchers have developed instruments for ethical decision making in various workplace settings. For instance, Mumford and colleagues (2006) created instrumentation for ethical decision making among academic researchers, while Kim (2011) did so for nurses providing end-of-life care.

Validity of an Instrument

Broadly speaking, validity means that an instrument is accurately measuring the construct in question. More specifically, DeVellis (2012) distinguishes among three types of validity (content, criterion, and construct).

Content validity means the instrument represents all aspects of the construct under consideration, while not capturing aspects of related but different constructs. For instance, PMC comprises five components; failing to capture one of them, such as moral agency, would jeopardize the content validity of a PMC scale (Sekerka, Bagozzi, & Charnigo, 2009). Content validity can be ascertained from evaluations of the instrument by subject matter experts (e.g., Lawshe, 1975), though some authors also recommend consulting those to whom the instrument will be administered (e.g., Vogt, King, & King, 2004).

Criterion validity refers to an instrument's empirical association with an established criterion that measures a presumably related objective outcome. For the construct of ethical action, one objective outcome might be the presence/absence of ethics violations in the organization. However, using that particular objective outcome to establish criterion validity would be subject to limitations. As suggested by Sekerka, Bagozzi, and Charnigo (2009), the presence/absence of overt malfeasance might distinguish deficient from mediocre ethical performance but would not separate mediocrity from excellence. Moreover, if there were relatively few ethics violations, the statistical power to verify an empirical association could be quite low. Establishing criterion validity for an instrument measuring ethical action is therefore challenging, due to the dearth of objective outcomes capturing the full spectrum of ethical performance. Ironically, this scarcity may reflect the dependency on a compliance orientation that BEI attempts to overcome (cf., Sekerka & Zolin, 2007).

Following Cronbach and Meehl (1955), DeVellis (2012) describes *construct validity* as an empirical association between an instrument measuring the construct of interest and instruments measuring other presumably related constructs. Thus, construct validity is subtly different from criterion validity, in that an objective outcome is not involved. For example, we anticipate a positive relationship between the constructs of perceiving a moral issue and rendering a moral judgment (cf., Rest, 1986). In this case, construct validity would entail a positive empirical association between instruments for these constructs. On the other hand, care must be taken in interpreting the absence of an anticipated empirical association. This may occur due to low statistical power, a lack of construct validity, or even the theory itself being flawed.

Some authors impose a stricter standard for construct validity, namely that the random and systematic errors inherent to an instrument are modest (cf., Bagozzi, Yi, & Phillips, 1991; Bagozzi, 1993). As documented by Bagozzi and colleagues (1991), several techniques have been proposed to evaluate such errors, ranging from the multitrait-multimethod matrix procedure of Campbell and Fiske (1959) to confirmatory factor analysis (e.g., Joreskog, 1974; Werts & Linn, 1970) and its variants (e.g., Anderson, 1987; Marsh & Hocevar, 1988). These techniques assume the availability of multiple instruments for measuring the construct of interest. Sekerka, Bagozzi, and Charnigo (2009) applied some of these techniques to ascertain the construct validity of two complementary instruments for PMC, one based on themes from critical incident interviews (Flanagan, 1982) and the other derived from an examination of related literature.

Instrument Reliability

Besides validity, another fundamental attribute for an instrument is reliability. In fact, some authors (e.g., Cook & Beckman, 2006) maintain that validity is impossible without it. Reliability pertains to the precision, rather than the accuracy, of measurement. More specifically, Cook and Beckman (2006) describe reliability as the (preferably high) correlation between subjects' scores on two administrations of the same instrument. In practice, this correlation may be approximated by the correlation between the subject's subtotal score on one half of the instrument's items and the subject's subtotal score on the other half. However, such an approximation admits an ambiguity because there are many ways in which an instrument's items may be separated into halves. Cronbach's (1951) alpha circumvents this ambiguity by considering the average correlation computed over all possible divisions of an instrument into halves (cf., Cortina, 1993). To distinguish reliability as described by Cook and Beckman (2006) from Cronbach's alpha, some people refer to the former as *test-retest reliability* and to the latter as *internal consistency* (DeVellis, 2012).

Cronbach's (1951) alpha is very sensitive to the number of items in an instrument, such that scales with only three or four items may have surprisingly low values of alpha. That said, low values of alpha may also signal one of two problems. First, a collection of items may be measuring more than one construct. This possibility may be investigated empirically via exploratory factor analysis (DeVellis, 2012); the results may provide guidance on how to best partition a scale into subscales, each of which measures a single construct. Second, some items may be misinterpreted by a large proportion of respondents. For instance, Sekerka, Bagozzi, and Charnigo (2009) found that many respondents were confused by reverse-coded items (i.e., statements containing words such as "no" or "not"). Ultimately, these authors recommended that users of their PMC scales omit or alter the reverse-coded items.

Designing the Assessment Study

After valid and reliable instruments have been found (or created) to measure constructs along the theorized causal pathway, an empirical study may be conducted to assess the effects of the ethics training. There are several considerations for designing such a study, which we now discuss. We also refer the reader to other sources for additional guidance (Brewerton & Millward, 2001; Christensen, Johnson, & Turner, 2010; Stangor, 2010).

When individuals are administered instruments before and after participation in an ethics intervention, the changes in their scores on those instruments provide insight into the effects of their participation. Yet there are at least two difficulties with *change scores*. First, there is a possibility for temporal confounding: If an appreciable amount of time passes between the two administrations (before and after participation), then external factors unrelated to participation may affect participants' change scores. For instance, suppose that BEI is delivered to employees at a firm and that, between the first and second administrations, the organization's CEO receives a barrage of unfavorable publicity. In this case, employee morale may suffer from the negative media attention and cause the change scores to give a misleadingly bleak impression about BEI. This difficulty is largely avoided if the time interval between the two administrations is narrow. However, that imposes another limitation, namely the inability to perceive effects of participation that emerge gradually over a number of weeks or months.

Second, regardless of the time interval between the two administrations, there may be multiple reasons for favorable change scores. Individuals may (1) respond because they are aware that they are being studied, (2) benefit from the receipt of attention but not from the specific content of the intervention, or (3) benefit from the specific content of the intervention. The distinction between reasons (1) and (2) is subtle, relating to whether a participant consciously wishes to positively impress those conducting the study; however, the term "Hawthorne effect" may be used in either case. Reason (3), on the other hand, is what those conducting the study ultimately hope to conclude.

One way to parse explanations (1) and (2) from (3) is to use a control group that receives some other form of training. If individuals engaged in the intervention of interest have appreciably better change scores versus individuals engaged in the other form of training, then explanation (3) becomes more plausible. In addition, the presence of a control group mitigates temporal confounding, since external factors will ordinarily affect the control group as well. However, the possibility of a facilitator effect still remains. For example, if the facilitator for the intervention of interest is better prepared, inherently more skilled, or generally more likeable than the facilitator for the other form of training, then a more favorable assessment of the intervention may have more to do with the facilitator than the training itself. Therefore, having the same facilitator for the control group may be appropriate.

Assuming that a control group is included, care must be taken in deciding which individuals receive the intervention versus take part in the control group. Making these assignments randomly rather than by convenience reduces the risk that the two groups are significantly imbalanced on characteristics associated with individuals' scores. For instance, suppose that a study involves employees in the marketing and research/development departments of a company. Assigning the marketing employees to receive the ethics intervention and the research/development employees to the control group may be convenient. However, if the marketing employees are generally more extroverted than those in research/development, one may not be certain whether differences observed between the groups are attributable to the mode of training or to differences in personality. Such difficulties may be avoided, in this instance, by randomizing half of each department's employees to each group. In addition, combining stratification with randomization is sometimes helpful. For instance, suppose that the marketing department has 40 employees, 20 of each gender. Randomly assigning half of the 40 employees to the intervention of interest does not guarantee that the resulting groups will be balanced on gender; a significant imbalance between groups is unlikely but not impossible. However, such an imbalance may be avoided with certainty by randomizing 10 female and 10 male marketing employees to the intervention of interest.

As described, some participation effects may emerge over time. This suggests that some instruments, especially those measuring constructs further along the theorized causal pathway, should be administered more than once (e.g., immediately after the training, one week later, and one month later). While often difficult and costly, longitudinal studies have substantial benefits that are recognized within the field of organizational development (e.g., Avey, Luthans, & Mhatre, 2008). For example, besides addressing the possibility of gradually appearing participation effects, longitudinal studies can identify situations in which skills are learned quickly but also decay rapidly over time. If such situations are identified, then appropriate actions can be implemented, such as providing refresher training (Salas et al., 2012).

A standing issue with a control group in organizational settings is that management is rarely inclined to allot time and resources to a form of training other than the intervention of interest. Yet merely having some employees receive no intervention and calling that a "control group" is problematic because the Hawthorne effect cannot then be ruled out. One way for practitioners to overcome management's concerns about time and resources is to identify two interventions of interest rather than one and then put them up for a head-to-head comparison. In this way, the second intervention serves as a control for the first intervention, and vice versa.

Finally, the concept of statistical power is a concern for any empirical study: What is the likelihood that an intervention effect will actually be detected via the statistical modeling and analysis? This relates to both the magnitude of the intervention effect (often called the "effect size") and the number of participants in the study. An intervention that dramatically improves target outcomes is likely to be distinguished from a control condition, even with a small number of participants. An intervention that only subtly improves target outcomes is unlikely to be distinguished from a control condition, unless the number of participants is quite large. Although there may be difficulties in increasing the number of participants beyond a certain threshold in an organizational setting (e.g., one cannot recruit 100 participants from a firm that employs 50 people), consulting a statistician regarding power is always advisable.

Statistical Modeling and Analysis

Using data from an empirical study with a group receiving the intervention of interest and a control group, one can readily perform a T test of whether the intervention group mean is significantly different from the control group mean on a particular instrument; a "yes" to this question suggests that the group means also differ on the underlying construct. Likewise, one can readily perform T tests of whether there are significant correlations between two particular instruments among intervention participants and among control participants, respectively; a "yes" suggests that the two underlying constructs are also correlated. However, if one wishes to empirically examine all links in the theorized causal pathway using a single statistical model, then one needs methodology more sophisticated than the aforementioned T tests. A structural equation model is often appropriate (e.g., Bollen & Long, 1993; Hoyle, 1995; Kline, 2010).

A structural equation model simultaneously quantifies the relationships among constructs in a theorized causal pathway (depicted by arrows in Figure 7.1) as well as the relationships between each construct and its corresponding instruments. Readers familiar with linear regression modeling may relate it to structural equation modeling by noting two key differences. First, linear regression modeling does not distinguish between construct and instrument; in effect, zero measurement error is assumed. Second, each variable in linear regression modeling is unambiguously regarded as either an independent variable or a dependent variable; no variable would both "send" and "receive" an arrow in a theorized causal pathway. Thus, linear regression modeling may be considered a special, simple case of structural equation modeling. Or, put differently, structural equation modeling is an extension of linear regression modeling. Indeed, structural equation modeling provides great flexibility compared to linear regression modeling. In particular, multiple instruments may be (and often are) used to measure a given construct. For example, if PMC were a target outcome, then one might use both established scales (one based on critical incident interviews and one derived from related literature) to measure this construct (Sekerka, Bagozzi, & Charnigo, 2009). Moreover, a structural equation model can accommodate repeated measurements of the same construct at different time points and can even permit reciprocal relationships (e.g., Huddleston-Casas, Charnigo, & Simmons, 2009; Simmons, Braun, Charnigo, Havens, & Wright, 2008). For instance, ethical decision making immediately after participation in an intervention may influence the desire to act ethically one week later, which in turn may influence ethical decision making at one month after participation.

Software implementing structural equation modeling reports estimates of parameters describing the relationships among constructs and of parameters representing the relationships between each construct and its corresponding instruments. These parameter estimates are accompanied by p-values indicating statistical significance or lack thereof. The p-values are primarily of interest for examining associations among constructs, as a statistically significant association between a construct and a valid instrument for that construct is fully expected. Besides reporting parameter estimates, software for structural equation modeling presents various *goodness of fit* statistics. These may include a chi-square statistic, the root mean square error of approximation, and the comparative fit index, among others (e.g., Bollen & Long, 1993; Hoyle, 1995; Kline, 2010). The goodness of fit statistics help the data analyst to judge whether the data are faithfully portrayed by the structural equation model. Sometimes the data are not faithfully portrayed because of unrealistic technical assumptions (e.g., measurement error on one instrument is uncorrelated with that on another instrument), in which case a remedy may be to modify the technical assumptions. However, weak goodness of fit statistics that cannot be improved by modifying the technical assumptions may indicate that the theorized causal pathway itself requires refinement. Thus, examining not only the parameter estimates and p-values but also the goodness of fit statistics is important in structural equation modeling.

We refer the reader to the texts cited above for more information on structural equation modeling. Also, we note that Charnigo, Kryscio, Bardo, Lynam, and Zimmerman (2011) have reviewed three other statistical methods for analyzing behavioral data collected repeatedly over time: generalized linear mixed modeling, group-based trajectory modeling, and latent growth curve modeling. We do not describe these three methods in detail here, but we do offer a few comments. The first two methods are geared toward data analyses emphasizing objective outcomes (e.g., number of alcoholic beverages consumed among college students, in that paper's context of substance abuse prevention and intervention). As suggested by our earlier remarks on criterion validity, one may not be able to rely (at least not solely) on objective outcomes for evaluating ethical performance. Thus, the last of the three methods, which (like structural equation modeling) distinguishes between a construct and an instrument, is most potentially relevant to assessing an ethics intervention. What distinguishes latent growth curve modeling from structural equation modeling is that the former explicitly represents the mean level of a construct as a mathematical function of time. Estimating such a function entails having each participant complete instruments on several occasions (not just two or three), which an organization may or may not be prepared to do even if that organization wishes to assess an ethics intervention.

DISCUSSION

Having considered a variety of measurement and methodological issues, we now provide recommendations for conducting empirical studies to assess the effectiveness of organizational training programs. Our suggestions are not limited to the acquisition and analysis of data from intervention participants; our recommendations also encompass the groundwork of formulating the intervention process itself, proposing a theorized causal pathway, and finding (or developing) instruments to measure constructs on this pathway.

To begin with, those conducting an empirical study in the workplace must carefully define the target population, from which they will draw a sample of employees and to which they wish their results to generalize. This definition includes recognizing the job, function, organization, and/or industry of the employees. For example, they may be line managers or executives, employees at a Fortune 500 company or in a healthcare organization, or people representing a particular profession (e.g., accountants) rather than a specific firm. The choice of target population has clear implications for establishing a theorized causal pathway and instrument selection. One would not use a scale with an item asking managers about the pressure they felt from physicians, nor would one inquire of nurses how high-ranking government officials affected their morale. One might consider using scales that were sufficiently neutral in their wording to be potentially applicable to several different target populations. However, an overly generic instrument might not be as valid or reliable as a specifically focused one.

Once a target population has been chosen, both the formulation of a theorized causal pathway (including specification of target outcomes) and selection or development of instruments should entail input from subject matter experts and perhaps even members of the target population. In this regard, conducting focus groups is a useful tool for researchers and practitioners alike. Candid and open discussions provide valuable insights both for creating effective interventions and for assessing them. Focus groups can also help to establish buy-in to the ethics training effort. This can be especially important in settings where organizational-level attitudes heavily influence employees' motivation to learn (cf., Salas et al., 2012).

The involvement of a statistician and/or psychometrician to ensure the validity and reliability of the scales (if newly created or not previously applied to the target population) is highly recommended. We emphasize that work to ensure the validity and reliability of the scales is not itself part of the empirical study assessing an ethics intervention. Rather, such work is a prerequisite for conducting the study. However, even with instruments well suited to measuring the relevant constructs, care must be taken in other aspects of study design. In particular, temporal confounding can arise if external factors sway the target outcomes between pre- and post-intervention assessments. Additionally, subjects may respond to an intervention not because of its specific content but because they are participating in a study. Having a control group, preferably one engaged in another form of ethics training, is therefore important. Moreover, random assignment to the intervention group versus the control group is essential; otherwise subjects may be imbalanced *a priori* on characteristics related to the target outcomes. Even with randomization, an unintended bias may arise if facilitators have different capabilities or styles, so that having the same person serve as facilitator for both the intervention group and the control group may be appropriate.

A statistician and/or psychometrician can play a valuable role in helping to design the empirical study and analyze the resulting data. While a T test can be performed to compare intervention and control groups on their mean scores for any given instrument, empirically examining the links in the theorized causal pathway will generally warrant a more sophisticated analytic strategy. Structural equation modeling permits comparisons between groups and, in particular, allows estimation of direct and indirect effects of an intervention on target outcomes. This analytic strategy takes into account that multiple scales may be used to measure the same construct at a particular time and accommodates repeated measurements of the same construct at multiple time points. The latter feature is salient because some effects of ethics training may manifest gradually, while others may be transient.

CONCLUSION

We see a variety of avenues for future research on ethics training and its assessment. One is to determine whether and how processes like BEI impact ethical decision making. In terms of cause and effect, what constructs mediate the influence of the training process on ethical decision making? How large is the impact of this training process on ethical decision making? Does this impact appear immediately or emerge gradually? A broader, yet related, issue is to better understand the influence of an intervention on employees' perceived versus actual behaviors. Multiple studies will be required to address all of these questions, not merely because there are several of them but also because the answers may vary across populations.

To discover whether and how an intervention affects target outcomes, one must confront a variety of methodological issues. Attending to these issues in an informed and thorough manner will yield more useful organizational knowledge. In particular, carefully conducted intervention research is far preferable to simply assuming that a theorized causal pathway is correct. Indeed, the expectation that a training activity will favorably affect ethical decision-making is a hypothesis that should be tested empirically.

Without such a test, an ineffective training activity may be continued indefinitely; this not only wastes precious resources but may also preclude the implementation of a more effective program. Forethought and planning can make the application of organizational resources toward ethics training a much wiser investment.

Future scholarship should also address the implications of how empirical studies in organizational settings are designed. For example, a practitioner can conduct two parallel empirical studies on an intervention of interest, one study designed without focus group input and the other with such input. Here, the empirical study without focus group input essentially serves as a control for the empirical study with such input. Note that the question here is not whether focus group input improves an intervention (although that, too, is a worthy topic for future scholarship) but rather whether the process of assessing the intervention is enhanced by focus group input.

Finally, there are opportunities for statisticians to improve upon structural equation modeling as well as statistical methodology more generally, especially regarding the relaxation of technical assumptions that may not be upheld in practice. The statisticians' efforts must go beyond strictly mathematical justifications for their proposals to furnishing practitioners with user-friendly tools that capture methodological improvements. For example, structural equation modeling software accommodating non-random patterns of missing data would potentially increase practitioners' confidence in their conclusions regarding the effectiveness of ethics interventions.

Implications and Takeaways

Having considered the challenges associated with ethics training and its assessment, we close this chapter with several key takeaways:

1. Process techniques need to be designed that address the needs of adult learners and engage participants in ways that link ethics to their own personal experiences.
2. Management learning can be particularly effective when both positive and negative workplace experiences are tapped, generating change and development from strength- and deficit-based inquiry.
3. Assessing intervention effectiveness is not only of interest to researchers but also of vital importance to practitioners and managers who want to create positive organizational ethics change and development.
4. An ethics intervention needs to be grounded in theory. This entails careful consideration of what is expected of or desired from participants. Identifying specific learning objectives is essential, as is mapping them to carefully chosen constructs.

5. Once valid and reliable instruments are identified to measure constructs, an empirical study should be designed to assess the influence of the training on target outcomes.
6. The presence of a control group and a longitudinal structure are key considerations for designing an empirical study from which sound conclusions may be reached regarding positive organizational ethics change and development.
7. Appropriate statistical methods (e.g., structural equation modeling) can help to establish whether and how an intervention impacts target outcomes, including core elements of ethical behavior such as the desire to act ethically.

Our discussion has highlighted key issues and presented specific suggestions to promote more effective ethics interventions and future research about them. Perhaps most importantly, we have described the nature and importance of careful processes for developing and assessing ethics interventions. Ultimately, our hope is that these suggestions and descriptions will help managers to more effectively train employees for ethical action in the workplace. The opening quote of this chapter, suggesting that "we are what we measure" (Ariely, 2010), reminds us that where we direct our inquiry helps to shape our reality. Perhaps paying more attention to developing and assessing ethics training in organizational settings will help to create a world in which business and ethics are truly integrated.

REFERENCES

Ajuwon, A. J., & Kass, N. (2008). Outcome of a research ethics training workshop among clinicians and scientists at a Nigerian university. *BMC Medical Ethics, 9*(1). doi:10.1186/1472-6939-9-1

Anderson, J. C. (1987). An approach for confirmatory measurement and structural equation modeling of organizational properties. *Management Science, 33*(4), 525–541.

Ariely, D. (2010). You are what you measure. *Harvard Business Review,* June. Retrieved on June 1, 2012 from: http://hbr.org/2010/06/column-you-are-what-you-measure/ar/1

Ashkanasy, N. M., Windsor, C. A., & Trevino, L. (2006). Bad apples and bad barrels revisited: Cognitive moral reasoning, just world beliefs, rewards and ethical decision-making. *Business Ethics Quarterly, 16*(4), 449–473.

Avey, J. B., Luthans, F., & Mhatre, K. H. (2008). A call for longitudinal research in positive organizational behavior. *Journal of Organizational Behavior, 29*(5), 705–711.

Bagozzi, R. P. (1993). Assessing construct validity in personality research: Applications to measures of self-esteem. *Journal of Research in Personality, 27*(1), 49–87.

Bagozzi, R. P., Yi, Y., & Phillips, L. W. (1991). Assessing construct validity in organizational research. *Administrative Science Quarterly, 36*(3), 421–458.

Bollen, K. A., & Long, J. S. (Eds.). (1993). *Testing structural equation models.* Thousand Oaks, CA: Sage.

Brewerton, P., & Millward, L. (2001). *Organizational research methods: A guide for students and researchers.* London, UK: Sage Publications.

Brookfield, S. D. (1986). *Understanding and facilitating adult learning.* San Francisco, CA: Jossey-Bass.

Campbell, D. T., & Fiske, D. W. (1959). Convergent and discriminant validation by the multitrait-multimethod matrix. *Psychological Bulletin, 56*(2), 81–105.

Charnigo, R., Kryscio, R., Bardo, M., Lynam, D., & Zimmerman, R. (2011). Joint modeling of longitudinal data in multiple behavioral change. *Evaluation and the Health Professions, 34*(2), 181–200.

Christensen, L. B., Johnson, R. B., & Turner, L. A. (2010). *Research methods, design, and analysis* (11th ed.). Boston, MA: Pearson.

Cook, D. A., & Beckman, T. J. (2006). Current concepts in validity and reliability for psychometric instruments: Theory and application. *American Journal of Medicine, 119*(2), 166.e7–166.e16.

Cortina, J. M. (1993). What is coefficient alpha? An examination of theory and applications. *Journal of Applied Psychology, 78*(1), 98–104.

Cronbach, L. J. (1951). Coefficient alpha and the internal structure of tests. *Psychometrika, 16*(3), 297–334.

Cronbach, L. J., & Meehl, P. E. (1955). Construct validity in psychological tests. *Psychological Bulletin, 52*(4), 281–302.

Delaney, J. T., & Sockell, D. (1992). Do company ethics training programs make a difference? An empirical analysis. *Journal of Business Ethics, 11*(9), 719–727.

DeVellis, R. F. (2012). *Scale development: Theory and applications* (3rd ed.). Thousand Oaks, CA: Sage.

Flanagan, J. C. (1982). The critical incident technique. In R. Zemke & T. Kramlinger (Eds.), *Figuring things out: A trainer's guide to needs and task analysis* (pp. 277–317). Reading, MA: Addison-Wesley.

Granitz, N.A. (2003). Individual, social, and organizational sources of sharing and variation in the ethical reasoning of managers. *Journal of Business Ethics, 42*(2), 101–124.

Hoyle, R. (Ed.). (1995). *Structural equation modeling: Concepts, issues, and applications.* Thousand Oaks, CA: Sage.

Huddleston-Casas, C., Charnigo, R., & Simmons, L. A. (2009). Food insecurity and maternal depression in rural, low-income families: A longitudinal investigation. *Public Health Nutrition, 12*(8), 1133–1140.

Joreskog, K. G. (1974). Analyzing psychological data by structural analysis of covariance matrices. In R. C. Atkinson, D. H. Krantz, R. D. Luce, & P. Suppes (Eds.), *Contemporary developments in mathematical psychology* (Vol. II, pp. 1–56). San Francisco, CA: W. H. Freeman.

Kashdan, T. B., & Fincham, F. D. (2004). Facilitating curiosity: A social and self-regulatory perspective for scientifically based interventions. In P. A. Linley & S. Joseph (Eds.), *Positive psychology in practice* (pp. 482–503). Hoboken, NJ: John Wiley & Sons.

Kashdan, T. B., Rose, P., & Fincham, F. D. (2004). Curiosity and exploration: Facilitating positive subjective experiences and personal growth opportunities. *Journal of Personality Assessment, 82*(3), 291–305.

Kelly, M., Bernstein, S., & Kipp, B. (2012). *Broader perspectives; Higher performance. State of compliance: 2012 study.* PwC and Haymarket Media Inc. Retrieved from http://www.pwc.com/en_us/us/risk-management/assets/2012-compliance-study.pdf

Kim, S. (2011). Development and initial psychometric evaluation of nurses' ethical decisionmaking around end-of-life-care scale in Korea. *Journal of Hospice and Palliative Nursing, 13*(2), 97–105.

Kline, R. B. (2010). *Principles and practice of structural equation modeling* (3rd ed.). New York, NY: Guilford Press.

Knowles, M. S. (1968). Andragogy, not pedagogy. *Adult Leadership, 16*(10), 350–352, 386.

Knowles, M. S. (1980). *The modern practice of adult education: From pedagogy to andragogy.* Englewood Cliffs, NJ: Prentice Hall/Cambridge.

Kolb, D. A. (1984). *Experiential learning: Experience as the source of learning and development.* Englewood Cliffs, NJ: Prentice Hall.

Laditka, S. B., & Houck, M. M. (2006). Student-developed case studies: An experiential approach for teaching ethics in management. *Journal of Business Ethics, 64*(2), 157–167.

Lawshe, C. H. (1975). A quantitative approach to content validity. *Personnel Psychology, 28*(4), 563–575.

LeClair, D. T., & Ferrell, L. (2000). Innovation in experiential business ethics training. *Journal of Business Ethics, 23*(3), 313–322.

Marsh, H. W., & Hocevar, D. (1988). A new, more powerful approach to multitrait-multimethod analyses: Application of second-order confirmatory factor analysis. *Journal of Applied Psychology, 73*(1), 107–117.

Mayrath, M. C., Clarke-Midura, J., Robinson, D. H., & Schraw, G. (Eds.). (2012). *Technology-based assessments for 21st century skills: Theoretical and practical implications from modern research.* Charlotte, NC: Information Age Publishing.

Merriam, S. B. (2001). Andragogy and self-directed learning: Pillars of adult learning theory. *New Directions for Adult and Continuing Education, 2001*(89), 3–14.

Mumford, M. D., Devenport, L. D., Brown, R. P., Connelly, S., Murphy, S. T., Hill, J. H., & Antes, A. L. (2006). Validation of ethical decision-making measures: Evidence for a new set of measures. *Ethics and Behavior, 16*(4), 319–345.

Nunnally, J. C., & Bernstein, I. H. (1994). *Psychometric theory* (3rd ed.). New York, NY: McGraw-Hill.

Rest, J. (1986). *Moral development: Advances in research and theory.* New York, NY: Praeger Press.

Rust, J., & Golombok, S. (2008). *Modern psychometrics: The science of psychological assessment* (3rd ed.). London, UK: Routledge.

Ryan, R. M. (1982). Control and information in the interpersonal sphere: An extension of cognitive evaluation theory. *Journal of Personality and Social Psychology, 43*(3), 450–461.

Ryan, R. M., & Riordan, C. M. (2000). The development of a measure of desired moral approbation. *Educational and Psychological Measurement, 60*(3), 448–462.

Salas, E., Tannenbaum, S. I., Kraiger K., & Smith-Jentsch, K. A. (2012). The science of training and development in organizations: What matters in practice. *Psychological Science in the Public Interest, 13*(2), 74–101.

Sanyal, R. N. (2000). An experiential approach to teaching ethics in international business. *Teaching Business Ethics, 4*(2), 137–149.

Sekerka, L. E. (2009). Organizational ethics education and training: A review of best practices and their application. *International Journal of Training and Development, 13*(2), 77–95.

Sekerka, L. E. (2012). Compliance as a subtle precursor to ethical corrosion: A strength-based approach as a way forward. *Wyoming Law Review, 12*(2), 277–302.

Sekerka, L. E., & Bagozzi, R. P. (2007). Moral courage in the workplace: Moving to and from the desire and decision to act. *Business Ethics: A European Review, 16*(2), 132–142.

Sekerka, L. E., Bagozzi, R. P., & Charnigo, R. (2009). Facing ethical challenges in the workplace: Conceptualizing and measuring professional moral courage. *Journal of Business Ethics, 89*(4), 565–579.

Sekerka, L. E., Brumbaugh, A., Rosa, J., & Cooperrider, D. (2006). Comparing Appreciative Inquiry to a diagnostic technique in organizational change: The moderating effects of gender. *International Journal of Organization Theory and Behavior, 9*(4), 449–489.

Sekerka, L. E., & Godwin, L. (2010). Strengthening professional moral courage: A balanced approach to ethics training. *Training and Management Development Methods, 24*(5), 63–74.

Sekerka, L. E., Godwin, L., & Charnigo, R. (2012). Use of Balanced Experiential Inquiry to build ethical strength in the workplace. *Journal of Management Development, 31*(3), 275–286.

Sekerka, L. E., McCarthy, J. D., & Bagozzi, R. P. (2011). Developing professional moral courage: Leadership lessons from everyday ethical challenges in today's military. In D. R. Comer & G. Vega (Eds.), *Moral courage in organizations: Doing the right thing at work* (pp. 130–141). Armonk, NY: M. E. Sharpe.

Sekerka, L. E., & Zolin, R. (2007). Rule bending: Can prudential judgment affect rule compliance and values in the workplace? *Public Integrity, 9*(3), 225–244.

Sekerka, L. E., Zolin, R., & Goosby Smith, J. (2009). Careful what you ask for: How inquiry strategy influences readiness mode. *Organization Management Journal, 6*, 106–122.

Simmons, L. A., Braun, B., Charnigo, R., Havens, J. R., & Wright, D. W. (2008). Depression and poverty among rural women: A relationship of social causation or social selection? *Journal of Rural Health, 24*(3), 292–298.

Singhapakdi, A., Vitell, S. J., Rallapalli, K. C., & Kraft, K. L. (1996). The perceived role of ethics and social responsibility: A scale development. *Journal of Business Ethics, 15*(11), 1131–1140.

Stangor, C. (2010). *Research methods for the behavioral sciences* (4th ed.). Belmont, CA: Wadsworth.

Tenbrunsel, A. (1998). Misrepresentation and expectations of misrepresentation in an ethical dilemma: The role of incentives and temptation. *Academy of Management Journal, 41*(3), 330–339.

Turker, D. (2009). Measuring corporate social responsibility: A scale development study. *Journal of Business Ethics, 85*(4), 411–427.

Vogt, D., King, D., & King, L. (2004). Focus groups in psychological assessment: Enhancing content validity by consulting members of the target population. *Psychological Assessment, 16*(3), 231–243.

Watson, D., & Clark, L. A. (1999). *The PANAS-X: Manual for the Positive and Negative Affect Schedule–Expanded Form* (Revised edition). Unpublished manuscript, University of Iowa, Iowa City. Retrieved from http://ir.uiowa.edu/psychology_pubs/11/

Weick, K. E. (1995). *Sensemaking in organizations.* Thousand Oaks, CA: Sage Publications.

Werts, C. E., & Linn, R. L. (1970). Path analysis: Psychological examples. *Psychological Bulletin, 74*(3), 193–212.

CHAPTER 8

GIVING VOICE TO VALUES IN THE WORKPLACE

A Practical Approach to Building Moral Competence

Mary Gentile

Few business leaders would argue with the proposition that their companies need employees at all levels who are responsible, ethical, and who adhere to the organization's values, policies, and mission statement. This is especially true in the current climate of frequent corporate scandals, financial crises, and ever-growing consumer and investor mistrust. And yet, the time and resources invested in this outcome are often tightly constrained, and the impact of, and return on, even this minimal investment are often hotly debated.

Typically, organizations try to operationalize their commitment to ethics and values by means of a variety of strategies: recruitment screening efforts; corporate communications directed at both internal and external stakeholders; the creation or outsourcing of anonymous tip-lines and ombudsperson resources; internal training programs; establishment of ethics and compliance

Ethics Training in Action, pages 167–182
Copyright © 2014 by Information Age Publishing
All rights of reproduction in any form reserved.

officer positions and networks, sometimes reporting to the General Counsel office and sometimes reporting directly to the CEO or a dedicated board committee (reporting lines being another hotly debated question).

Most of these strategies focus upon trying to avoid bringing less than ethical individuals into the organization, or on identifying and dealing with them and the potential fall-out from their actions, once they are there. Training and communication initiatives are the only company investments that are aimed specifically at helping employees, at all levels, to understand what is acceptable behavior and, ideally, to help them to act on that knowledge when it is challenged. However, it is not unusual for major corporations to require only an hour or so of ethics and compliance training per year per employee, and often ethics training is satisfied through "online" courses provided by outside vendors, with limited customization.

This reality highlights the major challenges, for both individual managers and for organizations, around efforts to prepare oneself and other managers for values-driven leadership and ethical behavior in the workplace:

- Time—Dedicated training time around these issues is extremely limited, and even when it does exist, employees may not recognize the return on their investment. Too often they feel this is a kind of empty exercise that, at best, does not necessarily help them to meet the demands put upon them, and, at worst, is a distraction.
- Consistency—It is one thing to communicate about the importance of adhering to codes of conduct and regulatory/legal requirements in an ethics course, but when the pressures on a daily basis are toward short-term profit and maximizing quarterly returns, these messages can seem inconsistent or even hypocritical.
- Source—Training and communication programs are often delivered online or by trainers who do not have regular contact with employees and who don't necessarily understand the personalities, needs, and pressures of the employees. Messages from direct peers and managers will therefore tend to trump, whether they are in line with the ethics training content or not.
- Relevance—Communicating the rules and policies is important and helping employees decide whether a particular action is "over the line or not" is unquestionably important. However, it does not necessarily help employees to know what to say and how to say it, in order to ensure that the "right thing" is done without damaging key working relationships and while still achieving their work objectives.
- Impact—It is difficult to assess the impact of ethics training initiatives. Does a deeper knowledge of the rules and policies lead directly to better compliance? Can people's behavior really be changed through ethics training, and is that the goal? And if incidences of

reported misconduct go up, does that mean that the programs have failed, or does it mean that more employees are taking the rules more seriously and reporting problems?

These are some of the primary and ubiquitous challenges of organizational ethics training. They are ubiquitous because they are based in some all-too-familiar assumptions about the purpose and approach to ethics and compliance training that restrain and constrain organizational responses: assumptions about *what* is being taught, *who* is being taught; and *how* to teach them. However, by flipping or reversing these typical assumptions, managers can get out of this box. A new and innovative approach to values-driven leadership development, "Giving Voice to Values," has done just that; it tests many of the key assumptions around ethics education and in so doing can reenergize and revamp organizational and individual managers' approach to this challenge.

"GIVING VOICE TO VALUES"

The "Giving Voice To Values"[1] (Gentile, 2010a) curriculum and pedagogy is housed and supported by Babson College, and was developed with the Aspen Institute Business and Society Program as incubator and as founding partner, along with the Yale School of Management. Drawing on both the actual experience of business practitioners as well as cutting-edge social science and management research, "Giving Voice to Values" (GVV) fills a longstanding and critical gap in business training and education. It helps employees and students identify the many ways that individuals can and already do voice their values in the workplace, and it provides the opportunity to script and practice this voice in front of their peers. GVV has been piloted in hundreds of educational and executive settings and/or courses on all seven continents including Antarctica. In the following pages, the GVV approach will be explained, and learnings from companies who have begun to pilot it or to consider doing so will be shared.

THE FIRST "FLIP"

So just how does GVV reverse or flip some of the central assumptions behind ethical training and education? First, consider the traditional focus on *what* to teach employees.

Often when the subject of ethics comes up, someone will say: "You know, the clear-cut, right/wrong issues are easy. It's the grey issues, the complex issues—the ones that appear to be wrong vs. wrong or right vs. right—where ethics training really needs to provide some guidance." And it's true, many ethical challenges are quite complex. But the response to this comment is often to focus ethics training only or primarily on these thorny ethical dilemmas, or even worse, to present more clear-cut scenarios in such a way as to invite respondents to find complexity and ambiguity there, even when it should not exist.

For example, a training case may present an employee who is asked for a bribe in order to secure needed operating licenses and doesn't know what to do. The discussion of the scenario will often focus on questions like: "Well, is this *really* a bribe, or could it be considered some sort of facilitating fee?" or "Does the employee have the information needed to determine what is going on?" or "Isn't this just the way business is done in this industry or this geographic location, and perhaps there is no realistic alternative?" or "Does management want the employee to just look the other way?" or "If the employee says 'no,' won't the company's competitors just step in and pay the bribe?" The discussion becomes one of rehearsing all the reasons why the situation is unclear and why it is so very difficult and personally risky or even futile to try to address it. There are the so-called "preemptive rationalizations" that prevent employees from even getting to the discussion of how they might avoid the bribe. Nevertheless, somehow the employee is supposed to leave this training discussion emboldened to just step up and "speak truth to power," regardless of the concern that it might be a so-called career-limiting move.

A situation like the one above is somehow presented as one of those thorny ethical dilemmas, when it is actually not so grey. It is fairly clear that the situation is, in fact, about bribery. The dilemma is not one of ethics but rather one of implementation. For this reason, the "Giving Voice to Values" approach would present the scenarios differently. Using GVV, the cases shared are typically the so-called "black-and-white" or clear-cut choices, and the protagonists in the scenarios have already decided what they believe is the right thing to do. The discussion is no longer about *whether* the situation is over the line or not; instead, the discussion *starts* from that position and is framed as an action-planning and scripting exercise. Rather than literally "rehearsing" how to rationalize the less-than-ethical position, GVV starts from the premise that it will be appropriately addressed and focuses the training on that outcome.

This is not to say that true ethical dilemmas do not exist. Sometimes one really does have to struggle to figure out what the most appropriate and responsible course of action may be. But in such cases, it is clear that reasonable and intelligent people of good will can legitimately disagree. It is, on the other hand, in addressing the more clear-cut issues where employee training can make a significant impact. After all, most of the high-profile scandals that hit the front pages of the business press and that lead to an erosion in public trust are, in fact, those more "black-and-white" violations—cases of outright fraud and illegality.

So the first GVV "flip" is one of focus: the idea is to focus training on the clear violations more than on the ambiguous ones. After all, if employees become more skillful and confident in identifying, talking about, and effectively addressing these clear issues, they are bound to be better prepared to address the "grey" issues as well.

THE SECOND "FLIP"

The second assumption of traditional business ethics training that GVV reverses concerns the identification of *who* the audience is. Typically, the target for ethics and compliance training is the employee whom the company fears may pose a threat to the company's ethics and violate the relevant laws or policies. The goal is to influence such employees through information about the rules and the potential consequences of transgression, through peer pressure, and through organizational influence.

The GVV approach, on the other hand, assumes a different audience and begins from the premise that employees can be mapped on a bell curve. Assume that those individuals who would self-identify as "opportunists"—defined as those who will always pursue their personal material self-interest, regardless of values—map onto one tail end of the bell curve. Similarly, assume that those individuals who self-identify as "idealists"—defined as those who will always try to act on their values, regardless of the impact on their material self-interest—map onto the other tail of the bell curve[2] (Dees & Crampton, 1991). Then assume that the majority of the body of employees would fall under the bell and characterize those individuals as "pragmatists"—identified as those who would like to act on their values, as long as that did not put them at a *systemic* disadvantage. That is not to say that they would only act on their values if they were absolutely certain they would succeed, or that they would not pay a price. It simply means that they think they have a chance to be successful, that the deck is not entirely stacked against them. This interpretation is consistent with the research that suggests that one of the most significant deterrents to ethical action within organizations is the concern that it will be futile (Detert, Burris, & Harrison, 2010).

Accepting this premised bell curve as a working hypothesis, GVV focuses not so much on the so-called "opportunists." Those are the individuals for whom the recruitment screening initiatives exist in order to try to avoid hiring them in the first place, and for whom the monitoring, reporting, and punishment systems are designed in order to deal with them if and when they do make their way into the organization. An hour of training per year, online or not, is not likely to change those individuals and, in fact, can sometimes simply feed their cynicism. And the GVV approach is less focused upon the idealists, except that its initiatives will help those individuals to become more effective at values-driven action. Rather, GVV defines its primary audience as the pragmatists, with the objective of providing them with the tools, the skills, and, importantly, the practice and rehearsal to be who they already want to be, at their best.

Framing the target audience in this way allows organizations to focus their training dollars and time on the audience and on the topics that are most likely to make a difference. And it presents ethics and compliance training less as the assertion of a set of prohibited actions, and more as an opportunity to build employee capacity for innovative and effective ethical action. It is about "can-do" more than it is about "thou-shalt-not." And as organizations that have begun to pilot this approach have seen, it is about building employee capacity for action and leadership around any sort of challenging situation, not exclusively ethical ones.

THE THIRD "FLIP"

The third assumption of traditional business ethics training that GVV reverses is about *how* organizations teach ethics. Typically training responds to this "how" question with a focus on preparing employees for ethical *decision making*: that is, communicating the rules, regulations and policies and then, as described above, inviting them to consider various scenarios in order to decide whether a certain behavior is "over the line" or not. The assumption is that employees need to learn to answer the question "What is the right thing to do?" Training is about communicating the information, practicing how employees think through these challenges, and emphasizing the importance of compliance (and the consequences of noncompliance) so that they can make the best choice.

The problem with this approach is that it assumes that information about the right thing to do and practice with making ethical decisions is all that the well-intended employee needs, but experience and research both tell us that this is not so. Otherwise ethical and responsible employees may fear the threat of retaliation or they may be concerned that their efforts to do the right thing will not only be risky for their own careers, but also ineffectual in the face of colleagues who would be willing to pick up where they say "no."

The challenge is not entirely about analysis and decision making. It is about figuring out how to get the right thing done, even when peers, customers, suppliers, or managers are pressuring one to do otherwise. And importantly, it is about rehearsing the scripts and action plans that are most likely to be effective, creating a sort of "ethical action default" and engaging with colleagues in directed peer coaching activities where the goal of the training activity is less about determining "what is right" but rather about working together to find the most creative and likely effective approaches to the seemingly risky challenge of acting responsibly and insuring ethical outcomes for the organization. In practicing this approach, GVV provides positive examples of times when employees have found effective ways to enact values-based choices and it offers tools for reframing choices and building effective and persuasive arguments, based upon decision-making patterns and biases garnered from behavioral science research (Gentile, 2010a, pp. 170–210).

THE "GVV THOUGHT EXPERIMENT"

This shift from a focus on information to a focus upon action is rooted in the "GVV Thought Experiment." That is, consider the typical ethics case scenario: A challenge is described, and the case ends with the question: "What would you do?" This question invites participants to take one of two approaches: either assume the role of the "good employee/student" and offer the answer the trainer is assumed to want to hear—that is, "I would do the right thing"—or play the devil's advocate (often framed as the realist) and talk about how it's not so clear or it's not so easy to comply with the rules. Either approach fuels a sort of cynicism in all but the most idealistic of the employees, and no one walks out of this session with ideas about how to address the situation ethically without metaphorically "falling on one's sword."

On the other hand, instead of asking "What would you do?" the GVV Thought Experiment poses the question: Starting from the premise that the case protagonist knows what he or she believes is right and wants to do it, how can they be most effective? What should they say, to whom, in what sequence, and in what context? What data should they gather first? What arguments and objections—the "reasons and rationalization" (Gentile, 2010a, pp. 170–210)—are they likely to encounter, and then how will they respond to those? And is this something they should do on their own, individual-to-individual, or is this the kind of situation that requires finding allies and collaboration? And so on.

Then the training activity is about working together with one's colleagues to develop the literal scripts and action plans that are most likely to succeed, and to engage in a peer coaching experience where employees share their best solutions and work together to make them even better. A template of questions is provided to approach each scenario:

- What is the values-driven position the protagonist wants to support?
- What is at risk for all parties involved, individual and organizational, internal and external to the organization, including the case protagonist?
- What are the predictable reasons and rationalizations—the objections or push-back—the protagonists are likely to encounter when they pursue their objectives? For example, some of the most commonly heard are: "This is standard operating procedure"; "It's not material"; "It's not my responsibility"; and "It may be wrong but I don't want to hurt my friend, my colleague, or my boss." Each of these is predictable and vulnerable to counter-arguments that can be rehearsed (Gentile, 2010b).
- What data, levers, arguments, responses will be most effective in response to these reasons and rationalizations?
- Craft the script and action plan that will be most successful in this situation.

After working together in small groups to address these questions, trainees then present their best approach to the larger group, which engages in a peer coaching activity, providing constructive feedback and input on how to improve the plan. In this way, all participants have the opportunity to craft, practice, and hear as many different approaches to the challenging situation as possible. They have the chance to think creatively, without the specter of appearing unrealistic or naïve, about just how one might get the right thing done in such situations. The idea is not to focus on those instances when the infraction has already occurred and when reporting (or even "whistle-blowing") is required by law or policy. The idea here is to focus on all the many moments and choices that occur prior to the choice to violate ethics or laws, in an effort to find ways to prevent ending up at that juncture. Finally and ideally, the scenario has a follow-up case (a "B" case, if you will) that details what the actual protagonist did in order to effectively resolve the situation, with the understanding that there may be many effective approaches depending on the specifics of the challenge.

And with this thought experiment, both the idealists and the opportunists, as well as and most importantly the pragmatists, have the occasion to work together to craft a practical and workable approach. They are not required to take an ethical stand, responding to the traditional question of "What would you do?" before they even believe there are actual and workable options for action. Instead they are invited to develop those options, and they are provided with tools and examples of how to do so, so that now the decision to comply with their own and the organization's values is experienced as a viable strategy.

HOW GVV ADDRESSES THE CHALLENGES
OF ORGANIZATIONAL ETHICS TRAINING

So given the reframing of the traditional ethics training described above, how does the GVV approach respond to the primary challenges organizations face in this arena?

Time

GVV helps to address this challenge in several ways. First of all, if one starts from the assumption that the allocation of training time dedicated to ethics and compliance will not change (an assumption that could be fruitfully challenged, however), it becomes even more critical that the limited time spent be focused on objectives that can be influenced in such a time frame and that cannot be achieved as well or better via more economical means (e.g., rules and policies can be shared via written and online communication channels, as opposed to formal presentation in training sessions.)

With regard to the first criteria above, it is highly unlikely that an individual who does not care about ethical compliance will be changed by an hour's worth of training on an annual basis. However, the sharing of positive examples and empowering stories, and, in particular, skill-building by means of the opportunity to focus upon the application of preexisting skills and capacities to ethical questions can be a productive endeavor for those pragmatists and idealists (described above) if approached properly.

For example, the impact of this type of training will be amplified if a standard approach (a template of questions and tools, as mentioned previously) is utilized that can become familiar and is easily referenced in other training programs and managerial conversations, whether or not the topic is ethics-related. For example, Lockheed Martin has been using the GVV approach, adapted for their own organizational challenges, since 2011 and they are now exploring ways to bring the standard action-planning template into their leadership training programs, as well as their ethics and compliance training (www.givingvoicetovalues.org).

Similarly, the GVV approach does not rely upon teaching an entirely new approach to decision-making (as for example, a more philosophical approach might do with its emphasis upon duties, rights, and consequences-based models of analysis). Instead it is about using the *same skills* that make employees successful in any other area of their activities: for example, data-based decision making, an understanding of effective modes of persuasion and influence, sensitivity to the individual needs and preferences of one's target audience, effective use of both quantitative and qualitative arguments, and so on. In this way, employees are being asked simply to frame values-based decisions as normal business decisions, rather than as some sort of different animal that requires an entirely new set of priorities and capabilities, thereby amplifying the impact of the time spent on this training (Gentile, 2010a, pp. 72–85).

Consistency

GVV can counter the perception of inconsistency or even hypocrisy regarding an organization's sincerity concerning its commitment to ethical behavior, because it goes beyond communicating the rules and policies. It offers the chance to examine positive examples of individuals who did, in fact, find ways to address ethical challenges effectively; however, these are regarded not as presentations of heroic action, but rather as displays of strategic solutions to normal business challenges. There is nothing wrong with heroism and moral courage, but when doing the right thing is framed as something that requires such Herculean levels of bravery, it begins to feel out of reach for many employees. Instead, one of the pillars of GVV is that this type of values conflict is a normal part of business dealings—a normal part of life, actually—so why not approach it as such? Bring the emotional level down a few notches. Recognize that the challenges in one's particular industry or one's particular functional area, whether it is accounting or marketing or operations, are fairly predictable and that one can prepare for them. Rather than aiming for a grandiose dose of moral courage, focus upon moral competence—a matter of skill and rehearsal that is more within one's reach.

When framed this way, as normal, it is easier to talk about the normal tensions around cost-saving, time pressures, pursuit of sales, and so on that can appear to be in conflict—at least short-term conflict—with ethics. Perceiving this conflict does not mean that one is unconcerned about ethics. It simply means that we need to think more creatively, more broadly, and more effectively about how to be both ethical and profitable. Often business leaders and business educators think that the way to address the perceived inconsistency between messages around profitability and messages around ethics is to argue the so-called "business case for responsible management": that is, to prove that managing responsibly and ethically is also financially rewarding.

GVV, on the other hand, starts from the observation that although one can point to organizations that have been financially successful while behaving ethically, one can also point to organizations that have been financially successful—at least in the short term—while behaving unethically. The way to address this perceived inconsistency is to focus, then, not on making the case for *why* one should behave ethically by arguing that it will be lucrative, but rather to focus on figuring out *how* one can be both ethical and profitable. Name the tension openly and honestly, and rather than arguing that ethics inherently leads to profit (obviously it does not, as there can be ethical firms that are ineffectively managed and do not thrive anyway), it is more credible to provide the opportunity to work collaboratively to figure out how to effectively achieve both outcomes.

Source

As noted previously, messages from peers and from managers/superiors will tend to trump the messages delivered by training professionals, especially if they are external contractors, or if the messages are delivered via standardized online training programs. Some companies address this issue by using a cascade model of delivery for ethics training, with senior managers training their own direct reports, starting at the top with the CEO and cascading on down the line. Lockheed Martin, for example, uses such an approach to deliver the award-winning GVV scenarios-based training mentioned above. However, such an approach can still be challenged if the senior managers who deliver the program are less than skillful, if they offer conflicting messages when they are not in "ethics training mode," and if the messages from those peer colleagues with whom employees have more regular contact are not in alignment.

GVV helps to address these concerns in several ways. In addition to the potential benefits of a cascade model of delivery if implemented well, GVV relies upon a peer coaching model. Through the pre-scripting exercises described above, employees have the opportunity to practice communicating with peers as they problem-solve for values-driven action, thereby making it less novel or potentially uncomfortable to talk about these issues from an implementation planning perspective when they work together outside the ethics training context. They have the chance to actually practice, or rehearse, this kind of process; they can come up with the actual words and ways of expressing these concerns in a "safe space"—the laboratory of the GVV thought experiment. Additionally, organizations can train their own internal ethics officers (if they have such a role), whether those are line or corporate positions, to use the GVV approach in order to become a network of GVV peer coaches, distributed across the company. In this way, other employees can approach these coaches not only to ask whether a particular action is over the line or not, but also to help them to find effective ways to address and hopefully prevent infractions before they happen.

Relevance

Employees often feel that ethics training is not that useful or effective because it is more about communicating and stressing the importance of the rules than about how to actually enact them. Obviously, the whole idea behind the GVV approach is to respond to this charge. In fact, one of the most common questions (or sometimes objections) to the GVV approach is the observation that it is more about how to be effective in communicating and persuading someone to do the right thing than it is about identifying the right thing. Guilty as charged! And it is precisely this shift in emphasis from analysis (i.e., determining what is right) to action (i.e., crafting effective ways to get the right thing done) that is the most effective response to the charge that ethics training is not "relevant." In fact, GVV is based on the premise that although doing the right thing may be its own reward, it is more desirable to find a way not just to stand up for what is right, but to do so effectively, influencing others along the way and finding strategies that can maximize positive impact. As noted above, it is an approach intended to appeal to pragmatists.

Impact

Perhaps one of the most difficult challenges for any sort of ethics training is to assess impact, or, put another way, return on investment. There are many reasons for this. For one thing, there are many different inputs that influence an individual's ethical behavior, and any attempt to measure the impacts of a single input will be confounded by the problem of distinguishing correlation from causality. That is, there is a lot of "noise" in the system and it is difficult to design a measure that will be able to separate out the impacts of the training activity from other factors. On the other hand, with the exception of pure testing of factual knowledge or skill level, this problem is true for most training that focuses upon or includes behavioral factors. In fact, this challenge may be one reason why so much ethics education focuses upon communicating the rules and testing one's memory of them. For example, how does one truly measure the impact of leadership development programs? Or, put another way, does successful completion of a marketing training program insure that all subsequent new product launches will succeed? In other words, it is useful to make sure that ethics training is not held to a higher standard than other educational initiatives.

These caveats understood, however, it is still important to make an attempt to assess whether what is being done in the arena of ethics training is worthwhile. GVV addresses this question at three levels. First, the approach itself is based upon existing empirical research from behavioral science as well as cognitive neuroscience, which demonstrates that how one frames an argument can make it feel more actionable and which suggests that rehearsal for action is an effective way to impact behavior (Gentile, 2010a). Second, increasingly as the approach has been used, there have been anecdotal reports of individuals who have encountered challenges, remembered the approaches, and applied them effectively. Third, some educators have begun to do pre- and post-course surveys to assess impacts. It is this third approach that provides some important input for managers who want to crack the impact measurement code. Instead of simply measuring input (e.g., How many employees completed the course? How many hours were dedicated to training? etc.) or measuring satisfaction (e.g., asking employees to rate the clarity, relevance, or effectiveness of the instructor and/or the course content), GVV raises the potential to ask questions such as:

- How many ways could you respond to the arguments that "This is just standard operating procedure" or "It's not material" when a colleague asks you to "cook the books" in order to increase the quarterly sales bonus? And what are they?
- What kinds of factors would be helpful to consider when you try to change your colleague's mind about exaggerating a new product's specifications?
- How might you be most effective in pushing back on your manager if he or she is pressuring you to understate the time and cost of a project in the written bid to a prospective customer?
- How confident do you feel that you would be able to craft an influential and effective action plan to avoid unethical behavior?

These types of questions—ones that assess the number and types of strategies, tactics, and arguments employees have available to them for addressing ethical challenges, as well as their felt levels of comfort with them—can be asked both pre- and post-training, to assess whether their skills and options have increased. This type of criteria is measurable and the completion of the assessment is a form of educational intervention in itself, thereby increasing the impact of the program.

RECOMMENDATIONS FOR GETTING STARTED

For those managers and organizations who want to get started using the GVV approach, there are several things to remember:

- GVV places the focus on *how* a manager raises values-based issues in an effective manner—what he/she needs to do to be heard and how to correct an existing course of action when necessary (rather than on arguments for *whether* or not it is necessary to do so in a particular situation).

- GVV emphasizes the inclusion of *positive examples* of times when people have found ways to voice and implement their values effectively in the workplace.
- GVV offers opportunities to construct and *practice effective and persuasive responses* to frequently heard "reasons and rationalizations" for not acting on one's values.
- GVV focuses on the development of skills in providing *peer feedback and coaching,*

Some initial action steps for those who may want to explore the use of this approach in their organizations include:

- Background Preparation: Review the curriculum website at www. GivingVoiceToValues.org for ideas about how to use and adapt the approach. Although the free materials at this site—cases, exercises, assessments, readings—were developed for use in MBA and undergraduate business education settings, companies have used and/or adapted many of them. Review the book website at www.GivingVoiceToValuesTheBook.com for introductory videos (such as the free 8-minute McKinsey Quarterly interview), interviews, related articles, book excerpts, and so on.
- Training Exercise and Mechanism for Generating GVV Scenarios: Consider using a modified version of the foundational GVV exercise—"A Tale of Two Stories" (downloadable at www.GivingVoiceToValues.org)—as a mechanism to gather examples that can be developed into customized, organizationally specific GVV-style case scenarios. This is an especially effective way to gather the positive examples. The exercise involves inviting individuals to recall an instance when they felt directly or indirectly pressured to violate their values in the workplace and they found a way to effectively enact their values. They then answer a set of questions about that story: what motivated them, what made it harder (disablers), what made it easier (enablers), and how they felt about their decision. Then they are asked to recall another story when they faced a values conflict in the workplace and they failed to enact their values, and to answer the same set of questions.

  Although in an educational context this is used as a group exercise with small and large group debriefs, it will need to be modified for confidentiality and safety issues when used within an organization. For example, it may simply be used as an anonymous written exercise with a random set of employees to generate case examples, or it may be used as a personal reflection exercise followed by a group debrief that uses a standard and disguised set of stories (not those of the individuals in the group).

- Pilot Test: Consider using some GVV-style scenarios and some of the curriculum readings (available at the websites) to develop a GVV peer network: a group of employees who have experienced and mastered the approach and its tools and who can facilitate face-to-face GVV training, who can serve as embedded GVV peer coaches, and/or who can help to integrate the GVV methodology into other non-ethics training initiatives (e.g., leadership, team building, etc.).

CONCLUSION

Most people want to bring their whole selves to work. Yet experience and research demonstrate that values conflicts will occur during the course of a person's career—those times when what we believe and want to accomplish seems in opposition to the demands of clients, peers, bosses, and/or organizations. Focused on emerging leaders in the corporate sector, the GVV curriculum helps people build and practice the understanding and skills they need to recognize, speak, and act on their values when these conflicts arise.

The "Giving Voice to Values" approach to values-driven leadership development is post-decision-making, as Carolyn Woo, the former dean of Mendoza School of Business at Notre Dame University, observed. That is, rather than emphasizing the analytic process—figuring out what is right—it focuses upon the many instances where employees are already quite aware of what's ethical but may not believe it is feasible to get it done. This set of challenges does not cover the entire realm of ethics, admittedly, but it does address a very large number of them—and importantly, the ones that are most likely to be well served by training initiatives.

That is, the issues not directly addressed by GVV—the ones where reasonable people of good will might legitimately disagree about what is right and ethical—are likely to be endlessly discussed in an ethics case discussion but without any conclusive outcome or take-aways for the employees. These can feel like mere "academic" exercises. On the other hand, GVV addresses the issues where most employees (though not all) would agree that there is indeed a violation of law, ethics, and/or policy, but they still don't know how to do the right thing when colleagues, customers, even bosses are pressuring them to the contrary. This is an area where just understanding what the rules are will not help. Rather, in these instances, providing literal scripts and action plans—preferably ones that have actually been used in the organization itself—can be a more effective educational offering.

Although originally developed for use in management education settings, increasingly individual managers as well as companies have been attracted to the pragmatic and intuitive approach GVV offers for ethics training. GVV is distinguished by its emphasis on action and its plain-spoken acknowledgement that often the challenge is not a matter of employees' lack of knowledge concerning the relevant laws or ethical obligations, or of employees who want to be unethical, but rather a matter of inconsistent organizational messages and employees' lack of skill and confidence in dealing with them. GVV is all about addressing this concern and helping individuals as well as organizations learn and practice how to voice their values when they know what's right.

NOTES

1. For a full explanation of the GVV approach and the research upon which it is based, see Gentile (2010a). See www.GivingVoicetoValues.org for the program curriculum and www.MaryGentile.com for related articles, videos, interviews, etc.
2. This idea is adapted from Gregory Dees and Peter Crampton (1991).

REFERENCES

Dees, G., & Crampton, P. (1991). Shrewd bargaining on the moral frontier: Toward a theory of morality in practice. *Business Ethics Quarterly, 1*(2), 135–167.
Detert, J., Burris, E., & Harrison, D. (2010). Debunking four myths about employee silence. *Harvard Business Review, 88*(6), 26.
Gentile, M. (2010a). *Giving voice to values: How to speak your mind when you know what's right.* New Haven, CT: Yale University Press.
Gentile, M. (2010b, March). Keeping your colleagues honest. *Harvard Business Review, 82*(2), 114–117.

CHAPTER 9

FROM THEORY TO APPLICATION

What's Behind Case-Based Ethics Training?

Zhanna Bagdasarov, James F. Johnson, and Shane Connelly

In light of the recent U.S. mortgage crisis, the failure of financial giants previously deemed "too big to fail," and the apparent less-than-savory business practices of the banking industry, populist outrage has sought to better understand unethical behavior and culture in America's financial and corporate ranks (Congressional Budget Office, 2010; Simkovic, 2013). As a result of increasing scrutiny by both consumers and government/industry regulators, organizations are seeking to improve ethical business practices through training. While established law, regulation, and organizational codes of conduct delineate the most egregious black-and-white examples of ethical violations, they often fail to provide adequate instruction regarding ambiguous, gray areas of acceptable organizational behavior that are arguably the most common types of ethical dilemmas occurring in the workplace. Accordingly, there has been renewed interest in promoting and im-

Ethics Training in Action, pages 183–205
Copyright © 2014 by Information Age Publishing
All rights of reproduction in any form reserved.

proving ethical decision making (EDM) through training. One method of training that has shown merit in organizational settings is case-based training, or the use of cases to help learners to "interpret, reflect on, and apply experiences—their own or those of someone else—in such a way that valuable learning takes place" (Kolodner, Owensby, & Guzdial, 2004, p. 829). This chapter provides an overview of case-based training, reviews empirical findings from studies showing how cases positively impact ethics training effectiveness, and prescribes a list of best practices for using cases in organizational ethics training.

CASE-BASED KNOWLEDGE AND LEARNING

As people work in a specific domain and gain professional experience, they begin to develop case-based, experiential knowledge to draw from and apply to similar future situations (Hammond, 1990). However, this occurs slowly over time. This presents a unique problem for organizations that want shorter, more efficient ways of equipping novices and/or other organizational members with new knowledge (Kolodner et al., 2003). One option is to use a case-based approach to increase knowledge through vicarious learning. *Case-based learning* involves the systematic and careful examination of low-fidelity, real-world simulations (e.g., case examples), discussion and construction of inferences based on case content, and ultimately decision making based on available case information (Kim, William, Pinsky, Brock, Phillips, & Keary, 2006; Kolodner, 1997). Through the examination of cases, novices are able to quickly acquire specific, relevant case-based knowledge as they gain experience on the job.

Aside from providing a relatively efficient way of increasing knowledge, case-based learning offers additional benefits above traditional lecture-style learning. The use of realistic cases is generally preferred by learners over lecture-based learning because it facilitates learner buy-in and involvement and aids in overall engagement, and learners find it more enjoyable and motivating (Kolodner et al., 2004; Setia, Bobby, Ananthanarayanan, Radhika, Kavitha, & Prashanth, 2011). Case-based learning is a flexible approach that resonates with a wide range of learners, making it appropriate in organizations where trainees differ in age, learning style, distance-learning familiarity, and other learning preferences. At the concept and process level, case-based learning promotes critical thinking, decision making, inductive, and deductive thinking skills—all skills necessary in real-life decision-making scenarios (Falkenberg & Woiceshyn, 2007). Lastly, case-based education centers around the discussion and application of real-world cases, making knowledge gained highly relevant.

Because case-based learning successfully promotes in-depth analysis and emphasizes decision making, it has become a popular method of training in many disciplines, such as business, law, education, and engineering (Garvin, 2003; Mayo, 2002; Williams, 1992). Case-based learning is particularly important in ethics education because gaining knowledge via *only* firsthand experiences may unnecessarily expose organizations to risk. Vicariously building knowledge by having employees work through real-world ethical situations enables development of ethical judgment in a nonthreatening environment.

Case-based reasoning, an underlying function of case-based learning, aids learners in understanding the multifaceted, dynamic, and overall complex nature of ethical dilemmas (Kolodner, 1992). "In case-based reasoning, a reasoner remembers a previous situation similar to the current one and uses that to solve the new problem" (Kolodner, 1992, p. 4). Given this observation, it is crucial for case-based learning to successfully promote case-based reasoning. Fortunately, this process is facilitated via sensemaking (Mumford et al., 2008; Sonenshein, 2007). The following section provides a description of sensemaking, a popular method of problem solving in crisis situations, and explains how sensemaking can be enhanced by both case-based education and application of specific strategies in applied ethics training settings.

SENSEMAKING, MORAL REASONING, AND ETHICAL DECISION-MAKING

Sensemaking describes how managers successfully "make sense" of multiple streams of information in organizational crisis situations (Weick, 1988, 1995). The first phase of sensemaking involves information scanning and gathering; attending to incoming streams of information from external, environmental sources, internal organization-level sources, and one's own biases and emotions (Drazin, Glynn, & Kazanjian, 1999; Mumford et al., 2008; Thiel, Connelly, & Griffith, 2011). Integration and interpretation, the second phase, involves the prioritization of information, identification of relationships among information, and ultimately the formation of a mental framework to interpret the current crisis (Gioia, 1986; Thomas, Clark, & Gioia, 1993). The final phase of sensemaking involves implementing the mental model via action or change, which can occur at the personal, team, unit, or organizational level (Thomas et al., 1993). Because ethical issues are often demarcated by equivocality, Sonenshein (2007) proposed that individuals engage in sensemaking during the moral reasoning process. Specifically, when engaged in ethical sensemaking, individuals are subject to nonrational, visceral reactions and biases, rely on situation-specific intuitive judgments, and provide justification for their moral processes after the fact (Sonenshein, 2007). A major contribution of Sonenshein's work is recognizing the impact that internal biases and external constraints have on sensemaking ability and successful EDM.

The Sensemaking Model of Ethical Decision-Making

As a logical extension and application of Sonenshein's (2007) model, Mumford and colleagues developed the sensemaking model of EDM, a model that provides specific strategies to improve EDM via successful implementation of sensemaking processes (Mumford et al., 2006; Mumford et al., 2008). Ethical issues require you to simultaneously consider ethical guidelines and professional practices and competing goals of stakeholders, and evaluate effectiveness of multiple courses of action. Given the inherent complexity, ambiguity, and risk to multiple parties in ethical dilemmas, ethical sensemaking is a critical component of successful EDM (Brock et al., 2008; Mumford et al., 2008; Sonenshein, 2007). Mumford and colleagues (2008) have identified several strategies to improve information gathering, interpretation/integration, and decision/action in the context of ethical issues: framing, forecasting, self-reflection, and emotion regulation.

Framing

Following the initial appraisal of an ethical issue, an individual must frame, or define, the nature of the problem at hand (Mumford et al., 2008; Mumford, Reiter-Palmon, & Redmond, 1994; Tversky & Kahneman, 1974). Framing takes place multiple times in ethical sensemaking, first by framing the issue as having ethical implications or not, and later when gathering and interpreting information. For example, professional and personal values and goals not only frame whether or not a situation is deemed to be ethical in nature, but also how we perceive ourselves as part of the issue in comparison to others. Caughron, Antes, Beeler, Thiel, Wang, and Mumford (2011) demonstrated that framing an ethical issue from an organizational perspective improved information integration in participants and subsequent EDM quality. Additionally, framing an ethical issue in an "us-versus-them" context leads to decrements in information integration and subsequent EDM quality (Caughron, Antes, Stenmark, Thiel, Wang, & Mumford, 2013). One's framing of an ethical issue sets the trajectory of future interaction and, in turn, influences decision-making outcomes. Consequently, methods that enhance ability to consider multiple frames are likely to improve sensemaking and EDM via information integration.

Ethics training instructors can improve framing skills of their trainees by providing case content or implementing activities that challenge trainees to examine multiple frames of reference early and often in the EDM process, as well as emphasizing how competing frames-of-reference impact sensemaking and EDM quality (Caughron et al., 2011 Caughron et al., 2013; Mumford et al., 2008). A case-based approach is uniquely adaptable to training successful framing skills as it provides multiple case-based scenarios to practice experiencing multiple frames of reference.

Forecasting

Forecasting is the prediction of potential future outcomes based on observations of the present situation (Pant & Starbuck, 1990). Forecasting is particularly important because it promotes generation of multiple potential problem solutions, as well as aiding in identification of potential constraints, restrictions, opportunities, and other sources of uncertainty (Hogarth & Makridakis, 1981). However, the ability to accurately determine downstream outcomes in complex ethical dilemmas is a cognitively intensive process and is impacted by individual factors like available experiential knowledge (Marcy & Mumford, 2007; Mumford, Schultz, & Van Doorn, 2001; Stenmark, Antes, Thiel, Caughron, Xiaoqian, & Mumford, 2010). Xiao, Milgram, and Doyle (1997) demonstrated that novice problem solvers are much more likely to formulate overly optimistic, simplistic forecasts, while veteran problem solvers succeed due to extensive experiential knowledge. Recent studies revealed that forecasting and EDM quality can be improved among novices using case-based instruction and targeted forecasting strategies, including identification of (1) a large number of causes and consequences, (2) critical causes and consequences, and (3) positive and negative consequences (Johnson et al., 2012; Stenmark, Antes, Wang, Caughron, Thiel, & Mumford, 2010; Stenmark et al., 2011).

Ethics training instructors can improve forecasting skills of their trainees by providing initial summaries of real-world case studies and asking trainees to identify possible outcomes. Forecasting training should focus on identification of multiple positive and negative outcomes that are most critical (Johnson et al., 2012). The use of real-world case examples is particularly useful because forecasted outcomes can be compared to actual outcomes and discussed and explored hypothetically in a safe environment without real-world consequences. By forecasting, trainees improve sensemaking processes of information interpretation and hypothetically "test" potential case outcomes (Hogarth & Makridakis, 1981; Weick, 1995).

Self-Reflection

Self-reflection involves drawing upon one's past and potential future experiences to make sense of a situation (Gardner, Avolio, Luthans, May, & Walumbwa, 2005; Mumford et al., 2008; Scott, Lonergan, & Mumford, 2005). Self-reflection can be thought of as self-awareness, self-monitoring, or managing personal or situational influences on problem-solving ability (Brown & Treviño, 2006). Successful self-reflection assists in reflecting on one's own motives, biases, and previous experiences, and, when applied to the sensemaking framework, improves both information gathering and interpretation (Dorner & Schaub, 1994; Schwandt, 2005). Recent research reveals that reflecting on positive past experiences, as well as future, prospective experiences, improves sensemaking ability and subsequent EDM quality (Antes, Thiel, Martin, Mumford, Devenport, & Connelly, 2012; Martin et al., 2011).

Ethics trainers can improve self-reflection skills of trainees by emphasizing that the process of sensemaking is continually impacted by personal and situational constraints as well as biases. Successful self-reflection training should focus on identification and minimization of biases and constraints on EDM while acknowledging that everyone is subject to internal and external influences (Brown & Treviño, 2006). Ethics training can promote self-reflection in novice trainees by having trainees adopt case roles and reflect on potential biases, constraints, and motives each character may have.

Emotion Regulation

EDM is also susceptible to the influence of emotions (Coughlan & Connolly, 2008; Gaudine & Thorne, 2001; Haidt, 2003; Kligyte, Connelly, Thiel., & Devenport. in press). Experiencing emotion during a crisis situation is not inherently good or bad. According to Sonenshein (2007), emotions are vital to the successful formulation of intuition and judgment and can signal the presence of ethical situations. However, affective responses introduce potential sources of bias that should be acknowledged and minimized. Ethical issues are often affect-laden given their complexity, conflict, and potential negative outcomes. High levels of negative emotion are taxing in terms of cognitive processing, leading to decrements of initial appraisal and subsequent framing, forecasting quality, and affect such as anger can inhibit EDM while fear may help (Connelly, Helton-Fauth, & Mumford, 2004; Forgas, 1995; Kligyte et al., in press; Werhane, 2002). Behavioral and cognitive emotion regulation strategies help determine how, when, and what emotions are experienced; are helpful for managing negative affective states; and can minimize the negative effects of emotion (Cohen, 2010; Gaudine & Thorne, 2001; Gross, 1998). Both cognitive reappraisal and relaxation, two emotion regulation strategies, can successfully mitigate the influence of anger on ethical sensemaking and reduce the negative effects of fear on sensemaking strategies (Kligyte et al., in press; Thiel et al., 2011).

Ethics trainers can improve emotion-regulation skills of trainees by using case examples to demonstrate where and how emotions can impact successful EDM. By demonstrating that emotions can and do impact EDM, trainees understand that while emotions are not necessarily bad to experience during an ethical dilemma, the key is taking steps to minimize their negative effects on EDM (Gaudine & Thorne, 2001; Sonenshein, 2007). Ethics trainers can then use case examples enriched with emotional content to provide trainees with opportunities to identify emotion and provide a method to regulate emotion in a healthy, proactive manner (Kligyte et al., in press; Thiel et al., 2011).

THE RATIONALE FOR CASE-BASED ETHICS TRAINING

Success and effectiveness of sensemaking strategy application is contingent upon access to case-based knowledge, which may be gained vicariously via observational and case-based learning (Kim et al., 2006; Kolodner et al., 2003). The use of cases to facilitate decision making, known as case-based reasoning, is the primary function of case-based learning (Kolodner, 1992; Mumford et al., 2008). Case-based learning provides novices with a structured and educational environment to gain experiential knowledge, where carefully selected cases not only emphasize important elements of the sensemaking process, but also provide ample opportunities to practice application of ethical sensemaking strategies. However, before case-based ethics training can be deemed effective, one must first identify what characteristics of example cases promote EDM and application of sensemaking strategies.

What Constitutes a "Good" Case?

Despite the well-established usefulness of cases in learning and instruction across numerous disciplines (Rippin, Booth, Bowie, & Jordan, 2002; Williams, 1992), literature regarding recommendations for effective case construction, both in terms of case content and suitable methods for learning from cases, is fairly recent and still emerging. It is important to review the efficacy of case features for learning given the new evidence suggesting that poorly constructed cases can hinder the facilitating mechanisms of case-based learning and sensemaking (Bagdasarov et al., 2013; Harkrider et al., 2012; Johnson et al., 2012; Thiel et al., 2013).

Content and Presentation

Although investigations into effective case content are few and far between, some researchers have proposed that "good" cases must not only be relevant to the reader, but also engaging, realistic, emotion-laden, and challenging (Atkinson, 2008; David, 2003; Herreid, 1998; Kim et al., 2006). Such researchers include Kim and colleagues (2006), who identified five core attributes of cases (i.e., relevant, realistic, engaging, challenging, and instructional), and proposed 17 viable strategies for incorporating these attributes into each case. Some of these strategies included promoting realism and relevance by providing a reasonable setting for the case narrative; establishing goals and objectives of both learners and teachers within the case, delivering content in a rich format by identifying key characters, problems, and situations involved; ensuring that the case is challenging by increasing the degree of content difficulty; and assessing student learning via plausible evaluation methods.

Along similar lines, Herreid (1998) advised that a "good" case must tell a story and possess an interesting plot that appears relevant to the audience; it must concentrate on an interest-arousing issue and be conflict-provoking, and it should also be decision-forcing and have general applicability. Atkinson (2008) augmented these recommendations by proposing that case writing can benefit from prominent techniques found in creative writing. The author emphasized the importance of clearly portraying the setting of the conflict, describing the characters, and making their motivations and personalities apparent, while also providing sufficient information for plot enhancement. The author maintains that using such creative writing techniques will "breathe life into the case study method" (Atkinson, 2008, p. 33). The foregoing recommendations for effective case development, although theoretical, were not tested empirically by these authors. Thus, more recently, a group of researchers conducted a series of systematic investigations testing these suggestions (see Table 9.1).

Similar to the limited literature on effective case content, information concerning useful techniques for case presentation that result in more effective processing of case-based material is virtually nonexistent. Laditka and Houck (2006) are among the few researchers who investigated a technique for teaching ethics using cases. Students were asked to write their own cases using general guidelines provided by instructors. Analyses of student-developed cases provided evidence for the usefulness of this method in engaging students in ethical dialogue, as well as its usefulness as a general learning tool. Likewise, McWilliams and Nahavandi (2006) tasked their students with selecting a real-world event containing ethical implications and writing a case based on it. Students later presented their cases to the class and conducted debates highlighting the issues described in the cases. These examples involved students writing their own cases, a useful and valuable method for enhancing critical thinking skills and ethics instruction. Nevertheless, other methods for learning from cases have recently been explored using well-controlled, experimental designs (see Table 9.1). These studies, along with a description of general procedures for testing these inferences, are discussed in the next section.

TABLE 9.1 Summary of Case Content and Presentation Studies

Case Content and Presentation Studies	Key Findings
Thiel et al. (2013)	Rich descriptions of characters' emotions improved case-based knowledge acquisition and EDM
Harkrider et al. (2012)	Descriptions of ethical codes of conduct and forecasting information improved sensemaking and EDM
Johnson et al. (2012)	Details regarding key causes and negative outcomes improved sensemaking and EDM
Bagdasarov et al. (2013)	Rich description of the social setting increased realism and improved sensemaking and EDM
Bagdasarov et al. (2012)	Elaboration on structured cases can be useful
Peacock et al. (2013)	Provision of alternative case outcomes induced cognitive load and confused learners
MacDougall et al. (in press)	Provision of case material incrementally induced cognitive load and impeded forecasting
Harkrider et al. (2013)	Structure via comparison of cases or structured prompts is effective, but not both. Too much structure led to detrimental learning outcomes

Procedures for Testing Case Manipulations

Embedded case content factors, such as the social context (setting), goals/motives of character, codes of ethical conduct, forecasting, emotions, causes, and outcomes, were empirically manipulated and tested during a two-day responsible conduct of research (RCR) ethics training course for novice researchers. Case presentation techniques and exercises, such as elaboration-based learning strategies, case comparison tactics, incremental case building, and provision of alternative outcomes within cases were also tested using the same population and procedures.

This RCR training course is a university-wide, 16-hour, case-based program, designed to train students in research ethics and promote EDM. Graduate students from various disciplines, including social, engineering, biological, and health sciences, as well as humanities and performing arts, took part in the studies. All studies were conducted in the same manner, during the 7th block of a 10-block program. The 7th block took place during the first 1.5 hours of the second day of training.

All studies employed similar, completely randomized between-subjects designs with a separate comparison group. Participants began the study by receiving one of two packets containing study materials. The first packet included manipulated case materials for either case content (e.g., affective information provided vs. no affective information) or case processes (e.g., comparing cases vs. sequential cases). In the case of content variables, some participants were given ethics cases with manipulated content while others received the same cases without the additional content. For case process studies, some participants read an ethics case that was accompanied by particular exercises thought to ensure effective processing of information, while others were asked simply to read the case and provide a brief response to the case in writing (control group). After working with the case, participants completed three outcome measures. First, case-based knowledge acquisition was assessed using a multiple-choice knowledge test. Second, sensemaking processes and EDM were evaluated via performance on an EDM transfer task. The transfer task entailed reading two additional ethics cases and responding to questions designed to assess sensemaking processes (i.e., causal analysis, constraint analysis, forecast analysis), and sensemaking strategy application (i.e., recognizing circumstances, seeking help, questioning one's judgment, dealing with emotions, anticipating consequences, looking within, and considering others' perspectives). In terms of EDM, participants were asked to resolve the main ethical dilemma within each case and provide a rationale for their chosen solution. Responses were rated by a team of experts, all of whom underwent frame-of-reference training and practiced coding participants' responses prior to rating. Third, reliable and valid pre- and posttest measures of EDM (Mumford et al., 2006, 2008) were administered to all participants prior to and directly following training. These field-specific measures, consisting of six pre and six post overarching scenarios and followed by 3–4 items reflecting ethical dilemmas, included 25 multiple-choice questions with eight answer options. Measures for each field mapped onto and assessed the following constructs: (1) data management (data collection and data interpretation); (2) study conduct (data protection, maintenance of study conduct and safety standards, and research administration); (3) professional practices (objectivity in evaluating work, recognition of professional boundaries, protection of intellectual property, publication practices, adherence to professional commitments, protection of public welfare and environment, professional leadership, production pressure, meetings and presentations); and (4) business practices (conflict of interests, deceptive bid/contract and unrealistic expectations, and resource management). All answers were structured to reflect high (3), moderate (2), and low (1) levels of EDM based on subject matter experts on ethics and from the fields of interest. Participants were asked to choose the two most appropriate answers to each ethical dilemma. Answers to the questions were scored by averaging the selected responses for each question, resulting in one overall EDM score for the pre- and posttests.

Case Content Study Findings

Thiel et al. (2013) investigated the influence of emotional content embedded within cases. Specifically, the investigators provided information about emotional reactions of the characters in the case to increase realism and evoke greater identification with the challenges facing the characters in the situations. Results of this work demonstrated that individuals acquired more case-based knowledge and performed better on the EDM transfer task when descriptions of case characters' emotional experiences were included. This study suggests a need for more realistic and emotionally evocative cases in ethics education. Please see the appendix for a sample case with manipulated emotional content.

Harkrider et al. (2012) examined the usefulness of the presence of codes of ethical conduct and forecasting information within cases. These researchers inserted ethical codes with or without context (i.e., providing either an ethical code without any subsequent information or providing the same code with information that offers a rationale for it), and long- or short-term forecasting information (i.e., predictions regarding potential outcomes) in cases and assessed participants on various outcome variables discussed earlier. As hypothesized, presentation of ethical codes of conduct and forecasting information within cases led to an improvement in EDM, greater knowledge acquisition, and increased use of sensemaking strategies. Furthermore, interactions were observed between these variables, such that when forecasting short-term, ethical codes without context led to higher sensemaking strategy use, whereas when forecasting long-term, codes with context resulted in greater application of sensemaking strategies.

In another study, Johnson et al. (2012) provided evidence for the importance of considering causes and outcomes of ethical dilemmas when developing cases. The authors manipulated cause complexity (high vs. low complexity) and outcome valence (negative vs. mixed valence) in two ethics cases. Cause complexity was defined as the number of causes provided in each case, with high-complexity cases containing seven causes, and low-complexity cases containing three causes. Outcome valence was operationalized as providing either four negative outcomes for case characters, or mixed outcomes, which involved a presentation of both two positive and two negative outcomes for case characters. Findings of this work indicated that individuals who read cases containing strictly negative outcomes identified more critical causes, produced better quality forecasts, and exhibited improved EDM compared to participants who read cases with mixed or no outcomes.

Finally, Bagdasarov et al. (2013) explored the influences of case characters' goal focus and social context/setting information with reference to sensemaking processes and EDM. The social context of cases was manipulated to portray either an autonomy-supportive or a controlling environment. An autonomy-supportive social context was presented as a comfortable working environment in which the advisor trusted his students to complete their work on time and act professionally and ethically when conducting research. The controlling environment, on the other hand, was defined by exerting pressure on subordinates via deadlines, potential punishments, strict guidelines, and lack of autonomy. Characters' goal focus was portrayed as either promotion- or prevention-seeking. A character motivated by a promotion goal was portrayed as one with a desperate need to attain positive outcomes, succeed, gain the supervisor's approval, and acquire as much knowledge as possible while working in the laboratory. Conversely, a character assigned a prevention goal in a case was depicted as someone willing to do anything to prevent failure, circumvent angering the supervisor, and avoid losses at all cost. The central findings of this work indicated that study participants who were given autonomy-supportive case information performed better on certain sensemaking outcomes (i.e., constraint and forecast analyses) and showed an increase in EDM. Characters' goal focus appeared only to have an effect on forecast quality, with participants receiving prevention goal information producing better quality forecasts. Please see Table 9.1 for a summary of the case content studies.

Case Presentation Study Findings

In the first of four experiments, Bagdasarov et al. (2013) empirically tested two processes: elaboration and self-development of cases. Participants in one condition were asked to write their own cases based on a brief provided sketch to assist in idea generation; others were given a case and asked to elaborate on the case; the third condition required participants to elaborate on their own developed cases; and participants in the fourth condition performed an equivalent control task requiring them to write a brief response to the given case. Results indicated that participants who elaborated on a given case outperformed their counterparts in other experimental conditions on all outcomes of interest, providing evidence that clear, well-written, and structured cases lead to the best learning outcomes. Interestingly, the control group performed similarly to the group elaborating on a given case, suggesting that simply writing about the case may be sufficient to meet certain learning objectives. Please see the bottom of the appendix for a sample of elaboration questions asked in this study.

In another study, Peacock et al. (2013) presented participants with scenarios featuring alternative outcomes (i.e., other potential outcomes for each case character) to an ethics case, expecting that the provision of these additional pieces of information would lead to a decrease in knowledge acquisition, reduction in sensemaking processes and strategy use, and decreased EDM. As hypothesized, complexity resulting in cases with alternative endings gave rise to cognitive overload and confusion. This trend in findings continued when MacDougall et al. (in press) showed via another study that simplifying cases is most beneficial to learners. Investigators presented the material to participants in increments, providing new pieces of information in chunks as learners progressed through the case. This, too, proved to be cognitively demanding for novice researchers. Participants not only disliked the incremental building of information, but this method also had an unforeseen negative effect on individuals' ability to forecast.

Finally, Harkrider et al. (2013) examined the influences of case presentation (sequential vs. comparison) and follow-up prompt questions (structured vs. unstructured) on learning and EDM. Interactive effects between these variables revealed that comparing cases led to better performance on various outcome variables when participants considered unstructured rather than structured prompt questions. Alternatively, when cases were presented sequentially, individuals performed better when working with structured prompts. Interestingly, coupling comparison of cases with structured prompt questions resulted in decreased performance overall. Clearly some form of structure is essential; however, it is important to note that too much structure is detrimental to learning and EDM. Please see Table 9.1 for a summary of studies investigating case presentation studies.

Best Practices for Case Design and Presentation

Before we turn to our recommendations for case design and presentation, a few limitations of the aforementioned studies should be noted. Results of these studies may not generalize to some populations because the findings were based primarily on graduate student samples, made up of novice researchers in their respective fields. However, we also stress that all studies were meticulously executed, suggesting that only further research in this area will tell how useful these techniques are to other kinds of adult learners in applied settings. Another potential limitation is that the length of each training session involving the cases where content or process features were manipulated was relatively short. It is unclear how the outcomes of these studies would differ over longer periods of time and with more practice. Finally, individual differences could alter the effects of the manipulations on both perceptions and use of case material. Individual differences, especially those known to influence learning, should be controlled for in future replications of these investigations through theory-driven designs.

The initial efforts made to examine content of cases and strategies for presentation of case material culminate in several key ideas informing case design and ethics instruction. Particularly, the new evidence is considerable when it comes to the importance of simplicity and structure within the case method. When developing the content for cases intended for novices, instructors should consider structuring cases in a manner that simplifies the material for the learners and emphasizes key concepts (Kim et al., 2006). Evidence regarding case content attributes illustrates the need for integration of affect (Thiel et al., 2013), ethical codes of conduct and forecasting information (Harkrider et al., 2012), clearly defined causes of the ethical dilemma at hand and negative outcomes (Johnson et al., 2012), and socio-relational information that defines the setting for the ethical dilemma (Bagdasarov et al., 2013; Herreid, 1998).

When considering case presentation methods and exercises to accompany the cases, it is essential to structure the material. Structuring case-based learning will simplify cases for learners, making the task easier and more beneficial for knowledge acquisition and application of sensemaking strategies (Harkrider et al., 2013; Kim et al., 2006). Furthermore, new findings suggest that elaboration-based strategies can be effective when used in conjunction with the case method, but only if such elaborations are made on a fixed, well-structured case (Bagdasarov et al., 2012). Likewise, Harkrider et al. (2013) showed that having students compare cases or consider structured prompts (but not both) enhanced sensemaking and EDM. Finally, case developers should be wary of providing numerous alternative outcomes within a single case (Peacock et al., 2013) and presenting cases to learners in increments (MacDougall et al., in press). Although further research into effective case attributes and processes is necessary, simplicity and structure clearly count when it comes to cases.

Many trainers already use cases of some sort in ethics training that they would like to continue using. When training novices, making adaptations to these cases may improve training outcomes in terms of knowledge retention, the development of ethical sensemaking strategies, and application of those strategies to new ethical problems. First, it is important to take note of case length. This is especially critical since many business cases continue to be very long, including large amounts of information not pertinent to the ethical situation at hand (Richardson, 1994). Using existing materials that are concise and to the point will lead to the best learning outcomes (David, 2003; Herreid, 1998). Second, altering the cases to focus trainees' attention on the key principles is essential (Johnson et al., 2012). This can be accomplished by removing nonpertinent distractors from the case (Kim et al., 2006). Third, it is important to ensure that the off-the-shelf materials have relevance to the reader (Herreid, 1998). If the cases are based on real-world events, such events will be more relevant if they deal with current issues. Finally, one should adapt or choose cases that are engaging, structured, rich in emotion, and realistic (Bagdasarov et al., 2012; Kim et al., 2006; Thiel et al., 2013).

TAKE-AWAY POINTS AND SUMMARY

Case-based knowledge is critical to successfully navigating today's complex world of organizational ethics. While experiential knowledge is primarily attained via firsthand experience, risk management issues and the need to quickly train novice employees in EDM dictate that a "sink or swim" approach to gaining experience is simply unrealistic. In this chapter we have outlined how case-based ethics training can quickly facilitate experiential knowledge acquisition via case-based instruction. Additionally, we introduced a practical method to facilitate ethics training based on the sense-making model of EDM (Mumford et al., 2006; Mumford et al., 2008), which promotes knowledge acquisition via the sensemaking process. This process of ethical sensemaking provides specific, trainable strategies like framing, forecasting, self-reflection, and emotion regulation—strategies that rely, in part, on case-based knowledge and complement a case-based approach to ethics training.

In order to prepare trainees to learn effectively from cases, we recommend spending time up front helping trainees understand the complexities inherent in an ethical dilemma. First, we recommend that trainers address existing rules, guidelines, and regulations of the organization and industry, pointing out they may not be particularly helpful in making an ethical decision in "gray" ethical matters. Second, the authors recommend that participants are exposed to bias and constraint training, demonstrating the internal and external biases common in ethical dilemmas as well as common personal and situational constraints that inhibit successful EDM. Third, training should focus on specific, teachable strategies (e.g., Mumford et al., 2006; Mumford et al., 2008) trainees can use to overcome biases and constraints. Finally, trainers should make trainees familiar with the steps of sensemaking and practice to scan, interpret, and apply information in order to make better ethical decisions. Once trainees have adopted the proper frame-of-reference in understanding the impact of biases and constraints as well as multiple strategies to improve EDM, they will be more aware of the complexities of EDM and be better prepared to work with case material.

While case-based training has demonstrated utility in ethics training applications, content and delivery processes that improve knowledge acquisition and application are still being uncovered. Regarding case content, recent empirical findings demonstrate that to improve ethical sensemaking and application of sensemaking strategies, cases should contain rich descriptions of character emotions, as well as descriptions of applicable codes of conduct and forecasting information. Additionally, case content should detail the immediate social setting; focus content on a few, critical causes; include negative case outcomes; and have clear cause-and-effect reasoning. Case delivery processes indicate that trainees benefit more from elaborating on a standardized case as opposed to on a self-written case. A final, emerging trend in case presentation processes is the need to delicately balance between presenting cases in a clear, straightforward manner while also not over-structuring case delivery. Future research should examine additional case content and process variables that have a positive impact on case-based ethics training. The education literature is replete with teaching techniques and tips that have not yet been examined in a case-based training context. Furthermore, while case-based ethics training has demonstrated significant improvement in EDM scores, both short- and long-term (Brock, Vert, Kligyte, Waples, Sevier, & Mumford, 2008; Mumford et al., 2006; Mumford, et al., 2008), currently little research exists examining the effectiveness of case-based ethics training on "bottom line" indicators. These include hard metrics such as organizational profits as well as indirect outcomes such as perceptions of organizational efforts by the public. While more empirical work is needed to further delineate beneficial case content and processes, these findings have implications for the existing case method, and especially case-based ethics training in organizational contexts.

APPENDIX

Information that is underlined was manipulated in various case conditions. The type of case content manipulated is identified in italicized labels.

Big Pharma Case

Jason is in his second year and Robin is just finishing her first year of post-doctoral training in a cell biology lab where they share a good working relationship. They have generous fellowships thanks mostly to their mentor's enterprising associations with the pharmaceutical industry. Dr. Davis, their mentor, does contract work that requires review and approval by industry scientists before work can be submitted for publication.

His university has offered to negotiate with the drug companies for better publication terms. Davis has so far refused on the grounds that he does not want to compromise his competitive edge, which has won him a solid reputation along with continued funding for a team of first-rate graduate students and post-docs. <u>Davis was always disappointed with other funding sources and the lack of recognition he received from those projects. He decided long ago to compete for private funding because he knew the larger budgets could open the door to limitless research possibilities, and maybe even help him achieve that "break-through" finding he had dreamed of.</u>
(*Secondary Case Character Emotion*)

The two post-docs are using different animal models to test the efficacy of a gene product. It is hoped that this gene product will interfere with cancer cell-signaling and slow or arrest metastatic activity. Jason's results are extremely encouraging, but Robin's are not. <u>Frustrated</u>, she confides to her friend that she is disappointed with her failing project and a year's loss in productivity. <u>She is also frustrated because</u> Davis has hinted that she must be doing something wrong. After all, Robin is working with the same protein as Jason, and it is reasonable to expect that her results would at least show a similar trend. <u>This diverging pattern of results really makes Robin uncomfortable and worried, to the point that she starts to question her ability as a scientist. She wants to talk to others about the situation, but worries that their reactions will be similar to Davis'. Robin even begins to worry that she may not have been well prepared to enter such a challenging postdoctoral position.</u> (*Primary Case Character Emotion*)

In speaking with Jason, he replies candidly about what he learned in his first year—that the industry's emphasis is on getting results. He points out that if the Davis group does not produce, the project will be turned over to another team that will, and the fellowships will follow the money. <u>Jason admits that he was surprised when he came to know of this reality, but expresses the satisfaction he now feels for the opportunities provided from these industry funds. His rationale is that as long as everyone is benefiting, there is no harm in interpreting the results with industry goals in mind.</u> (*Secondary Case Character Emotion*)

What Jason said made sense, but Robin is uncomfortable with the implication she thought was being conveyed. She made a noncommittal remark and changed the subject. However, the new information preyed on her mind. Was she being naively idealistic about science?

<u>In the weeks following Robin and Jason's conversation, however, Robin feels less guilt and more anger. She is angry that her research abilities are being questioned because she has chosen to cleanly interpret her data. Robin's anger begins to influence her attitude about the lab in general and relationships with other members of the laboratory. More specifically, her anger is starting to cause some confrontational interactions with Jason, as she feels that he is to blame for her embarrassment.</u> (*Primary Case Character Emotion*)

Robin tries to think of solutions to the problem, but worries that whatever she tries to do would do more harm than good for herself. Dr. Davis is a well-respected researcher in the field and is quite established. It would be almost impossible to publicly question the integrity of his laboratory's research given his position and status. Furthermore, with that power and status, Dr. Davis could seriously threaten Robin's chances at finding future employment. Robin has thought about just confronting Jason, but worries that she would ultimately have to deal with Dr. Davis. Jason is more experienced and has already gained respect from Dr. Davis. Dr. Davis would most certainly trust Jason more than Robin, and it would be extremely difficult to make a case to him. Plus, she is confident that Dr. Davis is aware of the sloppy data practices and biased interpretations.

Robin continues to feel uncomfortable with the climate of the lab and her interactions with Jason. While her anger has somewhat subsided, she once again feels fearful about her involvement in what she considers to be highly unethical behavior. Robin's fears cause her to wonder what might happen to her and her career if she stays under Dr. Davis any longer. (*Primary Case Character Emotion*) She contemplates discussing the issue with Davis but fears he will react just like Jason. Ultimately, she decides that the best course of action is to not change her results and to leave the laboratory altogether. When she discusses her resignation with Davis he is surprised and asks for an explanation. She circumvents the real issue, simply telling him that she doesn't feel like she fits in very well and would like to take her career in a different direction. Robin, admittedly, is conflicted over her decision to withhold information from Davis, but fears that she might create a bigger issue if she shares the entire truth. Davis seems content with her response, and is actually happy that he will no longer need to deal with this semi-controversial student. His satisfaction causes him to ignore the other possible explanations for her departure, and to assume that business can operate as usual. (*Secondary Case Character Emotion*)

Six months later, Robin finds herself in an entry-level position at a small biomedical company. She is satisfied with her current work and is relieved that she no longer faces the pressures of her previous lab. She is even more relieved that she left her post-doc position when she receives word from a former lab mate that Davis's laboratory has lost its funding after being investigated by the Office of Research Integrity on data fabrication charges.

Elaboration Questions

1. Think about the central ethical dilemma in this case. Now, extend the case by discussing several other secondary ethical issues that are present in this case that may have contributed to the problem at hand. Be very detailed in your response.
2. Think about the central causes of the ethical dilemma and list them below. Then, consider other causes that may have played an important role in this case and discuss each one in detail.
3. Think about the situational constraints in this case (e.g., time). Extend the case by discussing how each one has contributed to the ethical dilemma at hand.

REFERENCES

Antes, A. L., Thiel, C. E., Martin, L. E., Mumford, M. D., Devenport, L. D., & Connelly, S. (2012). Applying cases to solve ethical problems: The significance of positive and process-oriented reflection. *Ethics and Behavior, 22,* 113–120.

Atkinson, T. N. (2008). Using creative writing techniques to enhance the case study method in research integrity and ethics courses. *Journal of Academic Ethics, 6,* 33–50.

Bagdasarov, Z., Harkrider, L. N., Johnson, J. F., Thiel, C. E., MacDougall, A. E., Devenport, L. D., Connelly, S., Mumford, M. D., & Peacock, J. (2012). An investigation of case-based instructional strategies on learning, retention, and ethical decision-making. *Journal of Empirical Research on Human Research Ethics, 7*(4), 79–86.

Bagdasarov, Z., Thiel, C. E., Johnson, J. F., Connelly, S., Harkrider, L., Devenport, L. D., & Mumford, M. D. (2013). Case-based ethics instruction: The influence of contextual and individual factors in case content on ethical decision-making. *Science and Engineering Ethics, 19*(3), 1305–1322. doi:10.1007/s11948-012-9414-3

Brock, M. E., Vert, A., Kligyte, V., Waples, E. P., Sevier, S. T., & Mumford, M. D. (2008). Mental models: An alternative evaluation of a sensemaking approach to ethics instruction. *Science and Engineering Ethics, 14*(3), 449–472. doi:10.1007/s11948-008-9076-3

Brown, M., & Treviño, L. K. (2006). Ethical leadership: A review and future directions. *The Leadership Quarterly, 17*(6), 595–616.

Caughron, J. J., Antes, A. L., Beeler, C. K., Thiel, C. E., Wang, X., & Mumford, M. D. (2011). Sensemaking strategies for ethical decision making. *Ethics and Behavior, 21,* 351–366.

Caughron, J. J., Antes, A. L., Stenmark, C. K., Thiel, C. E., Wang, X., & Mumford, M. D. (2013). Competition and sensemaking in ethical situations. *Journal of Applied Psychology, 43,* 1491–1507. doi:10.1111/jasp.12141.

Cohen, T. R. (2010). Moral emotions and unethical bargaining: The differential effects of empathy and perspective taking in deterring deceitful negotiation. *Journal of Business Ethics, 94,* 569–579.

Congressional Budget Office. (2010). *Fannie Mae, Freddie Mac, and the federal role in the secondary mortgage market.* Congress of the United States. Washington, DC: Author.

Connelly, S., Helton-Fauth, W., & Mumford, M. D. (2004). A managerial in-basket study of the impact of trait emotions on ethical choice. *Journal of Business Ethics, 51,* 245–267.

Coughlan, R., & Connolly, T. (2008). Investigating unethical decisions at work: Justification and emotion in dilemma resolution. *Journal of Managerial Issues, 3,* 348–365.

David, F. (2003). Strategic management case writing: Suggestions after 20 Years of experience. *S.A.M. Advanced Management Journal, 68,* 36–43.

Dorner, D., & Schaub, H. (1994). Errors in planning and decision-making and the nature of human information processing. *Applied Psychology: An International Review, 43,* 433–453.

Drazin, R., Glynn, M., & Kazanjian, R. (1999). Multi-level theorizing about creativity in organizations. *Academy of Management Review, 24,* 286–329.

Falkenberg, L., & Woiceshyn, J. (2008). Enhancing business ethics: Using cases to teach moral reasoning. *Journal of Business Ethics, 79,* 213–217.

Forgas, J. P. (1995). Mood and judgment: The affect infusion model (AIM). *Psychological Bulletin, 117,* 39–66.

Gardner, W. L., Avolio, B. J., Luthans, F., May, D. R., & Walumbwa, F. (2005). "Can you see the real me?" A self-based model of authentic leader and follower development. *Leadership Quarterly, 16,* 343–372.

Garvin, D. A. (2003, September-October). Making the case: Professional education for the world of practice. *Harvard Magazine, 105,* 56–65, 107.

Gaudine, A., & Thorne, L. (2001). Emotion and ethical decision-making in organizations. *Journal of Business Ethics, 31,* 175–187.

Gioia, D. A. (1986). Symbols, scripts, and sensemaking: Creating meaning in the organizational experience. In H. P. Sims. Jr., & D. A. Gioia (Eds.), *The thinking organization* (pp. 49–74). San Francisco, CA: Jossey-Bass.

Gross, J. J. (1998). The emerging field of emotion regulation: An integrative review. *Review of General Psychology, 2,* 271–299.

Haidt, J. (2003). The emotional dog does learn new tricks: A reply to Pizarro and Bloom (2003). *Psychological Review, 110,* 197–198.

Hammond, K. J. (1990). Case-based planning: A framework for planning from experience. *Cognitive Science, 14,* 385–443.

Harkrider, L. N., MacDougall, A. E., Bagdasarov, Z., Johnson, J. F., Thiel, C. E., Mumford, M. D., Connelly, S. & Devenport, L. D. (2013). Structuring case-based ethics trainings: How comparing cases and structured prompts influence training effectiveness. *Ethics & Behavior, 23*(3), 179–198. doi:10.1080/10508422.2013.774865

Harkrider, L. N., Thiel, C. E., Bagdasarov, Z., Mumford, M. D., Johnson, J. F., Connelly, S., & Devenport, L. D. (2012). Improving case-based ethics training with codes of conduct and forecasting content. *Ethics and Behavior, 22,* 258–280. doi: 10.1080/10508422.2012.661311

Herreid, C. F. (1998). What makes a good case? Some basic rules of good storytelling help teachers generate student excitement in the classroom. *Journal of College Science Teaching, 27*(3), 163–165.

Hogarth, R. M., & Makridakis, S. (1981). Forecasting and planning: An evaluation. *Management Science, 27,* 115–138.

Johnson, J. F., Thiel, C. E., Bagdasarov, Z., Connelly, S., Harkrider, L., Devenport, L. D., & Mumford, M. D. (2012). Case-based ethics education: The impact of cause complexity and outcome favorability on ethicality. *Journal of Empirical Research on Human Research Ethics, 7*(3), 63–77. doi:10.1525/jer.2012.7.3.63

Kim, S., William, P. R., Pinsky, L., Brock, D., Phillips, K., & Keary, J. (2006). A conceptual framework for developing teaching cases: A review and synthesis of the literature across disciplines. *Medical Education, 40,* 867–876. doi:10.1111/j.1365-2929.2006.02544.x

Kligyte, V., Connelly, S., Thiel. C. E., & Devenport, L. D. (in press). The influence of anger, fear, and emotion regulation strategies on ethical decision-making. *Human Performance.*

Kolodner, J. L. (1992). An introduction to case-based reasoning. *Artificial Intelligence Review, 6*, 3–34.

Kolodner, J. L. (1997). Educational implications of analogy: A view from case-based reasoning. *American Psychologist, 52*, 57–66.

Kolodner, J. L., Camp, P. J., Crismond, D., Fasse, B., Gray, J., Holbrook, J., Puntambekar, S., & Ryan, M. (2003). Problem-based learning meets case-based reasoning in the middle-school classroom: Putting learning by design into practice. *Journal of the Learning Sciences, 12*, 495–547.

Kolodner, J. L., Owensby, J. N., & Guzdial, M. (2004). Case-based learning aids. In D. H. Jonassen & D. H. Jonassen (Eds.), *Handbook of research on educational communications and technology* (2nd ed., pp. 829–861). Mahwah, NJ: Lawrence Erlbaum Associates.

Laditka, S. B., & Houck, M. M. (2006). Student-developed case studies: An experiential approach for teaching ethics in management. *Journal of Business Ethics, 64*(2), 157–167.

MacDougall, A. E., Harkrider, L. N., Bagdasarov, Z., Johnson, J. F., Thiel, C. E., Peacock, J., Mumford, M. D., Devenport, L. D., & Connelly, S. (in press). Examining the effects of incremental case building and forecasting outcomes on case-based ethics instruction. *Ethics & Behavior.* doi:10.1080/10508422.2013.824819

Marcy, R. T., & Mumford, M. D. (2007). Social innovation: Enhancing creative performance through causal analysis. *Creativity Research Journal, 19*, 123–140.

Mayo, J. A. (2002). Case-based instruction: A technique for increasing conceptual application in introductory psychology. *Journal of Constructivist Psychology, 15*, 65–74.

Martin, L. E., Stenmark, C. K., Thiel, C. E., Antes, A. L., Mumford, M. D., Connelly, S., & Devenport, L. D. (2011). The influence of temporal orientation and affective frame on use of ethical decision-making strategies. *Ethics and Behavior, 21*, 127–146.

McWilliams, V., & Nahavandi, A. (2006). Using live cases to teach ethics. *Journal of Business Ethics, 67*, 421–433. doi:10.1007/s10551-006-9035-3

Mumford, M. D., Connelly, S., Brown, R. P., Murphy, S. T., Hill, J. H., Antes, A. L., Waples, E. P., & Devenport, L. D. (2008). Sensemaking approach to ethics training for scientists: Preliminary evidence of training effectiveness. *Ethics and Behavior, 18*, 315–339.

Mumford, M. D., Devenport, L. D., Brown, R. P., Connelly, M. S., Murphy, S. T., Hill, J. H., & Antes, A. L. (2006). Validation of ethical decision-making measures: Evidence for a new set of measures. *Ethics and Behavior, 16*, 319–345.

Mumford, M. D., Reiter-Palmon, R., & Redmond, M. R. (1994). Problem construction and cognition: Applying problem representations in ill-defined domains. In M. A. Runco (Ed.), *Problem finding, problem solving, and creativity* (pp. 3–39). Norwood, NJ: Ablex.

Mumford, M. D., Schultz, R. A., & Van Doorn, J. R. (2001). Performance in planning: Processes, requirements, and errors. *Review of General Psychology, 5*, 213–240.

Pant, P. N., & Starbuck, W. H. (1990). Innocents in the forest: Forecasting and research methods. *Journal of Management, 16*, 433–460.

Peacock, J., Harkrider, L. N., Bagdasarov, Z., Connelly, S., Johnson, J. F., Thiel, C. E., MacDougall, A. E., Mumford, M. D., & Devenport, L. D. (2013). Effects of alternative outcome scenarios and structured outcome evaluation on case-based ethics instruction. *Science and Engineering Ethics, 19*(3), 1283–1303. doi:10.1007/s11948-012-9402-7

Richardson, B. (1994). Towards a comprehensive view of the case method in management development. *Industrial and Commercial Training, 26,* 3–8.

Rippin, A., Booth, C., Bowie, S., & Jordan, J. (2002). A complex case: Using the case study method to explore uncertainty and ambiguity in undergraduate business education. *Teaching in Higher Education, 7*(4), 429–441. doi:10.1080/1356251

Schwandt, D. R. (2005). When managers become philosophers: Integrating learning with sensemaking. *Academy of Management Learning and Education, 4,* 176–192.

Scott, G. M., Lonergan, D. C., & Mumford, M. D. (2005). Conceptual combination: Alternative knowledge structures, alternative heuristics. *Creativity Research Journal, 17,* 79–98.

Setia, S., Bobby, Z., Ananthanarayanan, P., Radhika, M., Kavitha, M., & Prashanth, T. (2011). Case based learning versus problem based learning: A direct comparison from first year medical students' perspectives. *Webmed Central Medical Education, 2,* 1–14.

Simkovic, M. (2013). Competition and crisis in mortgage securitization. *Indiana Law Journal, 88*(1), 214–271.

Sonenshein, S. (2007). The role of construction, intuition, and justification in responding to ethical issues at work: The sensemaking-intuition model. *Academy of Management Review, 4,* 1022–1040.

Stenmark, C. K., Antes, A. L., Thiel, C. E., Caughron, J. J., Xiaoqian, W., & Mumford, M. D. (2011). Consequence identification in forecasting and ethical decision-making. *Journal of Empirical Research on Human Research Ethics, 6,* 25–32.

Stenmark, C., Antes, A. L., Wang, X., Caughron, J., Thiel, C. E., & Mumford, M. D. (2010). Strategies in forecasting outcomes in ethical decision-making: Identifying and analyzing the causes of the problem. *Ethics and Behavior, 20,* 110–127.

Thiel, C. E., Connelly, S., & Griffith, J.A. (2011). The influence of ethical decision-making: Comparison of a primary and secondary appraisal. *Ethics and Behavior, 21,* 380–403.

Thiel, C. E., Connelly, S., Harkrider, L., Devenport, L. D., Bagdasarov, Z., Johnson, J. F., & Mumford, M. D. (2013). Case-based knowledge and ethics education: Improving learning and transfer through emotionally rich cases. *Science and Engineering Ethics, 19*(1), 265–286. doi:10.1007/s11948-011-9318-7

Thomas, J. B., Clark, S. M., & Gioia D. A. (1993). Strategic sensemaking and organizational performance: Linkages among scanning, interpretation, action, and outcomes. *Academy of Management Journal, 36,* 239–270.

Tversky, A., & Kahneman, D. (1974). Judgment under uncertainty: Heuristics and biases. *Science, 185,* 1124–1131.

Weick, K. E. (1988). Enacted sensemaking in crisis situations. *Journal of Management Studies, 25,* 305–317.

Weick, K. (1995). *Sensemaking in organizations.* Thousand Oaks, CA: Sage Publications.

Werhane, P. H. (2002). Moral imagination and systems thinking. *Journal of Business Ethics, 38,* 33–42.

Williams, S. M. (1992). Putting case-based instruction into context: Examples from legal and medical education. *Journal of the Learning Sciences, 2*(4), 367–427.

Xiao, Y., Milgram, P., & Doyle, D. J. (1997). Capturing and modeling planning expertise in anesthesiology: Results of a field study. In C. E. Zsambok, & G. Klein (Eds.), *Naturalistic decision making* (pp. 197–205). Hillside, NJ: Lawrence Erlbaum.

CHAPTER 10

STRENGTHENING MORAL COMPETENCIES AT WORK THROUGH INTEGRITY CAPACITY CULTIVATION

Joseph A. Petrick

Strengthening practical moral competencies at work through systematic individual and organizational ethics training has been demonstrated to have many beneficial impacts on stakeholder work performance and organizational effectiveness (Collins, 2012; Petrick, Cragg, & Sanudo, 2012; Weber & Wasieleski, 2013). Managers want to have access to and use practical tools that develop moral competencies that add value to organizational performance. Among the practical moral competencies that can be strengthened are the following: (1) the organizational competency to empirically voice, measure, and shape an ethical work culture and (2) the individual competency to analyze and resolve ethical issues at work by using words, numbers, and digital graphic images. Integrity capacity cultivation is one way to systematically enhance these two practical moral competencies and improve performance at work (Petrick & Quinn, 2000; Petrick, 2008).

Ethics Training in Action, pages 207–226
Copyright © 2014 by Information Age Publishing
All rights of reproduction in any form reserved.

This chapter will consist of four sections: (1) the integrity capacity concept and moral competency goals of business ethics training; (2) an organizational integrity context development tool, the Organizational Ethics Needs Assessment (OENA), to solicit and strengthen collective moral competencies at work; (3) an individual moral judgment development tool, the Judgment Integrity Capacity Model (JICM), to improve the uniform systematic consideration and multicultural usefulness of managerial moral judgments about workplace ethics issues; and (4) implications and key takeaways. The main focus of this chapter will be on increasing awareness of the nature and value of integrity capacity as an intangible collective and individual strategic asset and on empowering managers and other stakeholders with two practical tools to improve both their ethical work cultures and their professional moral judgments at work.

THE INTEGRITY CAPACITY CONCEPT AND MORAL COMPETENCY GOALS

Integrity capacity theory has been developed and applied in a variety of macro, meso, and micro contexts to enhance and organizational moral competency goals (Petrick & Quinn, 1997, 2000, 2001; Petrick & Scherer, 2003). Integrity capacity is defined as the personal, organizational, and social capability to coherently process moral awareness, deliberation, character, and conduct; to regularly render balanced and inclusive judgments regarding moral results, rules, character, and context; to routinely demonstrate mature moral reasoning and relationship development; and to design and/or sustain morally supportive intraorganizational and extraorganizational systems (Petrick & Quinn, 2001). Integrity capacity is both inherently valuable and instrumentally worthwhile. Adults honor their inherent human dignity by demonstrating their integrity capacity through responsible decisions and actions. In addition, workplace leaders are held accountable for the proper management of integrity capacity as a key intangible strategic asset that can either enhance or detract from organizational reputational capital domestically and globally. Given the intrinsic and instrumental value of integrity capacity, a survey of literature on goals of business ethics training reveals at least two measurable and reasonable moral competency goals: (1) context management competence and (2) cognitive decision-making competence (Petrick, 2008).

First, the goal of developing context management competence in integrity capacity training is to enable individuals to design, build, and shape supportive moral environments within and outside organizations that sustain cognitive and behavioral moral competence (Collins, 2012; Trevino & Weaver, 2003). Context management competence focuses on improving the "moral barrels" (organizations and other environments) into which the "moral apples" (good people) are placed organizationally and extraorganizationally, domestically, and globally (Arnold, 2009). If fully implemented, context management competence creates a morally supportive environment that facilitates stakeholder ethical actions (Petrick, 2010; Wood, Logsdon, Lewellyn, & Davenport, 2006). Among the major collective context management competencies is the systematic and ongoing empirical assessment and improvement of an organization's ethical work culture. Although there are a variety of organizational assessments, the Organizational Ethics Needs Assessment (OENA) provides one practical and systematic way of doing so.

Second, the goal of enhancing cognitive decision-making competence in integrity capacity training is to develop systematic and responsible moral judgments that demonstrate the ability to comprehensively identify, analyze, and resolve ethics issues using words, numbers, and digital graphic images. Although there are a variety of ethical decision-making models, the Judgment Integrity Capacity Model (JICM) provides one practical, systematic, and multiculturally useful way of doing so. We now turn to a discussion of both of these practical tools.

THE OENA AND COLLECTIVE
MORAL COMPETENCY DEVELOPMENT

The first developmental tool, the OENA (provided in Appendix A), is designed to systematically and empirically operationalize collective moral competency by obtaining data on perceived ethics issues at work and the level of support for specific improvements at work to address those moral concerns.

Ample evidence demonstrates that the moral competency and behavior of adults at work is positively influenced by the ethical culture of their workplace (Collins, 2012; Trevino & Weaver, 2003). As a moral competency, organizational context management can be developed through the customized design, quantified structured process, and professional implementation of the OENA to identify and resolve organizational ethics issues, while strengthening an ethical work culture. This tool, implemented on a 360-degree basis, can empirically address two questions normally directed at organizational leaders: (1) What were the three top organizational ethics issues in your workplace last year? and (2) What actions have you taken to resolve those organizational ethics issues? Too often, the perceptions of leaders and the rank and file in organizations regarding the ethical work culture context differ significantly, but there is no empirical process institutionalized to give voice to those disparities (Trevino & Weaver, 2003). This neglect of properly managing the system integrity capacity of the firm can be overcome by the regular and ongoing use of the OENA, with timely follow-up interventions and their results transparently disclosed to all stakeholders.

The OENA has two sections. The first section identifies the perceived seriousness of 40 standard organizational ethics issues in column A and the adequacy of their current treatment in column B. Respondents assign numeric weights in column A from 5 = Very Great to 1 = Not at All to quantitatively measure the perceived severity of the issue. For example, if workplace ethics issue #18, workplace bullying, is accorded a numerical rating of 5 by a substantial number of respondents in column A and in column B, then that issue is probably a very serious one that is not being adequately addressed at present in the workplace and urgently deserves attention. Furthermore, empirical data provide some objective measure for ranking organizational ethics issues, which can be transparently communicated to respondents to incentivize leadership accountability for ethical work culture improvement.

The second section of the OENA identifies the nature and extent of existing support for specific actions that would improve the ethical work culture in items 41–56. Respondents assign numeric weights in the sole column from 1 = Very Strong Support to 5 = No Support to quantitatively measure the nature and extent of support for different components of an organizational ethics system. Those components with the lowest scores have the strongest support for ethics development system implementation and/or continuance and are most likely to be accorded higher priority in the respondents' organizational ethics development actions. For example, if organizational ethics system component #47, whistleblower protection, is accorded a numerical rating of 1 by a substantial number of respondents, then that system component is likely to be more readily supported in the organization as a whole or in certain divisions of the organization than other components accorded a rating of 3. Furthermore, those components that are quantitatively supported by respondents in the organization provide the prioritized roadmap for ethical work culture improvement efforts, so that pilot programs can be successfully implemented in targeted divisions using the data and then rolled out to the rest of the organization.

The implementation of moral competence through the OENA, nevertheless, is not inevitable. It requires leadership and stakeholder courage. In the U.S., the U.S. federal sentencing guidelines for organizations and the Sarbanes-Oxley Act are two of a number of legal/regulatory enactments designed to prevent criminal misconduct in and from organizations (Collins, 2012). Many business leaders and their stakeholders choose to only comply with these mandates and often reluctantly so, but to do no more. There are pressures to build and sustain an organizational ethical work culture, but there is no requirement that the OENA be implemented to do so. In fact, many business leaders are reluctant to do more than what is legally required, since uncovering organizational ethics issues that are not being addressed may expose them to additional legal liability (Collins, 2012).

To move from legal compliance to moral commitment to improve organizational ethical work culture through the voluntary implementation of the OENA requires professional moral courage from leaders and their stakeholders (Sekerka, Bagozzi, & Charnigo, 2009; Sekerka & Godwin, 2010). Moral competencies associated with the display of moral fortitude include emotional signaling, reflective pause, self-regulation, and moral preparation (Sekerka, McCarthy, & Bagozzi, 2010). These moral competencies can and have been incorporated in integrity capacity training and OENA development.

THE JICM AND INDIVIDUAL
MORAL COMPETENCY DEVELOPMENT

A concrete business ethics minicase and the practical application of the second developmental tool, the JICM, is provided in Appendix B. Too often, managers, especially those located in different countries who speak different natural languages but need to communicate an urgent, cross-culturally useful warning of a corporate ethical risk, do not have the training to do so professionally. The JICM is designed to address that practical concern by systematically and empirically operationalizing individual moral competency in judgment-making regarding moral issues at work by using words, numbers, and digital graphic images to analyze and resolve the issues. Managers trained in the JICM can digitally transmit their local analysis and proposed resolution of a workplace ethics issue anywhere in the world within seconds and be understood.

The JICM is structured around ten questions. The first two questions determine the scope and focus of the business ethics case being considered by determining the extent of harm caused to market and non-market stakeholders, followed by a determination of the facts of the case along with the prioritized identification of the ethics issues that are to be the focus of the case.

Questions three through six of the JICM are the key moral analysis questions. They hone in, respectively, on the moral results, the moral rules, the moral character, and the moral context of the issue at hand. The ideal is moral judgment that achieves good results by following the right rules while simultaneously cultivating virtuous character and strengthening a morally supportive work context. The acronym, R^2C^2, symbolizing both results and rules by referring to the first letter of each word (R^2) and symbolizing character and context by referring to the first letter of each word (C^2) is a hermeneutic formula or shorthand to ensure that all key dimensions of moral analysis have been considered. It is the inclusive, moderate balancing of well-reasoned answers to these four dimensions of an ethical issue that constitutes sound moral judgment in managers.

A distinctive value of this structure, however, is that in addition to words, each dimension can be assigned a numerical rating and then be graphed onto a digital image that depicts the current situation in a closed quadrilateral figure and recommends the desired moral improvement in a dotted line quadrilateral figure. Managers trained in the JICM, therefore, can rapidly convey their cross-cultural corporate moral risks by the use of numbers and/or graphic images along with an indication of the relative urgency and severity of the issues by highlighting the nature and extent of stakeholder harms.

Questions seven and eight of the JICM, respectively, determine whether the status quo is tolerable or needs to be improved, and then pose possible solutions using divergent thinking followed by convergent thinking that recommends and justifies a proposed resolution. Too often managers engage in satisficing judgments that rely upon a narrow cost-benefit analysis of short-term results and prematurely converge on a resolution that can be easily implemented regardless of the long-term consequences: for example, automatically firing an employee for any misconduct since employment-at-will legal provisions in most states protect managers from legal accountability. The steady use of the JICM can professionalize the moral judgment of managers.

Finally, questions nine and ten of the JICM focus on the practical implementation, evaluation, and control of the moral judgment and its anticipated impact; procedures for dealing with unintended consequences; and provisions for ongoing improvement. The JICM is graphically represented in Figure 10.1 to visually distinguish the current moral situation from the normatively preferred or desired moral situation.

IMPLICATIONS AND KEY TAKEAWAYS

For those responsible for ethics training in the workplace, there are some implications and key takeaways from this chapter:

1. Consider reading published research on integrity capacity theory and its practical dimensions so that those who undergo ethics training at work become aware that the training is about enhancing their competency to manage a key intangible strategic asset that is critical to their own career advancement and the reputational capital of the organization that they represent.
2. Consider courageously adopting the OENA as a practical, systematic, empirical way to collectively identify organizational ethics issues and organizational support for ethical work culture improvement.
3. Consider using the JICM as a practical, systematic, empirical way to individually analyze and resolve ethical issues at work using words, numbers, and digital graphic images.

APPENDIX A: ORGANIZATIONAL ETHICS NEEDS ASSESSMENT (OENA)

Purposes: The purposes of this survey are to assess perceived organizational ethics needs and to determine the relative degree of support for individual components of an organizational ethics development system.

Instructions: This survey is divided into two parts. In Part I a number of issues, processes and work-related factors are listed below. Please indicate in Column A on a scale of 1 to 5 how serious this issue/problem is in your work environment. In Column B on a scale of 1 to 5 please indicate how successful your work environment has been in responding effectively to the problem. Check only one box per issue in each column. In Part II, components of an organizational ethics development system are indicated on a scale of 1 to 5 and by checking the appropriate box you can indicate your level of support for any of the system components.

PART I

Workplace Ethics Issues	A Seriousness					B Success				
	Not at All				Very Great	Very Successful				Needs Attention
	1	2	3	4	5	1	2	3	4	5
1. Dishonesty (lying, stealing or cheating at work)	☐	☐	☐	☐	☐	☐	☐	☐	☐	☐
2. Persons always looking out only for themselves at the expense of others	☐	☐	☐	☐	☐	☐	☐	☐	☐	☐
3. Unfair hiring, appraisal and/or rewards processes, e.g., favoritism	☐	☐	☐	☐	☐	☐	☐	☐	☐	☐
4. Applying discipline inconsistently	☐	☐	☐	☐	☐	☐	☐	☐	☐	☐
5. Perceived inequity of rewards, e.g., superior and mediocre performers	☐	☐	☐	☐	☐	☐	☐	☐	☐	☐
6. Lack of quality, rapid service to meet internal and external stakeholder expectations	☐	☐	☐	☐	☐	☐	☐	☐	☐	☐
7. Racial discrimination	☐	☐	☐	☐	☐	☐	☐	☐	☐	☐
8. Sex discrimination	☐	☐	☐	☐	☐	☐	☐	☐	☐	☐
9. Age discrimination	☐	☐	☐	☐	☐	☐	☐	☐	☐	☐
10. Other forms of discrimination (specify)	☐	☐	☐	☐	☐	☐	☐	☐	☐	☐
11. Unhealthy and/or unsafe work conditions	☐	☐	☐	☐	☐	☐	☐	☐	☐	☐
12. Lack of respect for privacy/confidentiality	☐	☐	☐	☐	☐	☐	☐	☐	☐	☐
13. Weak board governance/oversight	☐	☐	☐	☐	☐	☐	☐	☐	☐	☐
14. Conflicts of interest	☐	☐	☐	☐	☐	☐	☐	☐	☐	☐
15. Unjust compensation and benefit package	☐	☐	☐	☐	☐	☐	☐	☐	☐	☐
16. Inadequate monitoring for legal/regulatory compliance	☐	☐	☐	☐	☐	☐	☐	☐	☐	☐

Workplace Ethics Issues	A Seriousness					B Success				
	Not at All Very Great					Very Successful			Needs Attention	
	1	2	3	4	5	1	2	3	4	5
17. Nonexistent or vague code of ethics and moral standards at work	☐	☐	☐	☐	☐	☐	☐	☐	☐	☐
18. Workplace bullying	☐	☐	☐	☐	☐	☐	☐	☐	☐	☐
19. Unfair distribution of benefits and burdens at work, e.g., workload, status, gain-sharing and pain-sharing	☐	☐	☐	☐	☐	☐	☐	☐	☐	☐
20. Inadequate enforcement of moral standards at work, e.g., people get away with too much at work	☐	☐	☐	☐	☐	☐	☐	☐	☐	☐
21. Perceived gap between moral rhetoric and reality at work, e.g., neither managers nor non-managers "walk the integrity talk"	☐	☐	☐	☐	☐	☐	☐	☐	☐	☐
22. Top managers and/or board members are complacent and not good moral role models	☐	☐	☐	☐	☐	☐	☐	☐	☐	☐
23. Inadequate level of managerial and co-worker appreciation for personal contributions	☐	☐	☐	☐	☐	☐	☐	☐	☐	☐
24. Inadequate resources/training to do quality work	☐	☐	☐	☐	☐	☐	☐	☐	☐	☐
25. Lack of innovative teamwork and shared work pride	☐	☐	☐	☐	☐	☐	☐	☐	☐	☐
26. Lack of willingness to continually learn and innovate	☐	☐	☐	☐	☐	☐	☐	☐	☐	☐
27. Appraisal processes that unnecessarily intensify internal competition at work and penalize cooperative conduct	☐	☐	☐	☐	☐	☐	☐	☐	☐	☐
28. Lack of willingness to learn how to develop statistically stable work systems	☐	☐	☐	☐	☐	☐	☐	☐	☐	☐
29. Lack of accuracy in documents/records	☐	☐	☐	☐	☐	☐	☐	☐	☐	☐
30. Avoidance of addressing performance problems	☐	☐	☐	☐	☐	☐	☐	☐	☐	☐
31. Unclear role responsibilities	☐	☐	☐	☐	☐	☐	☐	☐	☐	☐
32. Negative and complacent work attitudes	☐	☐	☐	☐	☐	☐	☐	☐	☐	☐
33. Lack of commendation for exemplary moral conduct at work, e.g., people feel taken for granted	☐	☐	☐	☐	☐	☐	☐	☐	☐	☐
34. Excessive extra-organizational performance pressures to act unethically, e.g., global competition, industry norms, corruption	☐	☐	☐	☐	☐	☐	☐	☐	☐	☐
35. Inadequate impact of professional association standards on work conduct	☐	☐	☐	☐	☐	☐	☐	☐	☐	☐
36. Lack of whistleblowing policy to protect persons from retaliation	☐	☐	☐	☐	☐	☐	☐	☐	☐	☐

Workplace Ethics Issues	A Seriousness					B Success				
	Not at All			Very Great		Very Successful			Needs Attention	
	1	2	3	4	5	1	2	3	4	5
37. Organizational ethical climate that prevents people from getting things done without getting done in	☐	☐	☐	☐	☐	☐	☐	☐	☐	☐
38. Inadequate advisory and support services for doing the right thing at work	☐	☐	☐	☐	☐	☐	☐	☐	☐	☐
39. Inadequate organizational social responsibility	☐	☐	☐	☐	☐	☐	☐	☐	☐	☐
40. Collective unwillingness to benchmark work processes or engage in intra- and inter-organizational networking for system improvement	☐	☐	☐	☐	☐	☐	☐	☐	☐	☐

PART II

Components of Organizational Ethics System	Very Strong Support			No Support	
	1	2	3	4	5
41. Moral leadership by example at the top and system support	☐	☐	☐	☐	☐
42. Formal statement of prioritized organizational values	☐	☐	☐	☐	☐
43. Written code of ethics	☐	☐	☐	☐	☐
44. Annual ethical work culture assessment and/or organizational ethics needs assessment administered with results transparently communicated	☐	☐	☐	☐	☐
45. An organizational ethics steering committee	☐	☐	☐	☐	☐
46. Ethics training, development and education for improved moral competency at work	☐	☐	☐	☐	☐
47. Whistleblower protection	☐	☐	☐	☐	☐
48. Ethics factors considered in human resource selection and work performance systems	☐	☐	☐	☐	☐
49. Ethics factors considered in performance appraisal and reward systems	☐	☐	☐	☐	☐
50. People commended for exemplary conduct in organizational formal communications	☐	☐	☐	☐	☐
51. Organizational ethics officer or comparable position with authority to investigate ethics violations	☐	☐	☐	☐	☐
52. Clear ethics reporting/advisory processes, e.g., "ethics hotline" for obtaining guidance and reporting violations	☐	☐	☐	☐	☐
53. Clear ethics conflict resolution processes	☐	☐	☐	☐	☐
54. Swift and fair enforcement of ethics standards	☐	☐	☐	☐	☐
55. Organizational ethics audit to ensure legal/regulatory compliance and benchmark continuous organizational moral improvement	☐	☐	☐	☐	☐
56. Communication of organizational moral progress and remaining moral challenges	☐	☐	☐	☐	☐

A. Instrument Scoring of Part I and Part II

Step 1 in Part I: Assign Numeric Weights to Responses in Columns—(a) Assign numeric weights in Column A from 5 = Very Great to 1 = Not at All; (b) Assign numeric weights in Column B from 1 = Very Successful to 5 = Needs Attention.

Step 2 in Part I: Rank Organizational Ethics Issues—(a) Calculate the numeric average of all responses for each ethics issue in each column (b) Add the numeric averages for both columns for each issue and rank order each issue from the highest to the lowest average scores. Those issues with the highest scores are perceived to be the most serious ethics issues that urgently need attention. Transparently communicate results to participating stakeholders.

Step 3 in Part II: Assign Weights and Rank Support Levels for Organizational Ethics System Development Components— (a) Assign numeric weights from 1 = Very Strong Support to 5 = No Support; (b) Calculate the numeric average of all responses for each system component and rank order each component from the lowest to the highest average scores. Those units or components with the lowest scores have the strongest support for ethics development system implementation and/or continuance, and are most likely to accord higher priority to addressing the identified ethics system component.

B. Action Steps for Part I and Part II

Action Step 1 for Part I: Address High Priority, Identified Ethics Issues—In order to effectively and efficiently analyze and resolve ethics issues, allocate resources to the top three ethics issues (those that are regarded as most serious and require urgent attention) to focus on the most salient moral issues first. Document corrective actions taken on targeted issues.

Action Step 2 for Part I: Measure Organizational Moral Progress at Regular Intervals and Communicate Results—Use annual OENAs or ethics audits to measure moral progress at regular intervals and communicate results to participating stakeholders. Be able to truthfully and empirically answer two questions: (1) What were your three top workplace ethics issues last year? and (2) What have you done to address those issues to date? Benchmark ethics practices internally and longitudinally and externally with other organizations longitudinally.

Action Step 3 for Part II: Implement Strongly Supported System Components—Take immediate action to implement or continue any component with an average support level of 1.25 or less. Determine if there are any correlations between support for system components in Part II and prioritized ethics issues in Part I, e.g., strong support for #43 (written code of ethics) and high ranking of ethics issue #17 (nonexistent or vague code of ethics and moral standards at work). In terms of timing, implement ethics development system improvements first in the units or components with high support that are correlated with high priority ethics issues. Managers are more likely to be successful in organizational ethics development if changes are made where there is already strong support for particular ethics system components. Communicate early success stories to build momentum for future organizational ethics initiatives.

(*Source:* Modified from Frank Navran (1993). *The Ethics Inventory.* Navran Associates, www.navran.com).

APPENDIX B: SALES DISHONESTY CASE AND JICM ANALYSIS AND RESOLUTION

Sales Dishonesty Case

Two probationary employees, David Smith and Kara Jones, are sales associates in a U.S. retail furniture company. Both are in the fourth month of their six-month probationary period. They have been informed by top management that meeting their sales quota numbers will be the exclusive factor that will determine whether or not they will be hired full time.

Yesterday, David sold a two-year-old bedroom set to a former customer of Kara by telling the customer that the bedroom set was a brand new model. Kara confronted David about the sales dishonesty, but David replied that if the customer returned, Kara could have her back. Kara objected. In addition, David replied that selling is only a game in which the company tries to get the highest price while the customer attempts to get the lowest price, so, as in poker and other games, bluffing and lying are acceptable ways to win the game. Furthermore, he ridiculed Kara for being from a small town with parochial and idealistic expectations about selling and questioned whether Kara was cut out for sales work.

Kara went to see Glen Richards, a senior sales representative in the company, and expressed her concern about David's dishonest sales practices. She complained about David taking her customers, lying to them to make sales, and in general, not playing by the rules. She asked Glen if she should report David to top management. Glen responded that that would be ill-advised because, since there was no ethics reporting system or a whistle-blower protection policy in place at the company, she would be vulnerable to managerial censure and it would look as if she was making excuses for her own substandard sales performance. He advised her to bend the rules in order to make the sales quota during her probationary period.

JICM Case Analysis and Resolution

1. Who are the stakeholders involved and how severely are they impacted? Who is harmed and by how much?
   a. Market Stakeholders: (1) *Employee David:* chose to lie to customer to get his sales quota and hurt his character, Kara, and the company (high impact); (2) *Employee Kara:* unfairly treated by David and the company for being honest (high impact); (3) *Employee Manager:* absent as a role model for honesty and apparently did not institute or enforce an ethics development system at work (high impact); (4) *Other Employees:* are influenced by norms of sales dishonesty in their future performance (medium impact); (5) *Owners/Investors:* jeopardizing long-term financial returns displaces more risk on investors without their consent or input (medium impact); (6) *Customer:* disrespectful treatment is likely to result in lost future business and bad word-of-mouth publicity (high impact); (7) *Suppliers:* jeopardizing long-term financial returns displaces more risk of reduced future orders on suppliers without their consent or input (medium impact); and (8) *Creditors:* jeopardizing long-term financial returns displaces more risk on creditors without their consent or input (medium impact).
   b. Non-market Stakeholders: (1) *Governments:* possible fraud inviting local, state, and/or federal government regulation (medium impact); (2) *Communities:* community members become victimized and/or vulnerable to dishonest sales tactics by a local business (medium impact); (3) *Professional Business Support Groups:* legal professional services risk the loss of their reputation for advancing justice; accounting professional services risk the loss of their reputation for objective and accurate auditing of accounting/financial documents; financial professional services risk the loss of their reputation by economically supporting fraudulent business practices; industry/trade reputation is tarnished by dishonest industry sales practices perceived by stakeholders to be an accepted norm; sales professional associations risk the loss of their reputation for certifying and tolerating fraudulent sales tactics without professional code enforcement; educational institutions risk the loss of their reputation by credentialing the adequate academic performance of busi-

ness graduates who engage in illegal and/or unethical activity (medium impact); (4) *Media:* will likely not report a single episode unless a pattern of fraudulent sales tactics arouse consumer and/or general public concern (low impact); (5) *Activist Groups:* depending on the consumer activist group connections and resources of the victimized consumer, the consumer activist groups may engage other non-market stakeholders in forms of public complaints and demands for restitution (medium impact); and (6) *General Public:* erodes trust in business sales transactions in general (medium impact).

2. What are the central ethical issue(s) and the relevant facts in this case?
   a. Central Ethical Issue(s): (1) *dishonesty in sales transactions;* (2) unfairness in employee relations and performance appraisal; (3) risking loss of employee, managerial, and company reputation for integrity and future business; (4) lack of ethical infrastructure in company to support ethical conduct.
   b. Relevant Facts: (1) David lied to customer to make his sales quota; (2) David's lying hurt the customer and Kara and risked the loss of reputation and future business for company; (3) the infrastructure processes for reporting and resolving unethical conduct in the company did not appear to exist or to be used.

3. RESULTS: To what extent do (should) the results of the action produce more benefits than costs to stakeholders in the short and long range? (Current: 1/Desired: 6) This case demonstrates extremely unacceptable under-emphasis upon good long-term moral results.
   a. David's lying results in some short-term benefits for him but more short-term and long-term costs for Kara, other employees, the company, and other stakeholders. He is acting selfishly and by doing so he offends customers, generates dysfunctional competition and distrust between coworkers, and risks the loss of future return business.
   b. The full extent of the costs to other more remote stakeholders could be substantial if sales dishonesty provokes more regulatory, legal, and industry condemnation, domestically and globally.

4. RULES: To what extent do (should) the rules followed to achieve results respect the rights of others and adhere to standards of justice and fairness? Are appropriate duties and obligations fulfilled and properly prioritized? (Current: 1/Desired: 6) This case demonstrates extremely unacceptable under-emphasis upon following the right moral rules.
   a. **Rights**: The act of lying by David was wrong. It violated the customer's right to the truth and the duty to treat customers with equal respect rather than manipulative disregard. It insults the

dignity of customers by unilaterally depriving them of accurate information needed to make free, informed purchasing decisions. Without the truth, their freedom to intelligently use their purchasing power is taken (stolen) from them, and stealing is inherently wrong.

b. **Justice:** The act of lying by David was unjust to Kara and other salespeople. The outcome disproportionately benefited David while displacing the bulk of the burdens of lost sales, future disgruntled customers, untrustworthy colleague relations, and future negative performance appraisals on Kara and other salespeople. By lying, David procured benefits that he did not justly deserve or merit. There were no grounds for retributive justice claims.

c. **Fairness:** Lying was procedurally unfair to the customers who were deprived of their purchasing power and procedurally unfair to other employees who told the truth to customers. Deceived customers and honest employees were treated unequally and adversely from others. David did not use fair processes to "earn" his sales, but took advantage of customer ignorance by misrepresenting a product and took advantage of employee goodwill by stealing customers.

5. CHARACTER: To what extent is (should be) the character of affected stakeholders enhanced? Are intellectual, moral, social, emotional and political virtues (readiness to act ethically) being cultivated or corrupted? Are individuals becoming better persons through this transaction/relationship? (Current: 1/Desired: 6) This case demonstrates extremely unacceptable under-emphasis on cultivating virtuous character.

a. **Personal Character:** By lying, David is weakening his character; he will be less willing to act ethically in the future. He is becoming a worse (vicious) person rather than a better (virtuous) one by lying. By lying, he betrays the *intellectual virtue* of respect for the truth; he indulges the *moral vices* of cowardice and imprudence by being afraid to lose sales by telling the truth and downplaying the hurtful long-term consequences of his action. By lying, he erodes the *social virtues* of trust and cooperation, while fomenting the *emotional vices* of hatred and resentment among and between stakeholders. Finally, by lying, David is violating the *political virtues* of workplace citizenship and civility by unilaterally abusing information power to take advantage of others.

b. **Group Character:** Not only is David's character diminished, but his bad example adversely impacts the collective readiness to act ethically by others at work. If David's conduct is overlooked, condoned, or praised, it sends a message about the kind of self-ish, dishonest person who will succeed at that company. Collective character corruption could then exacerbate customer distrust, hateful resentment among co-workers, the rapid loss of workplace community, and the lack of readiness to act ethically in other transactions in the future.

    c. **Leadership Character:** The notable lack of the visible presence of a manager to serve as a positive role model and to set the tone for honesty in sales practices at work indicates a lack of strong leadership character in the workplace.

6. CONTEXT: To what extent are (should be) the intra-organizational and extraorganizational contexts (barrels) supportive of ethical conduct? (Current: 2/Desired: 7) This case demonstrates unacceptable under-emphasis upon sustaining an ethically supportive context.

    a. **Intraorganizational context:** The implicit condoning of David's lying to get sales indicates that either a company's *compliance or ethics development system* (with regular reporting of unethical acts without retaliation, a code of ethics, and an ethics audit) does not exist or is not routinely used. Nor is there any indication that performance appraisal and reward subsystems factor in ethical ways to achieve results so that unethical practices are penalized and ethical practices are commended. This lack of an ethically supportive company infrastructure indicates that the workplace moral context is poorly designed and risks the loss of company reputation.

    b. **Extraorganizational context:**

        i. *Legal and Regulatory Standards:* The extraorganizational context provides domestic legal and regulatory enforcement of fraud statutes to externally support honest sales transaction practices and related ethical conduct. Sanctioned sales dishonesty also exposes the company to other legal and financial risks under consumer protection laws, the U.S. Federal Sentencing Guidelines for Organizations (USFSGO) and/or the Sarbanes-Oxley Act (SOX).

        ii. *Business Functional Professional Ethics Standards:* Sales representatives are part of the marketing efforts of a company and as such are bound by the American Marketing Association (AMA) code of ethics. Part of the AMA code of ethics is to maintain standards of honesty in relating to all participants in the marketing exchange and to ensure that "communications about offered products are not deceptive." David's deception of his customer violated the AMA professional code of ethics.

iii. ***Industry and Social Standards:*** Standards of sales honesty and sound customer relations in the U.S. furniture industry advocate truthful disclosure regarding any furniture product. Socially, if family and friends found out, they would probably feel ashamed of David's lying and exert some social pressure to stop his lying. Shameful industry and socially irresponsible acts risk the loss of external industry and community reputation and future domestic and global business, so they should be condemned and avoided whenever possible.

7. (JUDGMENT INTEGRITY CAPACITY DECISION) Is there justification for improving the inclusiveness and balance of the current judgment? There is justification for improving the inclusiveness and balance of the current judgment.

8. What are two alternative resolutions for the case, with their advantages and disadvantages?

a. **Resolution A**: (*Immediately Fire David*) After considering any ethics rationalizations, Resolution A is to fire David. The *upside* would be that it would remove a negative role model from the work site and eliminate the risk of future customer complaints and lost business due to sales dishonesty. The *downside* is that it would not be fair to David, who assumed in the absence of formal sales training emphasizing sustained customer relations an explicit and enforced ethics development system, and managerial positive role modeling that "getting his sales numbers" any way he could (including lying) would be acceptable. Nor does it fix the corrupt system (intraorganizational context or barrel) that allowed the lying to occur in the first place. Without an ethics development system in place to retrain David and set future standards of sales honesty for all salespeople, a new hire with David's lying style would jeopardize the company again in the future.

b. **Resolution B**: (*Comprehensive Resolution to Rebuild Integrity Capacity*) After considering any ethics rationalizations, Resolution B is to comprehensively address results, means, character, and context to restore and rebuild a system that would institutionalize business integrity capacity in the firm. The *upside* would be that a comprehensive ethics development system would provide a supportive infrastructure to retrain David and other employees to develop "sales with integrity" practices that would sustain customer relationships through truth-telling. Such a system would meet compliance guidelines and include ethics training on positive customer relations practices, explicit and enforced standards of sales honesty, whistleblowing protections, character education, an ethics audit with public accountability and in-house ethics commendations, and visible managerial moral role modeling of integrity-building sales practices. To avoid unfairly firing David, he would have to change his sales tactics so that they would adhere to the new explicit standards of rightness and fairness. In the process, not only David, but others in the company as well, would be strengthening their characters—that is, their readiness to act ethically in the future as a cooperative, workplace community. Finally, by incorporating a broader range of results than mere sales numbers, such as the number of return customers, level of coworker perceived cooperation and teamwork, and the number of customer complaints to be considered in performance appraisal and rewards, the company will be rewarding rather than penalizing those employees who get sales by safeguarding the reputation of the company. The *downside* is that this resolution takes time and is more complex than Resolution A, but addressing moral complexity in a simple-minded way (i.e., taking the quick, decisive easy way out by firing) won't rebuild the system of business integrity capacity fairly. If David does not respond appropriately to the training, however, the manager should fire him.

9. What is your proposed resolution? What are your moral justifications for the resolution? To what extent will it enhance judgment integrity capacity? (see Judgment Integrity Capacity Profile) Resolution B is the preferred and proposed resolution.

   a. **Comprehensive Moral Justification:** The moral justifications for the resolution are the following: (1) *Results:* there are more benefits than costs to Resolution B in the long run because it comprehensively counters selfish impulses to lie to customers by expanding the results expected for appraisal and reward to include benefits to multiple stakeholders; (2) *Rules:* Resolution B requires explicit statement of company standards of sales honesty and provides a whistleblowing policy for reporting unfair practices with impunity, thereby clarifying explicit rules and improving the chances of right and fair sales transactions in the future; (3) *Character:* Resolution B takes the step to heal the wounds to group character inflicted by lying through community-building, character education training that commends virtuous, trustworthy conduct and raises the level of rewarded cooperation between and among employees; (4) *Context:* through the ethics audit and ethics commendations the company can measure and motivate its system moral progress and signal that moral integrity is important to protect the reputational capital of the firm. The whistleblowing policy will signal that unethical business practices, such as dishonesty in sales transactions, are to be reported. These practices would be investigated swiftly and adjudicated fairly so that employees in the company would know that unethical conduct is penalized and ethical conduct is commended and expected. In addition, the public announcement of the integrity capacity building resolution and audit serves notice to the public to expect higher standards of sales practice from the company and to consider that in their choice of places to do business. The improved company reputation can be used to "win back," attract, and retain future customers.

   b. **Benefits of Resolution:** Resolution B will directly enhance judgment integrity capacity (see Judgment Integrity Capacity Profile Sheet) by comprehensively, simultaneously, and realistically addressing moral results, rules, character and context to protect the company's reputational capital for sustained competitive advantage, domestically and globally.

10. How will your resolution be implemented, evaluated, and improved over time?

   a. **Resolution Implementation and Evaluation Processes:** Resolution B could be implemented either through internal managerial initiative with employee input or external organizational ethics consultant intervention or both. They would design a comprehensive ethics development system, beginning with an organizational ethics needs assessment to identify and prioritize perceived ethics needs and a structured ethics training program to address the prioritized issues. Resolution B would be evaluated by monitoring progress in ethics needs assessments, results of ethics training, and results of ethics audits over time, and perhaps benchmarking. Sharing the success of the approach with industry, professional associations, as well as community and customer audiences would further invite feedback for ongoing evaluation.

   b. **Resolution Improvement Processes:** Resolution B will be improved through regular structured feedback, corrective actions taken when (statistically) warranted, and continual openness shown to incremental and/or breakthrough progress recommendations. Suggestions for improvement would be regularly solicited from stakeholders and incorporated as warranted. Resolution B impacts will be coordinated with other organizational assessment and improvement efforts to promote ongoing business moral progress.

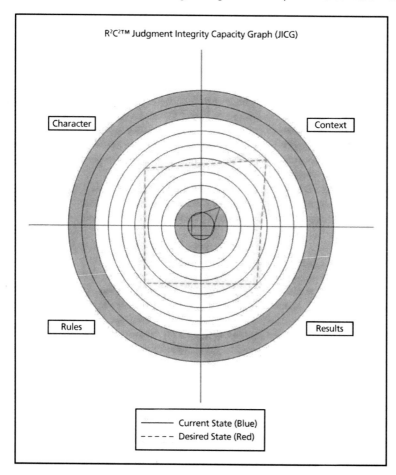

Figure 10.1 The JICG and global business ethics communication.

Ranges of Moral Judgment Evaluation using R²C²

The quantitative ranges for evaluation are based on a 0–10 scale using the qualitative key below:

Quantitative Ranges	Qualitative Anchors
0–1	Extremely Unacceptable Under-emphasis
2	Unacceptable Under-emphasis
3	Minimally Acceptable Emphasis
4	Below Average Emphasis
5	Average Emphasis
6	Above Average Emphasis
7	Optimal Emphasis
8	Unacceptable Over-emphasis
9–10	Extremely Unacceptable Over-emphasis

REFERENCES

Arnold, D. (2009). *Essentials of business ethics*. Hoboken, NJ: Wiley.

Collins, D. (2012). *Business ethics: How to design and manage ethical organizations*. Hoboken, NJ: Wiley.

Petrick, J. (2008). Using the business integrity capacity model to advance business ethics education. In D. Swanson & D. Fisher (Eds.), *Advancing business ethics education* (pp. 103–124). Charlotte, NC: Information Age Publishing.

Petrick, J. (2010). Sustainable stakeholder capitalism and redesigning management education: Lessons generated from the great global recession. *Journal of Corporate Citizenship, 40*, 101–124.

Petrick, J., Cragg, W., & Sanudo, M. (2012). Business ethics in North America: Trends and challenges. *Journal of Business Ethics, 104*, 51–62.

Petrick, J., & Quinn, J. (1997). *Management ethics: Integrity at work*. Thousand Oaks, CA: Sage.

Petrick, J., & Quinn, J. (2000). The integrity capacity construct and moral progress in business. *Journal of Business Ethics, 23*, 3–18.

Petrick, J., & Quinn, J. (2001). The challenge of leadership accountability for integrity capacity as a strategic asset. *Journal of Business Ethics, 34*, 331–343.

Petrick, J., & Scherer, R. (2003). The Enron scandal and the neglect of management integrity capacity. *Mid-American Journal of Business, 18*, 37–50.

Sekerka, L., Bagozzi, R., & Charnigo, R. (2009). Facing ethical challenges in the workplace: Conceptualizing and measuring professional moral courage. *Journal of Business Ethics, 89*, 565–579.

Sekerka, L., & Godwin, L. (2010). Strengthening professional moral courage: A balanced approach to ethics training. *Training & Management Development Methods, 24*, 63–74.

Sekerka, L., McCarthy, D., & Bagozzi, R. (2010). Developing the capacity for professional moral courage: Facing daily ethical challenges in today's military workplace. In D. Comer & G. Vega (Eds.), *Moral courage in organizations: Doing the right thing at work* (pp. 130–141). Armonk, NY: M.E. Sharpe.

Trevino, L., & Weaver, G. (2003). *Managing ethics in business organizations*. Stanford, CA: Stanford University Press.

Weber, J., & Wasieleski, D. (2013). Corporate ethics and compliance programs: A report, analysis and critique. *Journal of Business Ethics, 112*, 609–626.

Wood, D., Logsdon, J., Lewellyn, P., & Davenport, K. (2006). *Global business citizenship: A transformative framework for ethics and sustainable capitalism*. Armonk, NY: M.E. Sharp.

SECTION IV

FIELD APPLICATIONS

CHAPTER 11

INTEGRITY IN PUBLIC ADMINISTRATION

Lessons Learned

André van Montfort, Laura Beck, and Anneke Twijnstra

INTRODUCTION

In 2010, a number of civil servants of the city of Amsterdam were penalized because they had regularly accepted bribes from merchants. The market masters had offered merchants the best locations on the market place in exchange for kickbacks. After their corrupt behavior had been discovered, the civil servants were fired or otherwise punished by the local government of Amsterdam. At the beginning of 2012, there was bad news about the Amsterdam market masters again. Some of them were accused of applying the official rules too flexibly in exchange for kickbacks. The Dutch Public Prosecutions Department decided to set up an investigation (Verkerk, 2012).

Around the same period, another remarkable fraud came to light in the city of Rotterdam. Several local civil servants were suspected of having cooperated illegally with construction contractors. The contractors presented inflated invoices for their maintenance activities at public schools. Part of the amounts declared by the contractors was cashed by the local officials for their own

Ethics Training in Action, pages 229–248
Copyright © 2014 by Information Age Publishing

benefit. The Dutch Public Prosecution Service also started an investigation into this matter. The highest local official has already been fired by the board of the public sector organization in question (Rengers & Schoorl, 2012).

Such integrity violations do not only take place in the Netherlands. They are also observable in many other countries.[1] Therefore, all over the world, government organizations develop and execute integrity policies. Participation of officials in integrity training programs is often considered to be an important element of such policies (Beck, Van Montfort, & Twijnstra, 2010; Huberts, Six, Van Tankeren, Van Montfort, & Paanakker, in press; Van Montfort, Beck, & Twijnstra, 2013). Integrity training programs are expected to be useful for civil servants. Practitioners and scholars consider them a promising instrument to foster the integrity of public (or private) officials (Beck et al., 2010; Falkenberg & Woiceshyn, 2008; Hoekstra, Karssing & Kiebert, 2002; Huberts et al., 2013; Jonas & Sassenberg, 2006; Sims, 2002; Van Tankeren, 2010; Van Montfort et al., in press). In the past, integrity training programs were primarily conceived as being suitable for *integrity-based* ethics management. Civil servants should be empowered to recognize and handle ethical dilemmas. Nowadays, integrity training programs are increasingly considered an important element of *compliance-based* ethics management. Civil servants are provided with instructions and information in order to directly influence their behavior. Thus they are stimulated to act in accordance with the applicable regulations (Roberts, 2009; Van Montfort et al., 2013).

The aim of this chapter is to provide an overview of the literature about the effectiveness of integrity training programs offered to civil servants. This overview is complemented by the results of an empirical research project that we conducted from early 2009 until mid 2010.[2] First, several types of integrity training programs are distinguished. Subsequently, the effectiveness of such programs is assessed. Next, attention will be paid to three categories of factors that influence the effectiveness of integrity training programs, namely personal, organizational, and program-related factors. The chapter concludes with a number of concrete recommendations to create the most effective training programs.

VARIOUS TYPES OF INTEGRITY TRAINING PROGRAMS

Integrity training programs are aimed at enhancing the integrity of their participants. What does the term "integrity" mean?

The Concept of Integrity

A civil servant may be labeled as having integrity if three requirements are met. First, the civil servant must be aware of the possible moral aspects that may be distinguished in a certain situation. Second, he must be able to judge which decision should be made or which types of discussions should be held in this situation. Third, the civil servant has to act in accordance with the appropriate standards and rules. Therefore, three aspects of the concept of integrity can be distinguished: *moral awareness* (or moral conscience), *moral reasoning,* and *moral behavior* (Huberts, 2005; cf., Beck et al., 2010; De Groot, 2007; Van Montfort et al., 2013; Van Tankeren, 2010).

These aspects were deduced from the process model of ethical decision making introduced by Rest (1986) and elaborated by Jones (1991). According to this well-known model, an individual decision-maker goes through a staged process in which he subsequently recognizes a moral issue, makes a moral judgment about that issue, establishes an intention to act upon that judgment, and actually behaves in accordance with his intention (Davis & Crane, 2003; Jones, 1991; Rest, 1986; Van Montfort et al., 2013).

The Concept of an Integrity Training Program

There is a wide range of conceptions and descriptions concerning the term "integrity training program." In this chapter we choose a definition that fits with the conception of the term "integrity" discussed above. An integrity training program is defined as a number of mutually coherent activities that are offered by an internal or external agency to employees of an organization in order to raise their moral conscience, their level of moral reasoning, and the moral quality of their behavior (Beck et al., 2010; Van Montfort et al., 2013). This broad definition encompasses a variety of training programs. It includes, for example, a great number of different courses that are lately offered under the denominator of "ethics training programs" (Van Montfort et al., 2013).

Integrity training programs are aimed at promoting deliberate ethical behavior choices made by individuals. Such programs may be designed in various ways. The most common design is the dilemma training program (Van Tankeren, 2010).

Dilemma Training Programs

A dilemma training program aims at promoting ethical decision making in a situation where values and standards are at stake and where a choice must be made between several alternatives, while there may be good reasons for each of those alternatives (Maesschalck, 2005). The program may also aim at promoting an ethical culture in which people feel free to discuss the behavior and ethical choices made by themselves, their colleagues, or the organization (Van Tankeren, 2010). Dilemma trainings may take various shapes. They can, for example, be designed as one of the following basic forms or mixtures of these forms: scenarios (vignettes), the steps method, the Socratic method, and simulations (Van Tankeren, 2010).

With the *scenario or vignettes method* a situation is described. A number of operation alternatives are presented, one of which must be selected. The participants are asked to make a choice and to make this choice known. The discussion begins by asking the participants to substantiate their choices. In the simplest form, only one alternative is given and the participants can only make a yes-or-no choice (Van Tankeren, 2010).

The *step method* aims to apply stepwise one or more ethical theories in situations of moral decision-making. The number of steps may vary. Van Luijk (1993) and Karssing (2006), for instance, distinguish seven and five steps, respectively. In essence, however, the step method is based on the following approach: (1) there is a case; (2) the moral problem or dilemma is identified; (3) arguments for and against several practices are compiled; and (4) a conclusion is formulated with respect to the problem (Van Tankeren, 2010, p. 42).

The essence of the *Socratic dialogue* is that moral issues are analyzed by asking questions. Moral judgments are postponed. The dialogue should eventually lead to an objectified conclusion shared by everyone (Karssing, 2006; Kruisheer, 2005; Van Es, 2004). A major disadvantage of this method is that it may take a long time before a unanimous judgment is made (Van Tankeren, 2010).

Finally, during *simulations*, real situations are imitated in a game. The participants have to look for moral clues, additional information, and the opinions of other people. The method aims at deriving general ethical principles from concrete examples in which moral issues are at stake. This inductive approach differs principally from the deductive approach of the already discussed step method, in which general moral principles are applied to concrete moral dilemmas (Van Tankeren, 2010).

Other Types of Integrity Training Programs

Two other methods that enable the participants to reflect on ethical decision making are *collegial moral debate* and *training in open communication*. These forms are important for creating an ethical culture of accountability for moral decisions. They are also important for improving a participant's moral conscience, his level of moral reasoning, his ability to reflect on his own functioning, and his listening skills (Van Tankeren, 2010).

The *collegial moral debate* is a suitable method when a statement must be made about a complex ethical question. The moral debate aims at finding an outcome that is characterized by fairness, appropriateness, and solidarity (Van Es, 2004; Van Tankeren, 2010).

Training in open communication is particularly suited to promote a culture in which people address each other on behavior lacking integrity. In an open communication, no judgments are pronounced. People are encouraged to express their perceptions, their feelings, and their underlying values regarding certain situations. Open communication certainly is not common in our Western culture. Nevertheless, it is necessary for an adequate support of normative judgments and for an appropriate justification of the manner in which behavior lacking integrity is remediated (Van Tankeren, 2010).

THE EFFECTIVENESS OF INTEGRITY TRAINING PROGRAMS

In the literature, integrity training programs are often considered a promising instrument to promote the integrity of employees of governmental or private organizations. Such training programs have become a common phenomenon in public administration (Beck et al., 2010; Huberts et al., in press; Van Montfort et al., 2013; Van Tankeren, 2010). Consider, for example, the Dutch police. According to a recent survey among the 26 Dutch regional police forces, dilemma training programs are offered in almost all regional police forces. These programs are often intended for new employees. The majority of the programs are focused on creating a correct moral framework among their participants (Van Tankeren, 2010; Van Tankeren & Van Montfort, 2012).

Despite the popularity of integrity training programs in the public sector, the assumed positive effects of such programs are only to a limited degree supported by empirical data. There is little empirical research into the effectiveness of integrity training programs. The assumed positive effects have hardly been found in practice (Beck et al., 2010; De Groot, 2007; Delaney & Sockell, 1992; Menzel, 1997; Van Montfort et al., 2013; Weber, 1990; West & Berman, 2004).

Experiences with a Training Program for Policemen

One of the few studies on the effectiveness of integrity training programs in the public sector is the one conducted within the Amsterdam police force in 2006. The effectiveness of the program "Deliberate Choice" was examined by means of an organization-wide inquiry. The program aimed at stimulating employees to handle moral dilemmas consciously. To a certain degree it had the character of dilemma training. It was based on the

Socratic dialogue and consisted of several meetings. The meetings were attended not only by new employees, but also by employees who had already been affiliated to the police force (Huberts et al., in press; Van Tankeren, 2007; Van Tankeren & Van Montfort, 2012).

The results of the organization-wide survey at the Amsterdam police force made two things clear. First, the survey showed that three quarters of the participants appreciated the meetings. This applied especially to meetings that were characterized by clarifying discussions about how to act in certain situations. Meetings in which information about the concrete meaning of the concept of integrity in the daily life of policemen was delivered and discussed were also positively assessed. The same went for meetings that offered policemen the opportunity to express their own experiences on the broad area of integrity.

Second, the organization-wide survey revealed a number of statistically significant differences in the opinions, attitudes, and reported behavior between the employees who had attended the meetings and those who had not. According to these differences, the program "Deliberate Choice" seemed to be effective on the following points:[3] being transparent about events in which moral issues are at stake, discussing ethically cumbersome questions, addressing colleagues on unethical behavior, communicating unethical behavior to superiors, reducing racist jokes or remarks, and preventing the use of police force systems by employees for personal aims (Van Tankeren, 2007; Van Tankeren & Van Montfort, 2012).

Research on Two Training Programs for Municipal Officials

With the aim of supplementing the current limited number of empirical studies, we conducted a research project on the effectiveness of integrity training programs from early 2009 until mid-2010.[4] Our research project was aimed at answering the following question: To what extent do integrity training programs yield the desired results and to what extent is their effectiveness influenced by programs features and contextual characteristics? To answer this question, two different integrity training programs of two different training agencies were evaluated (Beck et al., 2010; Van Montfort et al., 2013).

The two evaluated training programs may be characterized as dilemma training programs. Both programs focused on the work situation of the participants. Practical examples related to the participants' tasks were discussed during the training sessions. This way, the programs aimed at stimulating the participants' moral awareness, contributing to their level of moral reasoning and providing certain methods to furnish the moral quality of their actions (Beck et al., 2010; Van Montfort et al., 2013).

The two programs were evaluated by means of an experimental research design. The data gathering was done by means of postal surveys in two Dutch municipalities in which the examined training programs were executed, and in two other Dutch municipalities in which no training programs took place. These postal surveys were conducted on multiple occasions. Thus it was possible to assess both the possible *short-term* effectiveness and the possible *long-term* effectiveness of the examined training programs (Beck et al., 2010; Van Montfort et al., 2013).[5]

The *short-term* effectiveness of a training program was assessed by comparing the respondents' results on the pretest (which took place immediately before the training) with their results on the first posttest (which was executed a short time after the training). Only one of the two examined training programs proved to be effective in the short term. The group of participants of this training program showed, on an average, a statistically significant increase of integrity. This applies both to the participants' *moral awareness* and to their *level of moral reasoning*.[6]

The second examined training program, however, was less beneficial for its attendants. The scores on the first posttest were, on an average, not statistically significantly higher than those on the pretest were. In other words, the second training program did not significantly increase the participants' moral awareness or their level of moral reasoning (Beck et al., 2010; Van Montfort et al., 2013).

The long-term effectiveness of a training program was evaluated by comparing the development of the surveyed civil servants of the experimental group (those who attended the program within their municipality) with the development of the surveyed employees of the control group (those who worked at the municipality where no training program was executed). The development of the *experimental* group in terms of integrity was measured on the basis of the scores on the pretest and the scores on the second posttest (six to nine months after the pretest). The development of the *control* group in terms of integrity was established on the basis of two consecutive tests which were executed at about the same time as the pretest and the second posttest in the experimental group were.[7] If the development of the *experimental* group is more positive (or less negative) than the development in the *control* group is, the training program may be considered effective.[8]

Unfortunately, both of the training programs examined did not prove to be effective in the long run. The development of integrity in the experimental group was not any more positive than the development in the control group for either training program. On an average, the scores of the municipal officials were not statistically significantly better with respect to the employees' moral awareness, their level of moral reasoning, or the moral quality of their behavior (Beck et al., 2010; Van Montfort et al., 2013).

Individual Differences in the Effectiveness of Training Programs

Based on the research findings presented above, it may be concluded that only one of the two examined training programs for municipal officials was effective in the short term and that both programs were not effective in the long term. This disappointing conclusion is based on analyses at a *group level*. However, it does not imply that there are no differences between *individual municipal officials*. Some officials benefited more from the training program than others. This applies to both the short-term effectiveness and the long-term effectiveness of the program (Beck et al., 2010; Van Montfort et al., 2013).

The foregoing may be illustrated by data on the long-term effectiveness of one of the two evaluated training programs. The program in question was not effective at a *group level*. The experimental group did not show a more positive development in terms of integrity than the control group did. *Within the experimental group* there were, however, remarkable differences in the extent to which individual officials had benefited from the program. For instance, more than one third (38%) of the participants showed a modest or substantial progress in their level of moral reasoning, whereas more than a quarter (27%) of the participants showed a modest or substantial decline in this respect (Beck et al., 2010). This can be seen in Table 11.1.

A fairly similar situation was found in the above-mentioned research project on the effectiveness of the integrity training program for Dutch policemen. The effectiveness of this training program seems to vary with each individual policeman. Some of the surveyed policemen seem to have profited more from the program than others (Van Tankeren, 2007).

TABLE 11.1 Long-Term Developments of Individual Participants Concerning Three Aspects of Integrity

	Moral awareness		Moral reasoning		Moral actions	
Strong progress	1	(2.2%)	3	(6.7%)	12	(26.7%)
Progress	2	(4.4%)	14	(31.1%)	20	(44.4%)
No change	41	(89.0%)	16	(35.6%)	3	(6.7%)
Decline	1	(2.2%)	10	(22.2%)	10	(22.2%)
Strong decline	1	(2.2%)	2	(4.4%)	0	(0.0%)
Total	46	(100.0%)	45	(100.0%)	45	(100.0%)

Source: Beck et al., 2010, p. 79–80 and 82; Van Montfort et al., 2013

FACTORS THAT INFLUENCE THE EFFECTIVENESS
OF AN INTEGRITY TRAINING PROGRAM

The fact that the effectiveness of an integrity training program varies with each individual employee implies that certain personal characteristics of an employee might influence this effectiveness. A number of such *personal characteristics* are discussed in the literature. The literature also presents several *organizational factors* and several *program-related factors* that influence the effectiveness of an integrity training program. We will discuss these three categories of influential factors.

Personal Factors

Characteristics of participants may influence the effectiveness of integrity training. Gender, level of education, and type of function are examples of characteristics that are distinguished in the literature.

With respect to the *participants' gender*, O'Fallon & Butterfield (2005) conclude in their literature review that there are hardly any differences between males and females with respect to moral awareness, ethical decision-making, and ethical behavior. Other articles indicate, however, a difference between the two sexes. Females tend to behave more ethically than males do. Research of Ritter (2006) for instance, shows that males are less sensitive to moral problems. Based on this research finding, we may hypothesize that integrity training programs will be more effective for male participants. More progress can be achieved for this category of participants.

This hypothesis is partly supported by our above-mentioned research on the effectiveness of two Dutch training programs offered to municipal employees. Male participants benefited more from one of the two programs than female participants did in the short term. They showed more progress with respect to the level of moral awareness (Beck et al., 2010; Van Montfort et al., 2013).

O'Fallon and Butterfield (2005) and Desplaces, Melchar, Beauvais, and Bosco (2007) point out the relevance of the *participants' level of education* for the effectiveness of an integrity training program. The higher one's educational level and/or the longer the duration of his education is, the higher his level of moral reasoning will be. This makes us suppose that well-educated civil servants will profit less from an integrity training program than their less educated colleagues will. Due to their lower initial level, there is more to gain for less educated employees.

This hypothesis, which specifically pertains to one's level of moral reasoning, is, however, not confirmed by our research findings about the effectiveness of two Dutch training programs for municipal officials. One of the two evaluated training programs was more effective for the lower educated participants with respect to their *level of moral behavior.* Contrary to our hypothesis, however, no significant influence of the participants' level of education on improvements to the *level of moral reasoning* was found (Beck et al., 2010; Van Montfort et al., 2013).

The *type of work that officials perform* is also a relevant factor. Huberts, Van Montfort, Doig, and Clark (2006) state that civil servants who often have contact with the outside world during their daily activities are more inclined to break the official rules than civil servants are who have less frequent contact with society. The contacts with society may seduce civil servants to empathize too much with the interests of citizens, private firms, and civil society organizations. The external contacts also make them susceptible to rule-breaking behavior like bribery.[9] Consider, for example, the vulnerable position of employees working at a municipal organization for construction and housing. Such civil servants who mainly fulfill executive functions are more susceptible to the temptations of behavior lacking integrity than are policymaking officials who perform their tasks from behind their desks. Therefore, integrity training programs are potentially more relevant for executive employees. It may be hypothesized that integrity training programs might have a more positive effect on the behavior of *executive employees* than on the behavior of their *policymaking* colleagues.

This hypothesis has been partly confirmed by our research findings. One of the two Dutch programs intended for municipal officials had a stronger effect on the level of moral behavior of the executive employees on the long term (Beck et al., 2010; Van Montfort et al., 2013).

Organizational Factors

The organizational context in which a training program is executed also influences the effectiveness of the program. In particular, the organizational factors discussed below may be considered relevant.

The *ethical climate* within an organization is described by Shepard and Wimbush (1994) as an unambiguous and shared conception by its employees about the way their organization should handle ethical dilemmas. The ethical climate includes the various interests by which an organization's employees are guided during their activities. An organization with a positive ethical climate is characterized by the fact that its employees are not guided by their own interests, but instead by the organization's and its clients' interests.[10] According to O'Fallon and Butterfield (2005), a positive ethical climate has a positive influence on ethical decision making. Based on this research finding, we hypothesize that the ethical climate within an organization determines which issues are considered ethically relevant and which criteria the employees use to solve a given issue. A positive ethical climate makes the employees feel "safe" so that they are more willing to discuss moral issues. An integrity training program shows the participants how to recognize moral issues and how to discuss them. Participants working in a less positive ethical climate will benefit more from the training program. Due to their less ethical work environment, there is more to gain.

This hypothesis is confirmed by our research findings about the effectiveness of two Dutch training programs for municipal officials. Participants working in an organization with a less positive ethical climate benefited more from the training program at the short term.[11] They showed more progress with respect to the level of moral reasoning (Beck et al., 2010; Van Montfort et al., 2013).

Ethical leadership is a type of leadership that implies that the relationship between the executive and his employees is such that the executive acts as a moral manager (Trevino, Weaver, Gibson, & Toffler, 1999). The executive places ethics on the agenda (Trevino, Brown, & Hartman, 2003). His ethical leadership encourages the employees not to accept any violation of integrity. Due to his leadership, the number of cases of integrity violations will be limited (Lasthuizen, 2008, p. 231). Participants in the training program whose managers are characterized as ethical leaders will probably be motivated to apply their knowledge about moral issues gained in the training in their daily work. The program is likely to be more effective for these participants than it will be for those participants whose managers display ethical leadership to a lesser extent (Beck et al., 2010, p. 25).[12]

According to several literature studies, the existence of a *code of conduct* within an organization is positively related to ethical decision making (O'Fallon & Butterfield, 2005, p. 397). Adams, Taschian, and Shore (2001) show that the existence of a code of conduct has a positive effect on employees' views on ethical behavior, even if the employees do not know the content of the code. The codes of conduct are even more effective when they are part of a more comprehensive integrity policy. Based on the foregoing, it may be hypothesized that an integrity training program is more effective if the participants' organization has established a code of conduct. The training will, in that case, be part of a larger integrity policy (Huberts et al., in press). Furthermore we hypothesize that the training program will be more effective if its participants also know the content of their organization's code of conduct. This is due to the fact that participants will be more sensitive to the tools that will be handed to them during the training (Beck et al., 2010).[13]

Program-Related Factors

The effectiveness of an integrity training program is also influenced by a number of program-related factors. The motivation of the participant of the training program is a relevant issue. The more motivated a participant is, the more he will benefit from the training program (Baldwin, Magjuka, & Loher, 1991; Facteau, Dobbins, Russell, Ladd, & Kudisch, 1995; Mathieu, Tannenbaum, & Salas, 1992; Switzer, Nagy, & Mullins, 2005). The participant's motivation is influenced by the circumstance of *whether the participant is participating voluntarily or involuntarily*. However, existing studies show different results in this respect (Baldwin & Magjuka, 1997; Collinson, 2000). On the one hand, it is argued that those who participate voluntarily are more motivated to learn than those who do not participate voluntarily (Aziz & Ahmad, 2011; Baldwin et al., 1991; Hicks & Klimoski, 1987; Mathieu, Tannenbaum, & Salas, 1990). On the other hand, it is stated that making a training program obligatory will be interpreted by the participants as a clear signal of the organizational importance of the program and therefore enhance the participants' motivation (Baldwin & Magjuka, 1991). Nevertheless, we hypothesize that voluntary participants are more motivated to actively engage in the training and to bring into practice what they have learned. A training program is therefore more effective for an employee if the person concerned participates in it voluntarily (Beck et al., 2010).

This, however, does not mean that it may not be wise to oblige all employees of the organization to participate in the program. According to some empirical studies, the obligatory participation of all employees in a training program creates better results for the organization as a whole than the voluntary participation of only a limited number of employees (Cotterchio, Gunn, Coffill, Tomey, & Barry, 1998; Penninger & Rodman, 1984; Rynes & Rosen, 1995).

In order to make a training program effective, the trainer must be competent and professional (Ponemon, 1996). Trevino et al. (1999) argue that a trainer from outside the participants' organization is not capable of giving any training. After all, *external trainers* are not involved in the participants' daily work. Therefore training is more effective if, for example, it is given by the executive of the participants. Kaptein (1998) disagrees with this argument. In his view an external trainer will not be felt to be a threat. An internal trainer may be considered an obstacle if he or she is considered by the participants to be part of the problem. We agree with Kaptein and hypothesize that the participants will speak and discuss moral issues more freely if a training program will be given by an external trainer (Beck et al., 2010).

One integrity training program is not enough to reach the goals of the training. It is essential to repeat the program's most important messages and theories in order to make it more effective (Ponemon, 1996). Weber (2006) also emphasizes that in order to stimulate moral behavior, the executives need to organize moral discussions. Thus the employees can discuss new moral issues they are experiencing. Based on these arguments, it is likely that *follow-up activities* will contribute to the effectiveness of the training program in the long run.

The two Dutch training programs for municipal officials in our research did not include any follow-up activities. For the program that was effective in the short run, the absence of follow-up activities may be considered as the main cause of its ineffectiveness in the long run (Beck et al., 2010).

Discussing cases clears the way for norms and values (Kaptein, 1998). It is important to give the participants in the program an active role by, for example, *selecting cases* (Weber, 2006). Cases that are derived from ethical dilemmas from real life contribute to the program's effectiveness. These dilemmas enhance the participants' motivation because they can identify with the examples that are presented in the cases (Felton & Sims, 2005).

Research into the effectiveness of a training program for employees of the Amsterdam police force confirms this. Participants who were able to share their experiences on integrity when discussing cases appreciated the program more than those who did not have any opportunity to communicate their experience (Huberts et al., in press; Van Tankeren, 2007).[14]

Finally, *group size* is also a relevant factor. A training program may be effective with both small and large groups of participants (Weber, 2006, p. 63). Small groups provide the opportunity to actively participate in discussions, while larger groups provide more views and experiences from their participants. The ideal group size is between 20 and 25 persons. The group should not be larger than 40 persons (Ponemon, 1996). Although different findings are presented in the literature, we hypothesize that training programs will be more effective when their participants are trained in small groups (Beck et al., 2010).

CONCLUSIONS AND RECOMMENDATIONS

What conclusions may be drawn from the results of our literature review and our empirical research? Both practitioners and scholars consider training programs as a useful instrument to promote the integrity of civil servants. The assumed positive effects of such programs, however, are only to a limited degree confirmed by the data of our empirical research. Only one of the two investigated training programs proved to be effective in the short run. Neither of them was effective in the long run. Therefore, one cannot simply assume that every training program is effective.

Another conclusion based on our empirical research is that integrity training programs have different impacts on individual employees. This applies both to programs that are effective at the group level (as is partly the case with one of the investigated training programs) and to programs that lack effectiveness at a group level (as is the case with the other investigated program). Some individual employees benefit more from the program than their colleagues do. Thus, training programs that are not effective on group level might, nevertheless, be useful for individual participants.

The program's effectiveness seems to be contingent on a number of factors. Some of these relate to characteristics of the program itself, whereas others pertain to characteristics of the individual participants or to features of the organizational context. Once again, it must be emphasized that empirical data are scarce. There are many plausible hypotheses, but empirical evidence is often missing.

Nevertheless, on the basis of our literature review and empirical research, a number of factors may be identified that probably influence the effectiveness of an integrity training program. The first *personal* factor is gender. The *gender* of the participant probably influences the effectiveness of the program. A training program is likely more beneficial for male participants than it is for female participants. This is due to the fact that females tend to be more ethical to begin with. Therefore, more progress may be achieved for the male participants. The second personal factor is the participant's *function*. Civil servants who mainly fulfill executive tasks that entail many external contacts are more susceptible to rule-breaking behavior like bribery than public servants are who perform policymaking tasks from behind their desks. Consequently, integrity training programs are likely especially relevant for executive employees who have frequent contact with society during their daily activities.

Regarding *organizational* factors it may first be stated that the *ethical culture* within an organization is relevant. Participants who work in a less ethical climate probably benefit more from the integrity training program. Because of their poor initial situation, they will show more progress in terms of integrity. Another relevant organizational factor is whether or not the training program is embedded in a set of coordinated policy instruments. If the training program is *part of a larger integrity policy*, the training will probably be more effective. The possible effects of the overarching policy reinforce the possible effects of the training program.

There are also some relevant *program-related* factors. An integrity training program is probably more effective for an employee if the person concerned participates in it voluntarily. Nevertheless, according to some empirical studies, a *general obligation* for all employees of an organization to participate in the training likely gives better results for the organization than when only some of the employees voluntarily participate in the training. Furthermore, a training program is likely to be more effective when it is given by an *external trainer*. The participants will discuss ethical issues more freely than when they receive the training from somebody from within the organization. The *types of cases* that are discussed during the training are probably another relevant factor. The training's effectiveness is increased if the program focuses on employees' practical experiences by using cases that are easily recognizable to the participants. Finally, *follow-up activities* probably also contribute to the effectiveness of an integrity training program. The absence of regular follow-up activities is detrimental to the effectiveness of the program.

The foregoing conclusions lead us to some concrete recommendations. First, if the managers of an organization decide to offer employees an integrity training program, they have to consider carefully the design and content of the program. Integrity training programs are not all equally effective. Some training programs are even ineffective.

Second, to optimize the chance of getting an effective training, at least the following requirements should be met. The training program should be an element of a more comprehensive integrity policy. The possible effects of the larger policy will then amplify the potential effects of the program. Furthermore, the cases discussed during the course should reflect the participants' work experiences. If so, the participants will appreciate the program more and will benefit more from it. A final requirement relates to the provision of follow-up activities. A training program must not have the character of a single event. The possible short-term effects of the training should be reinforced by appropriate follow-up activities. Thus, it will be ensured that long-term effects will also be realized.

Third, in addition to the just-mentioned requirements that are conducive to the extent to which individual officials benefit from the training program, it is also advisable to oblige all members of the organization to participate in the program. The obligatory participation of all staff probably creates better results for the organization as a whole than the voluntary participation of only some civil servants.

The final lesson to be learned, however, is that more research into the effectiveness of integrity training programs should be executed. The ultimate goal for future research should be to realize evidence-based programs.

NOTES

1. See, for example, http://www.bbc.co.uk/news/world-asia-16301515; http://tribune.com.pk/story/328610/embezzlement-five-including-two-civil-servants-accused-of-corruption/; and http://www.spiegel.de/international/europe/0,1518,729492,00.html (accessed on August 13, 2012).

2. We also published elsewhere about (aspects of) the literature review and research project (Beck et al., 2010; Van Montfort, Beck & Twijnstra, 2010; and Van Montfort et al., 2013).

3. There is no certainty about any positive effects of the program, as cause-and-effect is difficult to infer based on a study design without randomization.

4. The research project was executed by the three authors of this chapter. In the first phase of the project, a number of students of management and organiza-

tion sciences at VU University Amsterdam also contributed to the research activities.

5. Nearly all civil servants who took part in one of two examined programs filled in a questionnaire both directly before the training meeting and immediately after that meeting. This concerns 241 employees in all. More than half a year later, 86 employees filled in a questionnaire for the third time. There was a great loss of respondents in the course of the study. As a result, there might have been an overrepresentation of motivated respondents at the time of the third measurement, which might have resulted in too positive a picture of the long-term effectiveness of the programs. However, this situation did not occur. Both of the programs examined did not prove to be effective on the long term (see also hereafter). In the two municipalities where no training program was offered to civil servants, 108 and 78 employees, respectively, completed a questionnaire more than half a year later (Beck et al., 2010).

6. The third aspect of integrity (i.e., the moral quality of behavior) was not measured when assessing the short-term effectiveness of the program. The possible effect of the program on this aspect of the participants' integrity may be established only after a certain amount of time (Beck et al., 2010; Van Montfort et al., 2013).

7. The fact that the control group received a different number of tests than the experimental group had no potential to bias the long-term comparison. The first two tests for the experimental group were performed on the same day (and took place in the same period as the only pretest for the control group did).

8. The fact that the control group had no training at all, rather than an alternative form of training, does not imply the possibility of a "placebo effect" as an explanation for the increased moral awareness and level of moral reasoning of the participants of one of the investigated programs in the short term. Both the respondents of the control group and the respondents of the experimental group had to fill in some questionnaires. Thus, both groups of respondents received more or less the same amount of attention from the researchers.

9. While rule-breaking behavior like bribery is undesirable, empathy with the interests of citizens may not be entirely bad. In some situations it may be understandable that employees decide to bend the rules (Sekerka & Zolin, 2007).

10. In other words, employees use multiple value sets in their moral decision making. This is an important theme in professional moral courage as discussed by Sekerka, Bagozzi, and Charnigo (2009).

11. The ethical climate within (a department or unit of) an organization was established by means of several items in the questionnaire used in the first test for the experimental group and for the control group. Two relevant items are, for example, the degree to which employees are expected to obey laws and rules, and the degree to which they are expected to take care of their direct colleagues (Beck et al., 2010).

12. The opposite argument may also be made: Participants whose managers are not ethical leaders may benefit more from the training, as they may have a lower baseline and thus may have more to gain. However, neither the original hypothesis nor the opposite hypothesis is confirmed by the results of our

research into the effectiveness of two training programs for Dutch municipal employees. The same applies to the other hypotheses discussed below concerning organizational and program factors that influence the effectiveness of a training program. Part of these hypotheses were not confirmed because there were not enough data (i.e., too low expected counts in one or more crosstabs cells) or no suitable data available (i.e., a too skewed distribution of scores on variables) available to test them (Beck et al., 2010; Van Montfort et al., 2013).

13. Again, the opposite argument may be made: Participants whose organizations lack codes of conduct may benefit more from the training, as they may be more sensitive to the tools that will be provided during the training. Neither the original hypothesis nor the opposite one was confirmed by the results of our research into the effectiveness of two training programs for Dutch municipal officials.

14. This hypothesis is, however, not confirmed by our research findings about the effectiveness of two Dutch training programs for municipal officials. Participants who were not given any active role in deciding which dilemmas would be discussed during the training program profited more from the program in terms of moral awareness on the short term than participants who did have an active role (Beck et al., 2010). The only plausible explanation for this strange research finding is that the variable "participants' input of cases" perhaps was not measured correctly in our research project.

REFERENCES

Adams, J. S., Taschian, A., & Shore, T. H. (2001). Codes of ethics as signals for ethical behaviour. *Journal of Business Ethics, 29*, 199–211.

Aziz, S. F. A., & Ahmad, S. (2011). Stimulating training motivation using the right training characteristic. *Industrial and Commercial Training, 43*(1), 53–61.

Baldwin, T., & Magjuka, R. J. (1997). Organizational context and training effectiveness. In J. K. Ford, S. W. J. Kozlowski, K. Kraiger, F. Salas, & M. Teachout (Eds.), *Improving training effectiveness in work organizations. Series in applied psychology* (pp. 99–127). Mahwah, NJ: Lawrence Erlbaum Associates.

Baldwin, T. T., Magjuka, R. J., & Loher, B. T. (1991). The perils of participation: Effects of choice of training on training motivation and learning. *Personnel Psychology, 44*, 51–66.

Beck, L., Van Montfort, A., & Twijnstra, A. (2010). *Valt integriteit te leren? De effectiviteit van integriteitstrainingen voor gemeenteambtenaren [Can integrity be learned? The effectiveness of integrity training programs for municipal officials]*. Amsterdam, Netherlands: VU University Press.

Collinson, C.A. (2000). *Beyond training: An evaluation of transfer from the tertiary setting to the corporate environment*. Palmerston North, New Zealand: Massey University.

Cotterchio, M., Gunn, J., Coffill, T., Tomey, P., & Barry, M.A. (1998). Effect of a manager training program on sanitary conditions in restaurants. *Public Health Reports, 113*, 353–358.

Davis, I. A., & Crane, A. (2003). Ethical decision making in fair trade companies. *Journal of Business Ethics, 45,* 79–92.

de Groot, P. (2007). *Het dilemma van de training: Een exploratief onderzoek naar de effecten van een training morele oordeelsvorming [The dilemma of the training: An exploratory study of the effects of a training in moral judgments].* Unpublished master's thesis, Governance Studies, VU University, Amsterdam, The Netherlands.

Delaney, J. T., & Sockell, D. (1992). Do company ethics training programs make a difference? An empirical analysis. *Journal of Business Ethics, 11,* 719–727.

Desplaces, D. E., Melchar, D. E., Beauvais, L. L., & Bosco, S. M. (2007). The impact of business education on moral judgment competence: An empirical study. *Journal of Business Ethics, 74,* 73–87.

Facteau, J. D., Dobbins, G. H., Russell, J. E. A., Ladd, R. T., & Kudisch, J. D. (1995). The influence of general perceptions of the training environment on pretraining motivation and perceived training transfer. *Journal of Management, 21,* 1–25.

Falkenberg, L., & Woiceshyn, J. (2008). Enhancing business ethics: Using cases to teach moral reasoning. *Journal of Business Ethics, 79,* 213–217.

Felton, E. L., & Sims, R. R. (2005). Teaching business ethics: Targeted outputs. *Journal of Business Ethics, 60,* 377–391.

Hicks, W. D., & Klimoski, R. J. (1987). Entry into training programs and its effects on training outcomes: A field experiment. *Academy of Management Journal, 30,* 542–552.

Hoekstra, A., Karssing, E. D., & Kiebert, R. P. (2002). Instrumenten voor bevordering van integriteit binnen de publieke sector [Instruments for promoting integrity within the public sector]. *Openbaar Bestuur, 12*(1), 16–19.

Huberts, L. W. J. C. (2005, February). *Integriteit en integritisme in bestuur en samenleving: Wie de schoen past... [Integrity and integritism in governance and society: Whom the cap fits...].* Inaugural lecture, VU University, Amsterdam, The Netherlands.

Huberts L. W. J. C., Van Montfort, A. J. G. M., Doig, A., & Clark, D. (2006). Rulemaking, rule-breaking? Law breaking by government in the Netherlands and the United Kingdom. *Crime, Law and Social Change, 46,* 133–159.

Huberts, L., Six, F., Van Tankeren, M., Van Montfort, A., & Paanakker, H. (in press). What is done to protect integrity: policies, institutions and systems. In L. W. J. C. Huberts (Ed.), *Integrity of governance: Perspectives in research and policies on ethics, integrity and integritism.* Hampshire, UK: Palgrave Macmillan.

Jonas, K. J., & Sassenberg, K. (2006). Knowing how to react: Automatic response priming from social categories. *Journal of Personality & Social Psychology, 90,* 709–721.

Jones, T. M. (1991). Ethical decision making by individuals in organizations: An issue-contingent model. *Academy of Management Review, 16,* 366–395.

Kaptein, M. (1998). *Ethics management: Auditing and developing the ethical content of organizations.* Dordrecht, Netherlands: Kluwer Academic Publishers.

Karssing, E. (2006). *Integriteit in de beroepspraktijk [Integrity in the professional practice].* Assen, Netherlands: Van Gorcum.

Kruisheer, E. (2005). Toolkit voor integriteit. In A. Straathof (Ed.), *Integriteit in teams [Integrity in teams]* (pp. 65–80). Utrecht, Netherlands: Lemma.

Lasthuizen, K. M. (2008). *Leading to integrity. Empirical research into the effects of leadership on ethics and integrity.* Amsterdam, Netherlands: VU University.

Maesschalck, J. (2005). *Een ambtelijk integriteitsbeleid in de Vlaamse overheid [An administrative integrity policy in the Flemish government].* Leuven, Belgium: Steunpunt Bestuurlijke Organisatie Vlaanderen.

Mathieu, J. E., Tannenbaum, S. I., & Salas, E. (1990, April). *A causal model of individual and situational influences on training effectiveness measures.* Paper presented at the Fifth Annual Conference of the Society for Industrial and Organizational Psychology, Miami, FL.

Mathieu, J. E., Tannenbaum, S. I., & Salas, E. (1992). Influences of individual and situational characteristics on measures of training effectiveness. *Academy of Management Journal, 35,* 828–847.

Menzel, D. C. (1997). Teaching ethics and values in public administration: Are we making a difference. *Public Administration Review, 57,* 224–230.

O'Fallon, M. J., & Butterfield, K. D. (2005). A review of the empirical ethical decision-making literature: 1996–2003. *Journal of Business Ethics, 59,* 375–413.

Penninger, H., & Rodman, V. (1984). Food service managerial certification: How effective has it been? *Dairy and Food Sanitation, 4,* 260–264.

Ponemon, L. (1996). Key features of an effective ethics training program. *Management Accounting, 78,* 66–67.

Rengers, M., & Schoorl, J. (2012, May 25). Behalve fraude ook zelfverrijking bij Rotterdamse scholenkoepel BOOR [Besides fraud also self-enrichment at Rotterdam Schools Association BOOR]. *Volkskrant.* Retrieved from http://www.volkskrant.nl/vk/nl/5288/Onderwijs/article/detail/3261008/2012/05/25/Behalve-fraude-ook-zelfverrijking-bij-BOOR.dhtml

Rest, J. R. (1986). *Moral development: Advances in research and theory.* New York, NY: Praeger.

Ritter, B. A. (2006). Can business ethics be trained? A study of the ethical decision making process in business students. *Journal of Business Ethics, 68,* 601–617.

Roberts, R. (2009). The rise of compliance-based ethics management: Implications for organizational ethics. *Public Integrity, 11,* 261–277.

Rynes, S., & Rosen, B. (1995). A field survey of factors affecting the adoption and perceived success of diversity training. *Personnel Psychology, 48*(2), 247–270.

Sekerka, L. E., Bagozzi, R. P., & Charnigo, R. (2009). Facing ethical challenges in the workplace: Conceptualizing and measuring professional moral courage. *Journal of Business Ethics, 89,* 565–579.

Sekerka, L. E., & Zolin, R. (2007). Rule bending: Can prudential judgment affect rule compliance and values in the workplace? *Public Integrity, 9*(3), 225–244.

Shepard, J. M., & Wimbush, J. C. (1994). Toward an understanding of ethical climate: Its relationship to ethical behavior and supervisory influence. *Journal of Business Ethics, 13,* 637–647.

Sims, R. R. (2002). Business ethics teaching for effective learning. *Teaching Business Ethics, 6,* 393–410.

Switzer, K. C., Nagy, M. S., & Mullins, M. E. (2005). The influence of training reputation, managerial support, and self-efficacy on pre-training motivation and perceived training transfer. *Applied H.R.M. Research, 10*(1), 21–34.

Trevino, L. K., Brown, M., & Hartman, L. P. (2003). A qualitative investigation of perceived executive ethical leadership: Perceptions from inside and outside the executive suite. *Human Relations, 56*(1), 5–37.

Trevino, L. K., Weaver, G. R., Gibson, D. G., & Toffler, B. L. (1999). Managing ethics and legal compliance: What works and what hurts. *California Management Review, 41*, 131–151.

Van Es, R. (2004). Veranderfilosofie en ethiek van organiseren [Change philosophy and the ethics of organizing]. *Management en Organisatie, 58*(4/5), 102–115.

Van Luijk, H. (1993). *Om redelijk gewin: Oefeningen in bedrijfsethiek [For the purpose of a fair profit: Exercises in business ethics]*. Meppel, Netherlands: Boom.

Van Montfort, A. J. G. M., Beck, L., & Twijnstra, A. A. H. (2010). Op cursus voor de goede zaak [Participating in a course for a good cause]. *Openbaar bestuur, 20*(12), 20–24.

Van Montfort, A. J. G. M., Beck, L., & Twijnstra, A. A. H. (2013). Can integrity be taught in public organizations? The effectiveness of integrity training programs for municipal officials. *Public Integrity, 15*(2), 117–132.

Van Tankeren, M. H. M. (2007). *Het preventieve integriteitsbeleid van de politie Amsterdam-Amstelland: Onderzoek naar werking en effectiviteit [The preventive integrity policy of the Amsterdam-Amstelland police: Research into action and effectiveness]*. Amsterdam, Netherlands: VU University Amsterdam/Amsterdam-Amstelland Police.

Van Tankeren, M. H. M. (2010). *Het integriteitsbeleid van de Nederlandse politie: wat er is en wat er toe doet [The integrity policy of the Dutch police: What is and what matters]*. Amsterdam, Netherlands: VU University Amsterdam.

Van Tankeren, M. H. M., & Van Montfort, A. J. G. M. (2012). Schieten we er ook nog wat mee op? De effectiviteit van het integriteitsbeleid van de Nederlandse politie *[Do we benefit from it? The effectiveness of the integrity policy of the Dutch police]*. In A. de Schrijver, E. Kolthoff, K. Lasthuizen, P. van Parys & E. Devroe (Eds.), *Integriteit en deontologie [Integrity and deontology]*, Cahiers Politiestudies No. 24 (pp. 131–149). Antwerpen/Apeldoorn/Portland: Maklu.

Verkerk, C. (2012, February 28). Corruptie markt onderschat [Market corruption underestimated]. *Het Parool*. Retrieved from http://www.parool.nl/parool/nl/5/POLITIEK/article/detail/3207081/2012/02/28/Corruptie-markt-onderschat.dhtml.

Weber, J. A. (1990). Measuring the impact of teaching ethics to future managers: A review, assessment, and recommendations. *Journal of Business Ethics, 9*, 183–190.

Weber, J. A. (2006). Business ethics training: Insights from learning theory. *Journal of Business Ethics, 70*, 61–85.

West, J. P., & Berman, E. (2004). Ethics training in US cities: Content, pedagogy and impact. *Public Integrity, 6*, 189–206.

CHAPTER 12

EXPLORING BUSINESS ETHICS TRAINING PRACTICES IN SMALL FIRMS

Cathy Driscoll, Margaret C. McKee, and Wendy Carroll

In most developed countries around the world, small and medium-sized firms account for approximately 98% of all businesses, employ half of the workforce, and contribute one quarter to one third of a country's gross domestic product (GDP) (OECD, 2009). While large firms are more likely to conduct formal business ethics training than small firms (cf., Ethics Resource Center, 2007), small businesses still work to educate their employees to be mindful of ethical concerns. To date, little research has been conducted to explore the specifics of ethics training in small firms.

The purpose of this chapter is to obtain a better understanding of business ethics training in a small business context. We specifically focus on some of the barriers to and opportunities for ethics training in this type of organization. There are many definitions and categories of small business. For example, small businesses in the United States in the nonmanufacturing sector are operations with fewer than 500 employees and under $7 million in annual receipts (United States Small Business Administration, 2010). The European Union defines small business as operations with

Ethics Training in Action, pages 249–267
Copyright © 2014 by Information Age Publishing
All rights of reproduction in any form reserved.

fewer than 50 employees and balance sheet totals of less than 2 million Euros, while a medium size firm has fewer than 250 employees and balance sheet totals of less than 43 million Euros (European Commission, 2005). In Canada, businesses are classified as small if they have fewer than 100 employees, medium if they have 100–499 employees and large if they have more than 500 employees (Industry Canada, 2012).

To set the stage for this work, we begin with a review of the literature on small business, business ethics, and ethics training. We then discuss findings from our study of leading Canadian companies and their business ethics training practices, specifically comparing small businesses to larger firms. We conclude with a discussion of implications for practice and research.

ETHICS TRAINING IN SMALL BUSINESS FIRMS

An electronic search of the *Journal of Business Ethics,* one of the leading journals in business management and ethics, resulted in 284 journal records for "small business," 114 records for "ethics training," and no records for "small business and ethics training." Spence and Painter-Morland's (2010a) global commentary of extant research on ethics in small and medium-sized enterprises does not explicitly address the topic of ethics training. Perhaps the lack of inquiry is because many academics focus their study of ethics training on large rather than small and medium-sized firms (Fuller & Tian, 2006; Hillary, 2000; LePoutre & Heene, 2006; Spence & Painter-Morland, 2010a; Werner & Spence, 2004). Business ethics theories and their associated models often relate to large corporations rather than small and medium-sized enterprises (SMEs) (Spence & Painter-Morland, 2010a). Some scholars have criticized this lack of attention to the topic of small business in business ethics literature (e.g., Fassin, van Rossem, & Buelens, 2010; Longenecker, Moore, Petty, Palich, & McKinney, 2006; Spence & Painter-Morland, 2010a). After all, the relationship between firm size and organizational structures, processes, and behaviors is well represented in organizational studies. Despite this recognition, a content analysis of selected business ethics textbooks reveals little to no coverage of small business and/or entrepreneurial enterprise (Driscoll & Tesfayohannes, 2009).

In general, large companies are given more attention by business researchers and educators because they are more visible than small firms. Additionally, large multinational corporations are constantly under pressure to be more transparent and accountable (Karakowsky, Carroll, & Buchholtz, 2005). It is common for large organizations in the United States to have formal ethics programs (Weaver & Treviño, 1999) and to report on them. Spence and Painter-Morland (2010a) conclude that "ethical issues that SMEs face remain either hidden, or they are addressed in an informal, unstructured way" (p. 333). It is therefore not surprising that we find little academic work on the topic of business ethics training and small business.

The literature that does exist suggests that, compared to large firms, small business owner-managers are less likely to utilize training and learning activities (Bartram, 2005; Walker, Redmond, Webster, & LeClus, 2007). An early study of United States companies (Robertson, 1991) found that ethics training was carried out more in large firms (38%) than in small firms (7%). A Swedish study (Brytting, 1997) found considerably lower levels of ethics training among smaller firms (6% for firms overall but 11% for large firms). This is not surprising, given that the relative costs of training are higher for a small business than for a larger firm (Billett, 2001). We assume this is true for ethics training as well.

Context is critical with regard to ethics training. According to Baron (1998), small business owner-managers operate within different contexts and environments from managers in large companies. Moreover, small business owner-managers think differently than managers of large firms (Baron, 1998). Therefore, small businesses should not necessarily benchmark ethical business practice (including ethics training) against large corporations. There is often an assumption that SMEs are "little big firms" (Tilley, 2000, p. 33). As Spence and Rutherfoord (2003, p. 4) explain, "Business ethicists must acknowledge that the large multi-national firm is not a standard business form against which other types are benchmarked." To grasp this point, we turn to specific literature that focuses on the unique aspects of ethics in a small business and entrepreneurial context.

Ethics and Small Business

Justin Longenecker and his colleagues (2006) at Baylor University, who have been studying small business, entrepreneurship, and ethics for over three decades, have found that small businesses face different ethical issues and pressures than large companies. The literature suggests small business owners and entrepreneurs experience somewhat uniquely complex ethical challenges related to issues of ownership (Kuratko, Goldsby, & Hornsby, 2004); fairness, personnel, customer, and distribution issues (Hannafey, 2003); ethical dilemmas when introducing new technologies, products, and services (Hannafey, 2003); and ethical issues—in particular, conflicts of interest—involved in all stages of an innovative start-up (Fassin, 2005).

Longenecker, McKinney, and Moore (1989) speculated that perhaps the less formal control systems in a small firm lead to more unethical behavior because of fewer monitoring mechanisms. In addition, the particular traits common to many entrepreneurs, such as egoism and independence, have been reported to lead to questionable ethical practice (Hannafey,

2003; Longenecker, McKinney, & Moore, 1988). The scandals associated with some of the 1990s dot-com entrepreneurs and innovators (e.g., Global Crossing, WorldCom, and Nortel) highlighted the fact that innovation and entrepreneurial expansion are not morally neutral concepts. This was also evidenced in the creative development of overly complex financial products that were partly responsible for the 2008 financial collapse (Graafland & van de Ven, 2011). Entrepreneurs starting up new ventures often face time-related pressures, cash flow demands, and power build-up (Morris, Schindehutte, Walton, & Allen, 2002). Although small businesses often have a closer physical and social relationship to their stakeholders—especially employees, customers, the local community, their business partners, and the natural environment (Spence & Painter-Morland, 2010b)—some of the entrepreneurship literature reveals that the most relevant stakeholders for the entrepreneur include investment bankers, securities analysts, institutional investors, venture capitalists, certification gatekeepers such as ISO, and those who review products (e.g., Lounsbury & Glynn, 2001).

Others have discussed how small businesses face particular barriers (e.g., limited time, resources, and capabilities) related to ethical responsibilities (e.g., Karakowsky et al., 2005; Lepoutre & Heene, 2006). According to a study sponsored by Canadian Business for Social Responsibility, a nonprofit organization representing Canadian member companies, "Internal communications and training for employees on CSR [corporate social responsibility] practices is challenging for SMEs due to resource constraints and the lack of affordable, external support" (Princic, Floyd, & Bonham, 2003, p. 4). We suggest that this same concern is present for creating and implementing effective business ethics training. Graafland, van de Ven, and Stoffele's (2003) study of business firms in the Netherlands found that in contrast to large firms, which prefer an integrity strategy to promote ethical behavior, small businesses prefer a dialogue strategy. For example, small businesses often assign one board member to informally deal with ethical questions.

In general, small businesses are less likely to have formal ethics programs such as a written values statement and code of ethics or conduct. However, researchers examining small businesses practices have found that one of the reasons they may not have formal ethics programs in place is that they can more easily communicate corporate vision and instill the application of organizational values in the organizational culture (Heugens, Kapstein, & van Oosterhout, 2008). In short, their size permits direct and frequent dialog between and among members. In addition, the values of a SME are strongly influenced by the personal values of the business owner-manager (Jenkins, 2006). Although the values of a large company are often developed and instilled by its CEO, according to the work of Spence and her colleagues (e.g., Spence & Rutherfoord, 2003), the values of the small business owner more directly impact business practice than is the case in a large firm. Often, "the acceptable standards of behavior... [are] clearly conveyed by the readily accessible example, and guidance, of the leadership" (Spence & Lozano, 2000, p. 51).

The literature, therefore, suggests that small firms tend to approach ethics in an implicit, informal, unstructured manner on an ad hoc basis (e.g., Murillo & Lozano, 2006; Perrini, 2006). In other words, smaller firms rarely use formal instruments (like codes of conduct/ethics) to encourage ethical behavior (Graafland et al., 2003). In addition, terms such as "stakeholder" are unfamiliar to many small business owners and managers (Russo & Tencati, 2009). For many small businesses, responsible business practice or considering the "right thing to do" is most important (Fassin, 2008). Small firms do not necessarily see ethics in instrumental terms (e.g., "it pays to be ethical" or "CSR is strategic"). Rather, ethical behavior is just how business is done (Murillo & Lozano, 2006). At the same time, Fuller and Tian (2006) suggest that SMEs' "legitimacy with immediate stakeholders; employees, customers, suppliers, and their 'local' community is at stake in a far more direct and personal way than it is with major corporations" (p. 295).

Other studies specifically focused on family versus non-family business enterprises have similarly found that family-owned firms are more likely to have fewer policies, rules, and codes; rather, they focus their business ethics implementation efforts on informal methods such as role-modeling, storytelling, rituals, and language use (e.g., Adams, Taschian, & Shore, 1996; Belak, Duh, & Milfener, 2010; Craig & Dibrell, 2006). Family business founder-owners, like small business owner-managers, are found to be most influential with regards to setting firms' ethical culture and values (Blodgett, Dumas, & Zanzi, 2011). To add value to prior literature, we now turn to findings from a recent study of Canadian "top companies" and their ethics training initiatives.

THE CANADIAN CONTEXT

According to Industry Canada (2011), approximately 98% of Canadian businesses have fewer than 100 employees. Statistics Canada reported that approximately 48% of the total private sector labor force worked for small businesses in 2009. These small businesses contribute to approximately one quarter of Canada's GDP (Industry Canada, 2011). The goal of our research was to gain a better understanding of business ethics training practices of leading Canadian companies. We conducted previous research on the training practices of the top 101 firms in Atlantic Canada (Miciak et al., 2004) and wanted to use a similar approach to be able to make comparisons across the country. We recognize that such a purposeful sample does have limitations (Kemper, Stringfield, & Teddlie, 2003). But like others who have focused on leading firms (Knox, Maklan & French, 2005; Lindsay, Lindsay & Irvine, 1996; Sekerka, 2009; Singh, 2006), we believe important insights can be gained by examining what some of the most financially successful and potentially best resourced firms are doing relative to ethics training. As such, we created a database of firms using regional lists of top companies as measured by revenues published by Canada's largest national newspaper, the *Top 1000 Companies*™ (2010), and a regional business magazine (Top 101 companies, 2010). We sourced contact information for senior company personnel who bear responsibility for their operation's corporate ethics training. We then telephoned these representatives to explain the purpose of the research and asked them to complete our confidential online survey. We developed a questionnaire based on the academic literature on business ethics training and education best practices (Sekerka, 2009) and formal organizational cultural systems for ethics (Treviño & Nelson, 2011). We collected data over three phases: starting in eastern Canada, then central Canada, and finishing in western Canada. We were unable to include firms from Quebec due to limited funding (translations costs). A total of 253 surveys were completed (19 % from eastern Canada, 55 % from central Canada, and 26 % from western Canada). Response rates varied by region, with 45% of firms from eastern Canada, 20% from central Canada, and 25% from western Canada responding. The high response rate in eastern Canada is likely due to the fact that the research was conducted by professors from universities in this region.

Of the respondent companies, 27% self-identified their operations as small businesses with 0 to 99 employees, 30% as medium sized firms with 100 to 499 employees, and 36% as large companies with 500 plus employees. The industries represented in the sample included forestry, fishery, mining, and oil and gas (17%); finance and insurance (12%); manufacturing (14%); healthcare and health and social services (8%); professional services and sciences (7%), business services (4%);, public administration (3%); utilities (3%); accommodations and food services (3%); and other services (21%). Over 84% of the companies were Canadian, and 28% had a union presence.

RESULTS

Of the 253 firms, a total of 89 firms (or 35% of the total sample) reported that they conduct ethics training. Only 76 of the 89 companies conducting ethics training provided the data needed to classify their firm according to size. Given that surveys were anonymous, we were unable to source the size data ourselves, hampering our ability to conduct a full analysis. We determined that of the 76 firms, 10 were classified as small (under 100 employees), 23 as medium (between 100 and 499 employees) and 43 as large (with more than 500 employees). This translates into 15% of small firms, 30% of medium firms and 47% of large firms conducting ethics training.

We will now present the detailed results on the firms conducting ethics training. Given space constraints and the fact that 98% of Canadian firms are classified as small businesses, we present the results for small firms, and contrast this with large firms illustrative purposes. Not surprisingly, larger firms have conducted training for a longer period of time. Of the firms studied, 14 of 43 of the large organizations reported they started their ethics training seven or more years ago. None of the small firms reported having training in place for this length of time. In fact, three of the small firms had just begun their training in the last year, and for another three, less than three years ago. Taking this information together, 6 of 10 firms had training in place for less than three years. This is in spite of the fact that all but one of these small firms had been in existence for more than five years.

Stakeholders Receiving Training

We asked our respondents to provide us with information on who received the training and whether key internal and external stakeholders were taking part. Internally, the majority of our small firms (8 of 10) reported focusing their efforts on training all employees, as opposed to specific internal stakeholder groups. Large firms, on the other hand, were more likely to be training employees as well as specifically training other internal groups such as supervisors, middle managers, and senior management team members. Only four of our small firms reported training external stakeholders, with one firm training external partners, two firms training vendors, and one firm training both suppliers and partners. In contrast, 15 large firms reported training external stakeholders, with the greatest number (11) reporting training external partners and then suppliers (7).

Delivery of Training

We asked participating firms to provide us with information on who conducts their ethics training and if it was offered in-house or was outsourced. The overwhelming majority of our sample reported that training was done in-house (9 of 10 small firms and 34 of 43 large firms) and was more likely to be conducted by human resources staff (5 of 10 small firms and 21 of 43 large firms), with operational supervisors or managers being the second most likely group to conduct ethics training.

We asked respondents about when they schedule their ethics training. The majority of our small firms (8) reported conducting their training as part of new employee orientation, and only one small firm reported conducting such training annually for all employees. Most large firms (15) also reported conducting their training as part of new employee orientation, but significantly more large firms (18) reported conducting ethics training on an annual basis.

In addition, we asked about the focus of company ethics training programs and the degree to which this content was customized. For both small and large firms, the primary focus of our sample's business ethics training was "company values." Firms of small and large size categories reported that their training varied by organization level as opposed to company function.

In terms of training delivery, we found that face-to-face sessions were most popular with small firms, with large firms opting equally for self-study programs with an online component or programs combining face-to-face training and self-study. Firms participating in our study reported using a variety of instructional aids and approaches. With regards to instructional aids, both our small and large firms made the most use of ethical scenarios (6 small and 31 large firms), followed by videos with an ethics focus (3 small and 16 large firms).

To foster interaction and increase targeted learning, firms in our sample used various instructional approaches. Small firms made the most use of reflection opportunities, role playing, and sharing among participants (5, 4, and 4 firms, respectively), while large firms incorporated ethical decision making, polling of participants for ethical issues, and sharing among participants (19, 16, and 14 firms, respectively). In contrast, small firms made limited use of employee polling to identify ethical issues (only 2 firms), while large firms made limited use of reflection opportunities (only 9 firms).

As might be expected, firms tended to use a number of these tools and approaches in combination. Among small firms, the most frequent combination of two elements involved the use of ethical scenarios and role playing (used by 4 small firms). For large firms, 11 used this same combination, but 12 firms reported using ethical scenarios and employee polling or ethical scenarios and videos. The most common combination of the three elements were represented by three small firms who used ethical scenarios, role playing, and videos, while eight large firms combined ethical scenarios, role playing, and employee polling.

Assessment and Reinforcement

Most of the small firms in our study (6) used a "basic evaluation" of the training. For example, information was gleaned from participants on the appropriateness of content, speaker quality, training location and timing. For large firms, the greatest number (18 firms) used an "end-of-course" test and 12 firms assessed changes in learning with pre- and post-training tests.

The final question posed was about the use of mechanisms to support and reinforce the learning done as part of their training. We asked firms to report about mechanisms grouped into three categories: corporate ethics program elements other than training, firm communication activities, and human resource practices. We found relatively few differences between what small firms and large firms were doing to support their ethics training initiatives. For example, they made virtually equal use of codes of conduct/ethics, whistleblowing systems, and formal risk assessments. Not surprisingly, a lower number of small firms reported having a designated ethics officer (1 small firm versus 17 large firms).

In terms of ongoing communication about ethics-related matters, small firms reported doing relatively little formal communications as compared to their large firm counterparts. Only two firms reported asking ethics-related questions in employee opinion surveys, one firm reported including ethics-related content in the company newsletter and one firm reported including ethics on a department meeting agenda. Large firms were more likely to have included such ethics-related content in annual employee surveys, employee newsletters, internal meeting agendas, and discussions at company conferences/events.

Lastly, to assess the linkages between business ethics training and human resource practices, we asked firms to what degree they included ethics-related topics in key HR activities. Similar to their large firm counterparts, some of the small firms included ethics as part of the job applicant screening process (2 firms), performance appraisals (3 firms), succession planning (2 firms), and exit interviews (4 firms).

IMPLICATIONS AND RECOMMENDATIONS

Not surprisingly, most of the small firms in our complete sample (85%) reported having *no* formal business ethics training. This is in marked contrast with large firms (47%), but consistent with other academic studies related to particular pressures and barriers (e.g., limited time, resources, and capabilities) that small businesses face in relation to establishing and/or maintaining formal ethics programs (e.g., Karakowsky et al., 2005; Lepoutre & Heene, 2006). In terms of comparative data, our results are lower than those of studies carried out in small to medium-sized companies in the United States. For example, Altizer (2003) reported that 41% of the companies participating in their study used ethics training. We could not source any comparable Canadian studies that reported results based on firm size.

Of the small businesses with ethics training, most conduct their training only during new employee orientation, whereas larger firms in our study were more likely to conduct ethics training on an annual basis as well as during orientation. Most of the small firms in our sample who conduct ethics training report that the training places more emphasis on company values than on rules and regulations. This contrasts with previous findings that ethics training in large organizations typically bears a heavy compliance orientation (e.g., Bowen, 2004; Sekerka, 2009). Our finding is in line with work suggesting that the values of a small business are more apt to be closely aligned with the values of the owner-manager (Jenkins, 2006). It seems appropriate for the values fit to be emphasized from the onset of employment, especially if resource constraints do not allow for follow-up formal ethics training.

Following the work of Sekerka (2009) and Treviño and Nelson (2011), we are not overly confident in the benefits of one-time ethics training initiatives. As Sims and Felton (2006) suggest, research has found that ethical thinking and ethical behavior must be nurtured over time. We suggest that, like large businesses, small businesses need to provide ongoing support for ethics training and education. The completion of one ethics course or workshop during orientation is not necessarily going to create or support an ethical employee. In both small and large firms, there needs to be a substantial and ongoing role for ethics education. Related to this, Waples, Antes, Murphy, Connelly, and Mumford (2008) suggest that evaluation and feedback is critical. We were pleased to see that the majority of the small firms in this study who conduct formal ethics training were also incorporating some form of evaluation (although some was quite simplistic and likely to be of limited value in assessing actual learning). Additionally, with none of these firms indicating any pre- and post-training evaluations, there is likely little integration of a feedback loop in terms of ethics training and employee development. Where resources allow, we encourage small firms to implement ongoing education and support to accompany initial ethics training sessions.

We acknowledge that most of the small firms we studied did not conduct any formal business ethics training. However, this information does not imply that the employees, managers, or owners are any more or less unethical in these firms than those working in large firms (or firms in general that conduct ethics training). Although the first longitudinal study of the long-term efficacy of formal ethics training found strong support (Warren, Laufer, & Gaspar, 2012), there has been little empirical evidence to indicate that conducting ethics training necessarily translates into ethical business practice. Indeed, the very practice of conducting ethical training can mask unethical behavior. Anecdotally, consider how many of the firms in the past decade of corporate malfeasance and misconduct cases were conducting "ethics" training at the time of their ethical downfalls (e.g., Enron).

It should also be noted that while formal training programs may have been absent in the majority of the small businesses we studied, informal ethics management strategies likely exist in many of these companies. As Jenkins (2006) points out, SMEs largely "lack formal management structures"

(p. 242). When one probes into the vision, goals, and day-to-day activities of small businesses, many of these firms are taking good care of their employees, providing a quality product or service, trying to reduce their ecological footprint, and giving back in some way to their community. This is just the way good businesses act in the eyes of many small business owner-managers. Some small business owner-managers are likely doing informal ethics training and education without acknowledging it as such. For example, small business owner-managers often mentor employees, inculcate values through role modeling, and find other ways to carry out informal ethics training without ever formally integrating it into their management processes and without ever naming it "ethics training." As Sims and Brinkmann (2003) suggest, ethics tools such as codes and ethics officers (here we include ethics training) are secondary to leadership influence in promoting ethical behavior. As mentioned, it is understandable that leadership influence and closer proximity to the leader in a small business might have more of an impact than formal ethics programs and particular tools such as ethics training. Because small business employees often have a closer physical and emotional relationship to their stakeholders, there might be less need for formal ethics training than in a large firm where, for example, employees and customers are often disconnected from one another.

At the same time, if there is validity to Lepoutre and Heene's findings (2006) that small businesses are not aware of specific social responsibility issues, this may suggest a need for educating small business owners and managers as to their specific and relevant social responsibility issues. According to Walker et al. (2007), engagement in the learning process is critical for small business training. Because training costs are high and the small business owner-manager's time is limited, ethics training has to be seen as adding value. In that light, we turn to some specific recommendations for those implementing ethics training in a small business context.

Sharing Resources

We begin our discussion with some ways that training costs can be shared through synergistic and collaborative arrangements with larger firms who might have more ethics training resources available, with other smaller firms (geographically proximate as well as virtually), and with government and nonprofit organizations. Industry associations and other interested parties such as NGOs can play a role in increasing small business owners' awareness and understanding of the importance of ethical issues. They could also partner with small businesses in ethics training initiatives. According to Lepoutre and Heene (2006), small business owner-managers need to "seek partners in the market, government, society, or the entire supply chain" (p. 267) in order to develop capabilities and overcome barriers to social responsibility. We believe this argument transfers to ethical responsibilities as well. Such collective action could include the ethics education and development of small business employees, owner-managers, and relevant internal and external stakeholders.

There has been a recent growth in initiatives and alliances in the United States that have a mandate to encourage large firms to help small businesses. Examples include NYSE Euronext, Accion International, Entrepreneurs' Organization, and the Startup America Partnership. Although the recently launched NYSE BigStartUp, which connects small business owner-managers and entrepreneurs with large corporations, appears to be focused on economic growth and job creation, these developing networks could also provide opportunities for sharing information and educational resources on ethics training. According to a recent press release, "The program calls on the nation's corporate community to lend support, experience and resources to startups and small companies to improve procurement, networking, business development, *training*, marketing and information sharing" [italics added] (NYSE Euronext, 2012, para. 1). With ever-increasing advances in information technology and social media, there are additional opportunities for large firms to communicate with and share resources with smaller companies.

However, if as Baron (1998) suggests, small business owners think differently than managers of large firms, we would not expect business ethics training to be a "one shoe that fits all sizes" approach. Rather, it might make more sense for small firm owner-managers to share best practices in ethics training with one another rather than relying on large firm best practices. Weltzien Høivik, and Shankar (2011) propose a network model or cluster approach to implementing CSR among small businesses. A similar cluster approach could be used in ethics training, whereby small businesses in the same geographic location and/or same sector share training-related resources and expenses. A cluster approach to business ethics training would help smaller firms overcome some of the human and financial capital challenges. This mechanism would also prompt peer encouragement and help to legitimate business ethics training in the eyes of small business owner-managers.

Organizations such as the Global Reporting Initiative (GRI)[1] offer various materials for small businesses. The Caux Roundtable,[2] with their project for moral capitalism, provides ethics resources for small business. There are many other websites that offer cost-effective and even free ethics training resources for small businesses.

Training Delivery

Whereas in large firms the efforts that drive ethics training often come from mid-level human resources, in small firms the internal champion of ethics training is typically the owner-manager. And yet, in our study, half of the small businesses reported that ethics training was conducted by in-house human resource personnel. This suggests HR practitioners should seek out opportunities to educate themselves about trends in this area. Additionally, the small business firms in our sample stated that a lack of internal expertise was a barrier to implementing ethics training. To provide support to small businesses, professional HR associations could have an important role to play in supporting their members with such development opportunities—assuming HR practitioners make their needs known.

Waples and his colleagues (2008) found that development focused weekend seminars or workshop approaches tend to be more effective than shorter training sessions (e.g., 1–2 hours, offered over longer periods of time). This is good news for small business owners who might think that a more elaborate program is essential. Although these scholars found that a case-based approach was most effective in ethics training, it is considered most beneficial to have multiple experiential activities (Waples et al., 2008). In our study, small businesses most frequently reported using scenarios, role-playing, and videos as part of their training, with scenarios being the most common. Small firms developing training initiatives should incorporate a variety of such approaches, providing flexibility to their organizational members. For example, a multimedia program can be designed, one that includes online self-paced instruction and salient business scenarios in video format, along with face-to-face sessions emphasizing role-play.

It is important to note the research that suggests that ethics programs are only valuable if members at all levels of the organization are trained about what it is, how it works, and where they fit in (e.g., Palmer & Zakhem, 2001). Conine and Rowden (2006) found that small business employees who were expected to meet the legal and ethical expectations of their profession and organization were also more satisfied with their job. In a small business, it would seem to be easier to include all employees in an ethics training session than in a larger firm. Moreover, evidence supports that there is enhanced learning when participants are at varying career stages (Waples et al., 2008). Taking this information together, we suggest that a bottom-up versus top-down approach to ethics training might be better suited for those who work in small firms. We envision ethics training workshops in which employees are able to teach one another. Here, owner-managers and employees would work together to develop scenarios that focus on situation-specific ethical dilemmas that small business employees face on a day-to-day basis. Since personal reflection is an essential element of training (e.g., Cyboran, 2005; Sekerka & Godwin, 2010), employees can leverage this practice by reflecting on and sharing their ethical issues with others through either face-to-face or on-line formats. This material can then be organized and shared with other organizational members. Informal ethics training is more likely to take place in small firms; therefore, we encourage an ongoing dialogic approach. This means integrating ethics into everyday discussions and staff meetings and, as mentioned previously, it becomes a core theme brought forward in employee-mentoring efforts.

In Sekerka's (2009) study of ethics training and education, she found that practices are often limited to online activities, with additional face-to-face training reserved for employees in specialized roles and senior executives. Our study found that 40% of the small firms doing ethics training were using face-to-face ethics training initiatives and none of the companies were doing online self-study. Due to the fewer number of employees in small businesses, it might actually be easier to implement face-to-face training in these operations. At the same time, there might be opportunities related to the sharing of resources (discussed above) for the development of online and other self-study programs that could be used by small firms on an ongoing basis. Ethics-based courses in continuing education and professional development programs at educational institutions provide additional opportunities.

We strongly encourage firms to integrate ethics training as a part of employee development and performance appraisal. We also recommend training assessment for learning outcomes connected to course or workshop content and employee perceptions of the program's effectiveness. This information needs to be gleaned at the end of each training initiative and then shared with employees. Here again, we acknowledge that this may be difficult with the competing demands and scarce resources in the small business context.

CONCLUSION

Large multinational corporations have been called the dominant institutions in our world (Korten, 1995). However, as presented in this chapter, small businesses significantly contribute to society through job creation, the provision of products and services, taxes, and innovation and entrepreneurship. Small firms, therefore, also have a huge impact on economies, communities, and the natural environment, and are equally deserving of examination.

According to Walker et al. (2007), there has been little empirical study of ethics training initiatives in small businesses. Our findings pertain to ethics training among Canadian companies and are preliminary in nature. The data must be interpreted with caution, given the relatively small sample size and self-reported information. Limitations aside, our findings suggest an increasing trend in ethics training initiatives among leading small businesses in Canada, especially in the past three years.

We suggest that there is a need for further study of the activities of small businesses with regard to business ethics training. For example, in-depth interviews with small business owner-managers could assist in understanding and identifying the unique challenges and barriers that small firms face in conducting ethics training, as well as the opportunities that exist for determining context- and cost-effective means to implement ethics training. Furthermore, theoretical models built on large-firm assumptions cannot continue to be used to explain small business activities and outcomes (Spence & Painter-Morland, 2010b). If small businesses face unique ethical issues and challenges, then small business training needs to focus on building awareness of ethical issues and dilemmas relevant to this context. Spence and Painter-Morland (2010a) have called for "the development of ethics management strategies that are flexible and affordable enough to be implemented within small and medium sized organizations" (p. 335). We concur with this sentiment and encourage additional study to better understand how small business owner-managers and employees view the role and purpose of business ethics training, and to develop meaningful models designed and applicable for small business contexts.

ACKNOWLEDGMENTS

The second author wishes to recognize the Canadian Centre for Ethics in Public Affairs (CCEPA) for their financial support of this research.

NOTES

1. http://www.globalreporting.org.
2. http:www.cauxroundtable.org.

REFERENCES

Adams, J. S., Taschian, A., & Shore, T. H. (1996). Ethics in family and non-family owned firms: An exploratory study. *Family Business Review, 9*(2), 157–170.

Altizer, L. (2003). Why small organizations need our help. *Ethics Resource Center.* Retrieved from http://www.ethics.org/resource/why-small-organizations-need-our-help

Baron, R. (1998). Cognitive mechanisms in entrepreneurship: Why and when entrepreneurs think differently than other people. *Journal of Business Venturing, 13*(4), 275–294.

Bartram, T. (2005). Small firms, big ideas: The adoption of human resource management in Australian small firms. *Asia Pacific Journal of Human Resources, 43*(1), 137–154.

Belak, J., Duh, M., & Milfener, B. (2010). Informal and formal institutional measures of business ethics implementation: Exploring differences between family and non-family enterprises. *Proceedings from International Conference: An Enterprise Odyssey.* Zagreb: University of Zagreb, 1007–1021.

Billett, S. (2001). Increasing small business participation in VET: A "hard ask." *Education and Training, 43*(8/9), 416–425.

Blodgett, M. S., Dumas, C., & Zanzi, A. (2011). Emerging trends in global ethics: A comparative study of U.S. and international family business values, *Journal of Business Ethics, 99*(1), 29–38.

Bowen, S. (2004). Organizational factors encouraging ethical decision making: An exploration into the case of an exemplar. *Journal of Business Ethics, 52*(4), 311–324.

Brytting, T. (1997). Moral support structures in private industry: The Swedish case. *Journal of Business Ethics, 16*(7), 663–697.

Conine, C. T., Jr., & Rowden, R. W. (2006). Ethical climate and job satisfaction in small businesses. *Journal of Business and Entrepreneurship, 18*(2), 35–48.

Craig, J., & Dibrell, C. (2006). The natural environment, innovation, and firm performance: A comparative study. *Family Business Review, 19*(4), 275–288.

Cyboran, V. L. (2005). Moving beyond the training room: Fostering workplace learning through online journaling. *Performance Improvement, ∎44*(7), 34–39.

Driscoll, C., & Tesfayohannes, M. (2009). Big business ethics textbooks: Where do small business and entrepreneurship fit? *Journal of Business Ethics Education, 6,* 25–42.

Ethics Resource Center. (2007). *National government ethics survey.* Arlington, VA: Ethics Resource Center.

European Commission. (2005). *The new SME definition: User guide and model declaration.* Saint Giles, Belgium: European Commission, Enterprise and Industry Publications, EN NB-60-04-773-EN-C 92-894-7909-4.

Fassin, Y. (2005). The reasons behind non-ethical behavior in business and entrepreneurship. *Journal of Business Ethics, 60*(3), 265–279.

Fassin, Y. (2008). SMEs and the fallacy of formalizing CSR. *Business Ethics, 17*(4), 364–378.

Fassin, Y., van Rossem, A., & Buelens, M. (2010). Small business owner-managers' perceptions of business ethics and CSR-related concepts. *Journal of Business Ethics, 98*(3), 425–453.

Fuller, T., & Tian, Y. (2006). Social and symbolic capital and responsible entrepreneurship: An empirical investigation of SME narratives. *Journal of Business Ethics, 67*(3), 287–304.

Graafland, J., van de Ven, B., & Stoffele, N. (2003). Strategies and instruments for organizing CSR by small and large businesses in the Netherlands. *Journal of Business Ethics, 47*(1), 45–60.

Graafland, J., & van de Ven, B. (2011). The credit crisis and the moral responsibility of professionals in finance. *Journal of Business Ethics, 103*(4), 605–619.

Hannafey, F. T. (2003). Entrepreneurship and ethics: A literature review. *Journal of Business Ethics, 46*(2), 99–110.

Heugens, P. P. M. A. R., Kapstein, M., & van Oosterhout, J. (2008). Contracts to communities: A processual model of organizational virtue. *Journal of Management Studies, 45*(1), 100–121.

Hillary, R. (2000). *Small and medium-sized enterprises and the environment.* Sheffield, UK: Greenleaf.

Industry Canada. (2011). *Key small business statistics.* Retrieved from www.ic.gc.ca/eic/site/sbrp-rppe.nsf/eng/h_rd02488.html

Industry Canada. (2012). *Key small business statistics—July 2012.* Retrieved from http://www.ic.gc.ca/eic/site/061.nsf/eng/02714.html

Jenkins, H. (2006). Small business champions for corporate social responsibility. *Journal of Business Ethics, 67*(3), 241–256.

Karakowsky, L., Carroll, A. B., & Buchholtz, A. K. (2005). *Business and society, ethics and stakeholder management* (1st ed.). Toronto, CA: Nelson Education.

Kemper, E. A., Stringfield, S., & Teddlie, C. (2003). Mixed Methods Sampling Strategies in Social Science Research. In A. Tashakkori & C. Teddlie (Eds.), *Handbook of mixed methods in social & behavioral research* (pp. 273–296). Thousand Oaks, Calif.: SAGE Publications.

Knox, S., Maklan, S., & French, P. (2005). Corporate social responsibility: Exploring stakeholder relationships and programme reporting across leading FTSE companies. *Journal of Business Ethics, 61*(1), 7–28.

Korten, D. (1995). *When corporations rule the world.* West Hartford, CT: Berrett-Koehler/Kumarian.

Kuratko, D. F., Goldsby, M. G., & Hornsby, J. S. (2004). The ethical perspectives of entrepreneurs: An examination of stakeholder salience. *Journal of Applied Management and Entrepreneurship, 9*(4), 19–43.

Lepoutre, J., & Heene, A. (2006). Investigating the impact of firm size on small business social responsibility: A critical review. *Journal of Business Ethics, 67*(3), 257–273.

Lindsay, R. M., Lindsay, L. M., & Irvine, V. B. (1996). Instilling ethical behavior in organizations: A survey of Canadian companies. *Journal of Business Ethics, 15*(4), 393–407.

Longenecker, J. G., McKinney, J. A., & Moore, C. W. (1988). Egoism and independence: Entrepreneurial ethics. *Organizational Dynamics, 16,* 64–72.

Longenecker, J. G., McKinney, J. A., & Moore, C. W. (1989). Ethics in small business. *Journal of Small Business Management, 27*(1), 27–31.

Longenecker, J. G., Moore, C. W., Petty, J. W., Palich, L. E., & McKinney, J. A. (2006). Ethical attitudes in small businesses and large corporations: Theory and empirical findings from a tracking study spanning three decades. *Journal of Small Business Management, 44*(2), 167–184.

Lounsbury, M., & Glynn, M. A. (2001). Cultural entrepreneurship: Stories, legitimacy, and the acquisition of resources. *Strategic Management Journal, 22*(6/7), 545–564.

Miciak, A., Fullerton, G., Touche-Lightstone, K., Jutla, D., Driscoll, C., McKee, M., Kelloway, E. K., Haiven, J., & MacKinnon, G. (2004). TOP 101 companies make the grade. *Progress.* Halifax, NS: Progress Media Group.

Morris, M. H., Schindehutte, M., Walton, J., & Allen, J. (2002). The ethical context of entrepreneurship: Proposing and testing a developmental framework. *Journal of Business Ethics, 40*(4), 331–361.

Murillo, D., & Lozano, J. (2006). SMEs and CSR: An approach to CSR in their own words. *Journal of Business Ethics, 67*(3), 227–240.

NYSE Euronext. (2012, March 21). The NYSE big startup: A nationwide jobs growth initiative connects startups and entrepreneurs with corporate America to accelerate new business, funding and success. *NYSE Euronext* (news release). Retrieved from http://www.nyse.com/press/1332325195828.html

OECD. (2009, July) The impact of the global crisis on SME and entrepreneurship financing and policy responses. *OECD*. Retrieved January 10, 2013 from http://www.oecd.org/cfe/smesandentrepreneurship/theimpactoftheglobal-crisisonsmeandentrepreneurshipfinancingandpolicyresponses.htm.

Palmer, D. E., & Zakhem, A. (2001). Bridging the gap between theory and practice, using the students' moral reasoning, *Journal of Business Ethics, 29*(1), 77–84.

Perrini, F. (2006). SMEs and CSR theory: Evidence and implications from an Italian perspective. *Journal of Business Ethics, 67*(3), 305–316.

Princic, L., Floyd, M., & Bonham, J. (2003). Engaging small business in corporate social responsibility: A Canadian small business perspective on CSR. *Canadian Business for Social Responsibility*. Retrieved from http://www.cbsr.ca/files/ReportsandPapers/EngagingSME_FINAL.pdf

Robertson, D. C. (1991). Corporate ethics programs: The impact of firm size. In B. Harvey, H. van Luijk, & G. Corbetta (Eds.), *Market morality and company size* (pp. 199–136). North Holland, The Netherlands: Kluwer Academic Publishers.

Russo, A., & Tencati, A. (2009). Formal vs. informal CSR strategies: Evidence from Italian micro, small, medium-sized, and large firms. *Journal of Business Ethics, 85*(2), 339–353.

Sekerka, L. E. (2009). Organizational ethics education and training: A review of best practices and their application. *International Journal of Training & Development, 13*(2), 77–95.

Sekerka, L. E., & Godwin, L. (2010). Strengthening professional moral courage: A balanced approach to ethics training. Training & Management Development Methods, *24*(5), 63–74.

Sims, R. R., & Brinkmann, J. (2003). Enron ethics (or, culture matters more than codes). *Journal of Business Ethics, 45*(3), 243–256.

Sims, R. R., & Felton E. L., Jr. (2006). Designing and delivering business ethics teaching and learning. *Journal of Business Ethics, 63*(3), 297–312.

Singh, J. B. (2006). Ethics programs in Canada's largest corporations, *Business and Society Review, 111*(2), 119–137.

Spence, L. J., & Lozano, J. (2000). Communicating about ethics with small firms: Experiences from the U.K. and Spain. *Journal of Business Ethics, 27*(1/2), 43–53.

Spence, L. J., & Rutherfoord, R. (2003). Small business and empirical perspectives in business ethics, editorial. *Journal of Business Ethics, 47*(1), 1–5.

Spence, L. J., & Painter-Morland, M. (2010a). Conclusion: The road ahead for research on ethics and SMEs. In L. J. Spence, & M. Painter-Morland (Eds.), *Ethics in small and medium sized enterprises: A global commentary*. The International

Society of Business, Economics, and Ethics Book Series (Vol. 2, pp. 333–338). Dordrecht, The Netherlands: Springer.

Spence, L. J., & Painter-Morland, M. (2010b). Introduction. Spence, & M. Painter-Morland (Eds.), *Ethics in small and medium sized enterprises: A global commentary.* The International Society of Business, Economics, and Ethics Book Series (Vol. 2, pp. 1-12). Dordrecht, The Netherlands: Springer.

Tilley, F. (2000). Small firm environmental ethics: How deep do they go? *Business Ethics: A European Review, 9*(1), 31–41.

Top 101 companies. (2010). *Progress, 17*(5). Halifax, NS: Progress Media Group.

Top 1000 companies™. (2010). Report on Business Magazine, 2010. Retrieved from http://v1.theglobeandmail.com/v5/content/tp1000-2010/purchase.php

Treviño, L. K., & Nelson, K. A. (2011). *Managing business ethics: Straight talk about how to do it right* (5th ed.). Hoboken, NJ: Wiley.

United States Small Business Administration. (2010). Summary of size standards by industry. United States Small Business Administration. Retrieved from http://www.sba.gov/content/summary-size-standards-industry

Waples, E. P., Antes, A. L., Murphy, S. T., Connelly, S., & Mumford, M. D. (2008). A meta-analytic investigation of business ethics instruction. *Journal of Business Ethics, 87*(1), 133–151.

Walker, E., Redmond, J., Webster, B., & Le Clus, M. (2007). Small business owners: Too busy to train? *Journal of Small Business and Enterprise Development, 14*(2), 294–306.

Warren, D. E., Laufer, W. S., & Gaspar, J. (2012, August). *Promoting ethics in organizations: A longitudinal study of formal ethics training and outcomes.* Paper presented at the Academy of Management Annual Meeting, Boston, MA.

Weaver, G. R., & Treviño, L. K. (1999). Compliance and values oriented ethics programs: Influences on employees' attitudes and behavior. *Business Ethics Quarterly, 9*(3), 15–35.

Weltzien Høivik, H., & Shankar, D. (2011). How can SMEs in a cluster respond to global demands for corporate responsibility? *Journal of Business Ethics, 101*(2), 175–195.

Werner, A., & Spence, J. (2004). Literature review: Social capital and SMEs. In L.J. Spence et al. (Eds.), *Responsibility and social capital: The world of small and medium sized enterprises* (pp. 7–24). New York, NY: Palgrave MacMillan.

SECTION V

LEADERSHIP AND DEVELOPMENT

CHAPTER 13

DEVELOPING ETHICAL LEADERS

A Servant Leadership Approach

Charmine E. J. Härtel, Ivan Butarbutar, Sen Sendjaya, Andre Pekerti, Giles Hirst, and Neal M. Ashkanasy

Over the past decade, we have seen numerous high-profile scandals in both the private and public sectors: for example, Enron, Bernard Madoff, Lehman Brothers, WorldCom, Arthur Anderson, the BP Deepwater Horizon oil spill (Baker, Hunt, & Andrews, 2006). These scandals have raised important questions about the role that leaders play—and should play—in fostering and defining ethical conduct in organizations (Härtel & Ganegoda, 2008). In these examples, leaders modeled negative behaviors in the workplace, which research has shown to be associated with subsequent negative employee behaviors, including self-serving (Brown, Treviño, & Harrison, 2005; Schyns & Schilling, 2013) and deviant activities (Tepper, Carr, Breaux, Geider, Hu, & Hua, 2009). These behaviors are in contrast to the community expectation that leaders need to do the opposite: to model *ethical* leadership behaviors including fairness, integrity, and adherence to high moral standards. By so doing, leaders would be fostering positive employee

Ethics Training in Action, pages 271–291
Copyright © 2014 by Information Age Publishing
All rights of reproduction in any form reserved.

behaviors (Brown et al., 2005) and discouraging undesirable self-serving behaviors (Zhang, Walumbwa, Aryee, & Chen, 2013).

Thus, while most employees look to their leaders as a central source of ethical guidance in the workplace, contemporary critiques of leadership practices have been scathing, accusing business and government leaders of self-interest and greed (Brown & Mitchell, 2010). These troubling trends in organizational leadership have prompted urgent calls from all areas of society for a "new leadership"—one that focuses on ethics and service to society, especially in crisis situations (e.g., James, Wooten, & Dushek, 2011). For this call not to remain hollow, real organizational commitment must address, on the one hand, the need for leadership to be in service to others (as well as to promote followers' ethical and moral development) and, on the other hand, the need for leadership to chart a clear course and to deliver bottom line results.

In this chapter, we seek to address this issue by outlining some of the key practical findings of recent field research on the training of ethics in organizations undertaken by a team led by Charmine Härtel and funded by the Australian Research Council (ARC).[1] In so doing, we will:

1. Provide the business case for organizational ethics and explain why leadership should hold a focal role in ethics training. Related to this discussion, we describe how a strong, self-driven commitment is necessary for leaders to be motivated to develop their own ethical and moral compass.
2. Share the definition and model of ethical leadership that Härtel and her associates developed and applied in the ARC-funded ethical leadership training program.
3. Stress the importance of developing empathic leadership and its role in building an ethical leadership climate.
4. Provide examples of how such behaviors can be incorporated into an ethical leadership training program.

THE BUSINESS CASE FOR ETHICAL ORGANIZATIONS

Why should organizations care about business ethics? Ostensibly, the answer is clear. Studies examining this question reveal that ethical organizations tend to have better financial performance (Hitt & Collins, 2007; Margolis & Walsh, 2003; Orlitzky, Schmidt, & Rynes, 2003), better customer relations and customer loyalty (Collins, 2009; Luo & Bhattacharya, 2006), a better reputation (Roberts & Dowling, 2002), and higher levels of employee organizational commitment (Gong, Chang & Cheung, 2010; Sharma, Borna, & Stearns, 2009; Treviño, Butterfield, & McCabe, 1998). On the flip side, unethical behavior in organizations has huge costs, estimated in the billions annually in the U.S. alone (Detert, Treviño, Burris, & Andiappan, 2007).

As such, the evidence is clear: Ethical business practices *do* make good business sense. Given that this is the case, why do we hear of so many instances of unethical behavior? It isn't because people don't know what is right or don't want to do what is right. Mary Gentile's (2010, 2012) work in the area of business ethics shows the contrary; that is, most people can distinguish right from wrong and most people would like to do the right thing. The underlying problem, Gentile notes, is the perception of great personal risk to addressing an unethical issue or going against unethical norms, along with the concomitant lack of skills and confidence to handle the situation successfully. Creating the context for ethical behavior—an ethical climate—reduces the perception of personal risk in confronting unethical behavior. As such, ethical leaders who model ethical behavior and coach staff in handling ethical dilemmas constitute an important part of the solution.

DEVELOPING ETHICAL LEADERSHIP: THE LINCHPIN OF ORGANIZATIONAL ETHICS

As Sauser (2005) emphasized, leaders play an essential role in shaping followers' ethical orientation and enforcing ethical practice in organizations. Accordingly, leaders with unwavering integrity and ethical judgment are in great demand (cf., Aguilera, 2005; Dealy & Thomas, 2006). In an analysis of ethical issues in business, Sauser (2005) stressed in particular that leaders effectively shape the climate for ethics in an organization by influencing their followers' perceptions of ethical events, ethical practices, and ethical procedures in organizations. Moreover, according to Sauser, leaders do so through their example, including the behaviors they reward (and enforce), the goals they emphasize, and the policies and procedures they produce. The importance of not just being an ethical leader, but also building an ethical climate, is underscored by recent research by Mayer, Nurmohamed, Treviño, Shapiro, and Schminke (2013), which showed that, while ethical leadership behaviors have a positive influence on internal reporting of unethical conduct by staff, the effect is magnified when coworkers also engage in ethical behaviors and voice support for leaders' messages about the importance of ethical conduct.

Research (e.g., see Ahmed & Machold, 2004; Arnaud, 2010; Douglas, Davidson, & Schwartz, 2001) has consistently demonstrated that ethical climate is also a key factor affecting individual ethical behavior. Concomitantly, Victor and Cullen (1987) define ethical work climate as "the shared perceptions of what is ethically correct behavior and how ethical issues should be handled" (pp. 51–52). Moreover, and as Kozlowski and Doherty

(1989) note, the formation of climate in an organization is embedded in the leadership process, so that each leader in an organization can be seen to be a key figure who promotes and fosters a particular organizational climate (see also Mayer, Nishii, Schneider, & Goldstein, 2007).

Some may ask whether ethical leadership's positive effects extend beyond promoting ethical organizational activities. In a review of the ethical leadership literature, Brown and Treviño (2006) identified evidence showing that employees are willing to put in extra effort at work when they perceive their leaders as ethical. Other studies identify a link between ethical leadership and the ability to attract and to retain talent (Collins, 2010) and to foster higher levels of employee motivation (Piccolo, Greenbaum, Den Hartog, & Folger, 2010), job satisfaction (Toor & Ofori, 2009), organizational commitment (Upadhyay & Singh, 2010), and employee performance (Resick, Hanges, Dickson, & Mitchelson, 2006).

Before we get to a model of ethical leadership, however, it is important to address the concerns of a skeptic who might say, "Yes, but can we *really* develop ethical leaders?" In fact, the evidence appears to tell us that it is not possible to *make* someone learn these moral decision making skills through either testing or simply indoctrinating them in classroom-based training (Gentile, 2012). As an example of the futility of much ethical training, Bogomolny (2004) outlines the case of a leading Canadian financial company that developed a sophisticated electronic role-play involving a series of scenarios that required employees to make ethical judgment. Participation in the exercise strategy was mandated throughout the organization so that every employee was required to take a test every two years. The results of follow-up evaluation were then reviewed to ensure employees understood and were acting upon the firm's code of conduct. To management's delight, employees in regional offices that previously lagged behind began to increase their scores. So far so good, but the company then sent out representatives to develop a case study and considered using this information in an advertising campaign. What these representatives uncovered surprised and shocked the executive team. They reported back that managers and employees in regional sites had begun to think these exercises were a waste of time. Their solution was simply to ask coworkers who performed well on the test to complete the online test for their peers. In the words of one former employee "I would just knock these things out" (Bogomolny, 2004, p. 77). So, if we cannot *make* people ethical, what can we do?

To answer this conundrum, we argue, along with Gentile (2010, 2012), that development of more ethical leadership behavior requires ensuring that people have their *own* sense of why it is important to develop their *own* ethical and moral compass. As a consequence of this, it is clearly essential to build a case as to the importance of ethical behavior in people's lives and how it can have a positive influence on the world around us. Gentile argues further that it is also equally important to understand that, if people have little or no interest in engaging in ethical practices, it is better at least to give them the option to quit the organization.

So far, we have discussed the importance of ensuring an ethical climate in organizations, the key role leaders play in this, and the difficulties encountered in running ethical leadership training programs. Nonetheless, and as Giessner and van Quaquebeke (2010) point out, the number of reported ethics breaches in an organization indicates ongoing failure by leaders to attend to the organization's ethical climate. In consequence, ethics training for organizational leaders would seem to be a critical imperative, despite the difficulty of such training. Moreover, in order to develop ethical leaders, it is essential to identify a leadership model that focuses on the leadership behaviors that *actually* can produce ethical outcomes. In their review of the literature, Härtel and her team identified in particular *servant leadership* as an ideal candidate. We describe this model and its significance as a means to develop ethical leadership behavior next.

THE LEADERSHIP MODEL: SERVANT LEADERSHIP

Barbuto and Wheeler (2006) and Sendjaya, Sarros, and Santora (2008) define servant leadership as an altruistic and service orientation whereby leaders view employee growth and service to the community as worthwhile ends in themselves. In particular, researchers (e.g., see Hale & Fields, 2007; Hunter, Neubert, Perry, Witt, Penney, & Weinberger, in press; Liden, Wayne, Zhao, & Henderson, 2008; Sendjaya et al., 2008; Walumbwa, Hartnell, & Oke, 2010) have established that servant leadership promotes ethical behavior. Importantly for the case we make in this chapter, Graham (1991) has demonstrated that servant leadership is distinct from other leadership approaches because of its emphasis on the needs and welfare of stakeholders within the organization and outside community along with its development of followers' moral capacity reasoning.

Moral reasoning is an essential component preceding ethical decision making (Keeney & Raiffa, 1993; Kohlberg, 1984; Murnighan, Cantelon, & Elyashiv, 2001), insofar as it enables individuals to make sense of and integrate moral values (Kohlberg, 1984). In line with this (and following up on Graham, 1991), we posit here that Kohlberg's concept of moral reasoning development is likely to be a foundational ingredient of ethical leadership. According to Rest (1986), moral reasoning requires a concern for others' welfare, empathy, and the ability to visualize different moral action-effect scenarios. As such, servant leadership can be seen as an example of what we call *moral-laden leadership*, where servant leaders engage in moral dialogue with their followers, ensuring that both the ends they seek and the means they employ are morally legitimized, thoughtfully reasoned, and ethically justified (Sendjaya, 2005). In this way, servant leadership is likely to build the socio-moral climate of the organization, namely, the ethical norms characterizing the work setting and influencing the likely moral decision making and behavior of the individuals within it (Sims, 1992)—and consequently organization performance (Christie, Kwon, Stoeberl, & Baumhart, 2003).

Servant leaders foster an ethical climate in their organization because these leaders offer explicit cues as to what is ethical versus unethical behavior (Hunter et al., in press). Such leaders also support ethical applications within and beyond the organization through examples such as enhancing employee capacity for moral action, taking a resolute stand on moral principles, or displaying morally justified means to achieve organizational goals (Sendjaya et al., 2008). These leaders thus serve as role models for ethical action, expecting and encouraging followers to stand for and to adhere consistently to ethical standards (Hunter et al., in press). For example, servant leaders are likely to put an emphasis on persuading followers to comply with laws and professional standards, to follow the organization's rules and policies, and to do what is right for the organization and the public. These leaders may also develop organizational policies and practices that reward ethical behavior and punish unethical behavior.

Also, from a follower's perspective, employees tend to perceive servant leaders as selfless, supportive, and authentic leaders who consider their followers' interests and needs (Hale & Fields, 2007). These positive perceptions can later affect employees' reactions to leaders (Bennis, 2002; Hall & Lord, 1995), such as showing higher trust (Bennis, 2002; Joseph & Winston, 2005; Sendjaya & Pekerti, 2010; Tschannen-Moran & Hoy, 1998), and they provide clues to identify norms or behavior that is appropriate and expected in the organization (Brockner & Higgins, 2001; Hunter et al., in press; Kark & Van Dijk, 2007).

Pepper (2003) provides an interesting insight into this, observing that servant-led organizations and servant leaders commit to people-*building* instead of people-*using*. To serve followers, servant leaders build personal relationships with them in which personal persuasion and leading-by-example function as the dominant approaches (Hunter et al., in press; Spears, 2004). As such, servant leadership promotes four critical behavioral sets: (1) the act of serving others; (2) the involvement of organizational members in the decision-making process; (3) a more sensible concern toward community well-being; and (4) the empowerment of members' potential (Spears, 2004). We expand on each of these behavioral sets next.

The Act of Serving Others

Servant leadership inevitably has been viewed as a paradox in "traditional" leadership perspectives owing to the idiosyncratic notion that, instead of being served by followers, servant leaders *deliberately* serve followers (Graham, 1991; Sendjaya & Sarros, 2002). In this respect, the concurrent use of *servant* and *leadership* together also seems to be a paradoxical and oxymoronic concept to some scholars and practitioners (see Locander & Luechauer, 2006; Spears, 2004). In this more traditional view, most leaders in a typical organization are those who *lead*, not *serve*. In servant leadership practice, however, this notion is reversed: Instead of being served by their followers, leaders start becoming "servants" for others.

Graham (1991) points out that servant leadership distinguishes itself from transformational leadership in two important ways: (1) sensitivity to the needs and welfare of stakeholders within the organization and outside community, and (2) its strong engagement with moral reasoning. Graham further notes, "Servant-leadership takes a further step because it encourages followers not only in intellectual and skill development, but also enhances moral capacity reasoning" (1991, p. 116). In addition, the three key tenets of (1) serve-first, (2) serving the community, and (3) encouraging employees to display service have become distinctive features of servant leadership that are not reflected in transformational leadership (Barbuto & Wheeler, 2006; Liden et al., 2008). Consequently, when put into practice, in servant-leadership-driven organizations, the fulfillment of employees' needs and interests would be taken into consideration.

Since servant leaders show genuine care and sympathy for the needs and interests of followers (Ehrhart, 2004; Liden et al., 2008), their followers may start to behave likewise (Hunter et al., in press). Such leaders are also likely to cultivate a social context that allows followers to start to consider their coworkers' benefits, so that a supportive environment may flourish. Individuals motivated to help others are also likely to contribute toward overall organizational goals (Zhang et al., 2013). Indeed, research shows a positive association between servant leadership and team performance (Schaubroeck, Lam, & Peng, 2011), innovation and creativity (Van Dierendonck & Rook, 2010), and ultimately financial performance (Melrose, 1998; Ruschman, 2002).

The Involvement of Organizational Members in the Decision-Making Process

Servant leaders affirm their trust in followers, respect them and treat them as equal partners in the organization (Sendjaya et al., 2008), and, by so doing, improve followers' willingness to contribute to decision-making processes (Fujimoto, Härtel, & Härtel, 2004). Servant leaders also promote and establish an environment where everybody is respected and treated fairly, regardless of their personal backgrounds. This treatment positively affects the way followers work and collaborate with their leaders and colleagues (Fujimoto et al., 2004; Härtel, 2008; Hunter et al., in press; Van Knippenberg, De Cremer, & Van Knippenberg, 2007).

A More Sensible Concern Toward Community Well-Being

Since the key tenets of serve-first, serving the community, and encouraging employees to display service are *distinctive* features of servant leaders (Liden et al., 2008), the practice of "serving others" will be prevalent in the relationships between servant leaders and followers (Hunter et al., in press). When organizational members exhibit a high degree of service toward other individuals, an atmosphere that encourages them to act beyond their personal interests and take the initiative to understand and support others' interests naturally emerges (Graham, 1991; Liden et al., 2008). As direct or indirect consequence, leaders and followers are likely to start to value the cogent importance of collective interests, which in turn should inspire them to act beyond their personal interests. In such a high service context (where leaders actually do care for others) followers can be expected to respond by serving community interests (Hunter et al., in press; Liden et al., 2008).

The Empowerment of Members' Potential

Servant leaders are keen to draw the best out from their followers' talents and capabilities and so can be expected to assist followers to grow and to develop their potential to the fullest and also to maximize their contributions to the organization (Liden et al., 2008; Luthans & Avolio, 2003). By doing this, these leaders are likely to enhance follower satisfaction that leads to better work performance not only in the tasks required, but also to go beyond these in the form of organizational citizenship behavior (OCB) (Butarbutar, Sendjaya, & Härtel, 2010; Hunter et al., in press).

Spears (2004) notes further that servant leaders intentionally perform "service" for their followers through the acts of listening, empathy, healing, awareness, persuasion, conceptualization, foresight, stewardship, commitment to the growth of people, and building community. From a more macro perspective, servant leadership-driven organizations tend to be characterized by followers who have greater autonomy and freedom to develop their own potential (Liden, Wayne, & Sparrowe, 2000). This is because servant leaders empower followers and facilitate personal and job satisfaction (Hunter et al., in press). Liden et al. (2008) emphasize further that servant leaders empower employees and inspire the spirit of service, which benefits the interests of the organization.

In summary, in the servant-led paradigm, leaders focus not only on their own interests, but rather they can be expected to emphasize the interests of followers. Driven by moral love (Patterson, 2010), servant leaders genuinely want to become *servants* to others (Sendjaya & Sarros, 2002), and therefore they cultivate followers' talents and aspirations to the fullest level. Servant leaders thus contribute to cultivating "a culture of serving others, both within and outside the organization" (Liden et al., 2008, p. 174). Additionally, servant leaders endorse moral practice in organizations (Graham, 1991) and foster moral integrity and display themselves as role models (Hunter et al., in press; Whetstone, 2002). The acts of servant leaders are moreover driven by ethically sound principles that benefit organizations and followers (Graham, 1991; Hunter et al., in press). In this case, Sendjaya et al. (2008) proffer that servant leaders offer explicit cues as to what is ethical versus unethical behavior by taking a resolute stand on moral principles and by displaying morally justified means to achieve organizational goals.

Empirical research into servant leadership and its effects has been highly supportive of this view (Hunter et al., in press). In this respect, servant leadership has been tested in various cultures and industries (e.g., see Pekerti & Sendjaya, 2010; Sarayrah, 2004; Taylor, Martin, Hutchinson, & Jinks, 2007; Vargas & Hanlon, 2007; Walker, 2006; Walumbwa et al., 2010). In addition, there is supporting evidence about the practicality and significant contributions of servant leadership in successful companies, such as Synovus Financial Corporation (Hamilton & Bean, 2005). Servant leadership has also been shown to contribute to team performance (Schaubroeck et al., 2011), financial performance (Melrose, 1998; Ruschman, 2002), innovation, and creativity (Van Dierendonck & Rook, 2010).

Stemming from the foregoing, it was clear to Härtel and her team that servant leadership provided the ideal framework for development of an ethics training program for leaders. In particular, and based on this literature, the team concluded that the following behaviors and attitudes should be included among the objectives of program development:

- To embrace the focus of leadership on people-*building* instead of people-*using*
- To seek the needs and welfare of stakeholders within the organization and outside community, and the development of followers' moral reasoning
- To develop empathy and the ability to visualize different moral action-effect scenarios

- To practice engaging in moral dialogue with followers, ensuring that both the ends they seek and the means they employ are morally legitimized, thoughtfully reasoned, and ethically justified
- To promote acts of serving others and a culture of service
- To serve as role models of moral integrity by taking a resolute stand on moral principles and displaying morally justified means to achieve organizational goals
- To develop empathic listening skills so that the needs of followers can be explicitly recognized and acted upon
- To empower employees and to facilitate development of followers' potential

In the next section, we share some of the key aspects of an ethical leadership training program that were incorporated in the ARC-funded project conducted by the team.

PUTTING THE LEADERSHIP MODEL INTO PRACTICE

In this research project, and consistently with the literature we reviewed above, the team developed and executed a training program that employed a new, simplified definition of ethical leadership to guide the training activities. The program proceeded in three stages as we outline next.

Personal Reflection

The program opened by asking leaders first to think of an example where a person has displayed both (1) high levels of ethical and moral behavior and (2) dishonesty or unethical behavior in their own life.[2] The leaders were then asked whether these events had a significant impact on their lives and attitudes. In so doing, trainees were asked in which of these two categories (i.e., ethical or unethical examples) would they as a leader like to be remembered as? As such, prior to commencing the journey of a leader's ethical development, this personal reflection exercise served to address a key pillar of the program, namely, ensuring both an honest and committed engagement from the trainee to her or his moral development. Similarly, this discussion helped trainees decide for themselves whether they were willing to commit to such ethical development

Six Dimensions of Effective and Ethical Leadership

Leaders were then introduced to the core model underlying the training program. This was based on the six dimensions of effective and ethical leadership identified in Sendjaya et al. (2008): (1) voluntary subordination (altruism), (2) authentic self, (3) covenantal relationship (intimacy), (4) transcendental spirituality, (5) responsible morality, and (6) transforming influence. We summarize the six dimensions next.

1. *Voluntary subordination (altruism)*: using power to serve the greater good rather than the leader's own ambition—in effect, helping others without expecting anything in return
2. *Authentic self*: consistently displaying humility, integrity, accountability, and non-defensiveness
3. *Covenantal relationship (intimacy)*: treating others as equals
4. *Transcendental spirituality*: being motivated by a sense of higher calling and helping others find their sense of purpose
5. *Responsible morality*: encouraging others to engage in moral reasoning and focusing on doing right rather than looking good
6. *Transforming influence*: leading by personal example and providing a shared vision

This expanded definition of ethical leadership combines Kohlberg's (1984) theory of cognitive moral development with the goal of fostering an ethical climate (see also Rest, 1986). Thus, the trainee leaders in the program were next introduced to Kohlberg's three levels of moral reasoning. This was on the basis that leaders need to behave in accordance with the highest level and also to encourage their followers to adopt such reasoning as well. In brief, the three levels, from lowest (least desirable) to highest (most desirable) are:

- *Preconventional*: People using this level of moral reasoning think about the morality of actions in terms of the personal consequences such actions would have for them. Reasoning at this level is based on an egoism criterion (Victor & Cullen, 1988).
- *Conventional*: People using this level of moral reasoning think about the morality of their actions in terms of what their peers, family, and society think. Conventional reasoning is normally thought to be based on a benevolence criterion (Victor & Cullen, 1988), although moral reasoning at this level can sometimes be subverted by a perceived need to conform (Windsor & Ashkanasy, 1995).
- *Postconventional*: People using this level of moral reasoning think about the morality of their actions in terms of personal conscience and universalistic principles. Reasoning at this level is based on principled criteria (Victor & Cullen, 1988).

To illustrate how the research team put the new definition into practice and encouraged trainees to aspire to the postconventional Kohlberg level, we consider the example of an individual ethical scenario that the trainee leaders completed. First, they were asked to reflect on their personal view of the case, writing down their response together with their reasoning behind their response. Next, trainees were introduced to Kohlberg's framework of moral development stages, and they were then asked to use Kohlberg's framework to analyze their individual responses. In this way, we assessed and worked on developing participants' moral reasoning and capacity for moral action in both individual and team settings.

Having developed leaders' understanding of the dynamics of various ethical challenges, the research team next worked with leaders to develop their own levels of empathy and, in turn, to develop their capacity to engage with their team in constructive interactions that model an ethical and moral concern for others. Subsequently, the research team discussed how the leaders could see themselves contributing towards an ethical climate. The capacity to understand people is particularly important; this is because knowing what the leader's team members are thinking and feeling (1) affords better insight into follower's motives, (2) enables more effective communication with them, and (3) helps them to understand their interpretations of potentially demanding and ethically challenging situations. As a result, the leader is provided with a capacity to lead and to influence people in an ethical manner. Notably, this part of the program is underpinned by the notion of empathy, which we discuss next.

Developing Empathy

When we think of leaders who build their team, engage colleagues, and develop a respectful ethical climate, a fundamental piece in this equation is the capacity of leaders to build strong, high-quality working relationships. In turn, the key to building strong relationships and demonstrating genuine relationship building is *empathy* (Thomas, Legood, & Lee, 2011). Such empathic behaviors are emphasized by the covenantal relationship dimension of servant leadership, which promotes intimate constructive relationships through listening and seeking to understand followers' motivations. Empathy provided by servant leaders thus enables leaders to understand and to capitalize on people's positive thoughts and feelings, to sympathize with people's frustrations and hurts, to preempt relationship conflict, and insightfully to negotiate effective solutions to problems. In other words, empathic behaviors can be likened to the glue that holds relationships together.

To develop higher levels of empathy, the research team adopted the coaching techniques pioneered by UK researcher Dr. Geoff Thomas. Over the last decade, Thomas has invested much time becoming one of the world's foremost researchers in understanding empathy. Thomas has developed a technique to study and help people develop greater levels of empathy. It is particularly powerful in that it can objectively measure and develop empathic ability (Thomas et al., 2011). In this activity, trainee leaders work in pairs to complete a challenging negotiation exercise with differing viewpoints, where one individual takes the role of the leader and the other the direct report (which is videotaped). After the session, the direct report views the video and takes note of significant emotions occurring during the session and the time at which they occur. The leader is then provided with a sheet outlining the times when their direct report experienced significant emotions (but no information is provided as to what these emotions were). The leader is finally asked to indicate the emotions going through her or his own mind, and also understand the emotions the follower is experiencing.

Applying Thomas's approach to the training program that we outline in this chapter, Härtel and her team observed and took note of the capacity of the leader trainees to assess the emotions of their group members accurately, and to interpret the thoughts and feelings of others. After, in confidence, the team later reviewed the video footage with their leaders in order to help them to understand where they succeeded in understanding others, as well as to provide tips to enhance this negotiation and discussion (such as describing active listening as well as assertive communication techniques).

This approach is a particularly promising and interesting way to develop leaders' empathic understanding, especially because people generally do not know their own level of empathic ability (Patterson, 1985). That is, do we actually show empathy with our colleagues? This approach is preferred to asking people whether they show empathy (e.g., using a questionnaire) because people are often poor judges of their capacity to show empathy (Mehrabian & Epstein, 1972).

Developing a greater understanding of other's thoughts and feelings was a key part of the research team's training program because a sense of care for others is a pillar of ethical behavior and an essential component of servant leadership. Empathy is thus key to developing a stronger sense of how others interpret events and connect with others. This in turn enables leaders to build supportive and intimate covenantal work relationships, which are fundamental to helping others develop empathy and concern.

Another exercise the team used to develop participant leaders' empathy was a simulation where participants were asked to adopt different cultural perspectives. Key behaviors we focused on in the training included:

1. Looking at issues from different cultural perspectives
2. Applying effort to understand different cultures

3. Whenever making a value judgment about others' behavior from a different culture, stepping back and trying to look at the behaviors from a cultural perspective
4. Building a professional relationship with others beyond the surface level

Empathic development is a strong antidote to the lack of care or disregard for the welfare of others, which often translates to dispassionate narcissistic self-serving actions characterizing so many of the recent corporate scandals.

Develop an Ethical Team Climate

Having worked on the participating trainee leaders' empathic behavior, the research team then moved from individual relationships to developing an ethical team climate. This is a critical final step because, without an ethical climate, teams will inevitably tend to revert to old practices (Ashkanasy, Falkus, & Callan, 2000). At the penultimate step, therefore, and in order to reinforce the steps needed to foster an ethical climate in organizations, the research team introduced trainees to eight key recommendations (Sauser, 2005): (1) to adopt a code of ethics, (2) to provide ethics training, (3) to hire and promote ethical people, (4) to correct unethical behavior, (5) to take a proactive strategy for corporate ethicality, (6) to conduct a social audit, (7) to protect whistle blowers, and (8) to empower the guardians of integrity. Finally, trainees engaged in a range of training activities, including video cases and examples from the workplace designed to enhance their moral reasoning and their ability to engage in moral dialogue.

Although analysis of the training program is still under way (and definitive findings are therefore not yet available), preliminary results indicate that trainees have benefited from their participation in the program and understand the basic principles of ethical servant leadership. We conclude this chapter with practical implications and key takeaways for those interested in or responsible for ethics training in the workplace.

CONCLUSIONS AND RECOMMENDATIONS

In this chapter, we explained why servant leadership should hold a focal role in ethics training and shared the ethical leadership framework developed and applied by a research team led by the first author of this chapter. Drawing from the leadership and ethics literatures, we articulated a set of objectives ethical leadership training programs should achieve. In particular, based on a synthesis of research on Kohlberg's theory of cognitive moral development with research on ethical climate, we outlined a new definition of ethical servant leadership to aid the design and discussion of training activities. We also emphasized the importance of developing empathy and building an ethical team climate. Below, we summarize the key takeaways and recommendations for the design of ethical leadership training programs based on the principles of servant leadership:

- A useful practical definition of ethical leadership (especially for training purposes) is: *Ethical leadership entails consistently acting in accord with the highest levels of moral development and actively fostering an ethical climate.*
- The servant leadership model presented in Sendjaya et al. (2008) is an appropriate framework for developing an ethical leadership training program.
- Reflective exercises asking ethical leader trainees to think about leaders who empowered them help trainees to embrace a follower-centered view. As a result, followers come to understand that the leader has entrusted to them (the followers) to be elevated to their better selves.
- Including self-assessment exercises in ethical leadership training helps trainees to identify their core values and to link them to ethical leadership.
- Sharing cases that illustrate the importance of core values in the lives of leaders and how they shape leaders' convictions and behaviors reinforces ethical leader trainees' understanding of ethical leadership.
- Connecting ethical leader trainees' understanding of their own values and experiences with the practice of empathy helps them to internalize the principles of ethical leadership.
- Engaging ethical leader trainees in discussions on ways in which they can help others helps them to generate a sense of the meaning of their everyday life at work.
- Helping ethical leader trainees to develop their ability to be empathic enables them to build supportive and intimate covenantal work relationships, which are fundamental to helping others develop empathy and concern, resulting in an ethical team climate.
- Providing an environment that allows ethical leader trainees to experiment and to be creative without fear (and have them reflect on how doing so with their own followers) allows them to have the confidence to put their new training into action once they get back to the workplace.

In addition to implications for training, the findings of the study presented herein point to the importance of recruiting the right candidates (or future employees) with the ability to elicit servant leadership behavior. Individuals with high ethical values and a people focus, for example, could be identified through a mix of recruitment methods such as interviews and ethically focused case study discussions. The exercises used in the training program described herein could be adapted for such purposes. This demonstrates that identifying and preparing leaders with the required leadership abilities can result in the effective functioning of the organization (Dirks & Ferrin, 2002).

Having recruited the right candidates, organizations need to follow this up by creating an environment and experience conducive to a servant leader's core values. Alas (2006) asserts that to foster ethical practice, organizations need to develop an organizational codes of ethics and train their members in using moral considerations in decision-making processes. We trust that the training program described in this chapter provides a model for achieving this goal.

NOTES

1. Australian Research Council Grant LP110200893 (2011-2014) "Serving the greater good: using servant leadership to build ethical and engaging work practices;" awarded to C.E.J. Härtel, S. Sendjaya, A. Pekerti, G. Hirst, and R. Clark.
2. The resulting vignettes can be provoking and can sometimes entail challenging questions, so the team was particularly sensitive to people when asking them to share these stories.

REFERENCES

Aguilera, R. V. (2005). Corporate governance and director accountability: An institutional comparative perspective. *British Journal of Management, 16,* S39–S53.

Ahmed, P. K., & Machold, S. (2004). The quality of ethics connection: Toward virtuous organizations. *Total Quality Management, 15,* 527–545.

Alas, R. (2006). Ethics in countries with different cultural dimensions. *Journal of Business Ethics, 69,* 237–247.

Arnaud, A. (2010). Conceptualizing and measuring ethical work climate: Development and validation of the ethical climate index. *Business & Society, 49,* 345–358.

Ashkanasy, N. M., Falkus, S., & Callan, V.J. (2000). Predictors of ethical code use and ethical tolerance in the public sector. *Journal of Business Ethics, 25,* 237–253.

Baker, T. L., Hunt, T. G., & Andrews, M. C. (2006). Promoting ethical behavior and organizational citizenship behaviors: The influence of corporate ethical values. *Journal of Business Research, 59,* 849–857.

Barbuto, J. E. J., & Wheeler, D. W. (2006). Scale development and construct clarification of servant leadership. *Group & Organization Management, 31,* 300–326.

Bennis, W. (2002). Become a tomorrow leader. In L. C. Spears & M. Lawrence (Eds.), *Focus on leadership: Servant-leadership for the twenty-first century* (pp. 101–109). New York, NY: John Wiley & Sons.

Bogomolny, L. (2004). Good housekeeping. *Canadian Business, 77*(5), 87–88.

Brockner, J., & Higgins, E. T. (2001). Regulatory focus theory: Implications for the study of emotions at work. *Organizational Behavior and Human Decision Process, 86,* 35–66.

Brown, M. E., & Mitchell, M. S. (2010). Ethical and unethical leadership: Exploring new avenues for future research. *Business Ethics Quarterly, 20,* 583–616.

Brown, M. E., & Treviño, L. K. (2006). Ethical leadership: A review and future directions. *Leadership Quarterly, 17,* 595–616.

Brown, M. E., Treviño, L. K., & Harrison, D. A. (2005). Ethical leadership: A social learning perspective for construct development and testing. *Organizational Behavior and Human Decision Processes, 97,* 117–134.

Butarbutar, I. D., Sendjaya, S., & Härtel, C. E. J. (2010, December). *The mediating effects of ethical climate on the relationship between servant leadership and organizational citizenship behaviour.* Paper presented at the 24th Annual Australian and New Zealand Academy of Management Conference, Adelaide. ISBN: 1-877040-82-7.

Christie, P. M. J., Kwon, I.-W. G., Stoeberl, P. A., & Baumhart, R. (2003). A cross-cultural comparison of ethical attitudes of business managers: India, Korea and the United States. *Journal of Business Ethics, 46,* 263–287.

Collins, D. (2009). *Essentials of business ethics: Creating an organization of high integrity and superior performance.* Hoboken, NJ: John Wiley & Sons.

Collins, D. (2010). Designing ethical organizations for spiritual growth and superior performance: An organization systems approach. *Journal of Management, Spirituality & Religion, 7*(2), 95–117.

Dealy, M. D., & Thomas, A. B. (2006). *Managing by accountability: What every leader needs to know about responsibility, integrity—and results.* Westport, CT: Praeger.

Detert, J. R., Treviño, L. K., Burris, E. R., & Andiappan, M. (2007). Managerial modes of influence and counterproductivity in organizations: A longitudinal business unit-level investigation. *Journal of Applied Psychology, 92,* 993–1005.

Dirks, K. T., & Ferrin, D. L. (2002). Trust in leadership: Meta-analytic findings and implications for research and practice. *Journal of Applied Psychology, 87,* 611–628.

Douglas, P. C., Davidson, R. A., & Schwartz, B. N. (2001). The effect of organizational culture and ethical orientation on accountants' ethical judgments. *Journal of Business Ethics, 34,* 101–121.

Ehrhart, M. G. (2004). Leadership and procedural justice climate as antecedents of unit-level organizational citizenship behavior. *Personnel Psychology, 57,* 61–94.

Fujimoto, Y., Härtel, C. E. J., & Härtel, G. F. (2004). A field test of the diversity-openness moderator model in newly formed groups: Openness to diversity affects group decision effectiveness and interaction patterns. *Cross-Cultural Management: An International Journal, 11*(4), 4–16.

Gentile, M. C. (2010). *Giving voice to values.* New Haven, CT: Yale University Press.

288 ■ C. E. J. HÄRTEL et al.

Gentile, M. C. (2012). *Giving voice to values: How to speak your mind when you know what's right.* Newhaven, CT: Yale University Press.

Giessner, S., & van Quaquebeke, N. (2010). Using a relational models perspective to understand normatively appropriate conduct in ethical leadership. *Journal of Business Ethics, 95,* 43–55.

Gong, Y., Chang, S., & Cheung, S. (2010). High performance work system and collective OCB: A collective social exchange perspective. *Human Resource Management Journal, 20,* 119–137.

Graham, J. W. (1991). Servant-leadership in organizations: Inspirational and moral. *Leadership Quarterly, 2,* 105–119.

Hale, J. R., & Fields, D. L. (2007). Exploring servant leadership across cultures: A study of followers in Ghana and the USA. *Leadership, 3,* 397–417.

Hall, R. J., & Lord, R. G. (1995). Multi-level information processing explanations of followers' leadership perceptions. *Leadership Quarterly, 6,* 265–287.

Hamilton, F., & Bean, C. J. (2005). The importance of context, beliefs and values in leadership development. *Business Ethics: A European Review, 14,* 336–347.

Härtel, C. E. J. (2008). How to build a healthy emotional culture and avoid a toxic culture. In C. L. Cooper & N. M. Ashkanasy (Eds.), *Research companion to emotion in organization* (pp. 575–588). Cheltenham, UK: Edwin Elgar Publishing.

Härtel, C. E. J., & Ganegoda, D. B. (2008). Role of affect and interactional justice in moral leadership. In W. J. Zerbe, C. E. J. Härtel, & N. M. Ashkanasy (Eds.), *Research on emotion in organizations* (vol. 4, pp.155–180). Bingley, UK: Emerald Group Publishing.

Hitt, M. A., & Collins, J. D. (2007). Business ethics, strategic decision making, and firm performance. *Business Horizons, 50*(5), 353–357.

Hunter, E. M., Neubert, M. J., Perry, S. J., Witt, L. A., Penney, L. M., & Weinberger, E. (2013). Servant leaders inspire servant followers: Antecedents and outcomes for employees and the organization. *Leadership Quarterly, 24,* 316–331.

James, E. H., Wooten, L. P., & Dushek, K. (2011). Crisis management: Informing a new leadership research agenda. *Academy of Management Annals, 5,* 455–493.

Joseph, E. E., & Winston, B. E. (2005). A correlation of servant leadership, leader trust, and organizational trust. *Leadership & Organization Development Journal, 26,* 6–22.

Kark, R., & Van Dijk, D. (2007). Motivation to lead, motivation to follow: The role of the self-regulatory focus in leadership processes. *Academy of Management Review, 32,* 500–528.

Keeney, R.L., & Raiffa, H. (1993). *Decisions with multiple objectives–preferences and value tradeoffs.* Cambridge, UK: Cambridge University Press.

Kohlberg, L. (1984). *The psychology of moral development.* San Francisco, CA: Harper & Row.

Kozlowski, S. W., & Doherty, M. L. (1989). Integration of climate and leadership: Examination of neglected issue. *Journal of Applied Psychology, 74,* 546–553.

Liden, R. C., Wayne, S. J., & Sparrowe, R. T. (2000). An examination of the mediating role of psychological empowerment on the relations between job, interpersonal relationships, and work outcomes. *Journal of Applied Psychology, 85,* 407–416.

Liden, R. C., Wayne, S. J., Zhao, H., & Henderson, D. (2008). Servant leadership: Development of a multidimensional measure and multi-level assessment. *Leadership Quarterly, 19*, 161–177.

Locander W. B., & Luechauer D. L. (2006). Freereign—Embrace the simultaneous loose–tight leadership paradox of structures. *Marketing Management. 15*(4), 46–48.

Luo, X., & Bhattacharya, C. B. (2006). Corporate social responsibility, customer satisfaction, and market value. *Journal of Marketing, 70*, 1–18.

Luthans, F., & Avolio, B. J. (2003). Authentic leadership development. In K. S. Cameron, J. E. Dutton & R. E. Quinn (Eds.), *Positive organizational scholarship* (pp. 241–258). San Francisco, CA: Berrett-Koehler.

Margolis, J. D., & Walsh, J. P. (2003). Misery loves companies: Rethinking social initiatives by business. *Administrative Science Quarterly, 48*(2), 268–305.

Mayer, D., Nishii, L., Schneider, B., & Goldstein, H. (2007). The precursors and products of justice climates: Group leader antecedents and employee attitudinal consequences. *Personnel Psychology, 60*, 929–963.

Mayer, D. M., Nurmohamed, S., Treviño, L. K., Shapiro, D. L., & Schminke, M. (2013). Encouraging employees to report unethical conduct internally: It takes a village. *Organizational Behavior and Human Decision Processes, 121*, 89–103.

Mehrabian, A., & N. Epstein (1972). A measure of emotional empathy. *Journal of Personality, 40*, 525–543.

Melrose, K. (1998). *Putting servant-leadership into practice.* New York, NY: Wiley.

Murnighan, J. K., Cantelon, D. A., & Elyashiv, T. (2001). Bounded personal ethics and the tap dance of real estate agency. In J. A. Wagner III, J. M. Bartunek, & K. D. Elsbach (Eds.), *Advances in Qualitative Organizational Research, 3*, 1–40. New York, NY: Elsevier/JAI.

Orlitzky, M., Schmidt, F. L., & Rynes, S. L. (2003). Corporate social and financial performance: A meta-analysis. *Organization Studies, 24*(3), 403–441.

Patterson, C. H. (1985). *The therapeutic relationship.* Monterey, CA: Brooks/Cole.

Patterson, K. (2010). Servant leadership and love. In D. Van Dierendonck & K. Patterson (Eds.), *Servant leadership: Developments in theory and research* (pp. 67–76). Houndmills, Hampshire, UK: Palgrave Macmillan.

Pekerti, A. A., & Sendjaya, S. (2010). Exploring servant leadership across cultures: Comparative study in Australia and Indonesia. *International Journal of Human Resource Management, 21*, 754–780.

Pepper, A. (2003). Leading professionals: A science, a philosophy and a way of working. *Journal of Change Management, 3*, 349–360.

Piccolo, R. F., Greenbaum, R., Den Hartog, D. N., & Folger, R. (2010). The relationship between ethical leadership and core job characteristics. *Journal of Organizational Behavior, 31*, 259–278.

Resick, C. J., Hanges, P. J., Dickson, M. W., & Mitchelson, J. K. (2006). A cross-cultural examination of the endorsement of ethical leadership. *Journal of Business Ethics, 63*, 345–359.

Rest, J. (1986) *Moral development: Advances in research and theory.* New York, NY: Praeger.

Roberts, P. W., & Dowling, G. R. (2002). Corporate reputation and sustained superior financial performance. *Strategic Management Journal, 23*, 1077–1093.

Ruschman, N. L. (2002). *Servant-leadership and the best companies to work in America.* Hoboken, NJ: Wiley.

Sarayrah, Y. K. (2004). Servant leadership in the Bedouin-Arab culture. *Global Virtue Ethics Review, 5,* 58–79.

Sauser, W. I. J. (2005). Ethics in business: Answering the call. *Journal of Business Ethics, 58,* 345–357.

Schaubroeck, J., Lam, S. S. K., & Peng, A. C. (2011). Cognition-based and affect-based as mediators of leader behavior influence on team performance. *Journal of Applied Psychology, 96,* 863–871.

Schyns, B., & Schilling, J. (2013). How bad are the effects of bad leaders? A meta-analysis of destructive leadership and its outcomes. *Leadership Quarterly, 24,* 138–158.

Sendjaya, S. (2005). Leaders as servants. *Monash Business Review, 1*(2), 1–7.

Sendjaya, S., & Pekerti, A. A. (2010). Servant leadership as antecendent of trust in organizations. *Leadership & Organization Development Journal, 31,* 643–663.

Sendjaya, S., & Sarros, J. C. (2002). Servant leadership: Its origin, development, and application in organizations. *Journal of Leadership and Organizational Studies, 9,* 57–64.

Sendjaya, S., Sarros, J. C., & Santora, J. C. (2008). Defining and measuring servant leadership behavior in organizations. *Journal of Management Studies, 45,* 402–424.

Sharma, D., Borna, S., & Stearns, J. M. (2009). An investigation of the effects of corporate ethical values on employee commitment and performance: Examining the moderating role of perceived fairness. *Journal of Business Ethics, 89,* 251–260.

Sims, R. R. (1992). The challenge of ethical behavior in organizations. *Journal of Business Ethics, 11,* 505–513.

Spears, L. C. (2004). Practicing servant-leadership, *Leader to Leader, 34,* 7–11.

Taylor, T., Martin, B. N., Hutchinson, S., & Jinks, M. (2007). Examination of leadership practices of principals identified as servant leaders. *International Journal of Leadership in Education, 10,* 401–419.

Tepper, B. J., Carr, J. C., Breaux, D. M., Geider, S., Hu, C., & Hua, W. (2009). Abusive supervision, intentions to quit, and employees' workplace deviance: A power/dependence analysis. *Organizational Behavior and Human Decision Processes, 109,* 156–167.

Thomas, G., Legood, A., & Lee, A. (2011). Why, when, and how motivation helps mind-reading. In J. L. Smith, W. Ickes, J. A. Hall, & S. Hodges (Eds.), *Managing interpersonal sensitivity: Knowing when—and when not—to understand others* (pp. 21–40). Hauppauge, NY: Nova Science Publishers.

Toor, S., & Ofori, G. (2009). Ethical leadership: Examining the relationships with full range leadership model, employee outcomes, and organizational culture. *Journal of Business Ethics, 90,* 533–547.

Treviño, L. K., Butterfield, K. D., & McCabe, D. L. (1998). The ethical context in organizations: Influences on employee attitudes and behaviors. *Business Ethics Quarterly, 8,* 447–476.

Tschannen-Moran, M., & Hoy, W. (1998). Trust in schools: A conceptual and empirical analysis. *Journal of Educational Administration, 36,* 334–352.

Upadhyay Y., & Singh, S. K. (2010). In favour of ethics in business: The linkage between ethical behaviour and performance. *Journal of Human Value, 16*(1), 9–19.

Van Dierendonck, D., & Rook, L. (2010). Enhancing innovation and creativity through servant leadership. In D. Van Dierendonck & K. A. Patterson (Eds.), *Servant leadership: Developments in theory and research,* (pp. 155–168). Houndmills, Hampshire, UK: Palgrave Macmillan.

Van Knippenberg, D., De Cremer, D., & Van Knippenberg, B. (2007). Leadership and fairness: The state of the art. *European Journal of Work & Organizational Psychology, 16,* 113–140.

Vargas, P. A., & Hanlon, J. (2007). Celebrating a profession: The servant leadership perspective. *Journal of Research Administration, 38,* 45–49.

Victor, B., & Cullen, J. B. (1987). A theory and measure of ethical climate in organizations. In W. C. Frederick & L. E. Preston (Eds.), *Business ethics: Research issues and empirical studies* (pp. 77–97). Greenwich, CT: JAI Press.

Victor, B., & Cullen, J. B. (1988). The organizational bases of ethical work climates. *Administrative Science Quarterly, 33,* 101–125.

Walker, T. (2006). Servant leaders. *Managed Healthcare Executive, 16,* 20–26.

Walumbwa, F. O., Hartnell, C. A., & Oke, A. (2010). Servant leadership, procedural justice climate, service climate, employee attitudes, and organizational citizenship behavior: A cross-level investigation. *Journal of Applied Psychology, 95,* 517–529.

Whetstone, J. T. (2002). Personalism and moral leadership: The servant leader with a transforming vision. *Business Ethics: A European Review, 11,* 385–392.

Windsor, C. A., & Ashkanasy, N. M. (1995). Moral reasoning development and belief in a just world as precursors of auditor independence: The role of organizational culture perceptions. *Accounting, Organizations, and Society, 20,* 701–720.

Zhang, X., Walumbwa, F. O., Aryee, S., & Chen, Z. S. (2013). Ethical leadership, employee citizenship and work withdrawal behaviors: Examining mediating and moderating processes. *Leadership Quarterly, 24,* 284–297.

CHAPTER 14

APPRECIATIVE INQUIRY AND ETHICAL AWARENESS

Encouraging Morally Driven Organizational Goals

**David S. Bright, Ilma Barros,
and Veer Raghava Kumar Marthy**

This chapter describes how appreciative inquiry (AI) can be used to encourage greater ethical awareness within an organization. The value of this chapter is its focus on the organizational environment within which ethical considerations occur, rather than on the specific character or cognitive processes of individuals. An ethical organization can be a significant influence on its members to develop their own ethics. AI encourages conversations that bring alignment between personal ethics and an organization's moral purpose (Van Vuuren & Crous, 2005). We will describe how AI was used by the second author in the Brazilian organization FIESP (a Portuguese acronym for the Federation of Industries for the State of São Paulo) to create momentum for work on the United Nations Millennium Development Goals (MDGs).

Ethics Training in Action, pages 293–310
Copyright © 2014 by Information Age Publishing
All rights of reproduction in any form reserved.

AI is an approach to leadership and change that encourages generative spaces in organizational life (Bright, 2009; Bushe, 2007; Cooperrider, 2001). AI works by creating opportunities for people to speak with one another about substantive topics that relate to their work. People discuss answers to well-crafted questions, and their conversations explore issues that are both organizationally relevant and personally meaningful. Participants often discover shared values and interests that enable them to work effectively together. AI creates an "appreciative effect," both by helping people to develop deep understanding of the strengths, values, and capacities of an organization, and also by increasing social capital, an ability to work effectively together (Bright, 2009, p. 3).

In this chapter, we introduce an advancement of AI that includes both inner work (through psychological, inwardly oriented questions) and collective work (through organizational, outwardly oriented questions). Next, we explain the basic assumptions for using AI, including how it nurtures the conditions for greater ethical awareness. We end with a discussion of the stages in AI, as it was used in FIESP, to show how the morally relevant MDGs were introduced to employees. In sum, we demonstrate how AI encourages ethical awareness through an alignment of personal and collective moral aspirations.

FIESP AND THE MILLENNIUM DEVELOPMENT GOALS

The UN Millennium Development Goals (MDGs) were created to address a variety of social issues of global importance. The eight goals are grounded in ethical principles that address poverty, education, gender equality, health, and environmental sustainability. The achievement of these goals should significantly improve the quality of life of people all around the world. For the last decade, the UN has worked to promote these goals in regions around the world.

In Brazil, FIESP (www.fiesp.com.br) is one of the most powerful potential partners on these issues. FIESP is a membership organization of 132 business associations, representing more than 140,000 companies in the state of Saõ Paolo. It is an affiliate of the National Confederation of Industry of Brazil (www.portaldaindustria.com.br), a network of industry federations that are organized at the state level across Brazil. Each state-run federation operates on a budget generated through payroll taxes on industry partners to provide a variety of social and business services.

From a non-Brazilian perspective, FIESP is an unusual organization. It is part union, part chamber of commerce, part social services. FIESP engages in lobbying efforts to promote business; it owns and operates a full range of primary, secondary, and technical schools; it runs training programs that serve the employment needs of its industry partners; and it provides health-care, childcare, and cultural and sports programs for industry partner employees and their families. By reputation, the quality of these operations surpasses those offered by the government, literally touching the lives of millions. If there were one organization that could generate social change on a large scale in Brazil, it would be FIESP.

In 2005, UN officials first introduced the MDGs to the country by convening a regional summit in Brazil's capital, Brasilia, working with then-President Lula's Council for Social and Economic Development (CSEC). Through these efforts, summit participants determined to promote the goals as a social movement, sponsoring stakeholder meetings and training in partnership with the federation of industry for each state in Brazil. These efforts created significant momentum for a variety of business, industry, nonprofit, religious, and government organizations to accept and promote the MDGs throughout the country. FIESP, because of its position in the largest and most influential state, was considered perhaps the most important potential partner in these efforts.

In 2012, after nearly six years of discussions with council members of the CSEC, FIESP's president, Mr. Paolo Skaff, agreed to sponsor a two-day AI summit, involving over 500 people, to discuss FIESP's potential role in promoting the MDGs. The project was conducted through one of FIESP's subsidiaries, SESI-SP (Social Services for the Industries of Sao Paolo). From an applied ethics perspective, the event was intended to help employees become aware of FIESP's institutional impact on and its connection to the MDGs.

ORGANIZATIONAL ASSUMPTIONS IN APPRECIATIVE INQUIRY

The key mechanism of change in AI is inquiry, a process of asking and exploring through questions. The process of engaging one another through questioning should encourage an atmosphere of openness in which people feel psychological safety, are able to explore new ideas, and develop new insights and perspectives (Taylor & Bright, 2011).

We next describe the logic used to plan the two-day FIESP event, to illustrate how AI can be used to foster ethical awareness. Three mechanisms—social construction, moral imagination, and purpose and meaning—serve as levers of influence to shape or produce particular organizational effects. We present each mechanism as an assumption with its essential ideas, its application to the FIESP case, and its design implications.

Assumption #1: Change Is Stimulated Through an Exploration of Foundational, Socially Constructed Images

Several scholars have discussed the theory that organizations are driven by socially constructed images: assumptions, expectations, and metaphors about the nature of organizational reality (Hatch, 2011; Morgan, 2006; Weick, 1979). In this perspective, the reality of organizational life is the product of an intersubjective, meaning-making social process. Social reality is intersubjective in that it depends on shared perceptions, opinions, and emotions for its existence. Most people consider social reality to be an objective reality because it exists outside of their individual perceptions. However, as Hatch (2011, pp. 53–54) explains: "It is still subjective, just in an interpersonal domain.... Even if people are wrong about their situations, their beliefs will affect their behavior just the same as if beliefs were objective facts. What is more, the material consequences of behavior *are* objective facts." The essential idea here is simple: If an organization is an artifact of social construction, then we can change the nature of an organization by shifting the nature of the social constructive process that produces that organization.

Cooperrider (2001) provides a strong case for the practical potential of the social constructionist insight, reviewing several theories from mainstream research: Theory X vs. Theory Y, the placebo effect, the Pygmalian dynamic, positive self-talk, and sensemaking, among many others. In every instance, the organizing image—representing the assumptions, expectations, and beliefs about what is possible—provides a repertoire of action possibilities toward which people are naturally drawn in their enacted behaviors. Thus, if we understand how the social construction process unfolds, we can work with and stimulate this process to generate an understanding of reality that aligns with and advances ethical/moral causes.

Relevance

One way to encourage a focus on morally driven organizational goals is to shift the nature of the discourse within an organization. Social constructions are formed and perpetuated through conversations (Hardy, Lawrence, & Grant, 2005) and thus, greater awareness comes when diverse perspectives are activated through conversation. For example, FIESP, like any capitalistic organization, is grounded in a pro-industry identity and enacts actions that are commensurate with this identity. A shift in ethical awareness requires the introduction of images and conversations that include an understanding of ethics-in-action. In FIESP's case, it would be important that those images include an understanding of the MDGs as an integral part of the organization's identity.

Design Implications

To get people excited about the possibilities found in moral and ethical issues, it is essential to activate and explore existing organizational narratives about the institution when it is functioning as a moral force in society. The main way in which this is done is through questions that encourage people to think about "high point experiences" (Ludema, Whitney, Mohr, & Griffin, 2003) in their work or life, when they have felt that an organization was engaged in moral or ethical activities. Typically, we ask participants to think about moments when they felt that their work was achieving something of significance.

When people share high point experiences with one another, they intuitively become attuned to the social constructions that enable and support these positive experiences. Once these social constructions are activated, they can be leveraged to develop future action possibilities that go beyond what has previously occurred within the organization.

Assumption #2: The Presence of Moral Imagination Increases Ethical Awareness

Moral imagination is "an ability to imaginatively discern various possibilities for acting within a given situation and to envision the potential help and harm that are likely to result from a given action" (Johnson, 1993, p. 202). In this sense, moral imagination is a perceptive capacity. A person who has moral imagination has the capacity to evaluate, from a moral point of view, a moral or ethical issue not only in its original context of dominating mental models or social constructions, but also in terms of new possibilities that work outside these constructions (Werhane, 1999, p. 93).

Moberg and Seabright (2000, p. 845) argue that moral imagination is an essential reasoning process that functions to suppress "the organizational factors that corrupt ethical judgment." For example, if employees believe that their organization has no moral core, they are more likely to behave in ways that are aligned with an understanding that unethical behavior is acceptable.

Relevance

A stronger capacity for moral imagination could help employees to understand the broader potential impact of FIESP's institutional activities. For instance, employees could be encouraged to think about their work not merely as contributing to corporate benefit, but also as generating and creating significant societal and environmental benefit.

Design Implication

People are more likely to be in a mental state that activates their moral imagination when they find themselves in an environment of creativity and emergent thought. Activities that encourage dreaming, playing, designing, and laughing are all associated with positive emotionality and greater imagination (Fredrickson, 1998). When guided by a serious objective, such activities should activate a significant capacity for moral imagination.

Assumption 3: Inner Purpose Motivates Ethical Action

An important advance in motivation theory of the last decade is the awareness that people are more motivated by a sense of purpose than they are by extrinsic rewards. Barrick, Mount, and Li (2013, p. 133) explain that purposeful work can be understood in terms of two general "motivational strivings."

First, *purposefulness* indicates that a person aspires to some end state, like excellence or virtue, that provides guidance and direction to one's behavior. For instance, many people have a highly developed sense of personal virtue, whereby they strive to cultivate excellence of character, irrespective of context or environment (Ray, 2005). This aspiration provides personal guidance that allows a person to pursue a more excellent course, even when it is not required or even expected. A person behaves with integrity—even when a colleague pledges to look away, or chooses to forgive another—even when the offender refuses to apologize or admit wrongdoing (Bright, Fry, & Cooperrider, 2006).

Second, *experienced meaningfulness* describes the inherent "significance or meaning" that a person may draw from work itself. Often, work itself can acquire a character that conveys significance or meaning. Many people acquire a sense of calling in relation to their work (Wrzesniewski, McCauley, Rozin, & Schwartz, 1997). When people view their work as having purpose and significance, they are typically motivated to perform this work at a much higher level.

Relevance

In practical terms, morally relevant organizational goals are fostered when they align with a sense of purpose in people. People tend to support organizational goals if they understand how such goals fit with their own personal ethical frameworks; they are then more likely to be intrinsically inclined to promote an ethical organization.

Design Implications

Activities should encourage deep personal reflection and introspection. Activities such as journaling or meditation—guided by questions that ask participants to consider beliefs and issues of character—can activate the values and assumptions that provide people with a sense of purpose and personal meaning in their work.

In addition, activities should help participants to understand the ethical and moral impact of the organization's work. Participants should develop connections between this potential impact and their own sense of purpose. Ideally, people should be allowed to shape the direction of future organizational objectives. They might design initiatives that leverage an institution's ability to create impact in society.

PLAN AN APPRECIATIVE INQUIRY PROJECT

In this section, we focus on how to plan and facilitate an AI-based initiative to encourage change in an organization. Specifically, we describe how these ideas were used to create the two-day AI summit at FIESP.[1]

Nearly all variants of AI make some reference to the four elements shown in Figure 14.1: *discover*, a process that encourages exploration of an organization's current and past state; *dream*, a step that envisions future possibilities; *design*, activities that allow people to prioritize and choose from among future possibilities; and *destiny*, procedures that allow for the implementation of priorities. The approach described in this chapter synthesizes

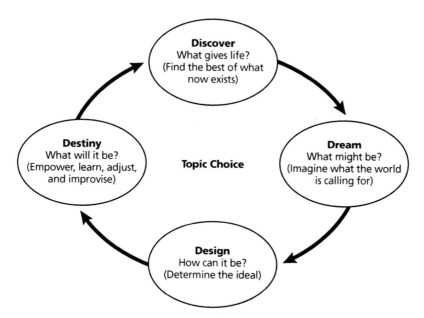

Figure 14.1 The appreciative inquiry cycle.

not only inner, reflective work that allows people to understand their own virtues and beliefs, but also collective work that encourages co-construction and shared narratives to advance organization-level initiatives.

Stage One: Planning

Planning is essential to the success of an AI-based project. Gaining the support of top-level leaders and selecting a provocative topic statement are the most important steps (Ludema et al., 2003).

Obtain Institutional Support

In the FIESP case, a member of the Brazilian Council of Social and Economic Development, Mr. Rodrigo Loures, was persistent in working with FIESP's leadership. Mr. Loures had used AI extensively in many settings, and he was well positioned to encourage support from FIESP's top leaders. Further, a planning committee dramatically increases the likelihood of success. This group guides and promotes the project and provides insights into the organization's common social constructions. Members should be selected from all the major affected stakeholder groups.

The FIESP committee members included Rodrigo Loures, the Director for Corporate Social Responsibility, a liaison from the office of the president, and four other mid-level and senior-level leaders. The facilitator met with the committee at least four times over two months before the initiative's main event.

Topic Selection

From the view of social construction, the topic is like a seed: It encompasses the range of potential actions that might flow from the initiative if it is successful. The topic guides all interactions and conversations. It should be provocative in that it encourages people to think beyond the current reality to an ideal possibility. At FIESP, the facilitator interviewed several senior leaders about their perspectives on FIESP's future with respect to the MDGs. She discovered a common desire: They all wanted employees at all levels to begin thinking of themselves as ethical, moral leaders. With this information, she worked with the planning committee to develop the topic "Leading for Transformative Action."

Identification of Stakeholder Groups

Next, it is essential to invite the right people to participate in the process. Typically, this is done through a stakeholder mapping exercise. Members of the steering committee discuss the parts of the organization that are influenced by the topic. They may also consider constituencies outside of the formal organization, such as suppliers or customers. After identifying the relevant stakeholder groups, the committee determines how to identify specific people to invite.

FIESP's design included two groups of invitations. Over 450 people from several different facets of the organization were invited to participate on the first day of the summit. Many of these were tapped because of their unique perspective, even though they may not have played an integral role in the organization. Of these, 120 were invited to attend on the second day. The steering committee created an appropriately compelling invitation to solicit attendance at the desired levels of participation.

Logistics

Much of the work in AI occurs in small groups. A space that nurtures discussion is helpful. At FIESP, there were significant constraints around the use of large spaces. Thus, the first day's activities were scheduled to be held in an auditorium with approximately 450 participants, while the second day's activities were held in a flat space that could comfortably accommodate around 120 people.

Another consideration is how to assign participants to groups. Diverse conversations are likely when participants interact in unusual configurations. A popular approach is to assign participants to sit with others in diverse groups. When people arrive, they pick up a name badge with a number, and then they sit at the corresponding table. At FIESP, because of space issues, pre-assigned groups were planned for the second day only.

Finally, plans should be made to capture the event's key, emergent themes. One method is to hire a graphic facilitator, an artist who captures themes in real time. Figure 14.2 shows an example from FIESP's event. The artist draws images on large sheets of paper as the event unfolds. This emergent display not only creates a visual record of the conference, but also sparks creative thought and innovative thinking.

Stage Two: Discovery

The *discover* phase establishes a foundation of understanding about the organization's capabilities, values, and strengths. It does so by activating the social constructions that enable organizational success and by linking these to personal purpose and meaning.

Introduction

Within the first few minutes, participants need to understand the event's purpose. The topic should be introduced, along with some explanation of the thought and intention behind it. They also need to know that the

Figure 14.2 Example of graphic facilitation at FIESP.
Translation from Portuguese to English
Upper left bubble: "You need to feel the power that exists within you. Know that you have the capacity to make the ordinary, extraordinary."
Lower left bubble: "We come from other parts of the world to learn from you."
Upper right corner: "We have reached the Millennium Development Goals in three years. MISSION POSSIBLE."
Lower middle scroll: "A dream that is dreamed alone is only a possibility, but if you dream it together it becomes a reality."

institution supports the effort. FIESP's President, Mr. Skaff, delivered the initial welcome and introduced the topic: "Leading for Transformational Action." He emphasized that the purpose of the event was to create a culture of active participation within FIESP in support of the MDGs. A handful of other key stakeholders, including the Brazilian Minister of Education, also presented their perspectives about the MDGs and FIESP's potential role to embrace them. A strong introduction establishes the legitimacy of the endeavor, and it establishes the importance and relevance of the work to participants.

In addition, participants are more engaged when they understand what to expect. The facilitator may explain the history of AI, the steps involved, and the need for deep listening. In FIESP, the facilitator emphasized the need for reflection and imaginative thought. She explained that each stage of the process would include moments for guided personal reflection, followed by collective activity.[2]

Reflection of meaningful work

As an introductory inner-work exercise, the facilitator asked participants to think silently about the meaning of their work. She asked them to consider the significance of performing meaningful work in connection with others. She showed them a video of a musical performance in which the musicians demonstrated palpable synergy. Then, she asked them to write their reflections about the meaning of their work in a journal for a few minutes. The intent was to help participants to become attuned to their deepest beliefs about the significance of their work.

Appreciative Conversations

An appreciative conversation is a paired interview that immediately engages all participants in discussion. The best pairs combine people who do not know or rarely have occasion to speak with one another. The facilitator reads several carefully designed questions, as illustrated in Appendix A, that explore high point experiences, strengths of the people in an organization, and an ideal vision of the future. Then, each person interviews his/her partner in a conversation that lasts up to one hour. Following the conversation, pairs are linked together to form groups of four or six members. The members of each group introduce their conversation partners to the group, describing the stories they heard and the key themes that surfaced. The group analyzes the stories and themes, and then prepares a report to share.

At FIESP, the facilitator introduced the activity through a discussion about listening and learning. She shared thoughts from experts about the difference between factual and active listening. She also suggested four levels of learning—judgmental, factual, empathic, and generative. She encouraged the participants to think about how they could listen and learn most effectively. Then, she read the questions and asked each person to jot down a few thoughts. Participants chose partners from among others who were sitting in close proximity to them. Small groups were formed in the auditorium for more discussion. The short reports from each of the small groups were the final activity for the first day.

It is difficult to describe in writing what happens in an event of this nature. Typically, participants are surprised to discover the energy they have to engage in conversations in this way. As FIESP participants exited, they commented about their surprise. Many stated that they had been skeptical at first. They expressed surprise about the focus on learning and listening at a deeper level. They had thought the discussion would focus on how to implement the MDGs, rather than on the personal significance of these goals. They were also surprised to discover that much of their current work was in alignment with the MDGs. Many participants also described a transformation in attitude from apathy or skepticism to intense engagement. In fact, the personal impact of the first day's event inspired many participants to invite other employees and stakeholders to join the next day's discussion: instead of the 120 expected second-day participants, over 170 arrived.

Root Causes of Success

This technique is a variation on the practice of root cause analysis (Ishikawa, 1976). Typically, the analysis is done to determine the causes of a problem. In AI, the analysis aims to find the causes of success. These causes comprise a "positive core" (Ludema et al., 2003), or the strengths, values, and factors that lead to desired outcomes. The facilitator asks each group to analyze the high point stories, looking for the common causes of success in them. The results are then shared with the larger gathering.

At FIESP, this step was accomplished on the second day of the summit. When they first gathered in the morning, the facilitator organized the 170 participants (of which 50 were new, self-invited participants) into 17 groups of 10 people. Each group was seated around one of 17 circular tables. She then asked participants to review their notes and share their answers from the interview questions discussed the previous day. She explained how to perform an analysis for root causes of success, directed them to conduct this analysis as a group, and asked them to prepare a report to share. Each report was to include three themes about the positive core and an illustrative example.

During the reports, participants expressed a strong interest in the results of each group's analysis; they insisted that they wanted to hear from all the groups. Again, one of the side effects of AI summit activities is often intense energy and excitement for the discussion.

Stage Three: Dream

The *dream* phase focuses conversation on the future of the organization and an exploration of potential opportunities for action. The process should encourage moral imagination at a very high level to produce a higher number of actionable ideas.

Moment of Reflection

The dream phase can be enhanced by giving participants an opportunity to reflect upon their deepest personal goals and aspirations for the future. This technique requires participants to consider how to translate their deepest values into practice. One approach is to provide an example that shows how ethics, morals, or virtues shape actions. Then, ask participants to write in a journal about how they do this in their own lives.

The FIESP facilitator introduced participants to the idea of "highest goal" or "highest purpose" (Ray, 2005) to show how many people have desires to do something of significance. She asked them to write answers for ten minutes in response to three questions: What is my highest goal? What is the purpose of my life? Which of my activities today are consistent with my highest goal? The intent of this exercise was to create awareness of these inner aspirations as preparation for a discussion with others about collective aspirations.

Share a Vision of the Future

The next step is to help participants develop a potential shared vision for the future. The facilitator creates an activity that helps participants to become attuned to existing ideas about the future. Participants discuss these ideas in groups to select and build on the best ideas. The process should encourage imagination and creative thought.

The FIESP facilitator asked participants to refer to their notes about the future. For example, one of the appreciative questions had asked participants to describe the future as if they had awoken a few years later. She instructed them to share their notes with their group. She encouraged a focus on FIESP's role in the achievement of the MDGs, not just for São Paolo, but also for all of Brazil. Next, she asked each group to create a shared vision of the future that represented all the best ideas in the group. She told them to develop a headline that described this vision. Finally, she instructed them to create a skit that would serve as a prototype of best ideas in action. She encouraged them to be creative in this process (e.g., stage a play, host a television show, create a song, etc.). Most important was to include a few "sizzling statements" or "zinger phrases" that would promote the most essential themes. Each group was allotted 3–5 minutes for its presentation.

FIESP participants found this to be a very engaging activity, and they again insisted on viewing every production. During the performances, the facilitator asked participants to take notes on the ideas that were invited within each presentation. She asked them, "What is new, interesting, innovative, challenging?" These notes would serve as a resource for the next stage.

Stage Four: Design and Destiny

The *design and destiny* stage focuses on prioritizing and selecting several ideas for actual work and implementation. These stages are often done separately. The key is to encourage the emergence of new social constructions and organizational actions.

Deep Creativity Exercise

Another moment of personal reflection can help to maintain a creative state during a discussion on action priorities. The FIESP facilitator asked participants to think of a moment when they felt especially creative, perhaps as a child. She asked them to consider what happened, what they felt when it happened, and what they were feeling upon remembering the event. She then asked, "What lessons can be drawn from this experience that might influence the way that you go about working with the MDGs?" Participants were given five minutes to write in a journal.

Actionable Ideas and Priorities

The next step is to establish a list of actionable ideas, then to select the most viable ideas. The facilitator might ask participants to brainstorm in groups about any idea that was prompted by the earlier presentations witnessed. After compiling a comprehensive list, each group should prioritize and highlight the best ideas.

The FIESP facilitator asked each group to create a list, and then asked each group to choose the top five initiatives from this list. She instructed them to rank these based on their viability, importance, and urgency. Finally, she asked them to analyze the top three ideas. For these, she asked them to consider the resources required for implementation, the stakeholders who needed to be involved, a potential timeline, and any other factor that would ensure the initiative's success. Each team presented its top three initiatives.

Values-in-Action Activity

A final, integrative reflection may be useful as a way to bring closure. At FIESP, the facilitator asked participants to consider, "Who do I need to be in order to accomplish my dream for my highest goal and the collective that we've just created together?" She instructed them to write an answer for about one minute and to reflect in silence for a few moments more. Next, she told them to think about the highest goal they had identified earlier and asked them to consider how their deepest personal values might support their highest goals. She asked, "Try to remember a time when you had a difficult decision you had to make, a decision that challenged your values, but in the end, you feel like you did the right thing. What value supported that decision and your action?"

Finally, she asked the participants, "Consider that you will encounter difficult experiences in the future. Write down three values that you consider of most importance to help you achieve the collective dream that we have just created together. To the right of each value, write three behaviors that will illustrate your value in action." To conclude, she asked participants to share one thought with a partner.

Final Invitation

The summit should be closed with an activity that invites participants to act. Asking participants to make specific commitments increases the likelihood that actions will be put into practice.

Follow-Up

One-time events rarely produce a lasting effect unless significant follow-up occurs. At a minimum, the participants and organization should receive feedback about the event and its outcomes. The planning committee should meet to discuss potential lessons, next steps, and how to follow up appropriately. In addition, a report should be developed that captures the work produced by the summit. Any visuals from the event should be preserved and shared in an appropriate way. Most important, the actionable steps identified as priorities should be cataloged and quickly considered by the relevant decision-makers.

At FIESP, the facilitator met with the planning committee several times after the summit. They were particularly excited about the level of participant engagement, and they were also pleased by the ideas that came from the process. The facilitator worked with this group to produce a report that was given and distributed in FIESP with specific recommendations.

Outcomes

The outcomes from an AI-based meeting generate both direct and indirect benefits. The most visible direct benefit is the catalogue of potential action initiatives. These ideas are important because they come from participants acting on their own initiative—this process increases the likelihood that resulting actions will be supported by employees.

FIESP benefited in several specific ways. First, most participants had no familiarity with the MDGs before this meeting. Through the summit, they developed an understanding for how their ongoing work might already integrate with the MDGs. Indeed, numerous examples of ongoing FIESP activities were identified as being in alignment with the MDGs.

Second, the event became a catalyst for FIESP to become a signatory in support of the MDG social movement in Brazil—FIESP has now officially partnered with the UN and Brazilian Government to promote the MDGs.

In addition, FIESP has adopted the MDG goals as an essential part of their mission and strategy. Key leaders have been given specific assignments to oversee projects that focus on the achievement of desired MDG-related outcomes.

Perhaps the most important benefit was an increase in ethical awareness for employees. They began to see that their work in FIESP creates important, societal impact, helping to establish a sense of calling and mission in connection with their work.

CONCLUSION

Ethics professionals may find that AI-based strategies are useful for a variety of purposes. The FIESP case illustrates how this approach may be used on a large scale to encourage broad social change. However, it also has utility at all levels of organizational intervention. AI has been used to shape coaching, leadership training, and both small-group and organizational interventions. It is especially useful when the intent is to establish a positive capacity for ethics, rather than to resolve an ethical dilemma or problem.

In sum, this chapter has described how appreciative inquiry can be used to build ethical awareness in an organization. We have explained several of the important assumptions that frame the practice of AI when it is used in this way. We have illustrated how these assumptions can be used in practice to create an AI-based event. We encourage colleagues to explore how to use AI in a variety of situations to encourage greater ethical awareness and the implementation of morally driven organizational goals.

RESOURCES

Of necessity, this introduction has been brief. Many resources are available for those who are interested in learning more about AI and its many uses. The seminal work on AI was written by Cooperrider and Srivastva (1987). Good introductory works include Whitney and Trosten-Bloom (2010), Ludema et al. (2003), and Cooperrider, Whitney, and Stavros (2008).

NOTES

1. A detailed description of the summit methodology is beyond the scope of this paper. See Ludema et al. (2003) for more information.
2. Inner, reflective work is not commonly used in AI-based events. However, it seems particularly useful when there is need for a deep reflection or conversation about values.

APPENDIX: EXAMPLE QUESTIONS
FOR AN APPRECIATIVE CONVERSATION

Question 1: Everyone here, no doubt, has had both positive and negative experiences of leadership. Think for a moment about the positive experiences, moments of real, transformational change, those times when you felt proud of your work. Think about what motivated your involvement in these experiences.

- Choose the most remarkable experience. It could even be a simple experience, but one that you remember as a highlight.
- Tell the story of what happened. Describe the experience, the most memorable moments, the challenges and innovation.
- Reflect on the roots of success in this story. What were the three main factors or the three qualities you demonstrated in this experience that contributed to success?

Question 2: Imagine that we are talking to/with people who know you very well. They know your full potential and your qualities and strengths. What will they talk about when they describe you?

Question 3: Imagine that tonight you go to bed and fall into a deep sleep. When you wake up it is the year 2015. As you listen to the radio while traveling to work, you hear a story about FIESP's role in achieving one or more of the Millennium Development Goals. You realize that FIESP's mobilization processes have already led to the social changes that achieve the Millennium Development Goals. What are the consequences and outcomes of this success?

Question 4: What one action would most help to make your vision of the future come true?

REFERENCES

Barrick, M. R., Mount, M. K., & Li, N. (2013). The theory of purposeful work behavior: The role of personality, higher-order goals, and job characteristics. *Academy of Management Review, 38*, 132–153.

Bright, D. S, Fry, R. E., & Cooperrider, D. L. (2006). Forgiveness from the perspectives of three response modes: Begrudgement, pragmatism, and transcendence. *Journal of Management, Spirituality & Religion, 3*, 78–103.

Bright, D. S. (2009). Appreciative Inquiry and Positive Organizational Scholarship: A philosophy of practice for turbulent times. *OD Practitioner, 41*(3), 2–7.

Bushe, G. R. (2007). Appreciative Inquiry is not (just) about the positive. *OD Practitioner, 39*(4), 33–38.

Cooperrider, D. L. (2001). Positive image, positive action: The affirmative basis of organizing. In D. L. Cooperrider, P. F. Sorensen, T. F. Yaeger, & D. Whitney (Eds.), *Appreciative Inquiry: An emerging direction for organization development* (pp. 9–29). Champaign, IL: Stipes Publishing. Retrieved from http://www.stipes.com/aichap2.htm

Cooperrider, D. L., & Srivastva, S. (1987). Appreciative Inquiry in organizational life. In R. W. Woodman & W. A. Pasmore (Eds.), *Research in organizational change and development*, Vol. 1 (pp. 129–169). Stamford, CT: JAI Press.

Cooperrider, D. L., Whitney, D., & Stavros, J. M. (2008). *Appreciative Inquiry handbook: For leaders of change* (2nd ed.). San Francisco, CA: Berrett-Koehler.

Fredrickson, B. L. (1998). What good are positive emotions? *Review of General Psychology, 2*, 300–319.

Hardy, C., Lawrence, T. B., & Grant, D. (2005). Discourse and collaboration: The role of conversations and collective identity. *Academy of Management Review, 30*, 58–77.

Hatch, M. J. (2011). *Organizations: A very short introduction.* Oxford, UK: Oxford University Press.

Ishikawa, K. (1976). *Guide to quality control.* Tokyo, Japan: Asian Productivity Organization.

Johnson, M. (1993). *Moral imagination: Implications of cognitive science for ethics.* Chicago, IL: University of Chicago Press.

Ludema, J. D., Whitney, D., Mohr, B. J., & Griffin, T. J. (2003). *The appreciative inquiry summit.* San Francisco, CA: Berrett-Koehler Publishers.

Moberg, D. J., & Seabright, M. A. (2000). The development of moral imagination. *Business Ethics Quarterly, 10*, 845–884.

Morgan, G. (2006). *Images of organization* (Updated ed.). Thousand Oaks, CA: Sage.

Ray, M. (2005). *The highest goal: The secret that sustains you in every moment.* San Francisco, CA: Berrett-Koehler.

Taylor, S. N., & Bright, D. S. (2011). Open-mindedness and defensiveness in multisource feedback processes. *Journal of Applied Behavioral Science, 47*, 432–460.

Van Vuuren, L. J., & Crous, F. (2005). Utilising Appreciative Inquiry (AI) in creating a shared meaning of ethics in organisations. *Journal of Business Ethics, 57*, 399–412.

Weick, K. E. (1979). *The social psychology of organizing* (2nd ed.). New York, NY: McGraw-Hill.

Werhane, P. H. (1999). *Moral imagination and management decision-making.* New York, NY: Oxford University Press.

Whitney, D., & Trosten-Bloom, A. (2010). *The power of Appreciative Inquiry: A practical guide to positive change* (2nd Ed.). San Francisco, CA: Berrett-Koehler Publishers.

Wrzesniewski, A., McCauley, C., Rozin, P., & Schwartz, B. (1997). Jobs, careers, and callings: People's relations to their work. *Journal of Research in Personality, 31*, 21–33.

CHAPTER 15

EMBODIED ETHICS

A Mentoring and Modeling Approach to Ethics Training

Emi Makino and Jeanne Nakamura

Now more than ever, there is a pressing need for organizations to expand their ethics training repertoire. New scandals erupt on such a regular basis that one begins to wonder if big business can *ever* behave ethically. In this chapter, we explore how recent developments in cognitive science encourage us to rethink the methods used to promote ethical behavior in the workplace. We focus in particular on mentoring and modeling as modes that can better deal with the embodied dimension of ethics. The chapter echoes the insights offered over 30 years ago by Peter Drucker. In 1981, Drucker wrote a scathing critique of one of the biggest issues in management at the time: business ethics. "There are countless seminars on it, speeches, articles, conferences and books, not to mention the many earnest attempts to write 'business ethics' into the law" (Drucker, 1981, p. 18). Drucker's greatest concern stemmed from the very concept of *business* ethics. Implicit in the wording was the assumption that ethics in the business context is fundamentally different from ethics in general. Drucker thought this approach

Ethics Training in Action, pages 311–328
Copyright © 2014 by Information Age Publishing
All rights of reproduction in any form reserved.

was seriously misguided. It promoted casuistry, as captured in the famous 18th century pun: "An ambassador is an honest man, lying abroad for the good of his country" (Drucker, 1981, p. 26). In Drucker's view, there is no business ethics, only ethics. He noted that authorities of moral philosophy in the Western tradition, from the Old Testament to Spinoza to Kant to Kierkegaard, have been unanimous on one point: "There is only one ethics, one set of rules of morality, one code, that of individual behavior in which the same rules apply to everyone alike" (p. 19). Just because one becomes CEO does not exempt a person from the rules of behavior that apply to other employees.

In the context of ethics training, Drucker worried that courses on business ethics were superficial (Williams, 1982). Such courses have a tendency to teach people to distinguish right actions from wrong actions by evaluating the *consequences* of their behavior (Drucker, 1981). Should an executive pay a bribe to lock in a contract that would guarantee the jobs and livelihood of thousands of Americans? It could be argued that the answer is yes, if one takes a consequentialist approach. Such reasoning can easily be used to justify ethical misconduct by those in power. Instead, Drucker advocated for an approach to ethics in business that emphasized self-development, one that could deal with issues of prudence and interdependence.

Unfortunately, essentially little has changed since Drucker's classic article on business ethics was published in *Public Interest* and reprinted a year later in *Forbes* in 1982. The ethical breakdowns at Enron and WorldCom prompted the U.S. Congress to once again try writing ethics into law, this time through the Sarbanes-Oxley Act. Companies and business schools are addressing the problem by introducing more courses on business ethics. According to a meta-analysis conducted by Ethan Waples and his colleagues (Waples, Antes, Murphy, Connelly, & Mumford, 2009), business ethics instruction has focused on goals such as ethical decision making, ethical awareness, moral reasoning processes, and ethical perceptions. Such goals assume that human beings are in full control of their cognitive capacities, that through effortful deliberation one can make moral judgments, and that moral action will follow from them.

In this chapter, we argue that traditional training methods for cultivating responsible practices in business overlook the significant developments that have been made in the cognitive sciences over the past few decades. They fail to fully take into account the tacit and embodied nature of much ethical know-how. Not all wisdom can be made explicit in the forms of rules and principles. Teaching people to make ethical decisions must take on new forms if we take the notion of embodied ethics seriously. An embodied ethics depends on tacit awareness as much as deliberate reasoning. The automatic, nonconscious nature of much moral intuition and its formation encourage us to reconceptualize moral education as building an individual's capacity for intuitive pattern matching. Classroom training is exchanged for learning through practical experience situated in the workplace. We explore, in particular, the potential of mentoring and modeling in the workplace, including alternatives to formal mentoring programs such as manager–subordinate mentoring.

The chapter proceeds as follows. First, we review some of the research in the cognitive and behavioral sciences that support the notion of an embodied ethics. We then consider the ramifications for ethics training in the workplace. An embodied approach to ethics encourages building our capacity to activate and extend our knowledge and feelings in situations where the correct action could be unclear. Modeling ethical behavior in the context of the employee's specific job situation is an effective way to show rather than tell people how values translate into real work. It gives people the sophisticated imagistic models necessary for ethical decision-making so that it is conducted effortlessly rather than through deliberate, rational reasoning. We draw on the findings of an empirical study of good mentoring to begin exploring the necessary conditions for developing professional virtue in employees through manager–subordinate mentoring. Recognizing that mentoring relationships can be prone to abuse, we emphasize the importance of aligning the integrity objectives of the company with its decisions regarding people. We highlight the efforts of two companies that have adopted steps to attract, select, and incentivize employees based on the organizations' espoused values. We conclude with some key takeaway points for building ethics into the workplace through mentoring and modeling.

EMBODIED ETHICS

Nitin Nohria took the helm of Harvard Business School (HBS) in 2010 as its tenth dean. He has made ethics a priority at the school, telling a columnist at *The Economist* that he wanted to improve both the competence and character of students to deal with the crisis of legitimacy in business ("Schumpeter: A post-crisis case study," 2010). Nohria has repeatedly mentioned in the media the danger of moral overconfidence. "Thinking hard about what it is about situations that are more likely to tempt us and what it is about situations that are more likely to give us moral courage is, in my view, one of the most important things that we need to understand," said Nohria in an interview for the online knowledge forum, Big Think (Honan, 2011).

Nohria equates at least some part of character building to deliberate reasoning. This approach has its merits. Indeed, cognitive control has been at the heart of ethical models that have dominated the West since the Enlightenment for nearly three centuries (Slingerland, 2010). Such a model of ethics requires individuals "to be conscious and aware of all the relevant factors, to suppress emotional reactions and social biases, and to arrive at and carry out an objective, dispassionately rational decision" (Slingerland, 2010, p. 247). Ethical behavior is guided either by rules and maxims (deontological ethics) or by a cost–benefit analysis (utilitarian ethics). This cognitive approach is consistent with older psychological models of morality that stressed capacity for moral reasoning, proposed in the late 1960s by Lawrence Kohlberg, "a towering figure in moral psychology" (Haidt, 2008, p. 67).

More recent literature in neuroscience and psychology suggests a different perspective. Social psychologist Timothy Wilson (2002) called attention to the importance of our nonconscious thinking in his book, *Strangers to Ourselves*. Our "adaptive unconscious" is what endows people with the ability to size up the environment very quickly to initiate behavior (p. 23). Researchers have estimated that our five senses take in 11 million pieces of information at any given moment, of which "people can process *consciously* about 40 pieces of information per second" (p. 24, emphasis added). If we see a truck careening towards us, wrote Wilson, we would feel a sudden fear in the pit of our stomachs and jump out of the way without consciously thinking about it. Our adaptive unconscious functions outside of our awareness; it lies out of our reach. But it is the adaptive unconscious that also makes it possible for us to learn a great deal of complex information implicitly and without much effort (Wilson, 2002). Experiments have shown that people can implicitly recognize complex patterns of data without being able to articulate how they know (Wilson, 2002).

Developments in neuroscience challenge the existence of the so-called "Cartesian split" between mind and body; it does not accurately reflect how our brains are wired. Technological advances in brain imaging have allowed scientists to explore the mind–body question empirically. Antonio Damasio (1994) conducted experiments on people who had brain damage and showed that emotions play an integral part in reasoning and decision making. According to Damasio, "emotion probably assists reasoning, especially when it comes to personal and social matters involving risk and conflict" (1999, pp. 41–42). Based on Damasio's somatic marker hypothesis, the gut feeling we experience when we sense something is wrong or right is a body-related signal that marks our options and outcomes as negative or positive. The range of decisions we can make in that situation is narrowed, increasing the likelihood of an action conforming to previous experiences (Damasio, 2004). Sometimes, the emotion is strong enough that a conscious feeling of the emotion follows. Other times, "the signal can operate entirely under the radar of consciousness" (Damasio, 2004, p. 148) resulting in an immediate, snap judgment of good and bad without even intending to make such an evaluation (Bargh & Chartrand, 1999).

The Chilean biologist Francisco Varela, with his mentor Humberto Maturana, developed a groundbreaking theory of cognition (Maturana &

Varela, 1980, 1987) that was foundational for the notion of an embodied mind (Varela, Thompson, & Rosch, 1991). Their theory of mind, called *autopoiesis* (self-reproduction), is based on properties of self-organizing and self-reproducing systems. It rejected the then-dominant view of cognition as an information-processing system based on inputs and outputs. According to Varela, "cognition consists not of representations but of *embodied action*" (1999, p. 17). This alternative theory of cognition is summed up in the aphorism: "All doing is knowing and all knowing is doing" (Maturana & Varela, 1987, p. 27). Varela explained that "most of our mental and active life is of the immediate coping variety, which is transparent, stable, and grounded in our personal histories" (Varela, 1999, p. 19). Few people paid attention to this kind of ethical know-how "until phenomenology and pragmatism, on the one hand, and new trends in cognitive science, on the other hand, brought it to the fore" (p. 19). Because such coping is so immediate, Varela wrote, "not only do we not see it, we do not see that we do not see it" (p. 19).

Responding to the needs of others feels reflexive and simple. Much processing is required by the brain to enable such a subconscious response. "Situations in which we exercise ethical expertise far outnumber those in which we must exercise explicit ethical deliberation" (Varela, 1999, p. 23). This is consistent with more recent literature in moral psychology that argues against the Kohlbergian cognitive reasoning approach to morality. Jonathan Haidt (2008), the most prominent researcher in this new line of research, has asserted that moral emotions and intuitions are the dominant phenomena in the psychology of morality. Conscious reasoning has its place in ethical decision-making. Otherwise, these skills would not have evolved so rapidly (Varela, 1999). Indeed, in the domain of moral psychology, the debate between intuitionist and rationalist theories is far from settled (Haidt, 2010; Narvaez, 2010a, 2010b). But it is important to recognize the limitations of a rule-based, effortful model of ethics, especially if so many of our decisions and moral judgments are formed automatically and beyond our conscious awareness.

INTUITIVE DECISION MAKING
AND EFFORTLESS ATTENTION

According to the Nobel Prize-winning psychologist Daniel Kahneman (2011), people are biologically endowed with two types of thinking systems. System 1 is fast, effortless, emotional, and subconscious. System 2 is slow, deliberate, calculating, and conscious. Traditional ethics training has emphasized the latter. Kahneman's main point in his book *Thinking, Fast and Slow* (2011) was that both systems have cognitive biases that affect how we make decisions. He provides a vivid example of the effects of priming on our fast, automatic thinking system (pp. 57–58). For many years, office workers at a British university had helped themselves to tea and coffee in their kitchen for which they collectively paid by dropping money in an "honesty box." A suggested price list was posted. One day, without warning or explanation, researchers displayed a banner poster above the price list. The first week, a picture of two wide-open eyes that stared at the coffee or tea drinkers was displayed. The average contribution was 70 pence per liter of milk. In the second week, the poster was replaced with one showing flowers. Average contributions plummeted to about 15 pence. The trend continued. On average, the users of the kitchen contributed almost three times as much in "eye weeks" as they did in "flower weeks" (pp. 57–58).

A symbolic reminder of social norms was all it took to improve behavior. A famous experiment on cheating by Dan Ariely and his associates achieved similar priming effects using the Ten Commandments. The researchers hypothesized that people simply knowing that the Ten Commandments were rules about morality "would be enough to increase attention to their own moral standards and thus increase the likelihood of behavior consistent with these standards" (Mazar, Amir, & Ariely, 2008, p. 635). It didn't matter whether the participants believed in God or even whether they remembered the Ten Commandments. Sure enough, cheating was eliminated in the group that wrote down the Ten Commandments before they undertook the assigned task.

The results of these and many other priming experiments support the argument that we need new approaches to ethics training that come to grips with the embodied nature of ethics. What prompts us to respond ethically in a given situation is not usually a rational calculation based on rules, but rather "the activation of stable, spontaneous, and at least partially emotional dispositions" (Slingerland, 2010, p. 266). It follows that building an individual's capacity for effortless attention in difficult ethical situations—as opposed to deliberate, effortful reasoning—is key to developing a more ethical workplace. Someone who has courage "can be counted on to correctly recognize situations that call for courageous action, effortlessly grasp what the appropriate 'courageous' response would be, and put that response into action in a spontaneous and unselfconscious manner" (Slingerland, 2010, p. 266).

Referring to the work of the Confucian philosopher Mencius, Varela (1999) pointed out that "people actualize virtue when they learn to extend knowledge and feelings from situations in which a particular action is considered correct to analogous situations in which the correct action is unclear" (p. 27). Describing a situation under a rule requires people to use cognitive categories. In contrast, when we orient our attention towards correspondences and affinities, we see the situation at hand in a more complex and textured way. All relevant factors are incorporated into the analysis, including aspects that don't fit neatly into predefined categories. This has implications for how we teach ethics in the workplace. "Moral education will involve training individuals—explicitly or implicitly—to develop more and more sophisticated imagistic models, as well as the ability to extend them in a consistent manner" (Slingerland, 2010, p. 257). Training in virtue ethics will inevitably need to incorporate general rules and principles to some extent. "But because the goal is to produce a self-activated disposition and a particular mode of perception, the primary tools tend to be role modeling, mentor-guided imaginative extension, and cultural practices that engage the body and the emotions, such as ritual and music" (Slingerland, 2010, pp. 266–267).

While rituals and music may have a place in corporate settings, they usually lie beyond the scope of ethics training. Mentoring and modeling to develop practical wisdom, however, are well within reach. Practical wisdom, or *phronesis* in the vocabulary of Aristotle, is the art of translating societal ethics into everyday work and activities (Schwartz & Sharpe, 2010). Aristotle posited that there are three types of knowledge. *Episteme* is scientific knowledge or universal truth (Aristotle, 2000). *Techné* involves craftsmanship using codified techniques or practical instructions (Chia & Rasche, 2010, p. 37). *Episteme* and *techné* represent knowledge that can be made explicit through language. These types of knowledge can be verified and falsified through empirical means. Conventional ethics training assumes that ethical know-how falls under these two categories, and neglects the third—*phronesis*, or practical wisdom. Practical wisdom requires both skill and will (Schwartz & Sharpe, 2010). Skill is the know-how; will is the desire to do the right thing. "Skill without will... can lead to ruthless manipulation of others, to serve one's own interests, not theirs. And will without skill can lead to ineffectual fumbling around—the sort of thing we see in people who 'mean well' but leave situations in worse shape than they found them" (Schwartz & Sharpe, 2010, p. 133).

Mentoring is effective because it addresses both skill and will. It takes seriously the tacit and embodied aspect of practical wisdom. *Phronesis* is qualitatively different from its two siblings, precisely because it is embodied in the individual. Unlike its siblings, one cannot distinguish between intent and behavior because "in *phronesis*, what one *does* is inextricable from what one *is*" (Chia & Rasche, 2010, p. 37). Being and doing are united. Practical wisdom is a form of tacit knowing, what the philosopher Michael Polanyi described as knowing "more than one can tell" (2009, p. 8). It is a type of knowledge that cannot be forgotten because it is so integral to one's identity (Chia & Rasche, 2010). While there is room for debate on whether integrity can be taught, Aristotle believed that "character and practical wisdom must be cultivated by the major institutions in which we practice" (Schwartz & Sharpe,

2010, p. 8). To do so, organizations need to expand models of mentoring beyond the formal approach commonly adopted today. In the next section, we turn our attention to the potential of alternative mentoring arrangements that emerge out of everyday work relationships. We then consider some of the preconditions for good mentoring and modeling at work.

GOOD MENTORING

Good mentoring practices within an organization evolve over a sustained period of time. It requires the alignment and commitment of individuals, mentors, and the institution. Mentoring has been defined in the empirical literature as "a relationship between a young adult and an older more experienced adult that helps the younger individual learn to navigate in the adult world and in the world of work" (Kram, 1985, p. 2). Mentoring in large organizations is often implemented through a formalized system of matching mentors with mentees. Formal arrangements for mentoring may be challenged by a hypercompetitive business environment in which corporations constantly have to restructure either through downsizing or rapid expansion. Scholars have been calling for broader conceptualizations of mentoring that can deal with the changing nature of work. Lillian Eby (1997) has suggested that organizations consider alternative forms of mentoring that include manager–subordinate mentoring.

The good mentoring study, conducted by Jeanne Nakamura, David Shernoff, and Charles Hooker, examined how professional values and conduct "are influenced organically through the extended mentoring relationships that emerge and evolve as novices enter a new profession" (Nakamura, Shernoff, & Hooker, 2009, p. xix). The study adopted a cultural evolution perspective by systematically studying the selection and transmission of values or "memes" related to work that is simultaneously excellent and socially responsible in a given profession. A meme is "a unit of cultural information, such as a cultural practice or idea, that is transmitted verbally or by repeated action from one mind to another" ("meme," n.d.). Biologist Richard Dawkins (1976) introduced the notion to suggest a cultural equivalent of genetic DNA. The good mentoring study asked if memes related to excellent and socially responsible work can be passed on to future generations through mentoring.

The study looked at three lineages of mentors and mentees in the field of genetic research. Labs headed by three exemplary scientists were selected. Most of the 36 study participants were research scientists. Some were clinical medical geneticists. Learning by apprenticeship is a cornerstone of graduate science education. Although the study was conducted in the context of higher education, it is important to note that the mentees in this study are graduate students, and the relationship with their advisors bears important parallels to the manager–subordinate relationship of a regular workplace. Graduate students are compensated for the work they do in their advisors' labs and evaluated by them. As a consequence, their advisor is essentially their supervisor. While recognizing its distinctive educational function, a scientific lab in academia is rather like a small-scale entrepreneurial venture in which the owner (the lab director) is responsible for managing various aspects of the business, from funding to the selection of new hires. Similar to the high-tech industry, research in genetics at the turn of the century was also characterized by cutthroat competition. Breakthrough research in biotechnology had the potential for lucrative financial returns in industry. Researchers in the field were hardly immune to breaches of ethics. The study's authors noted the highly publicized downfall in 2005 of South Korean scientist, Hwang Woo Suk, who succumbed to competitive pressures and falsified large amounts of data in stem cell research.

The study looked at 25 memes at the practitioner, domain, field, and societal levels. A domain meme contains values and practices which are aspects of the profession as "a sphere of cultural knowledge and practice" (Nakamura et al., 2009, p. 124), such as high standards of quality and mastery of specialized knowledge. A field meme relates to the profession's "social organization" (p. 124), including such values as collaboration and practices like authorship based on contribution. Societal memes go beyond the profession, encompassing values like treating people equally and fairly and humanitarianism. Audio-recorded interviews were conducted with the three lineage heads and two subsequent generations of 33 mentees (i.e., students and students' students). An interview protocol was used to probe the scientists' valued goals, beliefs, practices, apprenticeship and other formative experiences, obstacles, incentives, and experience as a mentor. The interviews were then transcribed, coded, and analyzed using qualitative analysis software.

The meme most inherited by the subsequent two generations was "Honesty, integrity, and ethics in research." It is one of the most crucial for the profession, yet is easily breached. These were followed by "Treating people equally, fairly," "Providing intellectual freedom and guidance," and "Creating a facilitative lab structure" (Nakamura et al., 2009, p. 133). It would be hard to disagree that such memes are important in any profession and organization, not just in the sciences and medicine. As Nakamura, Shernoff, and Hooker point out, honesty and integrity are so fundamental to society that "one might expect these memes to be absorbed primarily during childhood" (p. 133).

An important finding from the study was that "effective mentors teach their students the meaning of such virtues within the context of their profession" (Nakamura et al., 2009, p. 134). How, for example, do you handle the sensitive information related to a patient's genetic vulnerabilities? How do you allocate credit for publications? "These do not necessarily follow automatically from one's general disposition to do the right thing, however strong that might be" (p. 134), write the authors. Michael Davis (2002) calls this *ethical translation*. In theory, there may be no such thing as business ethics, only ethics. But in practice, how these ethics translate into a real work environment must be learned. A child can be taught the rule "do not lie" in kindergarten, but it is only through their lived experience that they learn how to tell a "white lie."

The central theme emerging from the good mentoring study is that "the practices and values that distinguish professionals as both ethical and excellent in their field often lose their force when conveyed in the context of a classroom or textbook" (Nakamura et al., 2009, p. 77). Benevolent caring for patients is a fundamental virtue of the medical profession (Pellegrino, 2002). Yet as one of the mentees in the study exhorted, "They don't teach that in medical school, for heaven's sake" (Nakamura et al., 2009, p. 77). When she was asked why, she responded: "I think it's because people don't put it into words well. When you talk in words, it's an intellectual process. And this is an emotional and spiritual process that is part of human interactions and medicine" (pp. 76–77).

According to Edmund Pellegrino, a professor of medical ethics, Aristotle singled out modeling as an effective way to teach practical wisdom. "The best practice is to follow a model of the virtuous person. In medicine this means we need virtuous physicians as teachers" (Pellegrino, 2002, p. 383). Arno Motulsky, an exemplary physician-scientist and founding father of pharmacogenetics, headed one of the three lineages in the good mentoring study. Motulsky's mentee eloquently articulated how modeling was an irreplaceable way of transmitting the situated and embodied expertise required in medical genetics:

> You tag along on rounds, watch this person function, watch whether it works with that patient or not. I think it's absorbed stuff. So when you start off, you think, "Oh, this is going to be this terrible tragedy situation." You read about the case. "Oh, this is awful." Then you watch this person walk into the room of the [patient] and uplift them by talking about what the options are, by helping them deal with [the fact] that they're going to die. By helping them to think about the preparations for dying. By talking about [the fact] that this life is special, you just have a different way you measure it. (Nakamura et al., 2009, p. 165)

One of the more surprising findings from the study was the importance of structuring a facilitative work environment to foster good practices. Motulsky was frequently away from his lab. He did not even hold regular lab meetings. Yet his protégés absorbed the values and practices of their mentor in spite of his absence. According to Hooker, who wrote the chapter on Motulsky's mentoring practices, several strategies were adopted to make this happen. First, Motulsky "selected trainees whose interests and inclinations were compatible with his own" (Nakamura et al., 2009, p. 71). He treated protégés collegially. He expected them to develop their own research questions, design their own experiments, and come to their own conclusions about the significance of their results. Closely mirroring the advice of management consultant Jim Collins (2001) of "putting the right people on the bus" or the principle of "first who, then what" when building great organizations, Motulsky essentially screened out those who could not direct themselves. Indeed, all three of the lineage heads deliberately selected students who could succeed in the environment they had created. This is in line with Benjamin Schneider's notion that an organization is defined by the people in it "as a natural outcome of an attraction-selection-attrition (ASA) cycle" (Schneider, Goldstein, & Smith, 1995, p. 747).

Motulsky strove to strike a balance between supervision and freedom. He did not micromanage. Mentees were urged to develop an inner sense for what is solvable—that is, to focus on questions with solutions that can be attained by available means. When they got stuck, however, Motulsky was very generous with his time. He created opportunities for students to collaborate with him on projects and journal articles. Other advantages for his protégés stemmed from Motulsky's perspective and position. Motulsky was a pioneer in the field of medical genetics. "He was really good at knowing where the field was going and putting you in a position of being able to participate in the process" (Nakamura et al., 2009, p. 73), recalled one mentee. He provided his mentees with the physical resources required to do research. In addition, he "created an environment that was dense in diverse human resources" (p. 74) and rich in social capital. Motulsky's standing enabled him to hire faculty and assistants with an intent to bring on board experts who had "skills and interests distinct from his own so that students could avail themselves of a broad range of know-how to help approach and solve any research question they might pursue" (Nakamura et al., 2009, p. 74).

PRECONDITIONS FOR GOOD MENTORING AT WORK

The good mentoring study examined mentoring from the perspective of a profession. A profession has a telos, or an aim that guides its practices. The professions studied—science and medicine—are well established. Medicine in particular is among the oldest of the knowledge professions. Those entering the profession take a Hippocratic Oath, pledging that they will do no harm. In contrast, organizational life in general is much messier.

An organization by definition is an assortment of people, often from different professions, performing different job functions. Large corporations, moreover, are a relatively new innovation. The concept of bureaucracy as an efficient form of organizing was introduced and popularized by the German sociologist Max Weber (1954) only in the 20th century through his posthumous book, *Economy and Society*, published in the 1920s. Rule-based decision-making is among the key organizing principles of a bureaucracy. Historically speaking, then, we have vastly less experience dealing with ethics in corporations in contrast to *any* profession, not just medicine or science.

The good mentoring study focused exclusively on moral exemplars. It was part of the study of good work, which sought to understand the conditions for work that is excellent and ethical (Gardner, Csikszentmihalyi, & Damon, 2002). Not all mentoring is good, however. In fact, bad mentoring can be toxic; it can be detrimental to an organization as well as to the individuals involved. Dennis Moberg and Manuel Velasquez (2004) warned that the mentoring relationship is also subject to abuse: "Although mentors are often heralded as virtuous agents of essential continuity, mentoring commonly results in serious dysfunction" (p. 95). Mentors may exclude people who are not like themselves. Tyrannical and manipulative behavior, harassment, dirty tricks, and backstabbing have surfaced on the dark side of mentoring. Citing a 2000 study by Eby and colleagues, they emphasized that dysfunctions in mentoring cannot be brushed off as phenomena with a low base rate. Of the 156 former protégés surveyed, just over half (54%) said they had been in at least one negative mentoring relationship (Eby, McManus, Simon, & Russell, 2000). The impact of managers and mentors whose conduct breaches ethics can be detrimental to the organization. A mentor may be emulated even when he or she models unethical behavior—that is, he or she may be a negative or deformative influence (Nakamura, 2011). Enron is an example that comes to mind. Practices such as good hiring and rewarding ethical behavior (through promotions, for example) are thus crucial. Moreover, unacceptable behavior must not be ignored.

Learning by watching and doing is fundamental to an embodied ethics approach to developing ethical behavior at work. Any sustained social interaction between employees in organizational life is an opportunity for modeling. Ethical role models are not confined to higher education and hospitals. In an article on ethical role modeling in organizations (Weaver, Treviño, & Agle, 2005), the authors gave an example of a senior vice president at American Express, who interrupted a meeting that was clearly getting antagonistic and personal.

> You guys may have thought this was an acceptable meeting. I did not," she told the participants in the meeting. "I will not lead another meeting where I feel like I need to hide the scissors in the room. You guys go and do whatever

you need to do to hammer out your differences, or figure out how to keep them out of our meetings. If you can't do that, you will not be part of my team. (Weaver et al., 2005, p. 313)

She gained some of the confidence to act with such boldness, she later reflected, "from having watched the actions of a highly respected senior executive she worked with very early in her career" (p. 313).

Clearly, managers influence employees by serving as ethical role models. Some of the characteristics of ethical role models Weaver and his colleagues found in their qualitative study overlap with the memes in the good mentoring study introduced earlier. These include honesty, trustworthiness, integrity, humility, care for others, taking responsibility for others, being uncompromising, having a consistent ethical vision, and putting ethics above personal and company interests. "Most striking is the fact that, with rare exception, the ethical role models identified by the interviewees were people with whom interviewees interacted frequently" (Weaver et al., 2005, p. 324); "Interviewees generally did not single out distant senior executives on the basis of official pronouncements or highly publicized actions" (p. 324). The 20 interviewees came from a diverse set of industries and organizations, and their age ranged from 27 to 50. These findings are further evidence of the need for a different kind of ethics training that addresses the ethical know-how embedded in the lived experience of work. It also is consistent with the argument that the definition of mentoring needs to be broadened if it is to be tapped as a vehicle for ethics training.

There are some aspects of organizational culture and structure in business that do make it challenging to develop ethics training using a mentoring or modeling approach. For example, Weaver and his colleagues noted how difficult it is to identify ethical role models within an organization. People were generally reluctant to identify themselves as an ethical role model, perhaps because it conflicts with their value of humility. The authors suggested that organizations try more subtle approaches to developing ethical role models, such as through leadership training (not ethics training).

Another, more pressing issue is the lack of alignment between an organization's ethical goals and its HR policies. The findings from a 2012 survey of compliance officers by the Consero Group are sobering. Of the survey respondents, "55 percent...indicated that their performance appraisal and incentive programs do not support their companies' compliance and integrity objectives" (Consero Group, 2012). Decisions related to people are the true controls of a company (Drucker, 2008). An organization's decisions "on placement and pay, on promotion, demotion, and firing...far more than the accountant's figures and reports, model and mold behavior" (Drucker, 2008, pp. 285–286). American Express not only explicitly includes being an ethical role model as part of its guiding principles; in its performance management system, it also defines and provides examples of the competencies expected of its senior leaders, some of which align closely with the competencies identified by the study of ethical role models (Weaver et al., 2005).

Compared to established companies, entrepreneurial startups have additional challenges. Successful ventures go through a rapid growth phase in which companies have to increase their employee count in a short amount of time. An organization may face an identity crisis if its values are not clearly articulated. Dealer Tire, an innovative tire distributor, has been incorporating some progressive methods to help move through that stage. First, instead of having its founders and top management develop a set of core values and guiding principles for the company, it used an approach called appreciative inquiry (Cooperrider, Whitney, & Stavros, 2008; see also Chapter 14, this volume) to engage all of its employees in deciding which values and principles matter. Second, the company's selection process for new hires is based heavily on the values that emerged. The HR department created a one-page purpose statement that describes four core values and ten guiding principles. It is sent to all potential candidates. The company's LinkedIn page features video testimonials of its executives and associates talking about their organizational values. The organization's efforts in values-based hiring have succeeded in attracting candidates who were initially reluctant to consider an unknown startup.

Mentoring and modeling are modes of ethics training that rely on the right people being on the bus. Another consideration is for organizations to pay more attention to modes of mentoring that are less formal but can nevertheless be purposefully embedded into an organization's structures. Eby (1997) introduced a typology of mentoring that divides mentoring into four categories along two dimensions—the relationship between mentor and protégé, and the skills that are developed. The mentor and protégé relationship can be hierarchical or lateral. The types of skills developed through mentoring can be job- or career-related. Formal mentoring arrangements fall within the hierarchical/job-related category. Eby's typology opens the door for a broader array of mentoring formats. The good mentoring study looked at manager–subordinate mentoring, an extension of hierarchical mentoring. Coworker mentoring and team mentoring are examples of lateral mentoring. Job-related mentoring could also provide support for relocations, as well as survivor mentoring (i.e., the survivors of a restructuring and staff cutbacks). Career-related mentoring is more oriented towards specific professions and broader career skills that are easily transportable. These are also the categories that are most frequently overlooked by researchers and practitioners, including mentoring partnerships developed through professional associations. Other scholars have drawn attention to the multiple relationships that comprise mentoring. Higgins and Kram (2001), from the perspective of social network theory, propose cultivating a "developmental network," which may encompass all of Eby's types. Compared to formal mentoring systems, alternative modes of mentoring such as developmental networks demand that the mentee assume a more proactive role in building and nurturing mentoring relationships.

An embodied ethics perspective encourages organizations to rethink their assumptions about ethics training. Here are some key implications and considerations:

- Good mentoring is a critical complement to traditional ethics training, contributing to cultivation of habits of ethical conduct in the context of a specific occupation and organization.
- Many spontaneous workplace mentoring relationships involve a supervisor of the mentee. A supervisor–supervisee relationship may be the naturally occurring locus of effective mentoring.
- It is important to appreciate how supervisors and managers shape the environment in which employees observe and learn to handle everyday ethical challenges. In contrast, formal mentoring relationships are limited to one medium—talk—and may not be as effective for developing ethical behavior of the immediate coping variety.
- There are risks inherent to mentoring. Performance evaluation systems must be capable of handling abuses in both formal and informal mentoring arrangements.
- Hiring for fit with organizational values—and for basic honesty and integrity—is a crucial support of good mentoring; the potential mentor is more likely to model the organization's form of good work and the potential mentee is more likely to be receptive.
- Publicizing examples of good mentoring amplifies the visibility of positive models.
- Performance metrics must be aligned with an organization's values and integrity goals.

Management by values promotes good mentoring and modeling. Can employees at every level clearly articulate the organizational values and guiding principles of the company? Are those values clear to external stakeholders such as customers and job candidates? Does the performance evaluation system incentivize ethical behavior? If the answers are no, it is probably premature to consider a mentoring and modeling approach to ethics. If the answers are yes, then mentoring and role modeling will have found a place in the organization for developing individuals to do good and do well.

REFERENCES

Aristotle. (2000). *Nicomachean ethics* (R. Crisp, Trans.). New York, NY: Cambridge University Press.

Bargh, J. A., & Chartrand, T. L. (1999). The unbearable automaticity of being. *American Psychologist, 54*, 462–479. doi: 10.1037/0003-066x.54.7.462

Chia, R., & Rasche, A. (2010). Epistemological alternatives for researching Strategy as Practice: Building and dwelling worldviews. In D. Golsorkhi, L. Rouleau, D. Seidl, & E. Vaara (Eds.), *Cambridge handbook of strategy as practice* (pp. 34–46). Cambridge, UK: Cambridge University Press.

Collins, J. (2001). *Good to great: Why some companies make the leap—and others don't.* New York, NY: HarperBusiness.

Consero Group. (2012). Consero survey reveals 55 percent of Chief Compliance Officers feel employees are not incentivized to support integrity objectives. PRNewswire. Retrieved from http://www.prnewswire.com/news-releases/con-sero-survey-reveals-55-percent-of-chief-compliance-officers-feel-employees-are-not-incentivized-to-support-integrity-objectives-182985761.html

Cooperrider, D. L., Whitney, D., & Stavros, J. M. (2008). *Appreciative Inquiry handbook for leaders of change* (2nd ed.). Brunswick, OH: Crown Custom Publishing.

Damasio, A. R. (1994). *Descartes' error: Emotion, reason, and the human brain.* New York, NY: Putnam.

Damasio, A. R. (1999). *The feeling of what happens: Body and emotion in the making of consciousness.* New York, NY: Harcourt Brace.

Damasio, A. R. (2004). *Looking for Spinoza.* London, England: Vintage Books.

Davis, M. (2002). *Profession, code, and ethics.* Burlington, VT: Ashgate.

Dawkins, R. (1976). *The selfish gene.* New York, NY: Oxford University Press.

Drucker, P. F. (1981). What is business ethics? *Public Interest, 63*, 18–36.

Drucker, P. F. (2008). *Management* (Rev. ed.). New York, NY: Collins.

Eby, L. T. (1997). Alternative forms of mentoring in changing organizational environments: A conceptual extension of the mentoring literature. *Journal of Vocational Behavior, 51*, 125–144. doi: 10.1006/jvbe.1997.1594

Eby, L. T., McManus, S. E., Simon, S. A., & Russell, J. E. A. (2000). The protégé's perspective regarding negative mentoring experiences: The development of a taxonomy. *Journal of Vocational Behavior, 57*, 1–21. doi: 10.1006/jvbe.1999.1726

Gardner, H., Csikszentmihalyi, M., & Damon, W. (2002). *Good work: When excellence and ethics meet.* New York, NY: Basic Books.

Haidt, J. (2008). Morality. *Perspectives on Psychological Science, 3*, 65–72. doi: 10.1111/j.1745-6916.2008.00063.x

Haidt, J. (2010). Moral psychology must not be based on faith and hope: Commentary on Narvaez (2010). *Perspectives on Psychological Science, 5*, 182–184. doi: 10.1177/1745691610362352

Higgins, M. C., & Kram, K. E. (2001). Reconceptualizing mentoring at work: A developmental network perspective. *Academy of Management Review, 26*, 264–288. doi: 10.2307/259122

Honan, D. (2011, May 20). We're not as moral as we think (and how that gets us in trouble). *Big Think.* Retrieved from http://bigthink.com/think-tank/were-not-as-moral-as-we-think-and-how-that-gets-us-in-trouble

Kahneman, D. (2011). *Thinking, fast and slow*. New York, NY: Farrar, Straus and Giroux.

Kram, K. E. (1985). *Mentoring at work: Developmental relationships in organizational life*. Glenview, IL: Scott, Foresman and Company.

Maturana, H. R., & Varela, F. J. (1980). *Autopoiesis and cognition: The realization of the living*. Dordrecht, The Netherlands: D. Reidel Publishing Company.

Maturana, H. R., & Varela, F. J. (1987). *The tree of knowledge: The biological roots of human understanding*. Boston, MA: Shambhala.

Mazar, N., Amir, O., & Ariely, D. (2008). The dishonesty of honest people: A theory of self-concept maintenance. *Journal of Marketing Research, 45*, 633–644. doi: 10.1509/jmkr.45.6.633

Meme. (n.d.). In *The American Heritage dictionary of the English language* (5th ed.). Retrieved from http://www.ahdictionary.com/word/search.html?q=meme

Moberg, D. J., & Velasquez, M. (2004). The ethics of mentoring. *Business Ethics Quarterly, 14*, 95–122. doi: 10.2307/3857774

Nakamura, J. (2011). Contexts of positive adult development. In S. I. Donaldson, M. Csikszentmihalyi, & J. Nakamura (Eds.), *Applied positive psychology* (pp. 185–202). New York, NY: Routledge/Taylor & Francis.

Nakamura, J., Shernoff, D. J., & Hooker, C. H. (2009). *Good mentoring: Fostering excellent practice in higher education*. San Francisco, CA: Jossey-Bass/John Wiley.

Narvaez, D. (2010a). The embodied dynamism of moral becoming: Reply to Haidt (2010). *Perspectives on Psychological Science, 5*, 185–186. doi: 10.1177/1745691610362353

Narvaez, D. (2010b). Moral complexity. *Perspectives on Psychological Science, 5*, 163–181. doi: 10.1177/1745691610362351

Pellegrino, E. D. (2002). Professionalism, profession and the virtues of the good physician. *Mount Sinai Journal of Medicine, 69*, 378–384.

Polanyi, M. (2009). *The tacit dimension*. Chicago, IL: University of Chicago Press.

Schneider, B., Goldstein, H. W., & Smith, D. B. (1995). The ASA framework: An update. *Personnel Psychology, 48*, 747–773. doi: 10.1111/j.1744-6570.1995.tb01780.x

Schumpeter: A post-crisis case study. (2010, July 29). *The Economist*. Retrieved from http://www.economist.com/node/16691433

Schwartz, B., & Sharpe, K. (2010). *Practical wisdom: The right way to do the right thing*. New York, NY: Riverhead Books.

Slingerland, E. (2010). Toward an empirically responsible ethics: Cognitive science, virtue ethics, and effortless attention in early Chinese thought. In B. Bruya (Ed.), *Effortless attention: A new perspective in the cognitive science of attention and action* (pp. 247–286). Cambridge, MA: MIT Press.

Varela, F. J. (1999). *Ethical know-how: Action, wisdom, and cognition*. Stanford, CA: Stanford University Press.

Varela, F. J., Thompson, E. T., & Rosch, E. (1991). *The embodied mind: Cognitive science and human experience*. Cambridge, MA: MIT Press.

Waples, E., Antes, A., Murphy, S., Connelly, S., & Mumford, M. (2009). A meta-analytic investigation of business ethics instruction. *Journal of Business Ethics, 87*, 133–151. doi: 10.1007/s10551-008-9875-0

Weaver, G. R., Treviño, L. K., & Agle, B. (2005). "Somebody I look up to": Ethical role models in organizations. *Organizational Dynamics, 34,* 313–330. doi: 10.1016/j.orgdyn.2005.08.001

Weber, M. (1954). *Max Weber on law in economy and society* (M. Rheinstein Ed.; E. Shils & M. Rheinstein, Trans.). Cambridge, MA: Harvard University Press.

Williams, O. F. (1982). Business ethics: A Trojan horse? *California Management Review, 24*(4), 14–24.

Wilson, T. D. (2002). *Strangers to ourselves: Discovering the adaptive unconscious.* Cambridge, MA: Belknap Press of Harvard University Press.

ABOUT THE AUTHORS

Lauren E. Benishek is a doctoral candidate in the industrial and organizational psychology program at the University of Central Florida and a graduate research associate at the Institute for Simulation and Training. She earned a BS in Psychology in 2007 from Virginia Polytechnic Institute and State University. Her current interests include individual and team training development and evaluation, enhancing learning and training effectiveness, integrating simulation into learning contexts, understanding team process and performance, and facilitating teamwork. Ms. Benishek has led and been involved with several training development initiatives sponsored by the Department of Veterans Affairs, the American Psychological Association's Coalition for Psychology in Schools and Education, and the Florida Medical Malpractice Joint Underwriting Association. She was awarded the University of Central Florida's Trustees Doctoral Fellowship in 2008.

Eduardo Salas is Trustee Chair and Professor of Psychology at the University of Central Florida, where he also holds an appointment as program director for the human systems integration research department at the Institute for Simulation and Training. Previously, he was the Director of UCF's Applied Experimental and Human Factors PhD program. Before joining IST, he was a senior research psychologist and head of the training technology development branch of NAWC-TSD for 15 years. During this period, Dr. Salas served as a principal investigator for numerous R&D programs, including TADMUS, that focused on teamwork, team training, decision-making under stress, and performance assessment. Dr. Salas has co-authored over 450 journal articles and book chapters and has co-edited

Ethics Training in Action, pages 329–339
Copyright © 2014 by Information Age Publishing
All rights of reproduction in any form reserved.

25 books. His expertise includes assisting organizations in how to foster teamwork, design and implement team training strategies, facilitate training effectiveness, manage decision-making under stress, and develop performance measurement tools. Dr. Salas is a past president of the Society for Industrial/Organizational Psychology, fellow of the American Psychological Association, Human Factors and Ergonomics Society, and a recipient of the Meritorious Civil Service Award from the Department of the Navy. He is also the recipient of the 2012 Society for Human Resource Management Losey Lifetime Achievement Award, and the 2012 Joseph E. McGrath Award for Lifetime Achievement.

Dr. David Bright is an associate professor at Wright State University in Dayton, OH. He received a PhD in organizational behavior from the Case Western Reserve University Weatherhead School of Management. His areas of expertise include virtue ethics and positive organizational scholarship.

Dr. Ilma Barros is a research fellow with the Fowler Center for Sustainable Value at Case Western Reserve University and a member of the Presencing Institute. She earned a PhD in organizational behavior from the Case Western Reserve Weatherhead School of Management. She has two decades of experience consulting with organizations throughout the world, but especially in Brazil.

Mr. Veer Raghava Kumar Marthy is an MBA student at Wright State University. He has also received an M.P.A from Wright State University, and he is a Certified Nonprofit Professional (CNP) with particular interest in social cause-related innovations and social entrepreneurship.

Richard Charnigo is an associate professor at the University of Kentucky, with joint appointments in the Department of Biostatistics (College of Public Health) and Department of Statistics (College of Arts and Sciences). His research interests in statistics include mixture modeling (including applications to microarray data analysis) and nonparametric regression (including applications to pattern recognition problems in Raman spectroscopy and light scattering by nanoparticles). His collaborative research interests include cardiology, psychology, public health, and organizational behavior.

Leslie E. Sekerka, PhD is a professor of management and the founder and director of the Ethics in Action Research and Education Center at Menlo College (Atherton, CA). Dr. Sekerka's teaching and scholarship is designed to create a proactive approach to applied ethics. Her interests in adult moral development stem from twenty years of work and research in business and military organizations. Her scholarship and teaching focuses on the promotion of strengths in support of personal and organizational growth, ethical decision-making, and professional moral courage in the workplace. Her award winning research appears in a variety of academic venues, including journals, books, and special issues targeting positive organizational ethics. Dr. Sekerka works closely with the Silicon Valley business community as an academic partner at Santa Clara University's Markkula Center for Applied Ethics. She is known globally as an ethics training specialist, providing workshops and seminars that help advance employees' moral competencies and build organizational ethical strength. Dr. Sekerka recently won the Charles B. Emerick Award for excellence in teaching.

Cathy Driscoll received her PhD in organizational behavior and marketing from Queen's University in 1994. She is professor in the department of management in the Sobey School of Business at Saint Mary's University in Halifax, Nova Scotia. Prior to Saint Mary's, she worked as a project manager and policy advisor with the National Round Table on the Environment and the Economy in Ottawa. She has served as a director on the Better Business Bureau of the Atlantic Provinces and the Canadian Centre for Ethics in Public Affairs, and was a founding board member for the Canadian Business Ethics Research Network.

Cathy's research interests include business ethics, ethical leadership, management education, stakeholder management, and spiritual and religious values in ethical decision making. She has published articles in the *Journal of Business Ethics, Business and Society*, and the *Journal of Management, Spirituality and Religion.*

Margaret C. McKee is an assistant professor in the management department of Saint Mary's University, which is situated in Halifax on Canada's east coast. Margaret earned a PhD in management in 2008 and is in her fourth year of a tenure-track position teaching a mandatory ethics course to undergraduate and master's business students. Margaret transitioned to academia after a 20-year career as a professional communicator with publicly traded companies, federal and provincial government departments, and consulting agencies in central and eastern Canada.

Margaret has a variety of research interests and has secured grants from several Canadian funding agencies, including the Social Sciences and Humanities Research Council and the Canadian Centre for Ethics in Public Affairs. In addition to research examining business ethics training and development practices in Canadian companies, she is midway through a project examining CSR practices in Vietnam. Margaret is also interested in organizational leadership and has several studies underway examining the effects of a transformational leadership style on various organizational and employee outcomes, with a particular interest in employee well-being. Margaret has presented academic papers in Canada, the U.S., and Europe, and has published articles in the *Journal of Business Ethics*, the *Journal of*

Leadership and Organizational Studies, and the *Journal of Management, Spirituality and Religion.*

Wendy R. Carroll is an associate professor at the University of Prince Edward Island (UPEI), School of Business, and the founder and faculty director of the UPEI Workforce Strategies Research Group. After a 20-year career working in national and multinational businesses as a senior leader and executive, Wendy completed her PhD in management and joined the faculty at Acadia University in July 2005 and then UPEI in July 2008. Wendy's industry experience spans strategic human resource management (SHRM), industrial relations, human resource management (HRM), employee relations, and operations and process management in various industry sectors including information technology, telecommunications, and financial services.

Wendy's research program focuses on human resource management, workforce strategies, employee and industrial relations, labor force dynamics, and evidence-based management. She has a number of peer-reviewed publications in HRM and employee relations journals (including a highly commended paper award by the Emerald Literati Network in 2011—Awards for Excellence), several book chapters, and numerous papers presented at leading management conferences. In her current role as faculty director of the Workforce Strategies Research Group, she works in partnership with the government of Prince Edward Island to examine future labor skills and demand, and workforce practices to assist with labor force planning and policy development. Wendy has recently become a member of the Human Resource Association of Nova Scotia's Board of Directors.

Wendy teaches management courses in both the undergraduate and graduate level at UPEI. She has won several teaching awards, including graduate faculty member of the year for UPEI in 2008, 2009, and 2012 as well as the Hessian Merit Award of Teaching Excellence in 2011.

Mary C. Gentile, Ph.D., is director of Giving Voice to Values and senior research scholar at Babson College; senior advisor, Aspen Institute Business and Society Program; and independent consultant. Previously Gentile was a faculty member and manager of case research at Harvard Business School.

Giving Voice to Values is a business curriculum launched by Aspen Institute and Yale SOM, now based and supported at Babson College. GVV is a pioneering approach to values-driven leadership that has been featured in *Financial Times, Harvard Business Review, Stanford Social Innovation Review, McKinsey Quarterly,* and *BizEd,* among other publications, and piloted in over 425 business schools and organizations globally. The book *Giving Voice to Values: How to Speak Your Mind When You Know What's Right* is published by Yale University Press (www.MaryGentile.com).

While at Harvard Business School (1985–1995), Gentile was one of the principal architects of the innovative educational program, Leadership, Ethics and Corporate Responsibility. Gentile coauthored *Can Ethics Be Taught? Perspectives, Challenges, and Approaches at Harvard Business School* (with Thomas R. Piper and Sharon Parks, Harvard Business School Press, 1993, translated into Japanese and Hungarian). Other publications include *Differences That Work: Organizational Excellence through Diversity; Managing Diversity: Making Differences Work; Managerial Excellence Through Diversity: Text and Cases*, as well as numerous articles, cases, and book reviews in publications such as *Academy of Management Learning and Education, Harvard Business Review, Stanford Social Innovation Review, Risk Management, CFO, The Journal of Human Values, BizEd, Strategy+Business*, and others. Gentile served as content expert for the award-winning interactive CD-ROM, *Managing Across Differences* (Harvard Business School Publishing, 1996).

Gentile holds a bachelor's degree from The College of William and Mary (Williamsburg, VA) and an MA and PhD from the State University of New York at Buffalo.

Lindsey N. Godwin, PhD, is an associate professor in the Stiller School of Business at Champlain College in Burlington, VT. She received her doctorate in organizational behavior from Case Western Reserve University. Her research focuses on moral decision-making in the workplace, the impact of business education on morality, and strength-based approaches to organizational change. Her work has been published in a variety of journals and books, appearing most recently in the *Oxford Handbook of Positive Organizational Scholarship*, and presented at national and international conferences, including the Annual Academy of Management Meetings. Currently she is serving as a guest editor for a forthcoming special issue on positive organizational ethics for the *Journal of Business Ethics*, and recently served as a guest editor for a special issue on advances in the AI Summit for the *AI Practitioner Journal*. She consults with a variety of organizations around the world, helping them apply strength-based change-management approaches.

Nicole S. Morris, CPA, CGMA, is an assistant professor in the Stiller School of Business at Champlain College in Burlington, VT. She is a graduate of Siena College and has held several positions, including senior auditor for KPMG and controller for a credit union. After obtaining her CPA license, she spent five years in various positions of increasing responsibility in the finance department at GE Healthcare. Her positions centered around the implementation of Sarbanes Oxley, software revenue recognition, managing system conversions, and Six Sigma process improvement. During her time at GE Healthcare, she obtained her MBA from Marist College. She is a dedicated and committed member of the CPA profession. Locally, she is a member of the Vermont State Society of CPAs. On a national level, she was selected as one of 28 young professionals from across the country to attend the AICPA leadership academy in the summer of 2009. In fall of 2009, she was honored to accept a nomination to become a member of the AICPA Student Recruitment Committee and currently holds a position on the AICPA EDGE Conference Planning Committee. Most recently, in 2013 Nicole has been accepted to the PhD in management program at Saint Mary's University in Halifax, Nova Scotia and is excited to begin her studies in May.

Charmine E. J. Härtel earned her PhD in IO Psychology at Colorado State University and is head of management and chair of human resource management and organizational development at UQ Business School, The University of Queensland, Brisbane, Australia. Dr. Härtel's pioneering work on the characteristics of positive work environments has identified a number of the individual, group, and organizational drivers of unhealthy and toxic work environments along with the leadership and human resource management strategies and practices to turn such situations around. She is a past president of the Australian and New Zealand Academy of Management (ANZAM) and a fellow of the Australian Institute of Management, the Australian Human Resources Institute, and ANZAM. Prof. Härtel is recipient of five awards for innovation in organizational practice as well as nearly $3 million in Australian Research Council funding. Her work appears in over 60 book chapters and 100 refereed journal articles. She has served as editor and associate editor of a number of journals and books, including *Academy of Management Learning and Education, Journal of Managerial Psychology, Journal of Management & Organization*, and the Research on Emotion in Organizations book series. Professor Härtel is also primary author of the wholly original textbook *Human Resource Management* (Pearson).

Dr. Ivan Butarbutar is currently a research fellow in the department of management at Monash University. He received his PhD from Monash University. Dr. Butarbutar was one of the Greenleaf Scholars Award recipients (2011), awarded by Greenleaf Center for Servant Leadership (in Indiana) for early career scholars who conduct a significant study of the impact of servant leadership in a wide range of organizational or social contexts. His research interests focus on leadership and employee performance.

Dr. Sen Sendjaya is a senior lecturer in leadership in the department of management at Monash University in Melbourne, Australia. He is passionate about servant leadership, as evidenced by his publications on the subject in various outlets, such as the *Journal of Management Studies, International Journal of Human Resource Management*, and *European Journal of Work and Organizational Psychology*. Dr. Sendjaya is currently part of a team examining the development of effective and ethical leadership on the basis of the servant leadership framework, funded by a large, nationally competitive grant. He conducts leadership field research in Australia, the U.S., China, and Indonesia, and has been invited to consult and speak on leadership in seminars and corporate workshops in these countries.

Dr. Andre Pekerti is a senior lecturer in the University of Queensland Business School at the University of Queensland, Brisbane, Australia. Dr. Pekerti has a multicultural background that complements his research interest in international management and organizational behavior. His primary research topics are attributions, cultural intelligence, family business and networks, multicultural individuals, servant leadership, and values. He has presented and published his work in a number of international conferences and in international journals, including *Career Development Quarterly, International Journal of Cross-Cultural Management, International Journal of Human Resource Management, Journal of Cross-Cultural Psychology*, and the *Journal of International Business Studies*. Dr. Pekerti is vice president of the Australia and New Zealand International Business Academy, and serves on the editorial board of the *Journal of World Business*.

Dr. Giles Hirst received his PhD from the Melbourne Business School, and is an associate professor and director of research in the department of management at the University of Melbourne, Australia. He serves on the editorial boards of the *British Journal of Management* and the *Journal of Organizational Behavior*. He has particular expertise in the fields of creativity, innovation, and leadership. Most recently, he has been engaged by the Australian Institute of Management to conduct a four-nation survey of managers and executives to examine the buffering role of positive psychological attributes on the effects of the global financial crisis. Dr. Hirst has published his work in the *Journal of International Business Studies*, the *Academy of Management Journal, The Leadership Quarterly*, and the *Journal of Organizational Behavior*, and has received more than half a million dollars of Australian Research Council funding.

Prof. Neal M. Ashkanasy is professor of management in the UQ Business School at the University of Queensland, where he received his PhD in social/organizational psychology. His research is in leadership, organizational culture, ethics, and emotions in organizations. He has published over 200 book chapters and journal articles, including works published in the *Academy of Management Journal*, the *Academy of Management Review*, the *Journal of Organizational Behavior, The Leadership Quarterly*, the *Journal of Applied Psychology*, and the *Journal of Management*. He serves on several editorial boards, including the *Journal of Applied Psychology* and the *Journal of Management*, and is editor-in-chief of the *Journal of Organizational Behavior*, associate editor of *the Academy of Management Review* and *Emotion Review*, and series co-editor of *Research on Emotion in Organizations*. Prof. Ashkanasy is a fellow of the Academy for the Social Sciences in the UK (AcSS) and Australia (ASSA); the Association for Psychological Science (APS); the Society for Industrial and Organizational Psychology (SIOP); and the Australia and New Zealand Academy of Management (ANZAM), where he also served as president. He has been a recipient of more than two million dollars of funding from the Australian Research Council.

Marianne M. Jennings, emeritus professor of legal and ethical studies, taught at the W. P. Carey School of Business, Arizona State University from 1977 through 2011. She has six textbooks and four monographs in circulation, with the 10th edition of her real estate law book published in December 2012 and the 22nd editions of her business law books published in January 2013. She was director of the Lincoln Center for Applied Ethics from 1995 to 1999. She has worked with government agencies, professional organizations, colleges and universities, and Fortune 500 companies on ethics training and culture. She is a contributing editor of *Corporate Finance Review* and *Real Estate Law Journal.* Two of her books have been named *Library Journal's* book of the year. Her books have been translated into three languages. Her book, *The Seven Signs of Ethical Collapse*, was published by St. Martin's Press and has been used as both an audit tool and a primer by numerous organizations for creating and sustaining an ethical culture.

In 2011, she was named one of the Top 100 Thought Leaders by Trust Across America, and in 2012 she was named one of the 100 most influential people in business ethics by *Ethisphere* magazine.

She served on the board of directors for Arizona Public Service (now Pinnacle West), the owner of the Palo Verde Nuclear Station, from 1987 through 2000. She has served on INPO's advisory council since 2005. She conducts ethics training and ethical culture assessments for businesses, including Fortune 100 companies, government agencies, professional associations, and nonprofit organizations.

Emi Makino, PhD is associate professor of management and entrepreneurship in Kyushu University's Robert T. Huang Entrepreneurship Center. She also teaches for the Education Center for Global Leaders in Molecular Systems for Devices at Kyushu University. Her research focuses on developing theory for novel methods of organizational knowledge creation. She is interested in the implications of embodied cognition for management and organization. She received her PhD from Claremont Graduate University. Prior to entering academia, she worked as a freelance conference interpreter in Tokyo. Her interpreting practice has given her a unique perspective on cross-cultural management in a wide variety of contexts and situations. She is trained as a journalist and was formerly a reporter for a leading Japanese business newspaper.

Jeanne Nakamura is associate professor in Claremont Graduate University's Division of Behavioral and Organizational Sciences. She received her BA and PhD from the University of Chicago. She co-directs the positive psychology concentration and the Quality of Life Research Center, and serves on the board of the International Positive Psychology Association. She helped direct the Good Work Project, a series of studies of excellence and social responsibility in professional life. She studies positive psychology in a lifespan-developmental context, including engagement and creativity, mentoring and good work, and aging well. Her current research and writing address meaning and engagement in adulthood, the formative influences of mentoring and the formation of good mentors, and social entrepreneurship and creativity after 60 as models for positive aging. She is coauthor of *Good Mentoring* (2009) and coeditor of *Applied Positive Psychology* (2011).

Dr. Joseph A. Petrick is Professor of Management and International Business and Founding Director of the Institute for Business Integrity at Wright State University in Dayton, Ohio. He earned his PhD from Pennsylvania State University, with postdoctoral work at the University of Bonn in Germany and the University of Tokyo in Japan. He has been a manager in the private, public, and nonprofit sectors. He has published widely in the field of business and professional ethics, including the book *Management Ethics: Integrity at Work*, which addresses private sector, public sector, and nonprofit sector administrative ethics issues.

In addition, he has over 80 refereed journal articles in the *Journal of Business Ethics, Business and Society Review, Journal of Corporate Citizenship, Human Resource Management Journal, Business and Professional Ethics Journal, Journal of Management Systems, Academy of Management Executive, Risk Management, Innovation: Management, Policy & Practice, Journal of Real Estate Practice and Education, Global Business and Finance Review, Journal of General Management, International Journal of Operations and Production Management, Journal of Management Development, Global Business and Economics Review, Interdisciplinary Environmental Review, Journal of U.S.-China Public Administration,* and *Journal of Managerial Psychology,* among others.

He serves as the executive president of the International Business Honor Society. He is also the CEO of two consulting firms based in Cincinnati—Integrity Capacity Associates and Performance Leadership Associates. His research interests have focused on integrity capacity theory, sustainable stakeholder capitalism, international human resource management ethics, business ethics education, and managerial leadership ethics.

Dr. Stephan Rothlin is the general secretary and vice director of the Center for International Business Ethics at the University of International Business and Economics in Beijing. He also serves as chairman of the Association of International Business Ethics of Hong Kong (AIBE). Born in Zurich,

Switzerland and educated in various cities throughout Europe in the disciplines of philosophy, economics, sociology, and ethics, Dr. Rothlin ultimately obtained his PhD in business ethics at the State University of Innsbruck, Austria in 1991.

Between 1992 and 1998 he taught business ethics in the Institute of Management and Economics at the University of Zurich. In 1998 he moved to Beijing, where he taught international business ethics at several universities, including Renmin University (Finance & Business School), Peking University (BiMBA-program), Beijing Institute of Technology, the University of International Business and Economics, and the Central Party School in Beijing. He is a permanent visiting fellow at the Institute for Empirical Research in Economics at the University of Zurich and is welcomed as a regular visiting professor at a number of business schools in Asia and France.

Dr. Rothlin's main research focus is the development of business ethics in Asia, with a special focus on China. In cooperation with Peking University Press, he directs a series of translations of major business ethics textbooks into Chinese. In 2004, Peking University Press published his book, *Becoming A Top-Notch Player*. He has considerable experience in cross-cultural projects and is fluent in six languages: German, French, Italian, Spanish, English, and Mandarin Chinese.

Dr. Dennis McCann is director of the Case Study Institute at the Center for International Business Ethics at the University of International Business and Economics in Beijing. Professor emeritus of Agnes Scott College, Atlanta/Decatur, Georgia, Dr. McCann obtained a PhD from the University of Chicago Divinity School in 1976 and an STL from the Gregorian University, Rome, Italy, in 1971. He has taught business ethics in the United States for over 30 years and has been involved in research, lecturing, and teaching business ethics in China and Southeast Asia for the past 15 years. Dr. McCann is particularly concerned with identifying culturally appropriate teaching materials for Asia, based on his ongoing research in the fields of philosophy and religious studies. Dr. McCann was formerly the director of research and development at the Hong Kong America Centre (HKAC) during his Fulbright year (2005–2006), and served as visiting professor in the department of philosophy and religion, Hong Kong Baptist University (2006–2008). Dr. McCann served as executive director of the Society of Christian Ethics, the premier academic association for professors of religious ethics in the United States (1996–2001). He is the author of several books and dozens of scholarly articles, most recently the coauthor, with Prof. Lee Kam-hon and Ms. Mary Ann Ching Yuen, of *Christ and the Business Culture*, published in 2012 by the Center for the Study of Religion and Chinese Society (CSRCS), Chinese University Press in Hong Kong. Over the past 15 years Dr. McCann has taught, given workshops, and lectured in universities in Hong Kong, China, the Philippines, Malaysia, Japan, Thailand, Indonesia, and India.

Dr. Denise Salin is associate professor of management and organization at Hanken School of Economics, Helsinki, Finland and adjunct professor of social psychology at Helsinki University, Finland. She teaches on organizational behavior, leadership, and gender in management.

Dr. Salin's primary research interests are workplace bullying and organizational justice. Her work has appeared in, among other journals, *Human Relations, Gender, Work and Organization, Journal of Managerial Psychology,* and *European Journal of Work and Organizational Psychology.*

André van Montfort, PhD, is an associate professor in governance studies at the department of governance studies and political science, faculty of social sciences, VU University Amsterdam (Netherlands). His research activities focus on, among others, the assessment and explanation of the quality of public governance.

Laura Beck, M.Sc., is graduated in governance studies at VU University Amsterdam (Netherlands). She is employed as civil servant at the Dutch Ministry of Security and Justice.

Anneke Twijnstra, M.Sc., is graduated in governance studies at VU University Amsterdam (Netherlands). She works as a civil servant at the Dutch municipality of Smallingerland.

CPSIA information can be obtained at www.ICGtesting.com
Printed in the USA
BVOW02s1203171014

371259BV00002B/4/P